HISTORICAL DIVERSITIES

Society, Politics and Culture

HISTORICAL DIVERSITIES

Society, Politics and Culture

(Essays for Professor V.N. Datta)

Edited by

K.L. TUTEJA
SUNITA PATHANIA

MANOHAR
2008

First published 2008

ISBN 978-81-7304-792-3

Published by

Ajay Kumar Jain *for*
Manohar Publishers & Distributors
4753/23 Ansari Road, Daryaganj
New Delhi 110 002

Typeset at

Digigrafics
New Delhi 110 049

Printed at

Salasar Imaging Systems
Delhi 110 035

Contents

Introduction

The present volume is a tribute to Prof. V.N. Datta, an eminent historian of our times. This project was initiated about two years ago when some of Prof. Datta's friends, colleagues and former students decided to bring out a collection of papers in his honour, as an expression of their affection and appreciation for him. This volume contains nineteen papers in all contributed mainly by historians and scholars associated with Prof. Datta in different capacities. The editors, however, decided to include a paper by a young scholar from the University of West Indies that explores a subject which, apart from its academic significance, falls within the area which is of deep concern to Prof. Datta. The papers included in this book cover a vast range of subjects cutting across time and space and are intended to highlight the multidimensional nature of historical studies. Hence, this *festschrift* is entitled *Historical Diversities.*

Prof. Datta is Emeritus Professor at Kurukshetra University in India. After his early education at Government College, Lahore, and Lucknow University, he went to Cambridge University where he was rigorously trained in historical studies under the guidance of Sir Herbert Butterfield. Prof. Datta endeared a liberal scientific approach in history and has never limited historical inquiry to narrow boundaries of time and space. As an inquisitive mind, he has always been receptive to different ideas and approaches relevant for a deeper understanding of history. Prof. Datta has an impeccable academic commitment that never allows space for 'shortcuts', which he rightly believes is a real threat to historical studies today. As a scholar dedicated to the cause of history, Prof. Datta has set high standards for those who wish to emulate him.

Prof. Datta has been engaged in the historical research for over half a century. Though his primary focus has been modern Indian history, the wide range of his writings reflect his diverse interests in the subject. He strongly feels that there is no 'final truth' in history and all historical researches at the most succeed in providing an 'interim report'. Prof. Datta is eclectic in methodology and firmly believes in the rigorous application of fundamental norms of historical research and abhors the mythification of history. We believe that the essays included in the present volume will not only reflect the issues and concerns that are dear to Prof. Datta as a historian but also help in a better understanding of some of the complex issues, trends and currents of history.

I

The volume opens with two essays dealing with the ancient Indian history. The first essay by K.M. Shrimali draws our attention to some aspects of land relations in central India on the basis of epigraphical evidence contained in the copper plates of Valkha chiefs covering the period between *c.* AD 350 to *c.* AD 450. The author discusses several terms used in these plates which have a direct bearing on the 'nature of agrarian structure' during this period. Re-interpreting some of these terms, Shrimali critiques the earlier historical perception of agrarian structure and the emerging land relations in central India. Since the purpose of these land grants was to 'further the cause of land cultivation', the author upholds that there was a conscious drive towards the establishment of new rural settlements. While emphasizing the role of religious establishments in actual agricultural production, Shrimali stresses that the land grants were in no way confined to Brahmanas alone. By his fresh interpretation of the Vakataka records, the author throws new light on the proprietary rights over land as well as the responsibility for the actual agrarian development. While discussing the nature of agricultural activities, Shrimali logically concludes that the donees appear to have enjoyed definite proprietary rights over the land with its well-demarcated boundaries. Furthermore, he emphasizes that even in the 'initial stage of land grant economy in an area with a tremendous potentiality for agricultural development', the possibility of 'misappropriation' of land was not overlooked, and care was taken against it. As a matter of fact, there were 'specific injunctions' whereby the donees cultivating and enjoying lands were not to be 'obstructed'.

The paper by Bhairabi P. Sahu seeks to explore the significance of a region in history. Sahu believes that 'regional history has a bearing on important questions such as causation, periodization and our understanding of larger patterns of Indian history'. Along with this, he challenges the notion of a 'unitarian Indian state' and also rejects the concept of India being 'equivalent to a confederation of regions'. The reality in his view appears to lie in the 'dynamic relationship between the two in the course of which they constituted each other'. Sahu sees the formation of regions through certain configurations of historical forces over time. In particular, he examines the evolution of Brahmanical ideology and the spatial spread of state society. It is argued in this study that the Brahmanical tradition in the course of its 'spread and evolution' developed a composite character evolved out of elements derived from other regions. At the same time, regional distinctiveness and specification too were assimilated in their own way in this tradition. Further, Sahu traces the formation of states outside the Ganga Valley and the extension of state society at local and trans-local levels. In this regards, he observes: 'In all periods of Indian history there were spaces outside the orbit of organized state intrusion. Such spaces, however, did not exist in immutable isolation, but in a state of interaction and change.' Hence, Sahu concludes that the process of regional or sub-regional identity formation and decentring of identities were at work simultaneously, leading to the making of composite and pluralist tradition.

II

Literature is the product of a given social situation. The pattern of social relations and values permeate and influence literature in a given historical context. As such the value of literature for the understanding of social history is of vital importance. Our next two contributors draw on indigenous tradition of love in medieval Punjabi literature for reconstructing the social life of medieval Punjab, particularly in the context of the idea of personal love and gender. Indu Banga's paper delineates the notions of love and deviance in medieval Punjab through her analysis of various versions of the *kissa* of Heer-Ranjha, a popular folklore entrenched deeply in the literature of Punjab between the sixteenth and eighteenth centuries. Banga argues that the *kissa* of Heer-Ranjha is suggestive of the tensions between the 'notions of personal love and fidelity on the one hand and those of family honour and appropriate rolès of daughters and wives' on the other. The author upholds that since marriage remained a social institution *par excellence* combining social reproduction with social control, the 'assertion of freedom' to love and marry by Heer and Ranjha was viewed not simply as deviance but an act of 'isolated rebellion'. This in turn also reflected the 'partial failure of social controls' setting in motion 'all modes of social controls like family honour, social customs, laws and institutions of State' to maintain a patriarchal social order. To Banga, the appeal of *kissa* of Heer-Ranjha in pre-modern times was as much 'for exaltation of love—whether spiritual or personal—as of fidelity and chastity so essential for the maintenance of patriarchal structure'.

J.S. Grewal takes up the Punjabi literary tradition during the reign of Akbar to highlight the notions of love and gender in medieval India. Contradictions between personal love and patriarchal social order, and steps taken towards its resolution are the highlights of this paper. Grewal states that even when the idea of love as popularized by the Sufis is cherished in the Punjabi literary tradition, there is also an awareness of social constraints imposed by the structures and values of patriarchy and the risks involved in flouting the social norms. As the society did not recognize or accept the notion of personal love, the tensions between 'personal predilections and social norms' remained unresolved. Instead of 'transcending the social realities', creative writers *took* recourse to 'evading' them. According to Grewal, the personal love either ended in tragedy as in the case of Peelu's *kissa* of Mirza-Sahiban or in Damodar Gulati's resolution of the conflict in the *kissa* of Heer-Ranjha where Heer and Ranjha defy the society but do not live within it.

The next two papers deal with the social and economic changes that took place in medieval times. Aniruddha Ray's paper contests the earlier understanding that the Sultans of Bengal followed a deliberate anti-Hindu policy resulting in an 'eternal conflict' between the Muslim rulers and Hindu *zamindars*. Ray emphasizes that for almost 250 years following the Muslim conquest, Bengal had remained fragmented and the contemporary records do not contain any references to the suppression of Hindus even during this period either as a 'state policy or at individual levels'. Ray, on the basis of contemporary Bengali literary sources, further maintains that from the fourteenth century onwards, when Bengal was brought under a unified administration, one discerns the beginning of the emergence of a composite culture in this region anchored on political 'identity and independence of Bengal'. The adoption of local customs and manners by the Sufis also helped in creating a regional Bengali identity among the Islamic organizations. The use of Bangla as a court language acted as a stimulus to the construction of Bengali identity. This process of acculturation impacted the Hindus as well. This is quite evident from the fact that tombs like that of Ismail Ghazi were venerated by the Hindus and the Muslims alike. The author stresses that political identity combined with regional Bengali identity gave further impetus to the growth of a composite culture. As the demands of increasing trade and overseas commerce from the end of the fifteenth century required more integration, this bolstered the composite culture in Bengal which reached its zenith by the sixteenth century under Sultan Alauddin Hussain Shah. While building up his case for the existence of a composite culture in Sultanate Bengal, Ray, however, qualifies that this was essentially a 'state sponsored' composite culture which can account for its inherent weakness as well.

Shireen Moosvi in her contribution has focused on the internal migration of skilled workers during the sixteenth to the eighteenth centuries. She forcefully contests the traditional view that 'caste rigidities and local ties often made migration of artisans a rare phenomenon'. Her paper aims at establishing that migration of artisans to both near by and far-off places was an important feature of the pre-colonial Indian society. However, Moosvi is well aware of the fact that it is not feasible to quantify such migration in medieval times. Her comprehensive account of the internal migration of skilled artisans is largely based on empirical data culled out intelligently from the records of the European trading companies and earlier indigenous sources. She contends that the migration of artisans equipped with special techniques was largely responsible for the growth of commodity production witnessed particularly in the textile industry before the onslaught of Lancashire products in the nineteenth century. Moosvi also draws our attention to the fact the Mughal state generally encouraged settlement of migrant artisans at new places when their services were needed by the state and people. Unlike the English East India Company, the artisans were not compelled by the Mughal state to stay if they showed any kind of interest to move to other parts of the country. The author mentions that sometimes the artisans moved out to other places either to save themselves from natural calamities or to raise their social position which could be described as an example of 'Sanskritization'. Finally, she observes that mobility of skilled labour in geographical terms was extensive enough to suggest that 'in a country as large as India, its different parts were connected well enough to rectify imbalances in productions through labour migrations'.

III

The next paper in this collection of essays links the medieval to modern phase of Indian history. In 1829, Raja Rammohun Roy was appointed as an agent by the Mughal ruler of Delhi, Akbar Shah II to represent his claims against the East India Company in London. This paper by Sabyasachi Bhattacharya is an analysis of a hitherto unexplored correspondence exchanged between Raja Rammohun Roy, the Mughals and the British authorities from 1829 to 1833. Bhattacharya emphasizes that both reasons of law and discourse of coercion were simultaneously used in the construction of British colonial state in India and provided 'theoretical underpinnings' for the British self-conception as a sovereign power. Thus, in the process of establishment and consolidation of British sovereignty in India, the colonial state spared no effort and let go no opportunity to delegitimize its predecessor. Bhattacharya contends that the British representation and redefinition of the notions of sovereignty were however, continuously questioned, contested and challenged by the Mughals, the chief 'native' power in India as per the political beliefs, the notions of rights and entitlements of the descendents of Mughal power in India in the early decades of the nineteenth century. According to the author, Raja Rammohun Roy in his defense of Mughal claims against the colonial state combined the contemporary English political idiom based on the discourse of law, legal entitlements, ideas of justice and equity and the traditional Mughal political and cultural practices. Bhattacharya further stresses that Raja Rammohun Roy's efforts 'met with failure as the British had superior power of coercion'. However, the challenge implicit in Roy's contestation of British claims to an extent, made the colonial state to rework its concept as a sovereign power in India and conceptualize its relationship with the Mughal rulers in new terms—a 'process that culminated in the post-1857 trial of the last Mughal on grounds of treason against the State'.

Sudhir Chandra's paper also deals with relations of power and dominance in a colonial situation though in a different context. He critically explores the career graph of an Indian missionary, Rev. Ganpatrao Raghunath Navalkar (1837-1912). Navalkar was associated with the Scottish Free Church. Sudhir Chandra's central concern in this study is to highlight the 'play of subjection and resistance' in the relationship of some 'more aware converts' with their European dominated missions. He observes that while not all European missionaries were necessarily conscious of power being implicit in their 'compassion and service', no 'thinking' Indian convert could miss it. In this case, Navalkar's 'ecclesiastical subjection' compounded 'political subjection which an unfree convert shared with his Indian compatriots. This realization and awareness of their predicament led many a Christian convert to varied forms of resistance as Christians and as Indians. In Navalkar's case, who perceived himself as Christian missionary *par excellence* if not by birth, certainly by 'taste, education and culture', the realization of 'ecclesiastical subjection' grounded in dominance and reflected through display of racial discrimination, took the form of heroic defiance. Navalkar questioned as to why Indian Christians should be 'degraded for their skin' and demanded that 'native missionaries must be respected and freed from European domination'. His resistance, based as it was on demands for 'justice and conformance with Christian ideal', was construed as an impudence by the Mission authorities. Finally, Navalkar was retired (a polite word for dismissal) from the Mission service without trial on grounds of indiscipline. Chandra concludes that the failure of the stirrings of 'Christian manhood' of Navalkar as an unfree native Christian convert reveals that Christianity in a colonial situation was inseparable from the 'hubris-and exploitation-of power'.

Satpal Sangwan's paper takes up one of the most contemporary of historical concerns, i.e. environmental history. Environmental history largely deals with the negative aspects of human interaction with nature unlike the history of science which is primarily the success story of human genius. Human history has been a progressive march from food gatherers to industrial producers. There is also a corresponding decline in environmental ethics. To judge the extent of human interference with nature and its consequences, Sangwan has taken up the study of man's relations with the forests in India from ancient, to medieval and colonial times. Sangwan concludes that throughout history of human civilization, men have tried to use and exploit the forests for their needs. However, there are variations in the nature of utilization/exploitation/conservation. While making a survey of human relations with forests since pre-historic times, he observes that as social relations become more and more defined and stringent and state formation begins taking a concrete shape, human relations with, forests in particular, out step the informal boundaries of community control model. Finally, Sangwan is more concerned with the issue of management of forests under the British rule which indeed 'marked the beginning of a new chapter' in the relationship of men with forests in India. He concludes that the war against the forests was not a new phenomenon since 'most of the cultivable plains of India had already been divested of its woodland when the British established their political authority'. At the same time, he accepts that the ideas of progressivism, the needs of empire and the forces of market aggravated the exploitation of forests during the colonial rule.

In his paper, Deepak Kumar offers a critical analysis of the work done by the Rockefeller Foundation in the field of public health during 1915-45. To start with, he states that public health refers to the organized efforts made under the direction of medical experts for preventing disease and improving the health of the people. Moreover, it is contended that public health is primarily a field of social activity, which includes 'applying practically every basic science directed towards a comprehensive programme of community service'. Deepak Kumar mentions that the issue of public health was extensively raised in the late nineteenth century, but the colonial government did not show much interest in it. In such circumstances, Rockefeller Foundation, which according to its charter claimed to have been promoting the welfare of mankind all over the world, made several efforts to remove hunger and disease in India. In this connection, the Foundation sent a number of its representatives to different parts of India to carry out its programme relating to public health in an effective manner. In particular, serious efforts were made to check diseases like hookworm and malaria which were quite harmful for the labour engaged in plantation industry. In this direction, the establishment of All India Institute of Hygiene and Public Health in Calcutta by the Rockefeller Foundation was an important step as this institution became a leading centre for research and development in this field. Deepak Kumar concludes that Rockefeller Foundation despite its considerable efforts neither replaced the government in this arena nor entered into any confrontation with the state. Rather, it adopted a very cautious approach on sensitive social issues which might have hurt and agitated the common people.

The last paper in the modern India section is by Radica Mahase who draws our attention to the attitude and concerns of the Indian nationalists on the condition of Indian emigrants abroad in general, and those working under the indentureship system in particular in the context of India's anti-colonial struggle. Towards the end of the nineteenth century, an organized movement emerged and developed in India that questioned and agitated against the emigration of Indians to overseas territories. Indian nationalists were the key players in this movement as they created a framework whereby colonialism was challenged and the mass emigration of Indians, as part of this colonial framework was also contested. This paper examines both structural and ideological factors that led to the inclusion of the issue of Indian indentured labour and subsequently the demand for the abolition of this inhuman system in the Indian nationalist discourse. It evaluates the extent to which nationalist agitation hindered the smooth operation of the scheme and forced the colonial authorities to implement structural changes in the system. Mahase also discusses the extent to which agitation in India presented a threat to the continuation of Indian emigration and evaluates the impact of such agitation on the system of indentured labour and the emigration of Indians in general. The paper finally assesses the role of the nationalists in the final termination of the indentureship system in 1920.

IV

The section on contemporary history begins with the paper of Suranjan Das who explores the ethnic assertion of Nagas in its historical context. Originally consisting of a number of tribes in the north-east, the Nagas evolved into a generic tribal identity in the late nineteenth century. The author observes that the colonial rule subjected the Nagas and other tribal population in north-east India to a 'circumscribed territorial existence'. What followed was a process of 'human territoriality', which entailed a mixture of 'territorial awareness with collective identity'. This generated amongst the Nagas like other hill tribes a feeling of separatism from the Indian mainstream. According to Suranjan Das, neither the Indian national movement nor the nation-building process in the aftermath of independence could effectively break the Naga isolation. He points out that the Naga ethnicity in post-Independent India gained strength because of their self-perception as 'victims of dual processes: commercialization of their resources and hegemonizing dictum of one state and one nation'. He also provides a comprehensive account of Nagas' response towards the centralizing ideology and practice of the Indian State. Both the insurgency and participation in constitutional processes within a larger framework of Indian nation state by the Nagas are taken up for discussion. These factors continue to influence and shape the society and politics of Nagaland. On the whole, this paper on Naga ethnic identity helps us in understanding the challenge posed to Indian federalism by the politics of ethnicity in the north-east.

Harish Puri in his essay takes up the question of changes in the lives of Dalits in Punjab after Independence. Here it is important to mention that the highest concentration of Dalit population in any state in India is in Punjab. This paper critically explores the changes that have taken place in the status and position of the Dalits since Independence along with shifts in the societal attitude towards them. Besides Dalits' perception of their own conditions is also taken up for analysis by Puri. He contends that the transformation though considerable has been partial and uneven both in terms of its extent and impact. This is particularly noticeable in the rural/urban context and between men and women comprising the various Scheduled Castes. Puri draws our attention to the fact that the focus of Dalit movement in a way has shifted from the goals set up by Ambedkar. Gradually, the struggle for equality has 'moved away from the issues of redistribution and access to opportunities and social justice' to that of 'identity'. The identity consciousness according to Puri is marked more by *jati* (caste) consciousness than Dalit identity. This has in turn resulted not only in the widening of internal hierarchies within the Scheduled Castes but has also strengthened the *jati*-based 'religio-cultural markers' among the Scheduled Castes in Punjab.

V

The following two papers take us beyond the boundaries of Indian history into the realms of Europe and Asia. Barun De in his paper takes up for discussion the ideas about forces that had led to the formation and shaping of modern Europe. Based on the premise that much of the 'thematics have been obscured by the historigraphical usages that are implicit in the unproblematic idioms of "Europe", "transition" and "modernity" De raises questions and doubts about the very meaning and usage of these terms, thereby providing a fresh insight into the processes that led to transition of Europe from medieval to modern. According to Barun De, modernity is not a past historical period but a 'neutral attribute of recent periodicity in historical development'. Hence as a concept, modernity can neither be treated as a definite category having a clear beginning or an end nor can the process of transition be reduced to a single path. Modernity is a multiplex formation. De states: 'Each formation is a set of practices including ideas and institutions that span different continents, countries, regions and social communities with different terminal boundings.' The patterns of modernity being different, the path of transition is also manifold. The important point, he argues, is to understand how and in which sector/class/region and with what velocity does transition from one predominant tendency to another takes place. Thus, departing from the 'smoothened out method of following the Eurocentric path of transformation', De draws our attention to forces other than Christian/European that influenced the process of transformation from medieval to modern in Europe. In this context, a change in the perception of the term Europe becomes highly relevant. Europe was not a geographic entity in ancient times. Its emergence as a composite continent was only a late Christian idea, i.e. in the second half of second millennium. Prior to this, the existence of Hellenic, Islamic, Indian and Chinese connectivity had created more or less a common zone of material culture. De emphasizes that these interconnectivities and extra European influences on Christendom have to be signified if Europe is not to be reduced to a 'medieval Christian concept' alone. This is, however, not to deny the influence of Christianity in the 'crystallization of ideas of sovereignty and ethics of power' in Europe. De further points out that the later distinctiveness of European continentality owes a lot to the development of colonialism in late medieval and early modern Europe. He argues that without the military and naval expansion of Europe into the wider world, Europe might not have 'gained its modern identity.'

The paper by Irfan Habib discusses the emergence, consolidation and the future direction of Asian identity. Habib draws our attention to the fact that the concept of Asia as a continent was unknown to the Asians till the arrival of the ideas of European geography along with colonialism. Even though an extensive knowledge of neighbouring civilization in other parts of Asia had existed in each of the subcontinents of Asia, it had not, however, taken the form of a 'spontaneous Asian consciousness'. Habib emphasizes that 'geographical designation' as Asia or Asians took a 'living form only when confronted by colonialism'. Colonialism by subjecting the Asian countries to a 'common system of oppression' did the initial spadework for the emergence of Asian consciousness. According to the author, colonialism despite its own exploitative and hegemonic agenda also produced the forces for the future regeneration of the colonies through the spread of modern western ideas in the colonies. Habib cautions against an approach that 'confounds colonialism with modernization' and contends that colonialism and modernization had twin impact on the colonies: one 'provoked resistance' while the other 'shaped the aims of resistance'. The idea of a nation, in particular the type of nation, manifest in the ideologies of nationalist movements in Asia was the product of ideas emanating from the Western mainstream. During the course of national liberation movements anchored on anti-colonialism and anti-imperialism, a sense of Asian identity began to emerge and grow among the peoples of Asia around the 'widely scattered fellow feeling' as victims of colonialism. Habib argues that the end of Second World War created conditions that further consolidated the process of Asian solidarity. However, the author upholds that the process has been neither smooth nor one of linear progress. The pressures of Cold War as well as the emerging territorial disputes between the Asian nations 'disrupted' and 'thwarted the growth of Asian spirit'. In the end, Habib builds up a case in favour of the strengthening of the Asian consciousness based on solidarity of the Asian peoples as opposed to religion specific appeals, which alone could give 'Asia for Asians' a new democratic substance.

VI

In this section on historiography, Kesavan Veluthat attempts to offer a critical analysis of historical tradition in pre-colonial India by undertaking a study of *Keralotpatti,* a historical narrative from Kerala. At the outset, he focuses on the weaknesses of the Rankean tradition of historical writings in which absolute reliance is placed on evidence from contemporary sources for understanding the historical past. He also contests the stereotyped view that unlike the West, India lacked a historical tradition. In other words, Kesavan questions the colonial writers for their refusal to accept existing forms of historical writing in India as valid. Kesavan argues that *Keralotpatti* is not merely a source of information for construction of Kerala history but actually represents the historical consciousness of pre-colonial times. He attempts to explain the form in which the Kerala society expressed its consciousness of past events and the events themselves which it chose to record. While doing so, he also logically explains the absence of *prasastis* in Kerala society as, in his opinion, there were other forms of expressing a consciousness of the past. He admits that *Keralotpatti* does not conform to the tradition of chronology, causation and generalization. Yet, he recognizes that it does express historical consciousness in a form which met the needs of that society. In essence, on the basis of his reading of *Keralopatti*, Kesavan endeavours to establish that India in general and Kerala in particular, was not a society entirely devoid of a sense of past. Different forms 'which that sense of history took to express itself eminently suited the needs of the society from time to time'.

In his paper dealing with historiography of the Sikhs, K.L. Tuteja makes a case study of Gokul Chand Narang's *The Transformation of Sikhism* which was generally recognized as an authoritative history of the Sikhs for a long time. Tuteja shows that Narang's own ideological predilections reflecting a Hinduized consciousness deeply influenced his reading of the Sikh past. It is argued in this study that Narang made use of historical evidence in an ingenious manner with a view to consolidating Hindu identity and, at the same time, projecting Muslims as the 'other' or as the enemy of Hindus. Narang's work was in a way similar in spirit to those writings of the Sikh reformers (*Tat Khalsa* Sikhs) who since the late nineteenth century were reconstructing Sikh past on the basis of religious faith and tradition, which sometimes did not necessarily correspond with actual historical reality. Tuteja explains that there was a vital difference that could be discerned between the study of Narang and *Tat Khalsa* writings. Narang, unlike the *Tat Khalsa* Sikh writers, zealously maintained that the roots of Sikhism lay in Hindu religion and therefore, it could best be described as a Hindu sect. Narang was certainly aware of the growing debate on the issue of separate identity of the Sikhs at the turn of the twentieth century. He, however, unhesitatingly describes the Sikhs as 'Hindus' throughout the book. In a wider perspective, Narang's work could be described as a part of the strategy of a section of Hindu intelligentsia trying to construct a broad Hindu identity at the turn of the twentieth century. Their ideological belief was that all those (including the Sikhs) who followed a religion whose founder was an Indian were 'Hindus'. This kind of approach along with an anti-Muslim stance actually makes Narang's study an early example of Hinduized version of communal history. The author further adds that Narang's work differs substantially from those nationalist writings on the Sikhs which have been highlighting human and spiritual content of Guru Nanak's message with a view to asserting common cultural heritage and composite nature of Indian nation.

K.N. Panikkar in his paper makes a critical analysis of the ideological aspects that surround the debate on history textbooks published by the National Council of Education, Research and Training (NCERT) and the efforts to replace them. The new textbooks were brought out 'to project a Hinduized view of Indian past'. This project, according to Panikkar, was inspired by the political 'purpose of seeking a rationale from history for constructing India as a Hindu nation'. The paper starts with a brief survey of the British historical writings that intended to 'fulfil the legitimizing role of colonialism'. It is well known that the British, in order to assert their superiority over Indian subjects, made use of historical knowledge and characterized Indian society as changeless and traditional with religion as one of its essential characteristics. Panikkar maintains that the Indian state after Independence endeavoured to de-colonize the educational system, and in that process NCERT brought out history textbooks written by a team of distinguished historians. The author argues that the latter offered scientific interpretation of India's past by 'adopting an interpretative framework which was different from colonial and communal' perspectives. These books, Panikkar observes, while locating the historical developments as a part of the social process, envisioned to shape the younger minds with the knowledge of rich Indian tradition comprising secular ideas and composite culture. This type of history writing is an enigma to the Hindu fundamentalists, who according to Panikkar, have been keen to recast 'textbooks as narrative of Hindu religious nationalism'. Finally, this paper in a wider perspective contests exclusivist and mythical description of Indian history devoid of lived reality and at the same time emphasizes the necessity of following basic norms and methods of historical discipline.

VII

We end the volume with a contribution by Amrik Singh. He raises some important questions hitherto ignored by the historians of Islam regarding its spread in India. Contrary to the general view that Islam is a 'religion of the sword' and that coercion was necessary for its spread all over the world, Amrik Singh draws our attention to certain contrary trends that led to the spread of Islam in India, given its slow and uneven growth. The author emphasizes the need not only for an in-depth study of the issue of spread of Islam in India but also highlights the importance of a better and scientific understanding of medieval Indian history. According to Amrik Singh, such an understanding based on objective realities is absolutely imperative as this can go a long way in facilitating the blossoming of a spirit of coexistence between the Hindus and Muslims on the Indian subcontinent. As such, Amrik Singh's paper foregrounds the important role that discipline of history can play in transforming the contemporary social realities.

Finally we express our deep sense of gratitude to our learned contributors for their admirable and generous support in bringing out this volume. We are also thankful to our friend Sanjay Subodh for his generous cooperation in finalizing the introductory section.

K.L. TUTEJA
SUNITA PATHANIA

ANCIENT INDIA

CHAPTER 1

Some Aspects of Land Relations in Central India

(*c.* AD 350 to *c.* AD 450)

K.M. SHRIMALI

In 1982 twenty-seven copper plates were discovered in a field at Risavala, on the outskirts of the present township of Bagh in Madhya Pradesh. These belong to five chiefs named Bhulunda, Svamidasa, Rudradasa, Bhattaraka and Nagabhatta who ruled at Valkha (identified with Bagh), most probably as feudatories of the Guptas. In addition to these plates, five more plates of some of the aforesaid chiefs had already been known. The thirty-two plates bear dates ranging between years 38 and 134 which are taken to be reckonings in the Gupta era, thus giving us a span of nearly a century (*c.* AD 357-453).[1]

Along with the land grant records of the Vakatakas,[2] the copper plates of the chiefs of Valkha represent a fairly comprehensive and one of the earliest evidences of the new socio-economic formation based on changing land relations. Despite a somewhat monotonous structure of these grants, their significance is considerably heightened by the light shed by them on some very complex phenomena of the rural landscape.

An idea of the region involved can be had by looking at the details of more than forty villages mentioned in the records under discussion. It can be said very easily that nearly 40 per cent of these places were located along the banks of the Narmada, for expressions such as *Narmada-dakshina tate*, *Narmada-para-kule*, *Narmada-uttara-tate* figure in many of these inscriptions.[3] The Narmada flows about 60 km south of Valkha and the topography of the region is, nowadays, marked by a very moderate annual rainfall ranging between 60 and 100 cm. Marked by black soil, the region is also noticeable for its forests which remind us of the *atavika rajyas* of central India in inscriptions of fourth-sixth centuries.[4]

The Valkha records use many terms having a direct bearing on the nature of agrarian structure in the concerned region.[5] Some of these terms are discussed here.

The earliest record in the series, viz., Bhulunda's grant of the year 38 (AD 357), refers to the donation of the village named Rohyanvahaka on the farther bank of the Narmada to eight Brahmanas of different gotras. Significantly, the donated villages is described as *Krishtaavasannaka* (कृष्टावसन्नक), which the editors have rendered as: 'Where cultivation has been terminated.'[6] Evidently, this rendering has been derived from the compound of *krishta+avasannaka*. It may be true from a literal lexicon point of view but makes little historical sense. When one of the ostensible purposes of land grants is to further the cause of land cultivation, why should a settlement be created after stopping cultivation in the area? It would perhaps be more appropriate to read the concerned term as *aavasaana* (आवसान) rather than *avasannaka*, which would mean a dwelling or living on the boundaries of a village. Such a rendering would not militate against the idea of a conscious drive towards the establishment of new rural settlements. It may be recalled that one of the three types of villages mentioned in the Pali texts of the post-Mauryan centuries included such establishments as were situated on the periphery of the countryside and almost merged into forests. Such areas could be expected to present enormous potential for fresh settlements. That the process of the land reclamation was still in its infancy is apparent from the grant of Rudradasa issued in the year 67 (AD 386). It records the donation of Bhutilakkhadaka, an uninhabited village (*shoonya graama*) in the Dasilakapallipathaka to a Brahmana named Bhagava.[7]

Another significant term used in the Valkha records is *pratyaya*. Though at one place it is used in the explicit context of the chief's injunction for the implementation of his order (*pratyaya upaneya aajnaavidheyaishcha*),[8] yet its more frequent and prominent application is seen in relation to land holdings. In all, it occurs at eleven places[9] and is invariably associated with *kshetra/kshetrapada/kshetrapatti*.[10] Despite numerous palaeographic variations and even some indistinctness,[11] the form of the word is clearly *pratyaya* (प्रत्यय) and not *pratyaaya* (प्रत्याय)—the latter being generally understood in the sense of dues payable to the king.[12] However, commenting on the use of *pratyaya* in the Valkha records, the editors note:

> This term primarily means 'entrusted with' or 'attached to' thereby leading to the conclusion that the land had already been brought under cultivation but was only a *temporary holding* of the individual mentioned. We may reasonably presume that when the Maharaj-donor succeeded in identifying a deserving brahmana donee he merely passed on the entrusted land to the latter for his enjoyment (*emphases added*).[13]

These assumptions and reconstructions raise many questions, not only about proprietary rights over land but also about responsibility for the actual agrarian development. Some of the relevant questions could be:

(a) Who was responsible for 'entrusting' or 'attaching' land to individuals? That the Valkha chiefs may have been instrumental in this is a matter of only inference rather than a positive indicator.

(b) Who all were entitled for getting the land entrusted to them? There are scanty indicators of the socio-economic affiliation of these fortunate or perhaps more unfortunate confidants. While references to the *pratyayas* of Moolasharma and Vaayusharma[14] may indicate that some of these people may have been respected brahmanas, there are also indications of a trader (*vaanijaka*) and even a potter (*kumbhakaara*) having *pratyaya-kshetrapada* under them.

(c) Was the identification of 'deserving donees' confined to Brahmanas? Apparently not. Of the eleven cases of *pratyaya-kshetras*, seven donees have been specifically referred to as Brahmanas[15] but in four cases the donees are deities rather than individuals.[16] The deities include Bhagavati (a female divinity of possibly non-Brahmanical affiliations) at Navatataaka Narayana at Valkah and Bappapishaachadeva[17] also at Valkha. It may not be out of place to mention that one of the Brahmana donees is called Hunadhyaka (हूणाढ्यक) in Rudradasa's Valkha grant of the year 67 (AD 386). Such an early epigraphic usage of Huna as a Brahmana is quite instructive.

(d) What persuaded the trustees to agree to the transfer of land which was cultivated by their sweat and toil? There are no indications in the records under references about compensation, if any, given to them.

(e) What types of land were 'entrusted' or 'attached' to individuals? In one case, *griha* (house) figures along with the *pratyayakshetra* of Indrasena.[18] However, a more intriguing allusion is to the *poorva brahmadeyakshetra* (the erstwhile *brahmadeya* land) which was also a *pratyaya* of Agnishvara to begin with and then donated to Bappapishaachadeva.[19] Moreover, the fact that the *pratyayakshetrapatti* of Khuddataka included marshy land (*mandalakachchha*), the (*pratya*)*ya-kshetra* of Dadhipanchaka lay in the vicinity of Vanavaasini – possibly a forested area, and *khila* (uncultivated or wasteland) was lying to the west of three *pratyaya-kshetrapadas* of Maheshvara, Nandipala and Nandi[20] show that all entrusted/attached lands were not developed or 'brought under cultivation' at the time of passing them on to Brahmana donees.

(f) How long were the trustees expected to keep *pratyayas* with them? What incentives were built into the structure to encourage them in undertaking the developmental work, particularly when holdings under them were only 'temporary'?

The editors have claimed that the term *pratyaya* occurs along with *bhujyamaana* and *poorva bhujyamaanaka*. This is far from being so. These terms occur three times each[21] but never in the context of any *pratyaya-kshetra*. Of these, *bhujyamaana* generally occurs in the context of facilitating the enjoyment of land by donees. Indeed in one case there is a special thrust on such an enjoyment from the day of the grant (*adya prabhritti*).[22] In the case of *poorva-bhujyamaanaka* as well, only one occurrence makes a distinction between the erstwhile enjoyer, i.e. Lohakaarapallikaa and the actual donee (Maattujja).[23] In the remaining two allusions of this usage there was a complete identity of the former enjoyer and the new donee, i.e. Bappapishachadeva. That the proprietary rights of donees were quite complete is evident from the use of *pradishata* along with *bhunjata* and *krishata* on two occasions.[24] People responsible for executing the grant are specially ordered both verbally and in writing that no hindrances should be caused to those who enjoy, cultivate, got cultivated, inhabit and sow the lands. In the light of these occurrences, the contextual affinity of *pratayakshetras* and *bhujyamaana/poorvabhujyamaanaka* seems somewhat untenable.

Keeping in view the textual and contextual allusions to *pratyayas*, it may perhaps be more appropriate to see them as lessees—may be of the donees. Such a connotation along with the notion of 'a dependent or subject' is discernible in the usage of *pratyaya* in the Veraval inscription of Chalukya–Vaghela king Arjunadeva who was residing at Anhillapataka in VS 1320/ Valabhi (Gupta) era 945 (AD 1264).[25]

The records from Valkha throw very useful light on the nature of agricultural activities. More than twenty inscriptions speak of donees enjoying and cultivating lands—this is not very unusual for the period under consideration. During the span of just two years—65 and 67 (AD 384 and 386), we get five grants from Svamidasa and Rudradasa which mention *krishaapayata* (getting land cultivated) along with *bhunjata* and *krishata*.[26] One may profitably undertake structural similarities between Valkha records and the Taleshvar (Almora district, Uttarakhand) copper-plate inscription of Dyutivarman.[27] Both speak of land grants for the performance of *bali, charu* and *sattra* sacrifices, the bathing of deities, worshipping them with perfumes, incense, flowers and garlands. However, it is the conspicuous reference to *krishi-karmaanushthaana*[28] (कृषिकर्मानुष्ठान) in the plates from the Himalaya *tarais* that makes the comparison pertinent, though Dyutivarman's grant was possibly made considerably after the Valkha grants.[29] The grants from Valkha speak of *vapa/vapanta/ vapamana* as an important agricultural operation carried on by donees. In these records these terms occur in two different contexts:

(a) Twice along with *bhunjata* and *krishata*—donees enjoying, cultivating and sowing[30] were not to be obstructed, and
(b) twice with *devakiyakarshaka* (देवकीयकर्षक) and *devaparichaaraka*[31] (देवपरिचारक) who were also cultivating donated lands.[32]

Valkha grants allude to numerous attendants, servants, dependants, officials as *devakulaashrita* (देवकुलाश्रित)[33] and *devaprasaadaka* (देवप्रसादक)[34]' but *devakiyakarshaka, devakarmaantika* (देवकर्मान्तिक) and *devakarmmika* (देवकर्म्मिकं) are of special significance in the context of the role of religious establishments in undertaking agricultural production. Of these, *devakiyakarshakas*[35] who were also responsible for sowing of seeds were certainly cultivators who functioned for temple establishments but they could also be the cultivators of irrigated fields. One may draw some sustenance for this pollution from the use of *vaapikaa* (a small well) in place of usual *vaapam* for *kedaara* field (which are either rice-fields or those which are largely under water) in the Taleshvar copper plates of Vishnuvarman.[36] It may also be mentioned incidentally, that Bhattaraka's grant of the year 102 (AD 421) from Valkha records the donation of a plot of land along with a paddy-field (*sahakedaaraih*).[37] Since some lexicographers use *karmaanta* in the sense of a tilled or cultivated ground,[38] *devakarmaantika* of Bhulunda's grant of the year 59 (AD 378)[39] could also be the tiller of such land for deities. It is perhaps not a mere coincidence that *devakarmaantikas, devakarmmikas, devakiyakarshakas, devakulaashritas, devaprasaadakas*, etc., figure alongside the Pashupatas, Pashupataachaaryas, Bhagavachchhishtas, Mantraganaachaaryas and Bappapishaachadeva.[40]

Finally, an idea may also be had of the pressure on land. Here two observations of the editors of Valkha grants may be mentioned:[41]

(i) There is a 'total absence of the mention of any boundaries of the gift-land as also their measurements', and
(ii) 'None of these charters contains any imprecatory passages or verses against misappropriation.'

Both these features are explained away as products of the 'initial stage of the system of land grants in the region'. From this, it may perhaps also be inferred that the pressure of land may not have been very acute. However, we also need to keep the following in view:

(a) It is not true that the Valkha records are totally silent on mentioning boundaries of donated lands. Apart from the Narmada figuring as an important indicator of the location of as many as fifteen gift-lands, Bhulunda's grant of the year 38 (AD 357), which incidentally is the earliest Valkha grant, delimits very specifically the village Rohyavaahaka. It was not only situated on the farther bank of the Narmada but also to the east of Ishvarasenaanaka and to the north of Karjurikaa in the Daasilakapalliraashtra.[42] Kukkutaanaka, the village donated by Svamidasa in the year 63 (AD 382) was lying to the east of Kattangapadra.[43] Another record of the same chief and dated in the year 65 (AD 384) describes the donated plot of land as lying to the north-west of Vanavaasini.[44] The donated field in Rudradasa's grant of the year 67 (AD 386) was situated on the 'south-western boundary' (*dakshina-apara-simaa*) of Daasilakapalli.[45]

(b) On the question of misappropriation of gift-land, the concern of the donors is clear right from the beginning. While it is true that the dharmashastric imprecatory verses against misappropriation, which become a conspicuous and persistent feature in later records, are not seen in the Valkha records, nonetheless specific injunctions such as *na vyahantavyam* (न व्यहन्तव्यं), *na vyaasedhya* (न व्यासेध्य) and *pratishedhashcha na kaaryah* (प्रतिषेधश्च न कार्य) are mentioned in many inscriptions.[46] All the kinsmen, king's partisans, police magistrates, messengers, soldiers and royal-heralds, were expected to see that no hindrance was caused to the donees who enjoyed, sowed, cultivated, got cultivated, inhabited and claimed rights over the donated lands. No less instructive is the explicit reference to the redressal of the situation arising out of *kapata-shaasana* (कपट शासन) (forged grant deed).[47] The earliest land grant of the Valkha chiefs made by Bhulunda in the year 38 was recounted about a decade later[48] at the request of *Brahmana Parishad* (Assembly of the Brahmanas) when the king's verbal orders were put down on the copper plate (*taamrapatta-sanniveshita*).[49] This also happens to be the record where officials and people in the donated lands are instructed not to cause any obstruction to the work of donees. Thus, the dangers of misappropriation of gift-lands were not overlooked even at this initial stage of the land-grant economy in an area with tremendous potentialities of agrarian development.

NOTES

1. All these plates of Valkha chiefs have been edited and translated. Cf. K.V. Ramesh and S.P. Tewari (eds.), A *Copper-plate Hoard of the Gupta Period from Bagh, Madhya Pradesh*, New Delhi, 1990. (henceforth *CHGPB*).
2. For their detailed analysis, see K.M. Shrimali, *Agrarian Structure in Central India and the Northern Deccan*, New Delhi, 1987.
3. Cf. *CHGPB*, nos. I, III, XI, XIII-XV, XVIII, XIX, XXI and Appendix I.
4. D.C. Sircar, *Select Inscriptions*, vol. I, Calcutta, 1965, pp. 265, 394-5. See also Hira Lal, 'Betul Plates of Samkshobha: the Gupta Year 199', *Epigraphia Indica (EI)*, VIII, 1905-6, no. 28, p. 287, l. 9.
5. The contention of the editors that the charters cover the Narmada Valley 'falling within 72°-80° longitude and 20°-40° latitude' (cf. *CHGPB*, Introduction, p. xxiii) is extremely far-fetched—it would mean an area of nearly 0.4 million sq km. Most probably, the region included only the western districts of Madhya Pradesh such as Mandsaur, Ratlam, Jhabua, Dhar, Khargaon, Indore, Ujjain, Dewas, Khandwa and so on.
6. *CHGPB*, App. I, l. 5 and p. 62. Earlier, G.S. Gai had translated the relevant line as 'village site was created by stopping the cultivation of the field there', Cf. *EI*, XXXVIII, 1970, no. 41, p. 243.
7. *CHGPB*, App. V, ll. 2-3.
8. Ibid., no. XXVI, l. 6.
9. Twice in Bhulunda's grant of the year 50; cf. ibid., no. II, ll. 3-4. Other occurrences are in IV, ll. 3-4; VII, l. 4; XIII, l. 5; XV, l. 4; XVI, ll. 4-5; XXIV, l. 4; App. II, l. 4; and App. IV. l. 4.
10. *Patti* is used not only in the sense of a plot of land (*EI*, IX, 1907-8, no. 20, p. 169, n. 4) but also as a synonym for the land measure

nivartana in south Indian inscriptions (*EI*, VIII, 1905-6, no. 24, p. 236, n. 2) as well as a 'share of the produce' (*Corpus Inscriptionum Indicarum* IV, p. 599).

11. E.g. grant XVI, l. 4, *CHGPB*, p. 35.
12. Commenting on both these terms, D.C. Sircar argues that they stand 'primarily for "income" and secondarily "a holding", the income of which is enjoyed', *Indian Epigraphical Glossary*, Delhi, 1966, p. 262.
13. *CHGPB*, Introduction, p. xvi.
14. Ibid., nos. II, ll. 3-4 and XXIV, l. 4.
15. Ibid., nos. VII, l. 4; XV, l. 4; XVI, ll. 4-5; XXIV, l. 4; App. II, ll. 4; App. III, l. 4 and App. IV, l. 4.
16. Ibid., nos. II, ll. 3-4; IV, ll. 3-4 and XIII, l. 5.
17. Bappapishaachadeva as a donee occurs in three additional non-*pratyaya* land/village gifts; cf. V, ll. 2-6; VI, ll. 3-4 and XII, ll. 2-4. It is very likely that he was the cult figure of non-brahmanical tribal community. As for Narayana too, his non-aryan affiliations and the processes of brahmanization up to the Gupta times have been discussed at length, cf. Suvira Jaiswal, *The Origin and Development of Vaishanavism*, Delhi, 1980, pp. 32-52.
18. *CHGPB*, no. VII, l. 4.
19. Ibid., XIII, ll. 4-5.
20. Ibid., nos. IV, ll. 4-7; XVI, l. 4 and App. II. l. 4.
21. For *bhujyamaana*, ibid., nos. I, l. 7; IX, l. 6 and XVII, l. 3 while *poorva bhujyamaanaka* occurs in V, l. 3; VI, l. 3 and XVII, l. 4.
22. Ibid., IX, l. 6 cf. also XXIII, l. 6 for similar usage and numerous occurrences of *adya divasaadaarabhya* (starting from this day), as for instance in XXIV, ll. 6-7 and XVII, l. 7.
23. Ibid., XVII, l. 4.
24. Ibid., XIII, ll. 7-8 and XXIII, l. 7.
25. The inscription is also dated in two other reckonings. For this as well as the connotations of *pratyaya*, see *EI*, XXXIV, 1960-1, no. 21, pp. 141-50.
26. *CHGPB*, nos. XVI, l. 8; XVII, l. 7; App. III, ll. 6-7; App. IV, l. 6 and App. V, l. 6.
27. *EI*, XIII, 1915-16, no. 7A.
28. Ibid., ll. 8-9, p. 115.
29. Y.R. Gupte considers Taleshvar copper plates to be forgeries made between the sixth and eighth centuries AD (ibid., p. 113). It is not improbable that the original grants were made earlier. Since the same record also mentions grants issued on cloth (*pata* in l. 11), the original grant may have been on some perishable material.
30. *CHGPB*, nos. XIX, ll. 6-7 and XXI, ll. 7-8. The editors have translated *vapataam* in the former as 'broadcast' (ibid., p. 43), though elsewhere it has always been translated as 'sowing'.

31. Ibid., nos. III, l. 5 and IV, l. 8.
32. The Taleshvar copper plate of Vishnuvarman refers to various compounds ending in *vaapam* such as *kshetra-kulyavaapam, drona-vaapam, jangala-kulya-vaapam*; *khaari-vaapam*, etc. Cf. *EI*, XIII, 1915-16, no. 78, ll. 13-26, pp. 118-21.
33. *CHGPB*, no. XII, l. 7.
34. Ibid., nos. III, l. 6; V, l. 6; VI, ll. 6-7; X, l. 7 and XIII, ll. 6-7.
35. Ibid., III, l. 5.
36. *EI*, XIII, 1915-16, no. 78, l. 21, p. 119.
37. D.C. Sircar takes *kedaara* as a corn field. Cf. 'Kendupatna Plates of Narasimha II', *EI*, XXVIII, 1949-50, no. 33, l. 188, pp. 193-4; idem, *Indian Epigraphical Glossary*, p. 152. Since Sushruta mentions *kedaaraka* as a kind of rice (Cf. M. Monier-Williams, *Sanskrit-English Dictionary*, New Delhi, Reprint, p. 309, col. 2), the rendering of K.V. Ramesh and S.P. Tewari (*CHGPB*, no. XXIV, ll. 5-6, pp. 52-3) as paddy-fields is preferred.
38. Monier-Williams, op. cit., p. 59, col. 2.
39. *CHGPB*, no. XIII, l. 7.
40. Ibid., nos. III, l. 5; V, l. 6; VI, ll. 7-8: IX, l. 7; X, ll. 7-8; XII, ll. 7-8 and XIII, l. 7.
41. Ibid., Introduction, p. xii.
42. Ibid., App. I, ll. 4-5.
43. Ibid., no. XIV, ll. 3-4.
44. Ibid., no. XVI, l. 4.
45. Ibid., App. IV, ll. 3-4.
46. Ibid., nos. II, l. 7; III, l. 8; IX, l. 9; XIII, l. 9; XXIX, l. 7 and App. I, l. 8.
47. Ibid., no. VIII, l. 9.
48. G.S. Gai reads the year of recounting as 77 (cf. 'A New Grant of Bhulunda, Years 38 and 77, *EI*, XXXVIII, 1969-70, no. 41, l. 10, p. 46) but K.V. Ramesh and S.P. Tewari have rightly restored it as 47, cf. *CHGPB*, p. 61.
49. *CHGPB*, App. I, ll. 9-10.

CHAPTER 2

Perspectives from the Regions and the Construction of Early India

BHAIRABI PRASAD SAHU

Perspectives on early India have undergone significant changes since the middle of the 1950s. Unlike the conventional historiography, the ascendant perspective which became the dominant historiography through the subsequent decades, analysed and explained changes and the significance of such changes in the socio-economic and political structures as well as the cultural domain. Over the last two decades some of the assumptions of this historiography have been amended and refined, particularly with reference to the historico-geographic transformation of the regions outside the Gangetic heartland and the changes coming from within local societies. It is emphasized that for a proper appreciation of Indian history the regions must be a central focus.[1] One can recognize and accept the significance of the regions while simultaneously emphasizing the all-India socio-political and economic processes. The multiple sources of cultural antecedents, varying across spatial segments, pluralistic tradition of the Indian historical experience and the reality of an overarching cultural ethos and civilizational universe have been mutually interacting, not exclusive, phenomena. We propose to draw attention to the enduring significance of the regions, the variegated historically constituted cultural entities,[2] while simultaneously arguing for the reality of a pan-Indian ideology and civilization, emanating from the operation of historical processes which intertwined elements of the local and the transregional, which in turn helped to universalize aspects of the local and the regional cultures.

We now come to one of the most basic oppositions in historical literature, viz., the opposition between the pan-Indian view from the top and perspectives from the regions. Colonialist writings characterized Indian history either in terms of its bewildering variety—constructing exclusive identities on considerations of region, caste, language, ethnicity, etc., rendering it impossible to be held together as a socio-cultural and political unit—or constructed a totalizing and consequently hegemonic picture where the unchanging caste system and 'the village community' were represented as the defining traits. The politics of imperial enterprise and administrative requirements dictated these shifts in perceptions.[3] Notwithstanding their rebuttal of many aspects of the imperialist reconstructions, the nationalists wittingly or unwittingly accepted the idea of India as an undifferentiated entity and, deriving from it, as a given cultural and political reality. R.K. Mookherji's *The Fundamental Unity of India* is a good example of the tendency to associate modern ideas with India's ancient past. In the context of the struggle for freedom the compulsions of the nationalist historians, including their fears of ascribing the continuing inheritance of the regions their due is understandable. However, the long shadow it has cast over the dominant historiography in post-Independence India is somewhat intriguing, especially because the uneven patterns in Indian history have been recognized within the same historiography and historians have engaged with the problem since the late 1950s.[4] This centrist or epicentric perspective, derived largely from the Gangetic valley and its fringes, fails to appreciate and address the cultural pluralism of the variegated regions. Paradoxically the point of strength also appears to be the weakness of the dominant historiography. While its ability to generalize allows for easy comprehension, the same tends to homogenize the variety of human experience and ignores the specificity of the regions, their comparable, but not similar, socio-political trajectories.[5]

Integrating regional histories into the history of India represents a condescending attitude and is not the same as writing history from within and in terms of the processes in operation across regions.[6] Besides, regional history has a bearing on important questions such as causation, periodization and our understanding of the larger pattern of Indian history. The Indian nation is not that frail and fragile as to disintegrate if its oneness is not overemphasized. It is better to recognize and address reality rather than falsify it, if we are to create a sense of enduring unity. The notion of a monolithic unitarian nation/state is not true. Neither is the concept of India equivalent to a confederation of the regions. There is no conflict here as the two share a harmonious coexistence. However, the priority of one over the other is context specific. If the subsumption of the regions under the overarching idea of India does not do justice to the Indian historical experience, the opposite position asserting regionalism to the exclusion of an underlying unity too is a falsification of history. The truth lies in the dynamic interrelationship of the two, in the course of which they constituted each other. Regions have not remained insular from evolutions within a larger unit. Regional history and the larger pattern of Indian history, to use a familiar expression, move *in tandem*.

Understanding the regions on their own terms or looking at the general pattern of Indian history from the perspective of the regions is not the same thing as encouraging regionalism. Bernard S. Cohn vividly makes the point:

> The obvious distinction, conceptually, between the terms 'region' and 'regionalism' is sometimes overlooked. 'Region' with all its difficulties as a concept refers to means of classification of a wide variety of kinds of data, which helps analyse particular or general situations. 'Regionalism' refers usually to conscious or unconscious development of symbols, behaviours and movements which will mark off groups within some geographic boundary from others in other regions for political, economic, or cultural ends. *The term 'region' relates to a form of analysis, 'regionalism' to a call for action. . . .*[7] (italics added).

The above quote is intended to show that providing the regions their due in historical analysis need not be viewed with apprehension. It is a necessary academic exercise and entails a corrective to tendencies to generalize from the perspective of Gangetic north India. It may be mentioned that regions are anything but fixed, they evolve historically.[8] While regions interact with and imbibe aspects of the pan-Indian, it is important to remember that localities and sub-regions also co-here in their making.

In two recent articles and an edited volume which focus on the conception of India as gleaned from textual references,[9] it is argued that the idea of India militates against the privileging of one region, community, language or religious group over the others. But then the important question is when and how did this concept of India emerge and crystallize? The works of Amir Khusrau and Abul Fazl, among others, in medieval India represent the richness of India's composite culture and the country as home to different interacting traditions.[10] How is it that despite some references to languages, scripts and territories outside northern India these traits did not attract the attention of Alberuni in the same way a few centuries earlier? Was it simply because his was an outsider's view of India addressed to an exogenous audience or was there more to it? It is recognized that what one writes is informed by the tradition within which he/she writes yet the important question to ask is did the spatial spread of the Sultanate and the Mughal state across the Vindhyas and beyond help in shaping a richer perception of India or, to put it differently, did the societal processes of change of trans-regional universality fructify and come into their own around the middle of the second millennium AD, forcing others to pay attention, to take them seriously? The truth may be rooted in the interplay of the two developments. The formation of regional polities, evolution of regional languages and the pursuit of regional historiographies[11] largely during AD 1000-1600 as significant markers of the evolution of regions bear out our assumption. Flowing from what has been already said it would be logical to ask how and through what stages were the regions constituted and what relationship did they have with the larger idea of India? Regions like nations did not exist from times immemorial, they were formed through certain configuration of historical forces over time. We wish to develop the argument with reference to two interrelated aspects: first, the evolution of Brahmanical ideology and, secondly the spatial spread of state societies.

Admittedly, Brahmanical ideology and Hinduism are not the only route to understanding the Indian reality. Indeed, the past was made of a variety of constituents. The heritage of heterodoxy, for example, from the middle of the first millennium BC onwards stares one in the face and the mutual influences and borrowings between the heterodox sects and Brahmanical tradition in fashioning ideas and practices cannot be swept under the carpet. We choose to focus on Brahmanical ideology because for a large part of our cultural past under discussion, it appears to have been the dominant cultural strand. Besides, through it we wish to also show the gamut of interactions, very often quite complex, that went into the making of a unified civilization. The preference for the term Brahmanical as against Hindu/Hinduism has the advantage of indicating continuity from the later Vedic period onwards. Though Hinduism is seen as a movement from below, involving religious and social practices with local and regional roots, which transformed Brahmanism in the post-Gupta and early medieval centuries,[12] it needs no emphasis that the normative texts while accommodating such changes continued to espouse the core values and the Brahmanas never really seem to have given up their dominance, notwithstanding the pressures, compromises and accommodation they had to encounter and endure. Finally, the word 'Hindu' is a later day social construct.

We are charting the progress and development of Brahmanical culture and tradition, which changed in the course of its adoption and adaptation in the varied regions, under the influence of the inheritance of the autochthonous people whom it encountered, as it first moved in an easterly direction in the Ganga Valley and subsequently beyond the Gangetic heartland. It is generally agreed that the earlier theory that India was colonized by light-skinned migrants from Central Asia was apocryphal and that there is a need to discard such history in favour of the evidence for interaction and symbiotic relationship between these migrant groups and speakers of non-Aryan languages.[13] The boundaries of Aryavarta as a cultural region were not very sharply defined. They were both porus and flexible, flexible in so far as it extended geographically and incorporated new regions within its ambit and porus because, contrary to general perception, it was inclusive. However, accommodation did not necessarily take place on a footing of equality. Brahmanical tradition since its early emergence and evolution simultaneously practised integration and hierarchization of peoples, places, customs and rituals by assigning them different positions within its fold,[14] with reference to the dominant structures. Constructs such as Aryan and non-Aryan, *dvija* and shudra, brahmana-kshatriya *versus* vaisya-shudra were ingenious devices for ensuring hierarchy and incorporation. The sphere of influence of Brahmanical tradition also expanded through the emulation of its rituals by people who considered them to be superior. Desirous of raising their own status, they started following and participating in Brahmanical rites and rituals. The widening geographical focus of Brahmanical ideology was thus, a two-way process since its inception.

Peoples and regions once considered outlying or perceived with hostility were amalgamated at another point.[15] As one moves from the Rig Vedic period to the later Vedic times and further through *Baudhayana Dharmasutra* up to *Manusmriti* one gets a sense of the changing contours of the conception of ideas such as Aryan and Aryavarta, with their substance and spatial dimensions being constantly modified. Kalinga, Vanga, Magadha and Surashtra, once placed outside the core, were made part of it with the passage of time. The ordering of peoples, places and their customs and beliefs continued over time and it demonstrates the complex processes involved in the spread of Brahmanical ideology as well as the assimilation of disparate groups of people. Compilers of *smriti* literature when confronted with practices they did not approve of, accepted them as of the other or outlying regions and even dismissed them as belonging to another *yuga*. However, the very act of the inclusion of local customs and practices ensured their integration with the mainstream.[16] The Brahmanical tradition in course of its geographical spread and evolution acquired a composite character, fashioned out of elements derived from different regions. The distinctiveness and specificity of regional contexts, traits and symbols were lost many a time in the process of syncretism.

With the horizontal expansion of state societies, from the Gupta period onwards and the requirements of royal legitimation, local cults associated with different social groups were sought to be assimilated and universalized on considerations of vertical and horizontal legitimacy, within local societies and supra-local contexts, including the fraternity of Hindu *rajas*, respectively.[17] Popular Puranic religion best illustrates the accommodation and assymetrical placement of different cults, sects and castes in the socio-religious hierarchy. Local state formation and land grants in regions largely outside the Indo-Gangetic plains created conditions for the interface between Brahmanical ideology and the tribal world, with a bearing on modes of worship, proliferation of deities and developments such as the hectic temple building activity. *Tirthas* in the outlying regions such as Jharkhand, Orissa, Chhattisgarh, Madhya Pradesh and Rajasthan were the meeting place and melting pot of varied influences and thus, they provided cultural connectivity and facilitated acculturation.[18] The rise of *tirthas* in a general context of state formation evidently brings out their interrelationship and the former's role in political validation. In the Hindu pantheon, comprising Vishnu and Shiva, Shakti represented the third stream. The incorporation of Shakta sects into Brahmanical tradition marked an important stage in the transformation of the latter. The absorption of Tantric elements too symbolized the same. In the process of acculturation, the Brahmanic tradition both incorporated and Sanskritized aspects of tribal life in the peripheral regions.[19] Vijay Nath vividly portrays this dialogic process—cultic appropriation and extension of Brahmanical ideology on the one hand and its tribalization on the other.[20] The cults of Jagannatha at Puri and Vitthala at Pandharpur exemplify Brahmanic adaptability. The appeal of these deities over wide social and spatial segments made them the focus of regional political interest.[21] Examples of this kind can be multiplied. The cult of Brihadishvara at Thanjavur and Ekalingaji in Mewar were manifestations of similar processes.[22]

Brahmanical ideology acquired a sub-continental identity largely through its socio-political functions such as the production of texts like the Puranas, creation of local mythologies, spread of Vedic-Shastric-Puranic ideas, invention of origin myths for ruling families, among others, and the use of Sanskrit as a common language. The network of temple-centric *tirthas*, mass bathing in holy rivers, *kirtanas* and the recital of Puranic stories to collective gatherings prepared the ground on which the sense of belonging of different kinds of groups, across regions, was created and fostered. There was a complex interweaving of the local, regional and national through which attitudes and ideas were produced and circulated. Lest one gets the impression of an entirely harmonious situation it may be added that there was integration, but as Hermann Kulke puts it was 'integration through contestation'.[23] It is also important to remember that in the lived history not every social group or segment of space adhered to the dominant world-view. The multitude of cults, sects, castes and beliefs, located in varied social and spatial situations, converged to shape an agglomerate; but it did not ever lead to the formation of a monolithic socio-religious identity.[24] The twin processes of fusion and fission impacted the religious and cultural world in the same way as they affected the political domain in the early medieval centuries.[25]

Early Indian texts and inscriptions mention the terms Jambudvipa, Aryavarta and Bharata, which are usually equated with the idea of India.[26] Notwithstanding the inadequate or inconsistent self-perception of the idea of India encompassed in these concepts, the authors of the texts seem to have shared a common value system, heritage and language with others of their status. As Ainslie T. Embree aptly notes this is quite striking because Bharata or India was more often, than not, a multitude of political formations.[27] The formation of the concept of India sans a unified political enterprise of considerable durability is significant and needs to be explained.

In conventional historiography, the Mauryas and Guptas are generally considered to represent the great moments of political unity in early India. Owing to their chronological precedence one may begin the discussion on the interrelated aspects of historical transformation of space and the spread of state societies across regions starting with the Mauryas. Although on the basis of the geographical distribution of Ashokan inscriptions a certain measure of material and cultural uniformity is generally assumed for the subcontinent, recent studies demonstrate that the prosperity in material culture, during the said period, was largely limited to Gangetic northern India and the fringes of central India.[28] The processes leading to the emergence of the early historical period in peninsular India are seen to have gathered momentum during and after the Mauryas. The archaeology of early historic settlements in peninsular India largely seems to endorse this argument.[29] The uneven patterns of growth within the Mauryan state as well as the differential levels of interaction between the core (Upper and Middle Gangetic plains) and the peripheral regions have been convincingly argued and, flowing from it, the problems in equating a political formation such as the Mauryan empire with an undifferentiated social formation have been highlighted. The recent perspectives[30] do not negate the existence of an empire; what they do is to bring into relief the different faces of the state in the varied regions (dependent on the socio-cultural levels and revenue potential of the latter) and the overall nature and structure of the state. The nature of the presence of the state, it is said, had a bearing on the level of interaction, which in turn influenced the pace of historical transformation in different regions.

The period under discussion was important in terms of the beginnings of wide ranging interactions across the subcontinent and the opening of communication routes. The distribution of Northern Black Polished Ware shreds (the deluxe ware which originated in the middle Ganga Valley around 500 BC and was in circulation up to the end of the millennium) in central India and the Deccan as far as Amaravati, in Andhra Pradesh, and the location of Ashokan edicts at Dhauli, Jaugada and Amaravati on the east coast point in that direction. The evidence for rouletted ware (a pottery of Mediterranean origin and inspiration dated to the post-Mauryan times) on the entire east coast at numerous sites from Bengal to Tamil Nadu together with the Tamil-Brahmi inscriptions from Tamil Nadu, supposedly derived from Ashokan Brahmi, make the more general point about the network of linkages which seem to have begun during the time of the Mauryas. In the western Deccan donations by craftsmen and merchants from far away places to Buddhist establishments at Sanchi, Bharut and numerous other centres show the movement of people, goods and ideas over long distances during the post-Mauryan period. Similarly, movements between the west and the east coast, on the Godavari, through Central Deccan endorse the wide ranging interactions. Mauryan presence in the Deccan seems to have paved the way for the subsequent flowering of Buddhism in the region.

It is in these aforesaid interactions and not in the administrative integration under the Mauryas that the transition to the early historical phase in the Deccan is located.[31] The Mauryas spread into the Deccan at a point when the Megalithic communities were on the road to the development of internal differentiation. Their subordination to the metropolitan state in the end enhanced the status of the evolving ruling strata because of the said association and they emerged wiser with experience in the management and control of labour as well as produce.[32] The withering away of the Mauryan state saw the emergence of localities, which corresponded to the earlier *janapadas* of north India.[33] To elaborate, the Maharathis and Mahabhojas, for example, represent the evolution of such locality-centred ruling elites as a consequence of the internal differentiation within local communities and related changes. Developments such as these not only problematise the question of administrative integration of the Deccan under the Satavahanas but also point to the phased socio-political integration of the regions. Continued manifestation of the process of locality formation is discernible in the post-Mauryan period in Kalinga, coastal Andhra and Karnataka, among others.[34] This process of secondary state formation, deriving from the combination of autochthonous forces and influences from developed spatial segments, continued throughout Indian history. State formation as late as the late medieval centuries in Chhotanagpur and north-eastern India bears testimony to that.[35]

The Kushana state in north India, covering large parts of Central Asia as well, comprised numerous socio-cultural entities. The persistence of the *Ganasamgha* tradition in the Punjab plains from the Mauryan times through the Kushana period and beyond, besides indicating weak property rights in land and poor agricultural growth, reflects this reality. Bactria and the Ganga Valley only added to the vibrant cultural mosaic. The numerous epithets such as *Maharaja*, *Devaputra* and *Shaonano Shao Koshano* (Kushana king of kings) that the rulers of the dynasty chose to bear and the accommodation of a variety of deities from different religions on the reverse of their coins (from Shiva to Buddha, even fire cult and the moon) were perhaps a recognition of the existing socio-cultural pluralism within their domain.[36] Through the adoption of various titles, incorporation of myriad religions and the representation of the rulers in supernatural contexts on the obverse of the coins (with the nimbus behind their head or their being shown as emerging from the clouds, among others) and the practice of *devakula,* the Kushanas sought to reach out to diverse groups and legitimize themselves in a situation of ethnic, linguistic and cultural plurality.[37] The idea of unity was hung on the state and the state was expected to deliver. It tried to do so by appearing to be responsive.

The Gupta and early medieval centuries were marked by the horizontal spread of state societies, largely into areas with little prior experience of organized state activity. The emergence of the *atavikarajyas* and *Pulindaraja rashtra* in different parts of central India sheds light on local state formation in tribal areas and their movement towards complex society. The Maitrakas of Gujarat, the Vakatakas of Maharashtra, Kadambas of Karnataka, Pallavas of Tamil Nadu, Vishnukundins of Andhra, Sarabhapuriyas of Chhattisgarh and the hill states of Punjab provide good examples of state formation and the extension of state society at the local and trans-local levels.[38] They also suggest the introduction of a comparable socio-political structure throughout the country. Local state formation in a big way outside the Ganga Valley and the corresponding rise in land grants unmistakably show the interrelationship between the two phenomena. On the basis of land grant charters, it is suggested that about fifty states spread over Maharashtra, eastern Madhya Pradesh, Andhra Pradesh, Orissa and Bengal between *c.* AD 400 and 650.[39] In the succeeding centuries they were replaced by fewer numbers of subregional and regional states. The evolution of such states points to the emerging configurations, leading to larger, expansive and integrated structures. The relationship between the monarch and *samantas* at different levels may have been more complex than is usually conceded. There was certainly more to it than loyal submission or affiliation on the part of the subordinates.[40] However, given the fact that early medieval polities were polycentred, graded and characterized by parcellization of sovereignty, integration was never complete; it was largely imperfect. State formation and socio-economic transformation were interrelated processes. The Gupta and post-Gupta periods were characterized as much by state formation as the step-wise formation of agrarian regions. The regional polities of the Palas and Senas of Bengal, Somavamsis and later Gangas of Orissa, Kakatiyas of Andhra, Hoysalas of Karnataka and Cholas of Tamil Nadu from the ninth-tenth centuries onwards thus, arose in a wider context of societal changes. B.D. Chattopadhyaya refers to this as the simultaneous operation of multiple interrelated processes of change,[41] involving agrarian expansion and peasantization of the tribes, caste formation, cultic integration and the gradual extension of state society.

Let us carry the story forward with reference to the region with which we have greater familiarity. In Orissa the formation of a regional agrarian base was achieved by the time of the Somavamsis and later Gangas, though the processes leading to it began much earlier at the local and supra-local levels.[42] It provided the basis for the gradual unfolding of the cultural personality of the region and the attendant larger political experiments. The region-specific caste system emerged with some measure of clarity during the Ganga-Gajapati period (twelfth-sixteenth centuries).[43] Although characteristics of the Oriya script began to develop in the thirteenth century, early Oriya inscriptions date between the fourteenth and mid-sixteenth centuries. The flowering of Oriya literature as manifested in Sarala Das's writings and those of the *Panca Sakhas* broadly converges with this time bracket. While the earliest use of the terms *Odisa* and *Odia* are dated to the middle of the fourteenth century, the identification of the region with *Odarastra* and *Odisa rajya* is observed in the *Sarala Mahabharata* and Gajapati inscriptions respectively in the fifteenth-sixteenth centuries. These simultaneous developments perhaps indicate the formation of a linguistic-historical region in itself. Efforts to reconstruct a trans-dynastic history of the region and a continuous regional tradition through the *Madala Panji*, the beginning of which is dated around AD 1600, would have strengthened the attenuated cultural identity.[44] The cult of Jagannatha too created a sense of affiliation and bonding and contributed to the making of a regional identity. In the south consequent to the evolution of a regional kingdom under the Kakatiyas and the gradual convergence of language and territory almost during the same period, i.e. eleventh-sixteenth centuries, Andhra too experienced nascent identity formation.[45] Later, the emergence of a sense of shared history going back to the Kakatiyas helped to strengthen the awareness of belonging to a region.

These developments were neither entirely unitary nor unilineal. It is difficult to argue for a pattern of uniform validity all over the country. The regions had distinct spatio-temporal trajectories.[46] Further, we may remind ourselves that regions themselves are constituted by sub-regions and localities. Punjab, for example, broadly comprised the plains and hills, but closer scrutiny allows for further demarcations.[47] Similarly, the Konkan, Khandesh and Vidarbha constitute Maharashtra. Visible manifestations of the importance of localities can be located in the assertion by local chiefs in the last phase of Chola history and the Nayakas following the military incursions of the Sultanate into the Kakatiya territories. Recent works on south Orissa and northern Andhra have reinforced the importance of such studies.[48] Historical transformation of spatial segments and their integration with the mainstream is a continuous process. In all periods of Indian history there were spaces outside the orbit of organized state intrusion. Such spaces, however, did not exist in immutable isolation, but in a state of interaction and change.[49]

This perspective, deriving from a desire to understand the structure and pattern of Indian history in terms of regions and trans-regional processes, focusing on the agency of local societies and constant interaction and change, constitutes an inversion of the dominant historiography which largely revolves around a narrative of colonization, crisis and fragmentation.[50] The alternative perspective has the advantage of presenting a coherent theory of historical change in pre-colonial India. Its emphasis on change within continuity helps to successfully engage with and negotiate the question of transition from the early historical to the early medieval and the early medieval to the medieval without having to address the curious problem of reconciling the fragmented world of early medieval India, as has been played out in the dominant historiography, with the centralized structures of the Sultanate. One may justly ask where does it leave the Purana-centred theory of Kali Age crisis which has been invoked to explain the passages from antiquity to the early medieval.[51] The notion of *Kali Yuga* was not symptomatic of a historical crisis, but represented a crisis of confidence; the fear of the loss of status and privileges and related anxieties of the Brahmanas in the face of unprecedented all-round growth and prosperity in the post-Maurya centuries. Besides, it alludes to the formation of local states within the framework of Brahmanical ideology.[52] Brahmanical ideology with its focus on the *dharmic* image of kingship had to distance the king from the concept of the Kali, which constituted the negation of *dharma* and all that it stood for. Inscriptions of the Pallavas, Kadambas, Vakatakas and numerous dynasties in Orissa yield evidence of it. Constructs such as the Kali Age provide unmistakable evidence for the ascendancy of Brahmanical ideology and its centrality in the making of the strategies of domination across the subcontinent from the Gupta and the post-Gupta centuries onwards.

Sanskrit emerged as the language of literature, administration and ideology or what Sheldon Pollock describes as the formation of 'the Sanskrit Cosmopolis' took shape largely between AD 300 and 1300 across the subcontinent (and beyond).[53] The trans-regional spread was actualized through a process of adaptation and appropriation of trans-local flows. The early medieval centuries witnessed the spread of Vedic-Shastric-Puranic ideas in course of the extension of the frontiers of state society. The influence of Gupta symbols, idioms and notions of power can be gleaned in the inscriptional records of numerous dynasties in early medieval India. The common political culture points to the unfolding of comparable socio-political processes across regions.[54] The question to be asked is how did it happen? The *prashasti* sections with their usually standardized messages of the images of kingship and the benedictory and imprecatory verses in the land grant charters, bearing influence of *Dharma-shastra* literature, in the process of their being read out on various occasions played an important role in the process of cultural communication.[55] Public records since the time of the Ashokan inscriptions were meant to be read or read out to the people. Numerous temples in peninsular India bear inscriptions charting the achievements of individual rulers and dynasties. Such inscriptions on temple walls as public documents may be invested with similar qualities.[56] Works such as the Puranas and Caritas, among other things, incorporated the past and transmitted it to the present and future. In the process, they tried to revitalize and reproduce society. Inscriptions, art and literature not only reflected society but through a conscious use of ideas and symbols, perhaps, also tried to change it, especially in regions experiencing the interplay of multiple processes of change.[57] In addition to political authority, exchange centres (*mandapikas* and *penthas*), trade and traders,[58] Brahmanic settlements, *mathas*, and temples as centres of cultural dissemination and integrative agencies provided the necessary supra-local and trans-regional linkages. The all-India Brahmanic ideology evolved through these network of linkages, engaging and coming to terms with different regions at different points of time. There was a constant appropriation of the local and localization of the trans-local flows, which created cultural arenas that went beyond those defined by the localities or regions.

There is no denying the fact that the number of people who thought of themselves as sharing a particular language or culture may have been small and confined largely to the elites. In spite of the fuzzy regional and trans-regional identities, the names of Mughal *subas* such as Bengal, Malwa and Gujarat remind us of the force of the regions in Indian history. The idea could be elaborated with reference to the history of the *Bhakti* movement, which at one level gives the impression of an inclusive, all-encompassing phenomenon and at another demonstrates the region-bound specificities, viz., Gaudia *Bhakti*, *Bhakti* in the Punjab and Braja.[59] However, simultaneously the depth and reach of an over-arching, unifying Brahmanical ideology can be seen in the hierarchies based on *varna*, gender and the patrilineal kinship structure as well as the caste-land-power pyramid through much of the country. The processes of regional/sub-regional identity formation and decentring of identities were at work simultaneously, leading to the making of a composite, pluralist tradition.

NOTES

1. See B.D. Chattopadhyaya, *The Making of Early Medieval India*, New Delhi, 1994, Introduction; idem, *Studying Early India: Archaeology, Texts and Historical Issues*, Delhi, 2003; H. Kulke, 'The Early and Imperial Kingdom: A Processural Model of Integrative State Formation in Early Medieval India' in idem (ed.), *The State in India 1000-1700*, Delhi, 1995, pp. 233-62; Romila Thapar, *Cultural Pasts: Essays in Early Indian History*, New Delhi, 2000, essay nos. 5, 6, 7 & 9 and B.P. Sahu Introduction, in his (ed.), *Land System and Rural Society in Early India*, New Delhi, 1997.
2. The concept of region can be defined in quite different ways. For the problems of definition see Bernard S. Cohn, 'Regions Subjective and Objective: Their Relation to the Study of Modern Indian History and Society', in his *An Anthropologist Among the Historians and Other Essays*, Delhi, 1987, pp. 100-35, and B.D. Chattopadhyaya, *Studying Early India: Archaeology, Texts and Historical Issues*, ch. 4.
3. See Bernard S. Cohn, 'African Models and Indian Histories', in Richard G. Fox (ed.), *Realm and Region in Traditional India*, New Delhi, 1977, pp. 90-113.
4. See, for example, D.D. Kosambi, 'The Basis of Ancient Indian History', reprinted in A.J. Syed (ed.), *D.D. Kosambi on History and Society; Problems of Interpretation*, Bombay, 1985, pp. 27-63; Idem, *An Introduction to the Study of Indian History*, Bombay, 1956, early chapters; also see R.S. Sharma, *Indian Feudalism (c. 300-1200)*, 2nd edn., Delhi, 1980, Appendix 1.
5. For a comprehensive critique see B.D. Chattopadhyaya, *The Making of Early Medieval India*; idem, 'State and Economy in North India: Fourth Century to Twelfth Century', in Romila Thapar (ed.), *Recent Perspectives of Early Indian History*, Bombay, 1995, pp. 309-46.
6. See note 1 above.
7. Bernard S. Cohn, op. cit., p. 119.
8. Ibid., pp. 100-35.
9. Irfan Habib, 'The Formation of India: Notes on the History of an Idea', *Social Scientist*, nos. 290-1, July–August 1997, pp. 3-10; idem, 'The Envisioning of a Nation: A Defence of the Idea of India', *Social Scientist*, nos. 316-17, September–October 1999, pp. 18-29; Irfan Habib (ed.), *India: Studies in the History of an Idea*, New Delhi, 2005.
10. See the articles by Imtiaz Ahmad, Iqtidar Alam Khan and S.A. Nadeem Rezavi in Irfan Habib (ed.), *India: Studies in the History of an Idea.*
11. For regional historiographies centering around a regional deity and its *kshetra* see Kulke, *Kings and Cults: State Formation and*

Legitimation in India and Southeast Asia, New Delhi, 1993, essay nos. 9, 10, 11 & 12.
12. See Vijay Nath, 'From "Brahmanism" to "Hinduism": Negotiating the Myth of the Great Tradition', Presidential Address, Ancient India Section, Proceedings Indian History Congress (hereafter PIHC), Calcutta session, 2001, pp. 26-56.
13. See Romila Thapar, *From Lineage to State (Social Formations in the Mid-First Millenium* BC *in the Ganga Valley*), New Delhi, 1984, ch. II; R.S. Sharma, 'Problems of Continuity and Interaction in Indus and Post-Indus Cultures', *Social Scientist*, nos. 320-1, January–February 2000, pp. 3-11.
14. See Kum Kum Roy, 'In Which Part of South Asia did the Early Brahmanical Tradition (1st millennium BC) Take its Form?' *Studies in History*, 9(1), 1993, pp. 1-32.
15. Ibid.
16. Richard W. Lariviere, 'Dharmasastra, Custom, "Real Law" and Apocryphal Smritis', in Bernard Kolver et. al. (eds.), *The State, the Law and Administration in Classical India*, Manchen, 1997, pp. 97-110.
17. H. Kulke, 'The Early and Imperial Kingdom: A Processural Model of Integrative State Formation in Early Medieval India', in note 1 above.
18. See Vijay Nath, 'Tirthas and Acculturation: An Anthropological Study', *Social Science Probings*, 10 (1-4), 1993, pp. 28-54.
19. See Romila Thapar, 'Imagined Religious Communities? Ancient History and the Modern Search for a Hindu Identity', *Modern Asian Studies*, 23(2), 1989, pp. 209-31; also in idem, *Cultural Pasts: Essays in Early Indian History*, pp. 965-89.
20. See notes 12 and 18 above.
21. See, for example, A. Eschmann, H. Kulke and G.C. Tripathi (eds.), *The Cult of Jagannatha and the Regional Tradition of Orissa*, New Delhi, 1978.
22. See George W. Spencer, 'Religious Networks and Royal Influence in Eleventh Century South India', *Journal of the Economic and Social History of the Orient* (hereafter *JESHO*), 12(1), 1969, pp. 42-5; James Heitzman, 'Ritual Polity and Economy: The Transactional Network of an Imperial Temple in Medieval South India', *JESHO*, 34, 1991, pp. 23-54 and Nandini Sinha, 'A Study of State and Cult: The Guhilas, Pasupatas and Ekalingaji in Mewar, Seventh to Fifteenth Centuries AD', *Studies in History*, 9(2), 1993, pp. 161-82.
23. H. Kulke, 'The Integrative Model of State Formation in Early Medieval India: Some Historiographic Remarks', in A. Tanabe (ed.), *The State in India: Past and Present*, Delhi, 2005. Also see B.D. Chattopadhyaya, *The Making of Early Medieval India*, p. 30.

24. See Romila Thapar, 'Imagined Religious Communities?', op. cit., pp. 209-31. Also see Suvira Jaiswal, 'Semitising Hinduism: Changing Paradigms of Brahmanical Integration', *Social Scientist*, no. 223, December 1991, pp. 20-32.
25. Thapar, ibid. For the political sphere see B.D. Chattopadhyaya, 'Political Processes and the Structure of Polity in Early Medieval India: Problems of Perspective', Presidential Address, Ancient India Section, Burdwan Session, PIHC, 1983, pp. 25-63.
26. Ainslie T. Embree, 'Brahmanical Ideology and Regional Identities', Idem, *Imagining India: Essays on Indian History*, New Delhi, 1989. Also see Ishrat Alam, 'Names for India in Ancient Indian Texts and Inscriptions', in Irfan Habib (ed.), *India: Studies in the History of an Idea*, pp. 36-44.
27. Embree, 1989.
28. See Romila Thapar, *The Mauryas Revisited*, New Delhi, 1987, pp. 1-31. For a different perspective see R.S. Sharma, *Aspects of Political Ideas and Institutions in Ancient India*, Delhi, 1991, pp. 392-402.
29. For example, see the diagram showing the history of sites in R.S. Sharma, *Urban Decay in India (c. 300-1000)*, Delhi, 1987, pp. 192-7. Also see D.K. Chakrabarti, *The Archaeology of Early Indian Cities*, New Delhi, 1995, on early historical cities.
30. See for example, I.W. Mabbett, *Truth, Myth and Politics in Ancient India*, New Delhi, 1972, ch. 6; Thapar, *The Mauryas Revisited,* op. cit., and G. Fussman, 'Central and Provincial Administration in Ancient India: The Problem of the Mauryan Empire', *The Indian Historical Review* (hereafter *IHR*), 14(1-2), 1987-8, pp. 43-72.
31. See S. Seneviratne, 'Kalinga and Andhra: The Process of Secondary State Formation in Early India', *IHR*, 7(1-2), 1980-1, pp. 54-69 and B.D. Chattopadhyaya, 'Transition to the Early Historical Phase in the Deccan: A Note' in B.M. Pande and B.D. Chattopadhyaya (eds.), *Archaeology and History*, vol. II, Delhi, 1987, pp. 727-32.
32. Seneviratne, ibid.
33. Chattopadhyaya, 'Transition to the Early Historical Phase in the Deccan: A Note', op. cit, pp 727-32.
34. For Kalinga see B.P. Sahu, 'Early State in Orissa: From the Perspective of Changing Forms of Patronage and Legitimation', in B. Pati, B.P. Sahu and T.K. Venkatasubramanian (eds.), *Negotiating India's Past: Essays in Memory of Professor P.S. Gupta*, New Delhi, 2003, pp. 29-51.
35. See Surajit Sinha, 'State Formation and Rajput Myth in Central India', *Man in India*, 42(2), 1962, pp. 35-80; K.S. Singh, 'A Study in State Formation Among Tribal Communities', in R.S. Sharma and V. Jha (eds.), *Indian Society: Historical Probings*, New Delhi, 1977,

pp. 317-36 and Surajit Sinha (ed.), *Tribal Polities and State Systems in Pre-Colonial Eastern and North Eastern India*, Calcutta, 1987.

36. See B. Puri, 'Ideology and Religion in the Kushana Epoch', in B.G. Gafurov et al. (eds.), *Central Asia in the Kushan Period*, II, Moscow, 1975, pp. 183-90.
37. Even in Gupta and post-Gupta times royal patronage was broad based. The compulsions of political power mostly made it necessary to recognize and address the rich socio-religious ground reality. For the Kushana state see R.S. Sharma, *Aspects of Political Ideas and Institutions in Ancient India*, pp. 291-309; A.K. Narain, 'The Kushana State: A Preliminary Study', in H.J.M. Ciaessen and P. Skalnik (eds.), *The Study of the State*, The Hague, 1981, pp. 251-73.
38. See for example, H. Kulke, 'Some Thoughts on State and State Formation under the Eastern Vakatakas', in Hans Bakker (ed.), *The Vakataka Heritage: Indian Culture at the Crossroads*, Groningen, 2004, pp. 1-9; Yogender Dayma, 'State Formation in Early North Karnataka: A Study of the Early Kadamba Inscriptions', M.Phil. dissertation, Department of History, University of Delhi, 2005.
39. Sharma, *Urban Decay in India*, p. 168.
40. For details of the argument see B.P. Sahu, 'The State in Early India: An Overview', PIHC, Aligarh Session, 1994, pp. 94-5. See the early chapters in Georg Berkemer and Margret Frenz (eds.), *Sharing Sovereignty: The Little Kingdom in South Asia*, Berlin, 2003.
41. Chattopadhyaya, *The Making of Early Medieval India*, Introduction.
42. See B.P. Sahu, 'Agrarian Changes and the Peasantry in Early Medieval Orissa (*c.* AD 400-1100)', in V.K. Thakur and A. Aounshuman (eds.), *Peasants in Indian History*, Patna, 1996, pp. 283-311.
43. B.P. Sahu, 'The Past as a Mirror of the Present: The Case of Oriya Society', *Social Science Probings*, 9 (1-4), 1992, pp. 8-23.
44. For the *Madala Panji* see Kulke, *Kings and Cults*, pp. 137-91. Regional historiographies elsewhere also seem to have served similar functions. See in the same volume essay nos. 11 and 12. Also see H. Kulke, 'Historiography and Regional Identity: The Case of the Temple Chronicles of Puri', in H. Kulke and B. Schnepel (eds.), *Jagannath Revisited: Studying Society, Religion and the State in Orissa*, Delhi, 2001, pp. 211-25.
45. See Cynthia Talbot, 'Inscribing the Other, Inscribing the Self: Hindu-Muslim Identities in Pre-Colonial India', *Comparative Studies in Society and History*, 37(4), 1995, especially pp. 710-19.
46. See Sahu (ed.), *Land System and Rural Society in Early India*, Introduction.
47. See Romila Thapar, 'The Scope and Significance of Regional History', Presidential Address, Punjab History Conference, 1976, reprinted in

Idem, *Ancient Indian Social History: Some Interpretations*, New Delhi, 1987, pp. 364-67.

48. B. Schnepel, *The Jungle Kings: Ethnohistorical Aspects of Politics and Ritual in Orissa*, Delhi, 2002; Georg Berkemer, 'Orissa Revisited: A View from the South', in Kulke and Schnepel (eds.), *Jagannath Revisited: Studying Society, Religion and the State in Orissa*, pp. 253-70.
49. See B.D. Chattopadhyaya, 'Autonomous Spaces and the Authority of the State: The Contradiction and its Resolution in Theory and Practice in Early India', in Bernhard Kolver et al. (eds.), *The State, the Law and Administration in Classical India*, Munchen, 1997, pp. 1-14. Also see his 'State's Perception of the "Forest" and the "Forest" as State in Early India', in B.B. Chaudhury and Arun Bandopadhayay (eds.), *Tribes, Forests and Social Formation in Indian History*, Delhi, 2004.
50. See fn. 1 above; also Kulke, 'The Integrative Model of State Formation in Early Medieval India: Some Historiographic Remarks'.
51. For the equation of the idea of the Kali Age with a systemic crisis see B.N.S. Yadava, 'The Accounts of the Kali Age and the Social Transition from Antiquity to the Middle Ages', *IHR*, 5 (1-2), 1978-9, pp. 31-63; R.S. Sharma, 'The Kali Age: A Period of Social Crisis', in S.N. Mukherjee (ed.), *India: History and Thought*, Calcutta, 1982, pp. 186-203.
52. See B.P. Sahu, 'Conception of the Kali Age in Early India: A Regional Perspective', *Trends in Social Science Research*, 4(1), 1997, pp. 27-36.
53. 'The Sanskrit Cosmopolis, 300-1300 CE: Transculturation, Vernacularization and the Question of Ideology', in Jan E.M. Houben (ed.), *Ideology and Status of Sanskrit: Contributions to the History of the Sanskrit Language*, New York, 1996, pp. 197-247.
54. See B.P. Sahu, 'Legitimation, Ideology and State in Early India', Presidential Address, Ancient India Section, Mysore session, PIHC, 2003, pp. 56 ff.
55. See H. Kulke, 'Some Observations on the Political Functions of Copper Plate Grants in Early Medieval India', in Bernhard Kolver, et al., (eds.), *The State, the Law and Administration in Classical India*, pp. 237-43.
56. See Georg Berkemer, ' "The Centre Out There" as State Archive: The Temple of Simhacalam', in Hans Bakker (ed.), *The Sacred Centre as the Focus of Political Interest*, Groningen, 1992, pp. 119-30.
57. B.P. Sahu, 'Profiling Daksina Kosala—An Early Historical Sub-Region?', paper presented at the International Conference of the Orissa Research Project on 'Centres Out There? Facets of Sub-Regional Identities', at Salzau (Germany), 13-17 May 2003.

58. See B.D. Chattopadhyaya, 'Markets and Merchants in Early Medieval Rajasthan' and 'Urban Centres in Early Medieval India: An Overview', in idem, *The Making of Early Medieval India*; idem, *Aspects of Rural Settlements and Rural Society in Early Medieval India*, Calcutta, 1990, ch. 3; and Ranabir Chakravarti, *Trade and Traders in Early Indian Society*, Delhi, 2002, chs. 9 and 10.
59. I am thankful to my colleague R.P. Rana for drawing my attention to it.

MEDIEVAL INDIA

CHAPTER 3

Love and Deviance in Mughal India: The *Kissa* of Heer and Ranjha

INDU BANGA

There was a strong indigenous tradition of love and war in the creative literature of medieval India. Drawn initially from the Puranas, epics and the local legends, these tales were often woven around the adventures of kings, princes, nobles and sometimes, merchants and others. Their appeal appears to have been as much for the social constraints over the expression of romantic love which was generally regarded as deviance, as for the societal appreciation of heroism as a value. Gradually, different expressions of love became the dominant theme of the creative literature emerging in regional languages. Love within wedlock, or with a happy ending, had a fascination for the writers and patrons of literature because love and marriage were not supposed to go together. At the same time, the tales of wifely devotion were popular because of their reinforcement of the patriarchal values. From about the fifteenth century, that is a little before the time of Chaitanya (1486-1533), the appeal of Radha's selfless devotion to Krishna and its superiority over

*An earlier version of this paper under the given rubric of love and deviance in literature, was presented at the seminar 'Literature, Art and Secular Thought in Mughal India', held in April 2005 at the Centre of Advanced Study, Aligarh Muslim University, Aligarh. I gratefully acknowledge the perceptive comments of the participants and the constructive criticism of Prof. J.S. Grewal. I also benefited from Prof. V.N. Datta's suggestion and my discussions with colleagues in Sociology and some other departments at the Panjab University, particularly Prof. Jagjit Singh of the School of Punjabi Studies.

conjugal love was growing in the devotional literature produced in Bengali, Maithili, Braj Bhasha, and other languages.[1]

It was in this context that the love tales in the Persian literary tradition found a congenial soil in medieval India. Amir Khusrau (1253-1325) rewrote the well-known tales of Laila and Majnun and Shireen and Khusrau, and composed the *Ashiqa*, a narrative poem (*masnavi*) on the tragic love of Prince Khizr Khan Khalji and Deval Rani, who were his contemporaries. Influence of the Sufi ideas of intense devotion to the Pir and God, pangs of separation, and union after death is evident in Khusrau's treatment of love.[2] Even human love was ennobled in the re-rendering by Jami (1414-92) of the Koranic tale of Zulaikha's passion for Prophet Yusuf in terms of her steadfastness and Yusuf's reciprocity which culminated in their marriage.[3] By the sixteenth century, adaptation of the Persian narrative poem to the love tales in regional languages, and often in the Sufi idiom of love of God, became increasingly evident.[4]

As may be expected, such poems were written mostly by Muslims who generally used the Persian script. The *Chandain* by Maulana Dawud, written in Awadhi in the 1370s, is the earliest known *masnavi* based on a local love legend (of Lorik and Chanda), and actually used for elucidating the Sufi doctrines. From the sixteenth century onwards more such tales came to be composed in Awadhi, the most notable being Malik Muhammad Jaisi's *Padamawat*. The Bengali Sufi poets like Alaol too composed narrative poems on some of the romantic tales, including that of Padmini and Ratan Singh.[5] Unlike Jaisi and Alaol, and some other poets in Awadhi and Bengali, whose stories revolved round the courts of petty rulers, the poets in the Punjab and Sindh 'based their themes on local romances thereby adding a touch of realism to their verses'. The Sufi idea of 'self-less love' as 'an approach to divine love', is also believed to have inspired the narrative poems in Punjabi (called *kissa* from Arabic *qissa*).[6]

I

Much before the emergence of Punjabi *kissa* as a literary form, love tales sung by professional bards like the Dhadis, Bhatts and Mirasis appear to have become part of the regional lore in north-western India. The romance of Sassi, an heiress, and Punnu, a Baloch merchant, was located in Sindh or the lower Sindh Sagar Doab. The locale of the story of Mahiwal, a merchant of Samarqand, and Sohni, a potter's daughter, happened to be the upper Chaj Doab, in the town of Gujrat founded in the reign of Akbar. The protagonists in the tales of Mirza and Sahiba and Heer and Ranjha belonged to the clans inhabiting the lower Rachna and lower Bari Doab in the Punjab.[7] Of these romances, regarded today as 'masterpieces of Indian literature',[8] the tale of Heer and Ranjha was the first to be put in writing some time during the late sixteenth century. As a saga of 'constant love', it is said to have acquired the same importance and sanctity in the Punjab region as did the love between Abelard and Heloise in Europe, Laila and Majnun in Arabia, and Shireen and Farhad in Persia.[9]

By the time of Akbar (1542-1605), the story of Heer was well-entrenched in the folklore and religious literature in Punjabi. The Punjabi Sufi poet Shah Husain (1538-1601) refers to Heer and Ranjha in about a dozen verses, using the female voice. For example,

> Crying *mahi mahi,* I have myself become Ranjha.
> Call me Ranjhan everyone and none should call me Heer.
> I have found the spouse I was searching for.[10]

Underlining the superiority of the disciple's love for the Guru, Bhai Gurdas (1551-1640), the Sikh divine and poet, refers to the fame of Heer and Ranjha 'for the love they bore each other'.[11]

Some scholars of Punjabi literature tend to emphasize the idealized aspect of this love and regard it as *'ishq-i majazi*, that is, love of God through love of His manifestation in the beauty of the beloved. The *kissa*-writers according to this view, elevated the lover to the status of a gnostic (*'arif*). Perpetual striving, pangs of separation, suffering, or even ruin in an earthly sense, are said to be built into this idea which is supposed to have no room for carnal (*nafsi*) love.[12] A 'spiritual significance' has thus been attached to the sacrifice of the lovers who are said to have attained perfection, that is 'joy, peace and knowledge' in the union after death.[13] It is maintained that even the poets believed that the narration of such stories of '*majazi* lovers' was 'a service to God', as much as listening to them.[14]

The first Punjabi version of the *kissa* of Heer and Ranjha was composed during Akbar's reign by Damodar Gulati, an Arora shopkeeper and perhaps a *patwari* in Heer's village of Jhang.[15] The first Persian version of this tale by Maulana Baqi, who had come to India from Badakhshan during Akbar's reign, is placed in the late 1570s.[16] From the seventeenth to the nineteenth century, a large number of Muslim and non-Muslim poets produced different versions of this tale. The historians of Punjabi literature list sixty such versions in Punjabi and over two dozen in Persian and Urdu and a few even in Hindi and English.[17] Three versions of this tale current around Jhang and Patiala and on the borders of Balochistan are reproduced in the *Legends of the Punjab* by Richard Temple, compiled soon after the annexation of the Punjab.[18]

II

By this time the story of Heer and Ranjha had entered a formal work of history. In the *Char Bagh-i Panjab*, a history of the region written in Persian in 1849, Ganesh Das, a hereditary *qanungo* of Gujrat, gives the essentials of this tale.[19]

1. Dhido, a Jat of the *got* Ranjha, was the youngest of the seven sons of Mauju, a *zamindar* and also the *chaudhari* of his area near the town of Takht Hazara, situated on the bank of the river Chenab. After the death of his father, Dhido (Ranjha) was given the poorest part of the land by his brothers, and he felt obliged to give up the effort to till it.
2. Ranjha dreamt of a sweet maid called Heer who was all kindness and affection to him. He left home in search of her, and on the way met the *panj-pirs* who pointed towards Jhang-Sial and gave him the blessing of union with Heer.
3. The boat in which Ranjha was ferried across the river Chenab carried a gorgeous bed for Heer, the daughter of Chuchak, the Sial, who was the virtual master of those parts. Treating that as a good omen, Ranjha gave his

golden ring to the boatman and persuaded him to let him sleep in Heer's bed. This happened to be the day when Heer was coming with her friends to the river for recreation. She was furious to find a stranger sleeping in her bed, but on seeing his handsome face, her rage gave place to compassion, ecstasy and love.

4. Heer persuaded her father to employ Ranjha as a cattleherd. They used to meet in the pasture lands in the low lying areas and share the food brought by Heer. Many months passed in this honeyed happiness.
5. Their love was discovered by Heer's uncle Kaido who reported to Heer's father Chuchak. Of the two alternatives of killing Heer or marrying her off suitably, the latter course was decided upon at the suggestion of her mother. Heer was hurriedly betrothed and married to Saida, a Jat of the Khera clan and son of the *chaudhari* of Rangpur. Heer remained deeply unhappy in her marital home and appeared to suffer from a serious malady which no medicine could cure and which enabled her to keep Saida away.
6. Ranjha became a *fakir* and went to every house in Rangpur in the garb of a *jogi*, wearing long ear-rings (typical of the *jogis*). He set up his *dhuni* (constant fire) outside the village and claimed to cure all ailments. Stories of his miracles soon became current.
7. Heer had shared the secret of her love for Ranjha with her husband's sister, Sehti, who thought of a strategem by which Heer managed to meet Ranjha and elope with him during the night.
8. When the fact of their flight became known in the morning, they were pursued by the Kheras, and caught near a village named Adilpur. They were taken to the nearest *hakim* (of Kot Qabula) who declared that Heer's marriage to Saida contracted against her will was unlawful. As it had not been consummated, she was free to go with Ranjha if she liked.
9. Instead of going straightaway with Ranjha as suggested by him, Heer preferred to return to her parents and get lawfully wedded before going to Takht Hazara. The *muqaddam* of the village of Maghiana near Jhang supported Heer in her

decision. He also assured Ranjha that he would himself take over the responsibility of a guardian if Chuchak refused to marry Heer to Ranjha.

10. Ranjha went to Takht Hazara to bring his marriage party. Heer was bitten by a cobra on the very night of their separation and died. When a fleet footed barber (*hajjam*) carried this news to Ranjha, he sighed, swooned and died in a few moments.
11. Chuchak refused to see the corpse of his daughter whose wayward love had cost him all his honour and reputation. She was buried on the way to Jhang. Four bare walls without a roof mark her grave. Ranjha was buried at Takht Hazara, without a memorial.[20]

The names of Heer and Ranjha 'are enshrined in the hearts of the people', says Ganesh Das. He places the death of Heer and Ranjha in the reign of Adil Shah Sur (1553-5).[21]

Empirically, this story covers the south-western tract of the region on both sides of the river Chenab, falling in the Mughal *subas* of Lahore and Multan. Among the important places figuring in this *kissa* are: Takht Hazara, the headquarters of the *sarkar* of Rachna Doab, located on the right bank of the Chenab; Jhang-Sialan on the left bank of the river; Rangpur, lower down the river to its west, in the *sarkar* of Multan; Kot Qabula, again across the river, in the lower Bari Doab, in the *sarkar* of Dipalpur.[22] The story is concerned with that segment of the rural society which owned property in land and cattle, and exercised influence and power in the countryside, also mediating between the rural people and the representatives of the state.

According to the *Ain-i Akbari*, the tract was inhabited predominantly by Jats.[23] In Ibbetson's *Punjab Castes* (1883), however, the Sials are mentioned as claiming descent from the Panwar Rajputs.[24] The Ranjha Jats were mainly the owners and cultivators of land. The Sials and Kheras, on the other hand, probably depended more on their cattle wealth. The low-lying areas close to the river where Heer and Ranjha are said to meet were particularly good for pasturage. It may be relevant to mention that this semi-agricultural but mainly pastoral situation continued down to almost the end of the nineteenth century when this tract was brought under canal irrigation by the British.[25]

Finally, the grave of Heer, located between Jhang and Maghiana, as mentioned by Ganesh Das, was actually in existence in the middle of the nineteenth century. Richard Temple describes the structure as under:

> Hir's tomb is about half a mile from the civil station of Jhang, and is marked on the survey map as 'Mookurba Heer', which stands for 'Maqbara-i-Hir', or Hir's monument. It is a brick building, resembling in style the ordinary Musalman tomb of the 16th century, with the exception that instead of being covered by a dome it is open to the sky. There are niches or windows on the four sides. That on the west is closed, while the other three are open, the reason assigned being that the wind should blow on Hir from every direction except that of her home Rangpur [*sic*], where she had been murdered. The tomb stands close to an old bed of the Chenab, and it is related that at the time of Hir's death the river was still flowing in this old bed, and that Hir appeared in a vision to a merchant who was travelling past in a boat, telling him to build her tomb in this place, and to build it so that the rain of heaven should always fall on it.[26]

The architectural term used for such a structure is 'hypaethral', that is 'without a roof, open to the sky', which was 'not a common feature', according to the historians of architecture.[27] In Temple's view, however, the architecture of the tomb accorded with the supposition that Heer and Ranjha 'flourished' during the sixteenth century. He further says that a fair of 'some local celebrity' was held at Heer's tomb in the month of *Magh* (February).[28] Notwithstanding the sanctity attached to Heer's grave (she is locally referred to as 'Mai Heer' according to Temple), this apparently was a much later structure, and the story associated with it is said to be a myth.[29]

III

Among the most notable literary presentations of the *kissa* of Heer and Ranjha in Punjabi in Mughal times are those of Ahmad Gujjar's, composed in the 1680s,[30] and Shahjahan Muqbal's, composed in the 1740s.[31] Sayyad Waris Shah built upon their works, and the status of a classic is accorded to his *Heer Waris* composed in the 1760s.[32] It may not be out of place here to mention that after about two centuries, the UNESCO commissioned an English rendering of this 'immortal classic'.[33]

As may be expected a priori, there are differences of language, meter, style, detail and even of some characters in the versions of the *kissa* of Heer and Ranjha. Writers also differ in the sequence of the story, its dramatic turns and invocation of the supranatural, including the role of the *panj pirs*, and the degree of suffusion of the Sufi idiom.[34] Even when the framework of Damodar Gulati's story is broadly followed by the later writers, there are some significant differences between his work and the compositions of Ahmad, Muqbal and Waris Shah.

Damodar focuses upon Jhang Sial (actually beginning the story from there), portrays the life of the people more faithfully, and uses the local dialects more effectively. He is appreciative of Akbar's rule, but his Heer accuses the *qazi* of dishonesty and injustice. Damodar's language may be termed Multani or Lahindi, and he mostly uses the *davayya* meter. It may be interesting to note that Damodar's description of Heer's marriage—combining Brahmanical rituals and Islamic practices with local customs—and his reference to Ramu Brahman as Sehti's paramour, suggest that though Islam had spread in the south-western parts of the region by the late sixteenth century, it had not yet penetrated the lives of the people deeply.

By contrast, Ahmad's *Heer,* composed a century later in the reign of Aurangzeb, upholds the orthodox Islam and, at the same time, deepens the mystic colour of the story. Waris Shah largely follows his points of emphasis, characters, sequence and dramatic turns, but written soon after the decline of the Mughal power in the region, the *Heer Waris* is more openly critical of the *qazi* and the *mulla*. Muqbal, a blind *fakir* writing in the reign of Muhammad Shah, too is critical of the *qazi,* though Muqbal's story is regarded as comparatively flat. Three of them name Heer's mother as Malki, which is more Islamized, whereas Damodar gives her name as Kundi. In his version, Heer's husband is called Sahiba Khera, but the trio call him Saida. Among other things, they differ with regard to the name and place of the *jogi* whose help was sought by Ranjha. Damodar ascribes Ranjha's leaving home to the unsympathetic behaviour of his three brothers' wives. Waris alludes to the jealousy of Ranjha's seven brothers for the youngest and the favourite son of their deceased father. In the accounts of Ahmad and Waris, poor quality of the land given to Ranjha and economic hardship become the reason for his leaving home, whereas Muqbal invokes a dream to explain it. The language of the three later poets may be termed standard Punjabi of the times, and Waris in particular makes an effective use of the popular *bait* meter.

However, all four of them end their tale differently. In the treatment of Damodar Gulati, Heer and Ranjha were able to live as *fakirs* till their death, retaining thus the essential aspects of idealized love and happy ending. The Sufiized versions of Ahmad, Muqbal and Waris Shah underline the pangs of separation, but vary with regard to the end. Muqbal sends them to Mecca where they lived ever after; in Ahmad's *Heer* they die, but as a concession to the popular sentiment, they were seen by the Hajis going to Mecca, Ranjha showing them the way and Heer serving them food. Waris Shah is the only one, initially, to make the story end in a tragedy: Heer was poisoned by her family and Ranjha could not bear to live after hearing the news.

There are differences also in the treatment of the idea of love. In Ahmad's *Heer*, love is 'subordinated to Islamic law and traditional piety'. Defeated by conservative forces in life, Heer and Ranjha are given 'high status as martyrs (*pak shahid*) of love.[35] For Muqbal, the love of Heer and Ranjha was pious (*pak*), and they became gnostics.[36] Waris Shah, who was affiliated to the Chishtia order of Sufism, professedly writes his story as an allegory. As he claims at the end of his narration, Heer symbolized the soul and Ranjha symbolized the body, the two consecrating their lives to *'ishq-i majazi*.[37] In Waris Shah's treatment, the emotions and experiences of *'ishq-i haqiqi* are transferred to the former, 'adding altogether a new dimension to his depiction of earthly love'.[38] In other words, idealized love (*'ishq-i majazi*) is presented as a stage in the progress towards divine love (*'ishq-i haqiqi)*. At the same time, Waris Shah is keen to give a refreshing version of the love of Heer, leading to her 'union' with Ranjha.[39] The *Heer Waris,* thus, remains somewhat ambivalent with regard to physicality between Heer and Ranjha. The scholars of literature are also divided on this issue.[40] The folk tales suggest that whenever Heer and Ranjha were together they kept a copy of the holy Koran between themselves.[41]

It may be interesting to note that this is reminiscent of the idea of the 'sword of chastity', or self-imposed restraint, in the Tristan (Tristram) legend, and general 'rejection of physical love' in the romances of Europe born in the twelfth century.[42] In feudal Europe despair and suffering was an essential ingredient of the experience of love because the norms of the courtly society did not approve of it. Before the Renaissance and the spread of individualism, love and marriage were considered incompatible in Europe.[43] It was the 'monumental integrity', 'self-denial', and the 'disturbing' image of the dying lovers that had an uplifting, aesthetic and exciting appeal which accounted for the popularity of the romantic myths in medieval European society.[44]

Just as romanticism gradually yielded place to realism in modern Europe, so the *kissa* lost its creative potential with the advance of colonial rule in the Punjab (1849-1947). Despite the availability of the print medium and widespread circulation of the *kissa*, it began to be replaced by new literary forms and tendencies by the beginning of the twentieth century.[45] Emotional appeal of the love tale of Heer and Ranjha seems to have been eroded apparently in the changed socio-economic and socio-cultural context of modern India.

IV

'Every work of literature is the product of a given social situation', and embodies its diversities, complexities and contradictions. As a 'social document' it also tells us 'something of the changing historical situations'.[46] Different facets of a changing world open up in the tale of Heer and Ranjha as rendered successively by Damodar, Ahmad, Muqbal and Waris over a period of nearly two centuries, but we are concerned here with the essential aspects of the story in the context of love and deviance, as suggestive of tension in a changing historical context.

Deviance signifies 'any behaviour which is not consonant with those expectations and norms for individual conduct which are shared and recognized within a social system'. Generally, it denotes a behaviour which is both 'infrequent and dysfunctional', and which violates the *mores* or other social rules 'commonly regarded as necessary to cohesion and order within a social group'.[47] In the Freudian sense, deviance represents 'an essential conflict between the desires and impulses of the individual and the constraints imposed by members of a social group'.[48] Moreover, different social groups in a society have different sets of norms for social control or maintenance of order and stability; deviance from these is punished and conformity is rewarded by implication.[49]

The *kissa* of Heer and Ranjha stood on the partial failure of social controls exercised by the privileged segment among the agri-pastoral clans of Jats, including the Sials. Some sort of deviant behaviour in fact was evident at several levels. By not tilling his share of land, by leaving home in search of a dream, by falling in love with Heer, and by becoming a *jogi* pursuing love, Ranjha was doing what is ordinarily not expected in the situation as known from other sources. But such lapses or idiosyncrasies on his part were nothing compared to Heer's transgressions. Her falling in love, and her stealthy meetings with Ranjha enraged her father sufficiently to consider killing her. Apparently, this was not an uncommon lapse in the countryside of the day, and Heer remained within the tolerance level by giving in to the pressure of the family and kin group to get married to Saida. However, she did that under protest, questioning the *qazi* and the system represented by him. She again deviated from the expected behaviour by not letting her lawfully wedded husband exercise his conjugal rights. Her final desperate act of elopement with Ranjha set all the modes of social control in operation—the family, social custom and the state.

The account of Ganesh Das differs from other versions which bring in the *qazi*, and later the local administrator, to enforce the social norms, and then invoke the supranatural to set Heer and Ranjha free, only for an idealized ending or the tragic parting (or union) in the Sufi idiom. Heer's death by poisoning in Waris Shah's version was the final resolution of the problem of social control. Rather, it was delayed action upon the course considered earlier by her kinsfolk. Her father's strong disapproval of Heer's deviance is evident even in Ganesh Das's somewhat prosaic account. Despite the social and spiritual resolution of the problem, the story leaves the reader acutely conscious of the tension between notions of personal love and fidelity on the one hand, and those of family honour and the appropriate roles of a daughter and wife, on the other. But, then, this was the *raison d'être* of the tale. Furthermore, its popularity through successive regimes—Turko–Afghan, Mughal, Sikh and even early British—reinforces, paradoxically, both its universality and autonomy. This points to the relative distance of the State from the day-to-day lives of the people, at least in the arid, pastoral and sparsely populated areas of the lower *doabs* in the Punjab.

V

We may now sum up the bearing of historical context on the *kissa* of Heer and Ranjha. The genre itself, and its emphasis on romantic or tragic love, was probably the product of political and cultural interaction between the subcontinent and the Islamic world. Moreover, when Ahmad, Muqbal and Waris were writing, the Punjab was experiencing economic distress, social upheaval, political turmoil, and even eternal invasions.[50] Some scholars of Punjabi literature maintain that this situation deepened the predilections of the *kissa*-writers towards tragedy.[51] Furthermore, as the first region to come into contact with the Turks, the north-west came to be suffused with Sufi tradition, and several Sufi orders flourished here.[52] The impact of Sufism was instrumental in the large-scale conversions to Islam which eventually made the Punjab a Muslim majority area. At the same time, orthodox Islam sat relatively lightly on the pastoral tribes in its south-western parts, the scene of the story of Heer and Ranjha. The customs and notions of honour particularly associated with the Jats of the area, in combination with the Sufi idiom, appear to have provided substantial bases for the tale as also for its appeal.

The crucial component of this story of personal love was, in all probability, the counterpart of the idea of personal devotion in the medieval Indian movements of 'devotional theism', a generic term used for the widespread phenomena that comprehended Sufism, Bhakti, Sants and Sikhism. These movements shared the individual seeker's intense devotion for the *pir*, *guru* or a personal God, which even permitted women to seek liberation through spiritual union with the object of devotion. Several women are known to have joined these movements of social and religious protest in different parts of India, including the Punjab. They could be accepted in these movements because they generally transferred the attitude of complete devotion and surrender woven into the patriarchal norms in secular life to the spiritual sphere.[53] It was likely that in most situations women joined these liberating movements after their husbands and other male members of the family had done so.

The *kissa* of Heer and Ranjha reflects the tension between the emergent social consciousness and the traditional patterns of social relations and values. Despite the changing social vision in medieval north India, love and marriage did not go together. Marriage remained a social institution *par excellence* (which it still is), combining social reproduction with social control, security and honour for the woman and her family, while to the man and his family it provided continuity, stability and economic, sometimes even political, advantage. Love outside marriage was also regarded as the man's prerogative. In this situation, the assertion of the freedom to love and marry by Heer and Ranjha and their reciprocity and steadfastness was not merely deviance. It was an isolated act of rebellion which was foredoomed in the given social situation. In Waris Shah's treatment, if seen independently of the idea of idealized love (*'ishq-i majazi*), this story becomes 'a saga of suffering which is human in nature but social in context'.[54] Its tragic finale, whether inspired by personal experience or spiritual affiliation of the poet, was in tune with the general trend and ethos of the Perso-Arabic love tales. The *Heer Waris* resolutely left behind the conventional or happy ending of the Sanskritic *prem katha* and its hesitant accommodation by Damodar, Ahmad and Muqbal. Nearly all the later versions of this *kissa* end in tragedy.[55]

Thus, the appeal of the story of Heer and Ranjha essentially lay in the daring to love and its failure or tragic end in conventional terms. It evoked compassion among its listeners, some of whom apparently believed that it also earned them religious merit. There probably were some other social and psychological reasons for its popularity. At one level, relief from daily drudgery was provided by the minstrels singing this tale of love. As the story of the dishonour and disrepute of the powerful sections in the rural society (the Sials disapproved of its recitation according to Richard Temple), it probably evoked the sympathies of the underdogs—the small peasants, artisans and labourers.[56] As J.S. Grewal puts it, 'empirically a symbol of threat to the social order, Heer becomes aesthetically a source of escape from the degradation of the world around'.[57]

Furthermore, even men and women belonging to the upper classes, or conforming to their norms and customs, appear to have empathized with Heer and Ranjha whose exercise of personal choice could probably have had a vicarious appeal. This would be largely true of the urban classes as well. Ganesh Das, at any rate, clearly expresses admiration for the lovers. Ironically, however, in his case, as evident from his great appreciation of *sati* elsewhere, this assimilates the idea of wife's fidelity and devotion so essential for the working of the patriarchal value system.[58] Thus, it appears that the appeal of the *kissa* of Heer and Ranjha in pre-modern times was as much for the exaltation of love—whether spiritual or personal—as of fidelity and chastity so essential for the maintenance of the patriarchal structure.

NOTES

1. For a general understanding of literature in regional languages in medieval north India, see S.K. Chatterjee, 'Language and Literature: Sanskritic', in R.C. Majumdar et al. (eds.), *The Delhi Sultanate, The History and Culture of the Indian People*, Bombay, 1960, pp. 490-521. Several scholars have contributed to the chapter on literature, in idem (eds.), *The Mughal Empire: The History and Culture of the Indian People*, 3rd edn., Bombay, 1994, pp. 555-84.
2. Wahid Mirza, *The Life and Works of Amir Khusrau*, rpt., Delhi, 1974, pp. 177-81, 195-9. Khusrau used Nizami (d. 1209) as his model, but the literary quality of Nizami's *Khusrau-Shirin* and *Laila-u-Majnun* could be matched only by the romance *Nal-Daman* (Raja Nal and

Damyanti) by Faizi (1547-95). S.A.A. Rizvi, *A History of Sufism in India*, 2 vols., rpt., New Delhi, 1997, vol. 1, pp. 362-3.

3. Thomas Patrick Hughes, *Dictionary of Islam*, rpt., Calcutta, 1988, pp. 250-55, 716-17. Jami's treatment, according to Hughes, turned the story into 'one of the most popular love songs of the East'. According to Rizvi, this 'masterpiece of mystic poetry' inspired poets not only in West Asia but also in different parts of India' who added 'their own delicate touches'. *History of Sufism*, vol. I, p. 371. Firdausi (d. 1020) was probably the first to render it in poetic form. However, in the Koran the role of Zulaikha has been depicted as satanic as she tries to seduce Yusuf whose righteousness and restraint have been emphasized. The earliest Punjabi version of this love tale was written by Hafiz Barkhurdar probably in AD 1679. S.R. Sharda, *Sufi Thought: Its Development in Punjab and its Impact on Panjabi Literature (from Baba Farid to 1850 AD)*, New Delhi, 1974, pp. 184, 189, and 208-9.
4. On the analogy of a medieval French poet, S.K. Chatterjee terms the transition in romances and story telling as 'the Matter of Medieval India' which 'took shape' between *c.* AD 1000 and 1400, and which entered a new cycle from the sixteenth century onwards, which he calls 'the Matter of the Islamic World—Persia, and Arabia'. 'Language and Literature: Sanskritic', *Delhi Sultanate*, p. 496.
5. Rizvi, *History of Sufism*, vol. I, pp. 364-71; vol. II, pp. 434-7. Badauni mentions that verses from the love story of Lorik and Chanda were recited even from the pulpit, and 'the people used to be strangely influenced by hearing them'. Abdul Qadir Badauni, *Muntakhab-ut-Tawarikh*, vol. I, tr. and ed. George S.A. Ranking, revised and enlarged by B.P. Ambashthya, rpt., Patna, 1973, p. 333. Among other such tales in Awadhi may be mentioned Kutban's *Mrigawati* and Manjhan's *Madhu-Malti*, both of which were composed in the early sixteenth century.
6. Rizvi, *History of Sufism*, vol. II, p. 437. See also, Sant Singh Sekhon and Kartar Singh Duggal, *A History of Punjabi Literature*, New Delhi, 1992, p. 74; Sant Singh Sekhon, *A History of Punjabi Literature*, Patiala, 1996, vol. II, pp. 56-64. The Punjabi *kissa* and tales of West Asian origin were somewhat different from the Sanskritic *prem kathas* popular in medieval India which were often secular in spirit and which generally had a happy ending.
7. J.S. Grewal and Indu Banga (tr. and ed.), *Early Nineteenth Century Panjab (From Ganesh Das's Char Bagh-i-Panjab)*, Amritsar, 1975, pp. 56, 145-52.
8. K.M George et al. (eds.), *Masterpieces of Indian Literature*, New Delhi, 1997, vol. II, pp. 1087-9, 1112-13, 1133-5, 1141-3.

9. Richard Temple (ed.), *Legends of the Punjab,* rpt., Patiala, 1963, vol. II, p. 177.
10. Here we are using the English rendering by Professor J.S. Grewal from his forthcoming paper entitled, 'Gender and Love in Medieval Punjabi Literature'. For some other Kafis using the symbolism of Heer and Ranjha, see Jeet Singh Seetal (ed.), *Shah Husain: Jeevan te Rachna* (Punjabi), Patiala, 1995, pp. 76, 95, 98 and 100. For some English renderings see, Sekhon, *Punjabi Literature,* vol. II, pp. 169-81, especially pp. 170, 171, 172, 175, 176 and 181.
11. The other classical lovers extolled by Bhai Gurdas in this verse, which serves as the prelude to a longish *Var*, are Laila and Majnun, Sassi and Punnu, Sohni and Mahiwal, and relatively less known Sorath and Bija. Giani Hazara Singh (ed.), *Varan Bhai Gurdas* (Punjabi), (7th edn.), Amritsar, 1962, *Var* 27, *Pauri* 1, p. 447. For an English rendering, Jodh Singh (tr. and ed.), *Varan Bhai Gurdas: Text, Transliteration and Translation*, Patiala, 1998, vol. II, p. 143.
12. Sharda, *Sufi Thought*, pp. 186-98.
13. Lajwanti Ramakrishna, *Punjabi Sufi Poets* AD *1460-1900*, rpt., New Delhi, 1973, pp. 9 and 10.
14. Sharda, *Sufi Thought,* p. 193. The Sufi poets are said to present the 'applied form' of Sufism through their *kissas*. Ibid., p. 187.
15. Gurdit Singh 'Premi' (ed.), *Damodar Rachnavali* (Punjabi), Patiala, 1974, pp. 3-5.
16. Muhammad Baqir, 'Heer-Ranjhe da Sabton Purana Malum kissa' (Punjabi), in Jeet Singh Seetal (ed.), *Waris Shah: Jeevan te Rachna*, Patiala, 1970, pp. 338-58. The author saw Baqi's manuscript containing around 2,400 verses at Karachi. Even Badauni quotes some of Baqi Kolabi's verses with appreciation. See Abdul Qadir Badauni, *Muntakhab-ut-Tawarikh*, vol. III, tr. and ed. Wolseley Haig, rpt., p. 270. Kolabi died in Jaunpur in 1579 during the rebellion of Masum Khan Kabuli. Ibid., vol. II, tr. and ed. W.H. Lowe, p. 284.
17. Joginder Singh, 'Hor Bolian wich Heer' (Punjabi), in Seetal (ed.), *Waris Shah: Jeevan te Rachna*, pp. 373-7; Shakir Pursarthi, 'Heer da *Kissa* Urdu-Farsi wich' (Punjabi), ibid., pp 379-72. Outside the Punjab the manuscripts of this tale are said to be available at Karachi, Delhi, Rampur, Patna, Kolkata and Hyderabad.
18. Temple, *Legends*, vol. II. pp. 177-81 and 506-80.
19. Ganesh Das, *Char Bagh-i-Panjab* (Persian), ed. Kirpal Singh, Amritsar, 1965, pp. 211-17. For an abridged version, see Grewal and Banga, (tr. and ed.), *Early Nineteenth Century Panjab,* pp. 148-50.
20. Temple, *Legends,* vol. II, pp. 177-8.
21. However, the historians of Punjabi Literature place the death of Heer and Ranjha before the time of Babur. Sekhon, *Punjabi Literature,* vol. II, p. 64. In fact, there is a good deal of hair-splitting among them

about the exact period of Heer and Ranjha. The consensus is that they were freed by the *hakim* of Kot Qabula in the time of Bahlol Lodhi, around AD 1472.

22. These places existed in the Mughal period and still do. See Irfan Habib, *An Atlas of the Mughal Empire*, New Delhi, 1982, Sheets 4-AB.
23. Abul Fazl, *Ain-i Akbari*, tr. H.S. Jarrett (2nd edn. rpt.), Delhi, 1997, pp. 331-5.
24. Denzil Ibbetson, *Punjab Castes*, rpt., Patiala, 1970, p. 147.
25. Indu Banga, 'Ecology and Land Rights in the Punjab', *International Journal of Punjab Studies*, vol. 11, no. 1, 2004, pp. 66-7.
26. Temple, *Legends*, vol. II, pp. 177-8.
27. *The Penguin Dictionary of Architecture*, rpt., Penguin, 1977, p. 140. See also, *Encyclopaedia Britannica*, 1959, vol. 12, pp. 12 and 20.
28. Temple, *Legends*, vol. II, p. 178.
29. This is maintained among others by Gurdit Singh 'Premi' (ed.), *Damodar Rachnavali*, p. 11; Kulbir Singh Kang, *Sayyid Waris Shah*, Amritsar, 1975, p. 68.
30. S.S. Padam (ed.), *Heer Ahmad*, Barnala, n.d., pp. 19-20. See also, J.S. Grewal, 'The Hir of Ahmad', *Proceedings Punjab History Conference*, 26th Session, Patiala, 1994, p. 116.
31. Shamsher Singh Ashok (ed.), *Muqbal Rachnavali*, 2nd edn., Patiala, 1947, p. 1.
32. Jeet Singh Seetal (ed.), *Heer Waris*, Delhi, 1963, pp. 10-12.
33. Sant Singh Sekhon (tr.), *The Love of Hir and Ranjha* (Waris Shah), Ludhiana, 1978, Preface. According to G.S. Talib, 'Waris himself and his creations Hir and Ranjha are the national figures of the Punjab, both in the Indian and Pakistani countryside'. 'Literature: Punjabi', in Majumdar (ed.), *The Mughal Empire*, p. 575. According to Sekhon, narration of the story of Heer came to be regarded as a kind of challenge and test for the aspiring poets of Punjabi. *Punjabi Literature*, vol. II, pp. 62-3.

    Some of the well-known poets of the early nineteenth century are Hashim, Ahmadyar, Fazal Shah and Miran Shah. The *kissa* of Heer and Ranjha came to the eastern part of the Punjab later in the century. Among some popular versions in this area are those by Bhagwan Singh, Lahora Singh, Joga Singh, and Kishan Singh Arif, Ibid., pp. 89-91 and 108-49.
34. This comparative understanding is based, among others, on the following works: Sekhon, *Punjabi Literature*, vol. II, pp. 65-73 and 87-95; Premi (ed.), *Damodar Rachnavali*, pp. 21-4; Padam (ed.), *Heer Ahmad*, pp. 67-118; Ashok (ed.), *Muqbal Rachavali*, pp. 16-18; Sharda, *Sufi Thought*, pp. 189-204; Kulbir Singh Kang, *Punjabi wich Kissa Heer Ranjha* (Punjabi), Amritsar, 1983, pp. 70-81.

35. Padam (ed.), *Heer Ahmad*, p. 285. See also, Grewal, 'The Hir of Ahmad', p. 117.
36. Ashok (ed.), *Muqbal Rachnavali*, p.111; see also, Sharda, *Sufi Thought*, p. 197.
37. Seetal (ed.), *Heer Waris*, p. 208.
38. J.S. Grewal, 'The World of Waris', in Sudhir Chandra (ed.), *Social Transformation and Creative Imagination,* New Delhi, 1984, pp. 114-16.
39. Ibid., p. 107.
40. The sceptics make much of the frequent use of the name 'Bhag Bhari' in *Heer Waris* to suggest that the poet probably had a romantic attachment with a woman of this name which 'remained unrequited'. He is believed to have 'sublimated his own love for Bhagbhari' in the romance of Heer and Ranjha. Kartar Singh Duggal, 'Heer Waris Shah', in George (ed.), *Masterpieces of Indian Literature*, p. 1087. The love of Heer and Ranjha is depicted therefore 'essentially as a human phenomenon' pitted against the social forces. Jasbir Singh Ahluwalia, *Punjabi Literature in Perspective*, Ludhiana, 1973, pp. 117-19. See also, Sant Singh Sekhon (ed.), *Heer Waris Shah* (Punjabi), New Delhi, 1969, pp. 14-18. For the opposite view, see Sharda, *Sufi Thought,* pp. 190-4.
41. Sekhon (ed.), *Heer Waris Shah,* p. 14.
42. Dennis de Rougemont, *Passion and Society*, tr. Montgomery Belgion (rev. edn.), London, 1956, pp. 34 and 98. There are five different versions of this myth referred to by Rougemont. For a brief reference, see Rhoda A. Hendricks (comp. and ed.), *A Dictionary of Mythologies*, London, 1981, p. 197.
43. There, in fact, was a judgement to this effect in Europe in AD 1174 Rougemont, *Passion and Society*, pp. 34, 44 and 45. Moreover, 'only a few instances of romantic love were known in antiquity' in Europe, and all ended tragically. Death was 'the inevitable fate' of love. Oswald Schwarz, *The Psychology of Sex,* Penguin, 1955, rpt., pp. 97 and 102.
44. Rougemont, *Passion and Society*, pp. 23, 25 and 51.
45. See, for example, Sekhon and Duggal, *History of Punjabi Literatrue,* pp. 107-19, 127-8, 138-9, 147 passim.
46. Grewal, 'The World of Waris', p. 107. See also, Sudhir Chandra, 'Literature and Changing Social Consciousness', *Indian Historical Review,* vol. VI, nos. 1-2, 1979-80, pp. 209-29.
47. G. Duncan Mitchell (ed.), *A Dictionary of Sociology,* rpt., London, 1977, pp. 167-8.
48. Ibid., p. 55. In other words, suffering arising from deviance is suggestive of the 'time honoured conflict between love and any sort of "ought", such as duty, loyalty, work, and the like'. Schwarz, *The Psychology of Sex,* p. 107.

49. See Peter Burke, *Sociology and History: Controversies in Sociology Series,* London, 1980, pp. 57-60.
50. Chetan Singh, *Region and Empire: Panjab in Seventeenth Century*, Delhi, 1991, pp. 229-308; Muzaffar Alam, *The Crisis of Empire in Mughal North India: Awadh and the Punjab, 1707-48,* Delhi, 1986, pp. 176-203; Veena Sachdeva, *Polity and Economy in the Punjab during the late Eighteenth Century*, New Delhi, 1993, pp. 8-13, 16-47 and 50-62. See also, Indu Banga, *Agrarian System of the Sikhs: Late Eighteenth-Early Nineteenth Century*, New Delhi, 1978, pp. 11-22.
51. See, for example, Attar Singh, 'Punjabi Kissian wich Dukhant te Honi' (Punjabi), in Seetal (ed.), *Waris Shah: Jeevan te Rachna,* pp. 24-30; Padam (ed.), *Heer Ahmad,* pp. 110-13.
52. For a discussion of Sufism in the Punjab, J.S. Grewal, *Guru Nanak in History*, rpt., Chandigarh, 1979, pp. 71-103. For some detail on the later period, see Rizvi, *History of Sufism*, vol. II, pp. 57-109, 196-244 and 264-79.
53. Indu Banga, 'Gender Relations in Medieval India', in J.S. Grewal (ed.), *The State and Society in Medieval India,* New Delhi, 2005, pp. 463-6.
54. Ahluwalia, *Punjabi Literature in Perspective,* p. 118.
55. Padam (ed.), *Heer Ahmad,* p. 111.
56. Sekhon (ed.), *Hir Waris Shah,* pp. 12-13.
57. Grewal, 'Gender and Love in Medieval Punjabi Literature'.
58. Marital love up to the point of *sati* is equated by Ganesh Das with *ishq-i haqiqi,* or the love for God. Indu Banga, 'Gender Relations in Medieval India', Grewal (ed.), *The State and Society in Medieval India*, p. 460. See also, Ganesh Das, *Char Bagh-i-Panjab,* pp. 179, 181-8, 211-17 and 265-72.

CHAPTER 4

Love and Gender in Medieval Times as Reflected in the Literary Punjabi Tradition

(In the Reign of Akbar)

J.S. GREWAL

> The love of Laila and Majnun is known in all the four quarters of the world. The praise of the love of Sorath and Bija [Sammi and Dhol] is sung sweetly by the ministrels. Well known is the love of Sassi and Punnun who belonged to different castes. Sohni is known to have swum across the river to meet Mahiwal. The tale of the love of Ranjha and Heer too is told. Among the Sikhs of the Guru, there is loving devotion to God whose praises they sing early in the morning.[1]

This statement comes from a *Var* of Bhai Gurdas, an eminent Sikh writer of the early seventeenth century. His preference for loving devotion to God is loud and clear. Nevertheless, he posits a parallel between human lovers and the devotees of God in terms which are not derogatory. In fact, he appreciates several dimensions of the known tales of love, mutual dedication, sacrifice, and disregard for the distinctions of social background. Bhai Gurdas assumes and reinforces the popularity of the tales of love in the Punjab.

It is interesting to note that the tales of Laila and Majnun, Sassi and Punnun and Sohini and Mahiwal were not indigenous. However, the tale of Heer and Ranjha was a product of the Punjab. Another such tale not mentioned by Bhai Gurdas was that of Mirza and Sahiban. Both these indigenous tales of love entered the growing literary tradition of the Punjab in the reign of Akbar.

The idea of love was made popular by the Sufis and it was inevitably linked up with gender. The first poet to talk of love in Punjabi was Shaikh Farid (1175-1265). He talked of love and separation; he talked also of the husband and the wife. The terms *piara*, *pir*, *pritam*, *sauh*, *kant* and *sohag* are used for God; the terms *sahib* and *pir* are used for the husband. Clearly, the husband is a metaphor for God.

Union being the goal, the woman who is not enjoyed by her husband when young grows old and dies and then she cries in the grave that she failed to meet the husband. The woman who fails to meet the husband regrets all her life. The woman who has found the spouse, the *sohagan,* does not look for anyone else. Humility is the word, to bear with him is the quality, and sweet tongue is the *mantra* which together induce the husband to come close. A woman should wear the garb that helps her to meet the spouse. In these *shalokas*, the wife's physical union with the husband is comparable to the spiritual union of man with God. The wife's union with the husband depends on his pleasure, just as man's union with God depends on God's grace.

These are not the only *shalokas* of Farid with a bearing on love and gender. The human life or soul (*jind*) is compared to a woman and death to the groom who weds her. Just as the exact time (*saha*) for marriage is fixed, so the time of death is fixed from the very beginning. There is a suggestion here that marriage for women is inevitable, like death. Shaikh Farid simply assumes that marriage is the norm for women. The assumption that a grown up girl could be married even to a child carries the implication that the individuals concerned had no discretion in the matter. The marital knot should be tied so tightly that it never loosens afterwards. This carries the possibility of the woman being divorced or simply abandoned. All the fragrance used by the wife in preparing herself for union with the husband begins to stink if she fails to keep awake for him. The young girl is keen to be wedded, but after marriage come problems; her misfortune is that she cannot become a virgin again. Formal marriage is meaningless if the husband does not care for the wife. The limbs of the wife whither if the husband does not sleep with her. The metaphors used in these *shalokas* presuppose the wife's dependence and subordination in a patriarchal family.

The primary concern of life, to find the 'husband', informs Shaikh Farid's attitude towards physical beauty. The eyes which lured the whole world and could not bear even a line of collyrium (*kajal*), are now used by birds for nestling. Love for the husband (God) is far preferable to youth (which is closely associated with beauty). Elsewhere, Shaikh Farid appreciates the beauty of the wife's arms round the neck of her husband in winter: they are beautiful like the cranes in the month of *Kattik*, the forest fires in the month of *Chait*, and the lightning in the month of *Sawan*. With no intrinsic value of their own, beauty and youth acquire meaning in the service of the husband (God).

Farid's *shalokas* generally consist of only two lines, with his name in the first or the second line. Therefore, though he uses the female voice in several of his *shalokas*, the metaphor is not sustained. In his *shabads*, however, there are more or less sustained metaphors. The wife pines for her husband in separation. She is madly in search of her spouse but he cannot be blamed for her plight because she herself has no merit. She did not appreciate the value of her spouse when she was young. Now that her youth is gone there is nothing but regret. She asks the nightingale (*koil*) why she is black; the *koil* tells her that she has been singed by the fire of separation. There is no peace (*sukh*) without the beloved. Only God in his kindness brings about union. This metaphor makes it clear that separation is due to the lack of merit in the woman; even if the woman has merit her union with the spouse depends on his pleasure. If the woman is lean (in merit), her spouse has nothing but harsh words for her.

However, the wife is not the only woman in the *shabads* of Shaikh Farid. There is the mother who gives birth to a *darvesh;* blessed is that mother. There is the young woman who feels encouraged to emulate the young men who swim across (the stream of life). There is also the woman who is alone at the well, with no companion and no friend. Through God's grace she is associated with *sadhs* (devotees of God) and discovers God as her everlasting friend.

We may be sure that Shaikh Farid's path was open to women. When the woman expresses her love, as a wife she gains spiritual equality with man but she is placed in a patriarchal family which ensures her social subordination. For creating spiritual space for women, Shaikh Farid reinforces the institution of patriarchal family. Conjugal love presents no threat to the social order.[2]

I

We enter a different world with Shah Husain in the time of Akbar. He addresses the self (*jind*) as a female. He tells her that this world is like the *sarai* in which the wayfarer stays for a night. The parting is for ever, like the leaves fallen from a tree: there is no return. Shah Husain tells the self that one reaps what one sows.

From addressing the self as a female to addressing the female herself, there is only a short step. Shah Husain exhorts the woman to turn to God (Rama), using the metaphor of fetching water from the well, invoking the image of the *paniharan*. He advises the young girl to turn to spinning so that she can prepare her dowry; a dowry-less bride is not honoured in the marital home. The woman who does not get rid of her inner dirt cannot hope to meet the spouse; good deeds are emphasized frequently through the metaphor of spinning. That she may never forget God is the prayer of the *faqirs*; she should cultivate the love of God and associate herself with the men of God; youth and beauty become dust in the end. In several other *kafis*, Shah Husain addresses women to express ideas and attitudes expressed in the male voice. In one of his *kafis*, Shah Husain betrays his assumption that the female he addresses is actually male. He starts with 'understand this o' innocent girl' but ends up by telling her that nothing goes with her after death, neither the mother, father, brother, son, nor the wife.

In many of his *kafis* Shah Husain adopts the female voice for addressing females. In one, the female friends are taken into confidence about the pangs of separation and an intense desire to see the spouse. In another, the separation and union are said to be due respectively to the woman's demerit and God's grace. One woman tells another not to be proud of wealth and youth which have duped even the wise women; every girl has to leave her father's house; life on this earth is the time to earn merit through good deeds. A woman invites others to come together for meditation on God (Rama). A female addresses her female friends on the loss of whatever little merit she had earned.

One particular form of address between two females is that of a daughter addressing her mother. A young daughter expresses her anxiety about the treatment she would receive on her first meeting with her spouse who is handsome and possesses all good qualities. Another daughter expresses her anxiety about the life hereafter because she has not earned any merit here. In a popular *kafi* of Shah Husain, the daughter sings the pangs of separation:

> To whom should I talk o' mother of the pangs of separation? The fire of the love of my *murshid* keeps smouldering; I find it red hot whenever I poke it. The thorns of pain have made me senseless; the sense of separation does not depart. Sorrows are my bread and pain is my *salan*; the sighs serve as the firewood. I wander in the wilderness but I have not yet found my Beloved?

Shah Husain goes on to add that satisfaction comes only on meeting the spouse. In another *kafi*, the daughter talks of the pangs of love. Unlike the *shaloka* of Shaikh Farid, the *kafi* of Shah Husain can lend itself to a sustained metaphor and, therefore, to a total immersion in the female voice. The woman addresses God directly, which is not the same thing as a wife addressing her husband. There are at least two scores of such *kafis*, nearly double the total number of Shaikh Farid's compositions with a bearing on love and gender. Their content is no different from that of the *kafis* in the authoritarian male voice. The man and the woman stand on the same footing in relation to God.

> I am all yours o' my Master. I have many omissions to my discredit but pray, do not forget me. I, the meritless one, have no merit; only through your gracious kindness can I be saved. Keep me as you wish my Loved One, I have taken refuge in you.

In another *kafi*, the female with the basket of love (*ishq*) over her head hawks from door to door: they who turn to God in love are good. Another woman proposes to become a *jogin*.

Another *kafi* in the female voice ends with a reference to the friend who knows all, who sees all, and who is the strength of the powerless. Another woman seeks grace rather than justice, from 'the river of mercy', accepting his will in gratitude. A woman who is betrothed to God says:

Whether bad or good I am your slave o' Master. The ignorant people think I am mad; they do not know that I am dyed in the Master's dye. My Friend fills my eyes and I roam freely in the streets.

In another *kafi* the woman is inclined to become a slave of God's devotees :

I shall become the slave of *sadhs* and do everything that the slave girls do. I shall cook, sweep the floor, and wash the vessels in which they eat.

Significantly, the slave-girl (*goli* or *bandi*) is the counterpart of the male slave (*das*).

Another woman sweeps the floor as a *chuhri*, of the divine court:

I am a *chuhri* of the *darbar*. With the broom of *gian* and the basket of *dhian* I remove *kam* and *krodh*. The *qazi* knows me and the *hakim* knows me; I have a letter of exemption from *begar*. The *mull* knows and the *mehta* knows that I serve the *Sarkar*.

She does this to have the sight of God: 'May I be a sacrifice to you my Master; you know my state my Friend; show me your face now my loved one.' The sight of the Beloved liberates the woman. 'See how wide is my stride; I trample cobras under my feet, and jump over the sleeping lions.'

Finally, Shah Husain speaks as Heer: 'I have been struck by the arrow of separation', says Heer. 'People heard and countries heard that Heer has become a *bairagan*. Not one but a hundred thousand may hear; what can they do? I am the slave of Sawal and Sawal is my master.'

'I too want to go to the abode (*jhok*) of Ranjha', says Heer. She wishes that someone may go with her, but she has to go alone. The stream she has to cross is deep and the boat she has is old (and unworthy); the fords are waylaid by lions. She is prepared to give the rings on her fingers to one who may bring the news of the friend. In pain during the night, she is helpless during the day; the wounds of love are raw. Ranjha, her friend, is said to be a great healer (*tabib*); only he can remove the strange ache of her body.

Heer is not prepared to hear of the Kheras: 'Ranjha is mine and I belong to him; the Kheras have a false hope'. People think that Heer is mad but Heer has chosen the *chak* (Ranjha) as her husband. This is known to God himself. The noise of the Kheras is futile. They can force her into the *doli* but her heart is with Ranjha. Without him, she is like fish out of water. She is in the hands of the Almighty who has preordained her love for Ranjha.

Uttering the name of God, Heer has appropriated love despite opposition from her father and mother. How can she turn back? From her very childhood she had nurtured love (*ishq*) and suffered the pangs of separation. The pain of a hundred years would vanish when Ranjha looked at her for a moment. Nothing but the sight of Ranjha can bring her peace. 'May I be a sacrifice to the path by which has Ranjha come from Takht Hazara', says Heer. 'God has sent the friend.'

'My heart longs for Ranjha', says Heer. She has wandered in the wilderness and in thickets in search of him. 'The buffaloes have come but not my friend', cries Heer in Jhang. Day and night she roams in the wilderness and thorns pierce her feet. But she must meet Ranjha, whatever way.

'Crying *mahi*, *mahi*, I have myself become Ranjha,' says Heer. 'Call me Ranjhan, everyone, and none should call me Heer. I have found the spouse I was searching for.' The identification between the lover and the beloved is complete. Heer, more than any other woman in the *kafis* of Shah Husain, sings of love and of its pangs and joys with abandon.

It is significant that Shah Husain uses the symbol of human lovers, Heer and Ranjha, to express his ideas of love. He could use them as symbols on the obvious assumption that people knew what he was talking about: their love tale must have become popular in the sixteenth century. His own preoccupation with Heer and Ranjha is evident from the fact that he refers to them in no less than a dozen of his *kafis*. The rebel Heer as the symbol of the lover presents a threat to the patriarchal social order.

In any case, Shah Hussain's world is crowded with women.

He refers to them in a wide range of situations: as a child, a young girl, a wife, and a mother; as a devotee, *jogin* and *bairagan*; as a slave girl cooking, sweeping the floor and washing utensils, and as an outcaste woman (*chuhri*) sweeping the courtyard; as a young girl at the spinning wheel with other young girls, playing and dancing in the courtyard; as a woman wearing a *salu*; enjoying a swing on the *peepal* tree, and playing in the moonlit night; going to the well for fetching water; going out into the lanes of the village as a peddlar; as a weaver woman settling accounts with the *sarraf* who had advanced money to get cloth made. Thus, Shah Husain is not concerned with the conjugal relationship. It is significant that he can virtually dispense with the metaphor of *sohagan*. In fact, his *sohagan* is the woman who dances with abandon in her dedication.

This does not mean that Shah Husain was not aware of the patriarchal family. The young maiden who has left her childhood behind is at the threshold of marriage. She spins with her friends in order to prepare her dowry. Her work in the home includes embroidery (*kashidah*), a household art appreciated by the in-laws (apart from enabling her to prepare some items of her dowry). She is expected to cherish the honour of her family and not to infringe any social norm. Her father looks for a suitable match for her, either directly or through an intermediary. The day of marriage is fixed and messages are sent to all close relatives. The bride uses *mehndi* on her hands and feet, puts on a large, coloured bangle on her wrist, and wears a *salu*. The marriage party witnesses the ceremony of marriage performed through *lavan* (not *nikah*). The newly-wedded girl sits in a palanquin to be taken to her in-laws. There she is received by her mother-in-law. The bridegroom's sisters taunt her if she has gone without adequate dowry. Her in-laws expect her to observe the norms of their home and to remain veiled. Otherwise, she would be called 'the unveiled one' (*ghungat-khulli*). Thus, Shah Husain is very much aware of the structure and the values of patriarchy. But conjugal love appears to have little relevance for his conception of love. The spirit of his *kafis* is extraordinarily free and liberal.[3]

II

We may turn to a contemporary of Shah Husain who wrote a narrative of Heer and Ranjha. As he himself says in his work, his name was Damodar and his caste name was Gulati. He refers to Akbar over a dozen times as the contemporary ruler, and claims to have seen every incident personally. But he places the meeting of Heer and Ranjha in the time of Bahlol Lodi, more than eighty years earlier than the coronation of Akbar. His claim to have been an eyewitness to the events amounts only to saying that he was narrating a true story in all its minute details.

Damodar's depiction of the social environment of the lovers appears to be realistic. Heer's father, Chuchak, is the head of the Sial clan of Jats and Dhido's father, Maujam, is the head of the Ranjha clan of Jats. They are referred to as the masters of land and water. Their wealth consisted of a large number of all kinds of domestic animals, grazing land, and culturable fields. Heer is betrothed at a young age because daughters in the long run are 'someone else's property'. The main consideration for selecting the groom is the position of his father. The matrimonial alliance is seen as a source of political strength.

Dhido Ranjha was also betrothed at an early age in an interesting situation. He was exceptionally handsome and impressive. His brothers began to feel that he would succeed to their father's position. Therefore, they wanted to get rid of him. Maiyam decided to betroth Ranjha to the daughter of Yakub Khan Waraich who was rich and powerful and who, therefore, could provide the necessary support for Ranjha. Maiyam died when preparations were being made for the marriage. Unable now to face the hostility of his brothers, Ranjha decided to leave his ancestral place, Takht Hazara.

Ranjha stayed in a mosque for the night and resumed his journey early in the morning to nowhere in particular. His meeting with Heer on her boat resulted in their mutual love and he became a personal servant (*chak*) of Chuchak so that the two could meet every day. Their love became a social scandal and the honour of the entire Sial clan was seen to be at stake. Heer is forcibly married to Sahiba Khera of Rangpur to whom she had been betrothed. Aware of the hostile reaction of the Kheras to his presence in Rangpur, Ranjha goes to Takht Hazara. There, the Waraich approach him for marriage to the girl he was betrothed to, but he refuses to get married. The girl is accepted as a suitable match for his nephew, uniting the two clans through this amicable settlement.

In Rangpur, Sehti, the sister-in-law of Heer, succeeded in discovering the secret of Heer's refusal to consummate her marriage to Sahiba: her love for Ranjha. With Heer's consent, she sends a messenger to Ranjha in Takht Hazara to persuade him to come to Rangpur in order to meet Heer. Ranjha goes to the Tilla of Bal Gundai and becomes a *jogi*. In this disguise he goes to Rangpur to meet Heer. Through a strategem devised by Sehti, they elope and take refuge with the Nahars who fight against the Kheras as a point of honour to protect them. A Sayyid of Rajoa intervenes to suggest that the two sides should seek justice from the court of Adli Raja (Awwal Fatta, Abu al-Fateh) of Kabula. There, the *qazi* and the *mufti* take up the case. The Kheras contend that Heer was duly betrothed and married to Sahiba and all customary rites and ceremonies were observed. Heer maintains that all this was done against her will and that she had always loved Ranjha. The *qazi* declares that the law (*shara*') recognized no love and it was socially forbidden. Heer asserts that the *qazi* was saying this out of greed. All the people knew that she belonged to Ranjha. She could not be married again. Her marriage with Sahiba had never been consummated. She preferred her love for Ranjha to all the wealth and luxury that the Kheras could offer. However, Adli decides in favour of the Kheras and Heer is entrusted to them. Fire breaks out in Kabula and the people attribute it to the power of *jogi* Ranjha who had been treated so unjustly. The *qazi* contends that he had given his verdict strictly in accordance with the admissible evidence. Nevertheless, he was willing now to give Heer to the party which would control the fire. The Kheras fail but Ranjha succeeds in this ordeal. Adli Raja does justice and gives Heer to Ranjha. Everyone recognizes Ranjha's greatness and bows to him. Thus, the steadfast love of Heer and Ranjha ends in their union. They go towards the south to build a house for themselves and are not seen afterwards.

Personal love triumphed against all social norms, even against the law of the land. However, this was made possible by supranatural forces. Damodar's social realism is combined with metaphysical forces in his treatment of personal love. In the first place, five-pirs (*panj-pir*) appear from nowhere to tell Ranjha that they were pleased with him and had bestowed Heer upon him. Similarly, they appear in Heer's dream to tell her that they had given Ranjha to her. On their first meeting, Heer and Ranjha come to believe that, as told by the *panj-pir*, they were meant for each other. The effect of Ranjha's flute on human beings, animals and birds is not exactly supranatural but it serves the purpose of demonstrating his closeness to God. The *panj-pir* come to Ranjha's support in all those situations which he could never handle on his own. Heer refers to him as *murshid* and even suggests that he had the power to do anything. He is almost divine. Damodar knows the strength of the social forces and tries to transcend them by invoking metaphysical entities. It is not without significance that Heer and Ranjha leave for the south never to be seen again. They defy the society but they do not live in it.[4]

III

Another contemporary of Shah Husain treats the love of Mirza and Sahiban much more realistically. Like the love of Heer and Ranjha in Damodar, or in Shah Husain, the love of Mirza and Sahiban in Peelu's *kissa* is preordained. Sahiban is exceptionally beautiful, with an extraordinary effect on the beholders. She goes to the shop of the local *pansari* for oil; the *bania* loses all sense and, instead of oil, pours out honey. Many a *bania* abandons his trade, and many a Jat leaves his plough for the sake of Sahiban. Three hundred men were wandering naked as *faqirs*, having abandoned their homes. Mirza falls in love with her the moment he looks at her. Had she given him a cup of poison, Mirza would have drunk it; had she pierced him with a spear, he would have felt no pain; he was willing to die for her. His foremost commitment is his love for Sahiban. For her, Mirza is like Mecca to the Muslim pilgrims (*hajis*).

Mirza is exceptionally handsome and brave, an unmatched

archer. And his valour is matched by his pride. He regards no warrior as his equal; he boasts that none dare attack him; he would kill all the warriors of Sahiban's brothers if they dared. As the hailstorm destroys all crops, he destroys all his enemies. Armies flee before him and he can plunder freely on the highway to Lahore, defying the authority of the state. Mirza's pride knows no bounds. Even God is afraid of him. His mare, named Bakki, is extraordinary. Her hooves thunder like a hammer on the anvil. Fed on the *ghee* of ten buffaloes, she could dive into the lower world as she could fly in the sky. Even the angels were afraid of Bakki. Indeed, she had descended from heaven, like her brothers and sisters: the mounts of Raja Rasalu, Hazrat Ali, Sakhi Sarvar, Gugga Chauhan, Dulla Bhatti, and Jaimal and Fatta. Bakki was the youngest, coming to Mirza of her own accord: she could never leave him in lurch. If his skill in archery made him invincible, Bakki made him virtually inaccessible to the foe.

Apart from pride, Mirza has a keen sense of honour, both clannish and personal. He receives a message from Sahiban that she was going to be married to a Chandhar Jat and that Mirza must come to her rescue, and his sister invokes the honour of his clan, the Kharal Jats, to dissuade him from leaving his native town Danabad. Her marriage had been fixed and the Bhattis were to arrive with their marriage party on the following day; Mirza was expected to ensure that all went well. Mirza replies that his four brothers would do their best for the honour of the Kharals but that he must leave. As he tells his mother, he could divorce a wife but he could not sully the honour of the Kharals by abandoning the girl betrothed to him. In personal terms too, on a call from his beloved he was honour-bound to go. Whereas the sense of clannish honour was cherished equally by the Chandhars and the Sials, the sense of personal honour was peculiar to Mirza as a warrior-lover.

Mirza was sent to the town of the Sials to study in the mosque with a teacher referred to as the *qazi*. He fell in love with Sahiban when they were studying together in the mosque. The *qazi* lashed Mirza but failed to separate them. Mirza returned to Danabad when the *qazi* died. The call from Sahiban came when her parents decided to marry her against her wishes. The alternative now was to elope. They were pursued by the warriors of both the Sials and the Chandhars. Sure of the efficacy of his archery and the speed of Bakki, Mirza sleeps a while under a *jand* tree. Sahiban is anxious to reach Danabad. When her brother Shamir appears on the scene, Sahiban wakes Mirza up and he shoots an arrow at Shamir who falls down from his horse. Sahiban exhorts Mirza to leave for Danabad but he is still intent on sleep. Sahiban puts away his quiver to save her brothers, and in the hope that Mirza would be persuaded to ride Bakki and reach Danabad. When an arrow strikes Mirza, he looks for his own bow, only to find that there are no arrows. He blames Sahiban for siding with the Sials. Without a companion in arms and without his brothers, Mirza dies fighting as a lonely warrior.

Peelu says that Mirza was brought down partly by his own pride but essentially by fate (*honi*) which overpowers prophets; Hasan and Husain, the sons of Ali, were swallowed by fate in their fight against Yazid; their mother, Bibi Fatima (the Prophet's daughter), could do nothing but cry that they never came back. If prophets were powerless before fate, Mirza was a small fry.

Peelu does not indicate how fate worked against Mirza, but a part of the answer is implicit in his narrative. The *qazi* in the first place is opposed to the idea of love, representing the orthodox Muslim position. Sahiban's father does not concede that his daughter had the right to choose a husband. In fact, as the head of the clan he is expected to ensure that no such right was exercised by girls. Mirza's mother, who is herself a Sial, tells him that the Sial women use their charms on men to gain their hearts; he should not stake his life for a woman. Friendship with women, she says later, is like friendship with tigers and cobras: the result inevitably is death. Mirza's father, Wanjhal, tells him that women are fickle-minded; their professions of love should not be taken literally; they fall in love with smiles but confess their helplessness with tears; they never step into the homes of men they profess love to; this is the essence of wisdom. However, Wanjhal's advice does not end there. He exhorts his son not to leave Sahiban behind: it was a point of honour for the Kharals.

In Peelu's story of Mirza and Sahiban there is an essential tension between love and honour, between personal predilections and social norms. The symbolic representative of Islamic orthodoxy is opposed to the notion of personal love as it infringes the social norms of a patriarchal family. Sahiban's father is opposed to her marriage to Mirza for the same reason: neither he nor Mirza's father has proposed the match; boys and girls have, and should have, no initiative or right in a matter that is strictly a prerogative of the elders. The honour of the family, and even of the clan, is involved in upholding and safeguarding the traditional practices. Sahiban's brothers are even more sensitive on this issue. The Chandhars are prepared to eliminate Mirza, and even Sahiban if necessary, for the sake of their honour. Mirza's father represents the other side of the same coin: his sense of honour dictates that his son should bring home the woman whom he has promised to wed. It is unlikely that Wanjhal would give the right of personal choice to his own daughter.

The poet is sympathetic to the idea of personal love. It is a noble feeling, justifying all kinds of sacrifice. In fact, sacrifices made for love make it memorable for others. The old Karmun Brahmana who is foolish enough to propose to Sahiban agrees nonetheless to take her message to Mirza. Sahiban's mother has no objection to her being married to Mirza. Mirza's mother is not opposed to the idea but is afraid of the inevitable risks involved in the venture. There are others, like Beebo and Jam the blacksmith, who actually help Mirza in eloping with Sahiban, not for any mundane gain but due to their concern for Mirza and his feeling for Sahiban. The young maidens who come together for spinning are sympathetic to Sahiban when they talk of her love for Mirza.

On the one hand thus, the idea of personal love is cherished or appreciated and, on the other, there is an acute awareness of social constraints and of the risks involved in flouting the social norms. It was almost impossible to resolve the contradiction between personal love and the patriarchal family. The tragic end was almost inevitable. Personal love as a social deviance demanded a very high price. Only a few were prepared to pay that price, and they were admired. Peelu feels the constraints of the patriarchal structure and values on the fulfilment of personal love, but he celebrates personal love nonetheless—notwithstanding Mirza's moral foible or his own conception of fate.[5]

IV

All the creative writers we have considered appear to have been fascinated by the idea of love, one way or another. They also reveal an awareness of the social situation in which personal love has no scope of fulfilment or survival. However, they handle the tension between personal predilections and social norms in different ways.

In Sufism, the essential relationship between human beings and God was that of love. However, the idea of love in relation to God was an anathema to the *'ulama*. One way of resolving the tension between Sufism and orthodoxy on this point was to overtly accept the social institution of patriarchal family and to draw metaphors from conjugal relationships in order to regulate love within the domestic walls. Shaikh Farid appears to do this, creating spiritual space for women but, at the same time, reinforcing the patriarchal family so that love holds out no threat to the traditional social order.

Shah Husain's affiliation to Sufism was rather loose. He did not belong to any order of the Sufis; he had no formal training from a *murshid*; he acknowledges no *pir* and looks upon himself as a *faqir*, a devotee of God whose sole aim in life is to offer loving devotion to God which subsumes the pillars of Islam: *kalima*, *namaz*, *rozah*, *zakat* and *hajj*. He remains silent about them. He is a liberated Sufi, if a Sufi at all. His *kafis* have a liberating effect through the bondage of love. It is possible to reconstruct the patriarchal family with the help of Shah Hussain's metaphors but he draws no metaphor from conjugal relationship, making the institution irrelevant for the pursuit of love. Taken out of the domestic walls, Shah Husain's women pursue love with abandon. At the top of them all is Heer, the symbol of love *par excellence*.

Damodar presents the love of Heer and Ranjha as a tale of triumph against all social obstacles and even the state law. But to take his narrative to this end he has to take support from metaphysical entities, attributing in the process divine powers to Ranjha. Even Heer is not an ordinary woman. The idea of personal love is valourized. Significantly, however, Heer and Ranjha do not live in the society as a married couple. Their existence after their triumph is etherealized. The hard social realities are not transcended so much as evaded.

Peelu is far more realistic in his treatment of the love of Mirza and Sahiban. They are ill-fated essentially in the sense that they are pitted against the structure and values of a patriarchal society which does not recognize personal love. The logical end is tragic. The essence of the tragedy lies in the unresolved, and unresovable, tension between the social norms and personal predilections. There is a suggestion that the love of Mirza and Sahiban is preordained. But Peelu has a great appreciation for their love without any religious dimension. His empathy is shared by several other characters. The idea of personal love has its own fascination.

NOTES

1. Giani Hazara Singh (ed.), *Varan Bhai Gurdas*, Amritsar, 1962, *Var XXVII, pauri 1*.
2. Shaikh Farid's *shabads* and *shalokas* are included in the Sikh scripture, *Guru Granth Sahib*. An annotated text has been published by Sahib Singh, and reprinted several times by Singh Brothers, Amritsar. Sant Singh Sekhon has discussed the poetry of Shaikh Farid at some length in *A History of Punjabi Literature*, Patiala, 1993, pp. 15-33, 163-81, and given an English translation of his poetry. Gurbachan Singh Talib has also given English translation of Shaikh Farid's *shabads* and *shalokas* in a monograph entitled *Baba Sheikh Farid Shakarganj*, New Delhi, 1974.

   For a brief discussion of Shaikh Farid's ideas and attitudes, see Denis Matringe, ' "The future has come near, the past is far behind": A Study of Shaikh Farid's Verses and their Sikh Commentaries in the *Adi Granth*', Anna Libera Dallapiccola and Stephanie Zingel-Ave Lallemant (eds.), *Islam and Indian Religions*, Stuttgart, 1993, pp. 417-43; J.S. Grewal, 'Shaikh Farid's Ideas and Attitudes', *Procedings Punjab History Conference*, Patiala, 1998, pp. 53-61.
3. Shah Husain's *kafis* have been edited and published by several scholars, notably Mohan Singh, Jit Singh Seetal, and Harjinder Singh Dhillon. The text used here is from Harjinder Singh Dhillon (ed.), *Sufi Kavi*

Shah Husain, Amritsar, 1992. For a brief discussion of Shah Husain's ideas and attitudes, see J.S. Grewal, 'Shah Husain's Devotional Theism', *Punjab Journal of Sikh Studies*, Amritsar, 1996, vol. XX, no. 2, pp. 67-92.

4. Apart from the complete works of Damodar in *Damodar Rachnavali*, Patiala, 1974, the following editions of his work on the tale of Heer have been published. Gurdev Singh (ed.), *Heer Damodar*, 2nd edn., Ludhiana, 1972, Gurdev Singh and Pritam Singh Saini (eds.), *Heer Damodar: Ik Punar Mulankan*, Ludhiana, 1986; Jagtar Singh (eds.), *Heer Damodar*, Patiala, 1987.
5. For Peelu's text, Piar Singh and M.S. Amrit (eds.), *Mirza Sahiban*, Amritsar, 1981.

CHAPTER 5

State and the Composite Culture in Sultanate Bengal (*c.* AD 1200–1600)

ANIRUDDHA RAY

It is generally assumed that composite culture would mean the integration of different cultural strands into one composite whole making it a syncretist one. It is believed that such a composition would be spontaneous, originating from the common people of different cultures. Here in this brief paper, we would look into the process or lack of it in Sultanate Bengal.

Since the conquest of Nadia and some time later Lakhnauti by Ikhtiyaruddin Bakhtiyar Khalji in 1204-5, a new polity began to develop in Bengal. Our only contemporary literary source of the period till AD 1260 is the narrative of Minhaj-us Siraj who describes the departure of the Brahmins and merchants from Nadia.[1] Actually Dinesh Chandra Sen had earlier suggested that the easy success of Bakhtiyar in conquering Nadia and Lakhnauti was due to the fact that most of the people did not want to support the Sena king due to the oppression of the Brahmins.[2] The Sena king, if we accept Minhaj and the inscriptions of the Sena dynasty, had fled to Dacca-Vikrampur area[3] where Senas ruled for nearly one hundred years. Nadia was a prosperous city from whose plunder Bakhtiyar had constructed many mosques and *madrassas* at Lakhnawati (later Lakhnauti and eventually Gaur).[4] This was the beginning of a new cultural strand that developed during the Sultanate period.

The establishment of the capital at Devkot by Bakhtiyar Khalji and his disastrous expedition to Tibet signalled the civil war among the nobles of the Sultanate. While the Sufis and other *darveshes* began to flock to Bengal and propagate the Islamic faith claiming converts, there was a brief interlude of independence. Basically Lakhnauti had remained under the jurisdiction of Delhi. Minhaj has described four different regions of the newly established kingdom of Lakhnauti with four nobles lording over each region with their fiefs generally termed as *Iqta*.[5] Below them the earlier Hindu zamindars had retained their internal autonomy with some exceptions of a few cases of struggle. During the thirteenth century, Balban had to undertake an expedition in Bengal to suppress his rebel noble, but there is no mention of his subjugating any Hindu zamindar. On the contrary, he made a pact with king Danujmardan Dev of Chandradwip (identified as coastal area near Sonargaon) to seize the rebel noble.[6] By the end of the thirteenth century, the expansion of the Sultanate brought conflict with the local Hindu chiefs. However, it appears that the pre-Sultanate administrative structure continued in an unchanging and fragmented form.[7] How far the Sultanate ruling class tried to extract revenue on the basis of the *Sharia* is not clear, but from later sources it seems that they had opted for fixed revenue in a particular area irrespective of the crop.[8]

Obviously there was no consciousness of the emergence of any new identity, since the country was divided in separate areas often ruled by both the Hindu and Muslim chiefs, not necessarily always eager to acknowledge the sovereignty of the Sultan. Since the Bengali sources do not start before the end of the fifteenth century, one does not find any clear description of cultural strands. There are certain other sources from which one could get a glimpse of the reaction of the Hindu or Buddhist society in Bengal as well as the gradually developing consciousness of a new identity of the inhabitants irrespective of faith and creed. Unfortunately, most of the late nineteenth and early twentieth century scholars have overlooked this aspect. Some of them even described the rapacity, rape, massacre, plunder and the destruction of temples by the invading Muslims for which however they have given very little contemporary evidence.[9]

The collection of the fragments of poems written from the eleventh to the thirteenth century AD, called *Charjyapada*,[10] obviously do not refer to the invasion of the Turks. These describe the chores of daily life of the people, their happiness and sorrow, in which the consciousness of an identity is clearly discernible. There is no reference to the 'foreigner'. On the other hand, a poem called *Shunya Puran*,[11] possibly written by a Buddhist, puts the blame of the invasion of the Turks and their easy victory entirely and squarely on the shoulders of the Hindus, particularly the Brahmins and the upper classes who were oppressing the lower classes and dominating the society with all sorts of rules and conventions created by them. This might be seen as the immediate reaction of a section of the society, caused obviously by the revival of Brahminism under the patronage of the orthodox Sena dynasty. The earlier Pala kings had emphasized on Buddhism but had not neglected the Brahmins as such. In the above poem, the strand of a new culture could be discerned as it describes how the gods and goddesses of the Hindus had appeared as Muslim saints, signifying not only a clear knowledge of Islam but also the spectacular spread of their faith. Thus, two strands of opposite cultures appear, creating a new dimension in the so far dominant Brahmanical cultural set up. It would, however, be unwise to look at these cultural groups—Hindus and Muslims—as two unified cultural power blocks, a point of view prominently displayed by some scholars of the modern period.

II

In the thirteenth century, the Hindu society was not unified and did not follow a particular god or goddess. The Bengali society was predominantly Hindu, dominated by the big landlords and high officials, except perhaps in the Rarh region, i.e. the western bank of the Bhagirathi. The landless formed the majority since they did not have the capital to exploit the agrarian resources and were considered by the upper castes as untouchables. The middle tier was composed of a variety of landowners. The collection of fragmented poems cited above[12] refers to the small artisans and traders but trade was not considered as the basis of wealth. The dominating Brahmins, who practised rigorous rules regarding untouchability, were patronized by the State and by the landowners.

Although the modern Bengali writers, mostly Hindus with some notable exceptions, blame the Muslims for breaking the temples and idols and despoiling the Hindu society, the Muslims did not interfere in the *Varnashrama* system.[13] The difference between the two social systems is highlighted by one of the earliest Muslim travellers, Alberuni,[14] who was sympathetic to the Hindu culture. One should however point out that there were indeed changes within the caste system. In the caste system, the Brahmins, Vaidyas and the Kayasthas were considered as higher castes, but new castes were emerging due to mixed marriages as listed in the Puranas. The concept of purity had so much obsessed the system that even the shudras were divided into 'pure' (*sat*) and 'impure' (*asat*). This was an attempt to include the shudras for their services into the system since occupations were integrated into a vast cooperative arrangement based on caste without much internal mobility and flexibility. The Turkish conquest and the Turk emphasis on equality in social matters, made the caste system far more rigorous and less flexible. After the passing away of the Sultanate, some kind of mobility could be seen creeping into the Bengali society.

At the time of the Turkish conquest, four religious opinions among the Hindus were current in Bengal. The first was the worship of the village gods and goddesses based on traditional lines in which the Vedic and Puranic gods and goddesses were there. The second had taken the form from Mahayana Buddhism in which local elements intermingled. The third was yogi thought that had similarities with that of Shaivism. The fourth was the Puranic opinion in which Vishnu, Shiva and Chandi dominated. Some of earlier Vedic gods had lost their predominance by that time. Indra, for example, was not dominant any more. It is assumed that the Turkish conquest made their integration far easier.[15] Obviously there was not one Hindu cultural strand.

Immediately after the Turkish invasion, smaller kingdoms began to emerge in Bengal. However, there is no evidence of conflict either between these kingdoms or between different cultural groups during the first one hundred years of Turkish rule. Impact of different opinions and thinkings began to enter into different sects. For example, the Buddhist thinking influenced the Brahmanical world-view. The Vedic and Puranic gods and goddesses came into the fold of village gods and goddesses. Various kinds of worship of stone or metal and *vrata* (fast), considered to be derived from the Buddhist form of worship, began to make appearance in Bengal society. The worship of Chandi was converted into worship of Durga and became a festival. In many areas *Dharma* worship or *Manasa* worship became the dominant feature of village life. Thus, one could see not only the existence of different sects within the fold of Hinduism, but also considerable mingling of other influences, creating new synthesis.

The social structure of the Muslims in Bengal had its own divisions that would be viewed later. Generally on a broader level, one finds, two immovable and contrasting if not conflicting blocks of cultural groups quite superficially though.[16] But below that level, there were divisions based on birth, occupation and wealth. Naturally from a superficial point of view, the cultural attitudes of these two groups would seem to be conflicting. But at a further lower level, one sees that the cultural attitude of ordinary people of these two groups were not so belligerent as made out to be. With the passage of time, these were coming closer to each other despite the presence of the Brahmins and the Mullahs. Perhaps such a convergence even on a small scale was possible due to the emergence of new economic forces in Bengal by the middle of the fourteenth century generating new social forces.

From *c.* 1204 till the end of the fifteenth century, one does not find any example of Bengali writing except the collection of fragments of songs called *Charjyapada* and the *Shunya Puran* cited earlier. However, at the end of the fifteenth century one finds the mature form of Bengali writing which was different from half-Prakrit and half-Bengali form used in the *Charjyapada*. Obviously, the language developed during the intervening period after the conquest of Nadia. It is generally surmised that the influence of Persian was responsible for bringing maturity to the Bengali language. This was perhaps due to the fact that with the establishment of the Turkish administration, the administrative procedure was done in Persian instead of Sanskrit, which made this kind of fusion possible, leading to the development of a mature form of Bengali language. Gradually the immigrant Muslims with some exceptions, began to use the Bengali language as well. This fact can be discerned, from the accounts of Chinese travellers in Bengal in the first half of the fifteenth century.[17] The influence of Chaitanya changed the language in the first half of the sixteenth century, using far more Sankritized Bengali, but Persian was never abandoned. In the absence of documents, one cannot precisely locate the chronology of the process of evolution of a common language. However, it is clear that by this time, a new language form had emerged, thereby creating a particular identity among different cultural groups. But this could be attributed to the emergence of new economic forces in Bengal.

After the Turkish invasion, Sufis and *darveshes* of different shades came from West Asia to north India and from there to Bengal. They carried with them the thinking and customs of north India, including its teaching methods. The Sufis' simple lifestyle, piety and donations irrespective of creed made them popular, which had some bearing on the process of conversion. However, from the middle of the fourteenth century, they began to include local customs and practices in their teachings. The Turkish Sultans encouraged the construction of mosques and *madrasas*, which helped the spread of Islamic culture that was not purely Islamic in the strict sense of the term. While Bengal was under the control of Delhi before the advent of Iliyas Shah, many Muslims came and settled in Bengal. Also, the commercial contacts between the countries of South-East Asia and the Middle East had led many Turkish, Persian and Arabs to come and settle in Bengal. Following the dominance of Mongols in Central Asia, many Muslim aristocrats, officials and learned men came to north India and some of them travelled to Bengal. These people brought their customs and lifestyle. Many aristocrats also came with their Abyssinian slaves. Therefore, by the middle of the fourteenth century, a new Muslim society evolved in Bengal that was a mixed cultural group with different cultural mores. But at least till the end of the fifteenth century, there is no evidence of any Hindu–Muslim conflict in the region. On the contrary, there are evidences to show that the two communities were living in peace and harmony. In the middle of the fourteenth century, the Moroccan traveller Ibn Battuta who came to Bengal, does not speak of any religious conflict. He states that peasants had to pay 50 per cent as tax irrespective of communal affiliations.[18]

In the early fifteenth century, Sultan Ghiyasuddin Azam was allegedly killed by Ganesh, named by the Persian historians as Kans, who married the Muslim widow of the late Sultan and ascended the throne of Bengal, although no coin in the name of Ganesh has been found so far. Sukhomoy Mukhopadhya has asserted that the coins of Raja Danujmardan Dev were actually those of Ganesh.[19] It is clear, however, from the correspondences of several Sufis, including those of Nur Qutb Alam of Pandua, that the Muslim aristocrats had actually supported Ganesh. There are no references to any civil war nor is there any mention of prolonged struggle over the issue. Actually in the letters, Nur Qutb Alam regrets that the Hindus were occupying high posts with the connivance of the Muslims.[20] Some scholars including R.C. Majumdar have called it a 'Hindu Revival', but there is no evidence that the Hindus had taken the lead either in getting the throne for Ganesh or in doing anything after his ouster. On the other hand, it is believed that since Ganesh had favoured the Muslims so much, after his death, the Muslims wanted to bury him according to the Muslim customs.[21] It may be mentioned that four Chinese travellers visiting Bengal between 1406 and 1436 had found everything peaceful, with cultivation and commerce going on in full steam. Evidently the 'Hindu conspiracy' behind the ascendancy of Ganesh as told by the sufi saints of rather orthodox opinion was merely a reflection of the stereotyped attitudes not much different from the Brahmanical usage for the Muslims.[22] It would be seen later that the Vaishnavas, at least in the sixteenth century, were critical of the Brahmins for their orthodoxy and the Muslims for their policy of persecution in which, according to the Vaishnavas, the State took a leading role. Significantly, this Vaishnava perception of the State was different from that of the Hindu writers, who almost unanimously praised the Sultan.

Several Sufi orders entered Bengal in the wake of the Turkish conquest and they generally looked towards north India and Central Asia. But the Chishti order was thoroughly indigenized. Akhi Sirajuddin was perhaps the first Bengal-born Muslim to adopt Sufism under Shaikh Nizamuddin Aulia. He returned to Bengal some time after 1325 and authorized his disciple Alaul Huq to help Iliyas Shah in his bid for independence of Bengal, which from the Sufi point of view was the will of god. The celebrated son of Alaul Huq was Nur Qutb Alam who had invited the Sharqi ruler of Jaunpur to drive out Ganesh from power. The formation of an independent State ruled by a Muslim king was helped by the Chishtis, which was a departure from other Sufi orders. The undercurrent of tension between the ruler and the religious order continued, often erupting into open hostility.[23] The Hindu poets were aware of the different sects of Muslim saints as seen from the writing of the late sixteenth-century poet Mukundaram Chakrabarty.[24] Another Muslim poet Alaol, writing in Bengali from Arakan, reveals the influence of Hindu ideas and beliefs among the Muslims. He admits the existence of lesser deities, which is a departure from the strict theology of Islam.[25] He also refers to the idols as shadows of god and his work shows his knowledge of Hindu mythology. Elsewhere, he however suggests the worship of formless god, showing the superiority of Islam.[26]

It may be emphasized that by the end of the Sultanate rule in Bengal, there were tombs and mausoleums which were venerated by both the Hindus and the Muslims. The tomb of Ismail Ghazi is a perfect example of such veneration.[27] That a particular identity of Bengali society was growing could be seen in the two invasions of Firuz Tughluq during the second half of the fourteenth century against Iliyas Shah and his son Sikandar Shah. Barni suggests that there was a treaty between them by which the king of Bengal acknowledged the sovereign ruler of Delhi and that Firuz Shah did not want to continue the fight for fear of killing the Muslims. In reality, Iliyas Shah left the capital Pandua and took refuge in the strong fort of Ekdala, still not properly identified. The same fate befell Sultan Firuz Tughluq when he invaded Bengal a second time during the reign of Sikandar Shah. What is important here, as given in the contemporary *Insha-i Mahru*, is that Firuz Shah in his exasperation had made a declaration promising land and money to both the Hindu and Muslim zamindars and peasants as well as Hindu and Muslim saints. Yet, none came forward to help him. On the other hand, he had perhaps the satisfaction of knowing that the Hindu general of Iliyas Shah, perhaps his chief commander, died in the battle fieldfighting for his master.[28] The identity of Bengal with its independence cherished by both the Hindus and Muslims of all classes of people could be seen very clearly. From the first half of the fifteenth century, what is interesting is that the Brahmins also began to get positions in the royal court and there were inter-marriages between both the communities.

Unfortunately we do not have much concrete evidence on the inter-marriages among the different communities in Bengal during the Sultanate period. From the *Nishan* of the Sultan Firuz Shah Tughluq as analysed by Abdul Karim and from the writings of Vipradas Piplai (late fifteenth century), one can see several grades of Muslims in Bengal. In the top group one finds Shaikhs, Sayyids and Maulanas, all belonging to the orthodox group of the Muslim society. Below them were the converted Muslims, many of whom had not forgotten their old Hindu customs and manners as stated by the late sixteenth-century poet Mukundaram Chakrabarty. The third group was composed of the Muslims who had married Hindu women. Their descendants were of mixed marriages but no stigma was attached to the descendants. The ancestor of the seventeenth-century poet Muhammed Khan had married a Brahmin woman and their descendants got high posts. However, it should not be construed that only the ordinary people had married the Hindu women or only the Muslims had such marriages. Sultan Iliyas Shah was supposed to have married a Brahmin woman named Fulmati of the village of Vajrayogini. As cited earlier, Ganesh too had married the widow of the slain Sultan Ghiyasuddin Azam Shah, named Fuljani. Two daughters of the Sultan Alauddin Hussain Shah were married to the sons of the Brahmin *zamindar* of Bhaduria. Pir Khan Jaban Ali had converted a Brahmin and his Hindu wife and their descendants were known as Pirali Brahmins. The Brahmin after conversion had a Muslim wife and the descendants were known as Taheria. Muslims also married Vaishnava women. One Murtaza Khan of Murshidabad married a Vaishnava woman named Anandamoyee. Obviously the State, in need of a large number of educated workers, was ready to forget some aspects of orthodox beliefs, while inter-marriages were growing to the consternation of the orthodox groups of both the communities. The mid-sixteenth-century Vaishnava poet, Vrindaban Das laments the laxity among the Hindus since even the Brahmins were getting converted. The Portuguese traveller Duarte Barbosa states that the Hindus converted for gains. Obviously there were some who wanted riches and positions, but a far larger number could get no such positions and resources. It is clear that the Muslim society did not oppose such marriages. There is no evidence to show that the orthodox Hindu society had opposed it either. Perhaps there were certain economic forces which favoured the obliteration of the divisions at least politically if not socially in Bengal during the Sultanate period.

III

As seen earlier, the *Charjyapada*, written between the eleventh and thirteenth centuries, did not contain any reference to overseas commerce. This seems to confirm the view of Niharranjan Ray that overseas commerce in Bengal had dwindled after the fading away of the Tamralipta port at the end of the eighth century AD.[29] But there are other evidences of the Pala and the Sena period which show that some form of overseas commerce existed in Bengal, perhaps through the port of Chittagong before and after the Turkish invasion. While Ibn Battuta mentions the ships of rulers of different regions of Bengal in the first half of the fourteenth century, Chinese visitors to Bengal in early fifteenth century spoke of Bengali merchants doing overseas commerce on their own ships. The description of ornaments used by the local women in abundance would suggest an affluent mercantile class. The declaration of independence of Bengal by Sultan Iliyas Shah and his establishment of a uniform administration certainly helped the process of commercialization. By the middle of the fifteenth century both Pandua and Gaur were becoming populous.[30] The inscription of Sultan Nasiruddin Mahmud, dated 1457, AD at Gaur,[31] seems to signify the transfer of capital from Pandua to Gaur, then fed by the overseas port of Satgaon.[32] The enhanced production that Ibn Battuta had seen in the earlier century and the peaceful cultivation along with the beginning of silk cultivation from worm on the Chinese model as stated by Ma Huan, the last Chinese traveller to Bengal in 1433,[33] seems to have helped in the increase of this commerce along with inland trade. The establishment of the mints in Bengal including one at Satgaon and perhaps supplemented by one at Gaur, might have helped the process.

The increased production, growth of commerce and greater circulation of money fostered the growth of towns by the end of the fifteenth century. In particular, the growth of Satgaon was phenomenal. Vipradas Piplai, writing around 1493-4, has given a telling description of the town of Satgaon (Saptagram in the Bengali documents), on the Sarasvati River coming out of Triveni confluence. He wrote that there were rows of houses, obviously on the southern bank of the river. Vipradas narrates that there were 36 castes doing their worships in the temples with loud music. At the same time he mentions the Muslim inhabitants, Sayyid, Mulla and Qazi, in that order, praying in mosques.[34] Later Krishnaram Das also provides similar narrative of a crowded and prosperous city of Satgaon.[35] Even towards the end of the sixteenth century, when Satgaon was on its way to decline, the French traveller Vincent Le Blanc had found loud music coming from the temples and he could buy live birds like chicken from the market for his meal.[36] Around the same time, Ralph Fitch describes the town of Satgaon as a 'Moorish town', meaning thereby the existence of mosques and *hammams*.[37] This means that a sizeable Muslim population lived there. It is obvious that both the communities were not only settled in the same town but were performing their own forms of worship without a problem. Another such town was Nabadwip, which was a small town in the middle of the fifteenth century but grew up to a big town even before the advent of Chaitanya. The description of the contemporary Vaishnava poets would suggest that the growth had taken place between 1450 and 1500, and it had become a known centre for Brahmanical teaching and learning.[38]

The capital Gaur was the most prosperous city. A Portuguese who visited Gaur in 1521 observed that different communities were living side by side in a peaceful manner.[39] There were ruins of several mosques and *madrasas* within an area of nearly 20 miles in length and 3 miles in breadth between the river on one side and marshy land having a population of nearly two lakh people[40] where different communities and racial groups were living in the city. However, there is no record of any conflict between them. As a matter of fact, the Portuguese travellers saw Sultan Nusrut Shah distributing non-vegetarian food for Muslims and vegetarian food for the Hindus on the occasion of his father's death anniversary.[41] It was a cosmopolitan city, obviously based on surplus of land revenue and commercial profits since there are references of the presence of Turkish and Arab merchants.[42] The rapid growth in urbanization could be seen also in small towns like Santipur on the bank of the Ganges due to the production of textile, rice and other commodities, as seen by the visiting traveller from the boats on the Ganges.[43]

Yet, the divisions and separation are there. Neither the producers of textile nor the merchants had a place of equality in the Hindu society dominated by the Brahmins. It may be suggested that Chaitanya by his preaching of equality without the aid of the Brahmin priests tried to unite the producers, distributors and the merchants into one socially cohesive society in which the Muslims were not unwelcome.

There is not much evidence of the contrasting cultures even in the early days of the Turkish rule whereas R.C. Majumdar and A.C. Bannerjee[44] have contended that there was a perennial Hindu-Muslim conflict in medieval Bengal. Their argument is on the basis of two documents written at the end of the fifteenth century in Bengali.[45] These were *Manasa Mangal* (Worship of the Snake Goddess) and described the oppression carried by the two high officials and the Qazi on the Hindus, particularly on the shepherds who had started worshipping the Snake Goddess. Obviously at the end, the Muslims were defeated. However, the historicity of these documents is questionable. There are differences between the two writings although these were written almost at the same time and on the same theme. Vipradas shows that Hasan and Hussain, high officials and living in style, were smoking tobacco in *hookah*, which had not appeared in northern India till early seventeenth century. Secondly, in the writing of Vipradas there are words like 'Muslim', which do not occur in case of the latter. It has, therefore, been assumed that the former had many interpolations of later years. Significantly, in both these texts, the Qazi did not initiate the oppression on the shepherds. But in both cases, the attack was against the Hindus among the lower classes. This would suggest that the Muslim preachers were targeting the lower classes with the purpose of spreading the tenets of Islam in which they had become successful in some areas. Given the circumstances of the conflict, one may assume that these were converted people. Even if true, this was possibly a rare case since there is no other reference to such a conflict till we come to the brief incident at Nabadwip, which might have occurred in the reign of Fateh Shah at the end of the fifteenth century. The late eighteenth-century author of *Riyaz-us Salatin*[46] spoke of the oppression of respectable Muslims of Gaur during the anarchical rule of the Abyssinians. There is no denial of the fact that the Qazi and the Mullah had the objective of converting the Hindus. They could get away due to the anarchical situation. The evidence of the orthodox strand of culture was becoming prominent during those turbulent years.

This kind of orthodox cultural strand could be seen clearly at Nabadwip in the conflict between the Qazi and Chaitanya. There are two sources on this—one by Vrindaban Das writing about 1563 and the other by Krishnadas Kaviraj writing in 1617. Vrindaban Das[47] clearly states that the Brahmins complained to the Qazi about the late-night *kirtan* (singing with instruments), and the latter prohibited Chaitanya to play such loud music at night. With a notice to the general people, Chaitanya started a torch-lit night procession, going round the city and finally ending at the house of the Qazi. Since Chaitanya was at the end of the procession, by the time he had reached the house, his followers had broken the outer gate of the house from where the sentries had fled and ransacked the garden of the Qazi. Chaitanya was on the point of putting fire to the house and burning the Qazi and his family alive, but some of his followers restrained him for fear of retaliation of the *Mlechchha* king, evidently Sultan Alauddin Hussain Shah. It is important to note that the *Kotwal* did not try to stop the procession nor any punishment was meted out to Chaitanya after the event, which boosted the Vaishnava movement.

In the writing of Krishnadas Kaviraj,[48] there is no reference to violence. One may also note that the writing of early Vaishnava writers, like Vrindaban Das called the Hindus by different names including 'villains'. Krishnadas also refers to the fact that Sultan Alauddin Hussain Shah had ordered his officials not to harass Chaitanya and allow him to preach.[49] Obviously the Sultan wanted to take advantage of the division within the non-Muslim society and see that the predominance of the Brahmins would be challenged from within.

IV

For nearly two hundred years following the conquest of Nadia by Bakhtiyar, we do not hear of the Hindus holding high posts. This had however changed by the early fifteenth century. Earlier, the Hindus were in the army of the Sultans as Ziauddin Barni refers to it as the 'Bengal army' and not Muslim army. The commander of Sultan Iliyas Shah was a Hindu who died fighting Firuz Shah Tughluq. The rise of Ganesh, a Hindu zamindar of Bhaduria Pargana, has been cited already. His son Jalaluddin Muhammed (who had a Muslim mother and had converted to Islam) had a Brahmin in his court named Brihaspati Misra, on whom he showered gifts and titles.[50] During the reign of Barbak Shah, Maladhar Basu wrote his immortal classic *Sri Kishna Vijaya* and was given the title of Gunaraj Khan.[51] According to Sukhomoy Mukhopadhya, the writer of *Ramayana* in Bengali, Krittibas Ojha visited the court of Barbak Shah.[52] The poet gives the names of several Hindu officials sitting close to the Sultan. For instance, Narayan Das was the principal physician of the Sultan and had received a title. One also finds mention of Kedar Ray in two contemporary Persian and Sanskrit texts showing that the latter was the Naib of Sultan Barbak Shah and after his conquest of Tirhut. Kedar Ray was also given charge of revenue collection of the area.[53] In a recently discovered Persian manuscript of Ibrahim Kayum Faruki, the names of Muslim scholars patronized by Barbak Shah have also been found.[54] Kuladhara, of Subarnabanik caste, was a high official of Barbak Shah.[55] Therefore, it is clear that Sultan Barbak Shah had a definite policy of taking Hindus in the Sultanate administration. This became the dominant trend of composite culture in the state. It may be mentioned that Barbak Shah was not particularly lenient to the *darveshes* who dabbled in politics and executed two such people, one of whose tomb still remains and is venerated by both the Hindus and the Muslims as Ismail Ghazi.[56] The other *darvesh* executed by Sultan Barbak Shah in 1476 was Shah Jalal Dakhini, perhaps because of his popularity in the city of Gaur, as suggested in a later book by Ghulam Sarwar. It is perhaps to reduce the influence of the orthodox Muslim nobles that Barbak Shah imported 8,000 Abyssinians.[57] Whatever the number, the Abyssinians became the Sultans of Gaur later and they had to be driven out of Bengal by Sultan Alauddin Hussain Shah around 1493-4 to stop their tyrannical activities. It has also been stated that Barbak Shah had begun to recruit Afghan, soldiers perhaps to reduce the influence of the Turks in the army.[58] There was, therefore, an attempt not only to patronize the Hindu scholars, but also to create a composite culture in the statecraft and in the army, the latter one being not so successful.

Shamsuddin Yusuf, son of Barbak Shah, was far more orthodox than his father and had built several mosques in and around Gaur. According to Firishta, he had asked the ulema to decide religious cases on merit. He built a mosque at Pandua in Hugli district in AD 1477 in which there are remains of Hindu icons, although there is no evidence that he had destroyed Hindu temples.[59] It is not clear what happened to the large number of Hindus who had held high posts under his father. The orthodox Muslim culture was becoming dominant during his reign.

In Bengal, Jalaluddin Fateh Shah has been praised by the contemporary poet Vijay Gupta.[60] The poet states that the king had ruled the world with his sword and during his reign the subjects were happy. Ghulam Hussain Salim in his *Riyaz-us*

Salatin states the same.[61] Strangely enough, as seen earlier, Vijay Gupta had described the oppression on the Hindu shepherds, which is in contradiction of his own praise of the Sultan. It has been suggested that the description of the oppression given by Vijay Gupta was a later interpolation. It is, however, possible that the officials and the Qazi had taken the powers in their hands and oppressed the shepherds without the knowledge of the Sultan. Obviously, the poet was aware of the difference in the attitudes of the Sultan and his officials. Also it remains to be seen how far both Vipradas Piplai and Vijay Gupta were writing the stereotyped story of the victory of the Snake Goddess over the Muslims. But it is true that some isolated incidents of oppression on the Hindus by the zealous Qazis did happen, since Vaishnava poets have referred to such activities. One can therefore, find the contrary strand of culture continuously present in the polity despite the different attitude of some of the Sultans.

Unfortunately we do not have an account of the oppression on the Muslims during the same period, of which the only reference can be seen in the narrative of Vrindaban Das. This was the incident of Yavan Haridas, obviously a Hindu name given by Chaitanya since Haridas used to utter the name of Krishna. The regional authority oppressed Haridas for this on the complaint of the Qazi. According to the narrative of Vrindaban Das, the Sultan behaved well with Haridas and he had to order the punishment on the repeated demands of the Qazi. This reflects the Sultan's liberal attitude.[62] The incident at Nabadwip before the birth of Chaitanya has been narrated by Jayananda, which shows that the Sultan was not happy with the Hindus there. The poet clearly writes that the Sultan acted on the complaints without making proper enquiries and his action was based on the prophecy that a Brahmin boy of Nabadwip would be the next King of Gaur. He ordered the destruction of Nabadwip and many Brahmins fled to Orissa and Varanasi. But the appearance of Goddess Kali in his dream made the Sultan change his mind and he instructed the next morning that no tax would be taken from Nabadwip and any one breaking the temple or oppressing a Hindu would be severely punished.[63] There is no confirmation from any other document of this incident, but one could get indirect support from the writings of Vrindaban Das.[64] One could therefore suggest that Sultan Fateh Shah had to accept the other strand of culture for some time but changed later. Furthermore there are examples of both Hindu and Muslim zamindars being kept in prison for non-payment of taxes. It is certain that during his reign local administrators and orthodox Muslim groups could get some prominence, but how far that affected the Hindu subjects is yet to be estimated properly. One of the reasons for such unbridled power enjoyed by the local administrators was the growing dominance of the Abyssinians, which finally resulted in ushering of large-scale anarchy in Bengal. From the recently discovered inscriptions, it has been estimated that from the second year of his accession, there were continuous conflicts between Sultan Fateh Shah and the Abyssinians.[65] It is quite possible that to gain support, the Sultan leaned more towards the Muslim orthodox group and their ideology in the court, which he gradually gave up towards the end of his reign.[66] Therefore, the entire question of oppression of the Hindus should be seen in the light of contemporary political circumstances and not necessarily from racial or religious point of view, as has been done so far.

The oppression of the Abyssinians on both the Hindus and the Muslims, particularly on those who had money, led Alauddin Hussain Shah, the Wazir of the last Abyssinian Sultan, to rebel and seize power. According to the author of *Riyaz*, Alauddin had driven all the Abyssinians out of Bengal but there are evidences that some of them had remained. Perhaps to make the operation successful, particularly at Gaur, Alauddin had transferred his capital from Gaur to Ekdala. Alauddin's father had come from the Middle East with his two sons of whom Alauddin was the eldest. If the later Vaishnava writing is accepted, Alauddin was a mere labourer. During his reign, the territory of Bengal Sultanate expanded tremendously which could be seen from his innumerable inscriptions and other buildings of note. Chaitanya's activities at Nabadwip occurred during his reign and as stated earlier, he was believed to have ordered his officials not to harass Chaitanya, although the latter never went to Gaur for fear of the *Mlechchha* king.[67]

The hallmark of the reign of Alauddin Hussain Shah, one of the greatest Sultans of Bengal, was that the composıte culture of the court reached its apogee during his time. A large number of Hindus were employed in highly confidential positions as is evident from the Vaishnava writings. Chaitanya flourished during his reign. The attitude of Alauddin Hussain Shah towards Chaitanya had been quite a liberal one. When Chaitanya reached the village of Ramkeli quie close to Gaur, Alauddin asked his Hindu officials to explain to him the influence of Chaitanya on ordinary people who had assembled there. After hearing them, he expressed, according to a Vaishnava poet, that such a man would certainly be a great man. This might be an exaggeration since there is no confirmation from other sources.[68]

The principal Hindus employed in the court, among many others, were Rup and Sanatan, the names given later by Chaitanya when they left the court and became Vaishnavas to go to Vrindaban to write commentaries on the Vaishnava philosophy. They were called *Sagir Mullik* and *Dabir Khas* in the court. There is some controversy as to who was what, but such titles and positions have been constantly referred to in contemporary and later Vaishnava literature. It has been generally assumed that Sanatan was *Sagir Mullik* and had a more important political responsibility than Rup.[69] Keshav Basu was named *Chatri*, whose job was to hold the umbrella over the head of the Sultan. He was also named Keshav Khan, a title given by the Sultan when he was appointed as the chief of the bodyguards. He was the nephew of the poet Maladhar Basu, who was probably a *Chatri* during the reign of Barbak Shah.[70] The other Hindu employee was Subuddhi Ray who was the *Chaudhury* or the revenue collector of Gaur during the rule of the Abyssinian Sultan, Muzaffar Shah, before 1493-4. According to the Vaishnava poet, Subuddhi Ray had whipped Alauddin when the latter was a mere labourer. After becoming the Sultan, Alauddin supposedly penalized Subuddhi Ray on the insistence of his wife. The latter went to Varanasi where he met Chaitanya and on his advice become a Vaishnava.[71] The incident is difficult to believe. Chaitanya came to Varanasi around 1516 and Subuddhi Ray might have come at least a year before that. Alauddin ascended the throne in 1493-4 and this whipping incident must have happened at least five to seven years before his accession when Alauddin was a young man with no proper employment. It is rather difficult to believe that the Sultan took revenge on the insistence of his wife nearly twenty years after his accession and at least twenty-five years after the whipping incident. The incident is referred to by Krishnadas Kaviraj, writing nearly one hundred years after the visit of Chaitanya to Varanasi. His account cannot be taken seriously as there is no other record that Chaitanya had met Subuddhi Ray at Varanasi. It is possible that Krishnadas might have heard this story from later sources. The near contemporary Vaishnava poets, Vrindaban Das and Churamani Das did not refer to the incident.

The personal physician of the Sultan Alauddin was Mukunda, whose father Narayan Das was the personal physician of the Sultan Ruknuddin Barbak Shah. Mukunda was a disciple of Chaitanya. The brother and son of Mukunda were close followers of Chaitanya and after the demise of the saint-poet became the leaders of the Vaishnava movement in Bengal. The *Iqta* system seems to be in vogue during the reign of Sultan Alauddin Hussain Shah. From the writings of Krishnadas Kaviraj we know that Hiranya Das and Gobardhan Das were *Muktas* of different areas.[72]

From *Rajmala* of Tripura, a literary text of this region, we get the name of Gorai Mullik, who was the commander of the Sultan Alauddin Hussain Shah in his wars against Tripura. There is mention of Vidyabachaspati, who used to live in Kulia village opposite Nabadwip and was the teacher of Sanatan. Apart from these people, there were other Hindus employed in the lower rung. Krishnadas Kaviraj wrote that when Chaitanya was returning from Orissa and was waiting on the border, a Hindu spy in disguise came into his party to find out all about him. From *Rajmala* it seems that there were many Hindu soldiers in the army of Sultan Alauddin in his war against Tripura and they used to worship a stone icon on the bank of the Gomati River. In the *History of Bengal*, A.B.M Habibulla has written that there was a Hindu minister by the name of Purandar Khan in the court of the Sultan Alauddin Hussain Shah.[73] This seems to be the title of Gopinath Basu who was a secretary in the court. His elder brother Govinda Basu was also working in the court of the Sultan and got the title of Gandharba Khan. There is, therefore, no doubt that during the reign of Sultan Alauddin Hussain Shah a large number of Hindus were employed in the court, which clearly proves that the State under the Sultan did not discriminate people on the basis of their religion. It may be mentioned that Sultan Alauddin Hussain Shah ruled over a large territory. His coins and innumerable inscriptions show that almost the entire of Bengal, and a large portion of Bihar, including Bhagalpur and Patna, were under his control. Large parts of Kamrup-Kamta and Orissa too came under his sway at least for a temporary period. For twenty-six years Sultan Alauddin Hussain Shah ruled this huge kingdom almost without any trouble. The Hindu poets also praised him highly as the best king and a learned scholar. The Vaishnava poets, even while referring to him as *Mlechchha* and Yavana, admired him for his learning and favourable attitude towards the non-Muslims.

There is a difference of opinion among the historians regarding Sultan Alauddin Hussain Shah's attitude towards the Hindus. Both R.C. Majumdar and A.C. Bannerjee describe Alauddin as anti-Hindu while A.B.M. Habibulla and M.R. Tarafdar characterize him as pro-Hindu.[74] It is pertinent to mention that R.C. Majumdar and A.C. Bannerjee based their assertion on Bengali poems but their authority is doubtful.[75] It may be mentioned that the breaking of temples or mosques of the enemy during war was common practice among the Hindu and Muslim rulers. There are records that the Vijayanagar rulers too had destroyed mosques during war, which did not necessarily reflect their anti-Muslim or pro-Hindu bias. It may be added here that Sultan Alauddin had constructed a large number of mosques throughout his kingdom[76] but there is no single evidence that he ever destroyed a Hindu temple to construct a mosque. Also, the contemporary and later Vaishnava sources are not unanimous in their opinions about the Sultan. It has already been mentioned that Alauddin ascended the throne through turmoil and had to transfer his capital to the fort of Ekdala. It is quite possible in the circumstances that Allaudin Hussain Shah might have taken a tough stand against the Hindus. One may mention that prior to the birth of Chaitanya in 1486 many Hindus from the outlying province of Sylhet had come to Nabadwip.[77] If the persecution of the Hindus had been a deliberate State policy they would have avoided coming near the centre of power. As a matter of fact, there were Brahmin and Vaishnava settlements within walking distance of the capital. When Chaitanya visited village Ramkeli close to the capital Gaur there was no prohibition against Vaishnavas holding their ceremonies in the village. The Brahmins of Nabadwip were fearful of the Yavana king, but were not converted to Islam nor were their temples destroyed. The Brahmins could carry on their teachings uninterrupted. Therefore, isolated incidents of oppression by a few Qazis should not be viewed as oppression by the State. Neither should it be taken as the presecution of the Hindus by the Muslims. It is quite possible that the Sultans did not try to restrain the zealous Qazis in the outlying areas. But the absence of any repressive measures against Chaitanya after his violent attack on the Qazi of Nabadwip would show that the State did not subscribe to such a policy of repression. The contemporary Bengali poets, particularly the non-Vaishnavas, were aware of this distinction and after narrating the role of the villain Qazi, they had praised the Sultan. Vijay Gupta's narrative of the persecution by the Qazi, which has been taken by R.C. Majumdar as an example of the persecution of the Hindus by the Muslims, omitting the praise of Sultan Jalaluddin Fateh Shah by the poet, is another example of the misrepresentation of the sources. The poet has categorically stated that the subjects were living in happiness under the Sultan.[78]

One notices three features in the appointments of Hindus by Sultan Alauddin Hussain Shah. The first was that he not only recruited larger number of Hindus compared to any other Sultan of Bengal, but some of them were given high posts of confidential nature. This shows that it was not lip service to take the Hindus into the administration, but a deliberate policy to make them part of the inner circle that took important decisions. There were, however, some conflicts within. When the Sultan proposed to undertake the expedition to Orissa ruled then by a Hindu king, Sanatan, the *Sagir Mullik*, refused to go with him. He was imprisoned, but he could escape by bribing the guard.[79] His brother Rup also left the job and went to Vrindaban. The second feature was that the Sultan recruited mostly from Rarh and Bakla areas. While Rarh was closer to the capital, Bakla was a distant place, which was becoming prey to the Arakan and later Portuguese onslaughts. The third feature was that he recruited mostly from a particular family. Sanatan and his three brothers along with their brother-in-law were recruited perhaps to ensure loyalty to the Sultan. This limited political integration to a few families.

Alauddin was succeeded by his son Nasiruddin Nusrut Shah in 1519. Nasiruddin was also a patron of Hindu literature, but we do not hear of any recruitment of Hindu officers. One reason was perhaps that by that time Chaitanya had gone to Orissa and the Vaishnava poets turned their attention from Bengal to Orissa. It may also be mentioned that at the end of his reign, Nusrut Shah was beset with the problem of the fleeing Afghans from northern India after the fall of Ibrahim Lodi in 1526. Nusrut tried to form a Bengal-Afghan alliance against the advancing Mughals which failed to materalize. It is possible that he had to recruit more Afghans instead of Hindus.[80] The reign of his son Feroz Shah was too short to have a decisive impact at the social level and the next Bengal ruler Ghiyasuddin Mahmud III remained involved in external problems.

V

In the first 250 years since the conquest of Nadia by Bakhtiyar Khalji, the kingdom of Bengal was fragmented and had rebelled against Delhi off and on. Till the middle of the fourteenth century, which marked the turning point in the history of the Sultanate, there are few references to Hindu culture. However, one does not find any evidence of the 'eternal conflict' with the Hindu zamindars some of whom held their own for a long time. For example, when Balban invaded Bengal to suppress the revolt of Tughril Tughan, he did not undertake any expedition against any Hindu zamindar. As a matter of fact, according to Barani, Balban had made a pact with Raja Danujmardan Dev of Chandradwip. Neither Minhaj nor the later Persian historians of Delhi speak of any suppression of Hindu zamindars, although the expansion of the Sultanate would suggest that conquests had taken place. Significantly enough, when these sources speak of the expansion of Islamic culture in Bengal, they do not mention the suppression of the Hindus either as a State policy or as an act of individual Sultan.

It is from the middle of the fourteenth century that Bengal began to be united under one administration, initiated by Sultan Iliyas Shah. By that time, the Hindus had begun to cooperate with the Sultan and one gets the idea of the beginning of the composite culture based on political identity and independence of Bengal. As cited already, Sultan Feroze Shah Tughluq's inducements to get the orthodox Muslims and the Hindus including peasants and zamindars to leave the Sultan of Bengal, did not bear fruit and his two invasions ended in failures. Without a composite culture, even of a political nature and restricted within the machinery of the government, such resistance to the two invasions of the Delhi Sultan could not have been successful. This was a turning point in another sense, which could be seen within the fold of the Islamic culture. Since the conquest of Nadia in the early thirteenth century, the Sufis and *darveshes* were coming to Bengal from northern India. They were following the customs and manners of their masters so far. But by the middle of the fourteenth century, these Sufis and *darveshes* became far more attuned to the Bengali culture and adopted the local customs and manners, thus cutting off their links with Delhi. Thus, a regional identity along with the political identity grew up within the fold of Islamic organizations in Bengal that helped the formation of a composite culture. More and more Hindus came closer to such a process of acculturation. The two tombs of Ismail Ghazi became points of veneration for both the Hindus and the Muslims. There are other such examples. At the end of the fifteenth century, the description of Satgaon by the poet Vipradas Piplai clearly shows a high degree of overseas commerce and of urbanization. By then, the smaller towns on the bank of the Bhagirathi were expanding and the weavers could be found in large numbers at Satgaon, Nabadwip, Santipore, and so on. In early sixteenth century both Duarte

Barbosa and Thome Pires have mentioned the rich overseas commerce of Bengal.[81] The Portuguese began to arrive in Bengal from 1517 for trade but the inhabitants of Chittagong refused to trade with them.[82] The demands of increasing trade and overseas commerce required far more integration and Chaitanya tried to get the producers, distributors and merchants into one cohesive society in which the dominance of the Brahmin priests would be less.

It was during the early sixteenth century that we see the growth of the composite culture, when Sultan Alauddin Hussain Shah gave the Hindus a share in the management of the State, a trend that had started from the beginning of the fifteenth century culminating in the rise of Raja Ganesh, as mentioned earlier. During this period, the Sultanate had reached its apogee of political unity. The new cultural ethos faded away after the death of Sultan Alauddin Hussain Shah, when the Portuguese, Afghans and the Mughals struggled to dominate Bengal. Although there was a brief interlude of independence during the reign of the Karranis, it faded away with the death of Daud Karrani in 1576. For the next forty years the Sultanate, then partly under the Mughals, remained fragmented till the Mughals established political unification to turn Bengal into a Suba of the Mughal Empire.

The composite culture in Bengal did not take root when the country was fragmented. It was only from the middle of the fourteenth century that a composite culture began to develop. It was to the credit of the Sultans of Bengal that they had helped the process of establishing a Bengali identity. Bengali language was used in the courts. One can therefore postulate that factors like centralization, emergence and consolidation of Bengal's political identity and independence, along with the developments of Bengali language and literature and overseas trade and commerce helped in the development of a composite culture in Bengal. It should be pointed out that this composite culture was largely a State-sponsored one. Therein lay its inherent weakness. Yet its emergence could keep the orthodox cultural activities in check and helped to create pockets of such acculturation, which grew later under the Mughals. One cannot therefore call this period of the Sultanate as the period of 'eternal conflict' between the Hindus and the Muslims, which would be a travesty of history.

NOTES

1. Minhaj-us Siraj, *Tabaqat-i Nasiri* (Eng. tr. Major Raverty), Calcutta, 1995, rpt., vol. I, pp. 537-58.
2. Dinesh Chandra Sen, *Vrihat Banga* (Bengali), Calcutta, 1993, rpt., 2 vols.; Kaliprasanna Bandopadhyay, *Madhyayuge Bangla* (Bengali), Calcutta, 2002, rpt.; Abanti Kumar Sanyal, *Banglar Adi Madhyayuga: Bhasa, Sahitya, Samaj O Sanskriti* (Bengali), Calcutta, 1999.
3. Ramaranjan Mukherjee and S.K. Maity, *Corpus of Bengal Inscriptions*, Calcutta, 1967, pp. 277 ff..
4. Minhaj, p. 244.
5. Ibid. Also see, Jadunath Sarkar (ed.), *History of Bengal*, Dacca, 1972, vol. II, rpt.
6. Sarkar, 1972, pp. 59-67.
7. Niharranjan Ray, *Bangalir Itihas* (Bengali), Calcutta, 1996, rpt., pp. 269 ff.
8. Minhaj is silent on this, but the system continued even at the end of the Sultanate period. See discussion in article by Aniruddha Ray entitled 'Middle Bengali Literature: A Source for the Study of Bengal in the Age of Akbar' in Irfan Habib (ed.), *Akbar and His India*, Delhi, 1997, pp. 225-42. Also see, Abdul Karim, *Banglar Itihas: Sultani Amal* (Bengali), Dacca, 1987, 2nd edn., pp. 395-6.
9. Jawhar Sircar, *The Construction of the Hindu Identity in Medieval Bengal: The Role of Popular Cults*, Calcutta, 2005, particularly Chapter III.
10. Sukumar Sen, *Bangla Sahityer Itihas* (Bengali), Calcutta, 1978, 3 vols., 6th edn., pp. 60 ff.
11. Bhaktimadhab Chattopadhyay (ed.), *Shunya Puran* (Bengali), Calcutta, 1977, pp. 159 post under the title 'Niranjaner Rushma'. See also Dinesh Chandra Sen, vol. I, pp. 500 ff.
12. Discussion of *Charjyapada* in Sukumar Sen, 1978, vol. I, pp. 54-76.
13. Dinesh Chandra Sen found that the easy victory of Bakhtiyar Khalji was due to the strengthening of caste rules and untouchability during the rule of the Senas; see Dinesh Chandra Sen, vol. I, pp. 500 ff.
14. See the article by Iqtedar Alam Khan entitled 'Concept of India in Alberuni' in Irfan Habib (ed.), *India: Studies in the History of an Idea*, New Delhi, 2004, pp. 110-21. For the comments of Alberuni,

see the Bengali translation of Alberuni's *Kitab-i Tahkike* by A.B.M. Habibullah, Dacca, 1974, pp. 66-9.

15. For discussion on the sectarian differences in early thirteenth century, see Sukumar Sen, 1993, vol. I, pp. 77 post. Also see J.N. Bhattacharjya, *Hindu Castes and Sects,* Calcutta, 1973.
16. Abdul Karim, *Social History of the Muslims in Bengal*, Chittagong, 2nd rev. edn., 1985. Also see Reena Bhaduri, *Social Formation in Medieval Bengal*, Calcutta, 2001.
17. Haraprasad Ray, *Trade and Diplomacy in India-China Relations*, New Delhi, 1993, p. 102.
18. Ibn Battuta, *Travels in Asia and Africa, 1325-1354* (tr. H.A.R. Gibb), New Delhi, 1986, pp. 267-71.
19. Sukhomoy Mukhopadhyay, *Banglar Itihas, 1204-1576* (Bengali), Dacca, 2000, pp. 274-315.
20. For the English translation of the letters of Nur Qutb Alam, see the article by Syed Hasan Askari in *Bengal Past & Present*, 1948, no. LXVII, pp. 38-9. The full text of the letter in English has been published by Abdul Karim in *Abdul Karim Sahityabisharad Commemoration Volume*, Dacca, 1972, pp. 341-3 under the title 'Nur Qutb Alam's letter on the Ascendancy of Raja Ganesh'.
21. Sarkar, 1972, pp. 120-9.
22. For a discussion on such terminology, see Brajadulal Chattopadhyay, *Representing the Other?*, New Delhi, 1998.
23. Muhammad Enamul Huq, *Sufism and Bengal*, Dacca, 1975, pp. 146-7. See also Richard M. Eaton, *The Rise of Islam and the Bengal Frontier*, Delhi, 1994, pp. 55-91.
24. Mukundaram Chakrabarty, *Kavi Kankan Chandi* (Bengali) ed. Panchanon Mandal, Calcutta, 1992, rpt., p. 88.
25. D. Bandopadhayay (ed.), *Padmavati* (Bengali), Calcutta, 1985.
26. Ibid.
27. Jagadish Narayan Sarkar, *Banglaye Hindu-Musalman Samparka* (Bengali), Calcutta, 1935, pp. 33-8.
28. See Mukhopadhayay, pp. 225-30. Ibid.
29. Niharranjan Ray, pp. 701 ff.
30. Ghulam Hussain Salim, *Riyaz-us Salatin* (English tr. Abdus Salam), New Delhi, 1975, p. 118.
31. Shamsuddin Ahmed (tr. & ed.), *Inscription of Bengal*, Rajshahi (Bangladesh), 1960, vol. IV, pp. 59-60.
32. Aniruddha Ray 'Morphology of Medieval Saptagram or Satgaon', *Journal of Bengal Art,* Dacca, 1999, vol. 4, pp. 217-34.
33. J.V.G. Mills (tr. into English), *Ma Huan*, Cambridge, 1979, pp. 161-3.
34. Vipradas, *Manasa Vijay* (Bengali), ed. Sukumar Sen, Calcutta, 1958, p. 143.

35. Krishnaram Das, *Shasti Mangal* (Bengali), Calcutta, n.d., p. 25.
36. Vincent Le Blanc, *Les Voyages Fameux* (French), Paris, 1648, pp. 133-4.
37. Account of Ralph Fitch in W. Foster (ed.), *Early Travels in India*, New Delhi, 1985, rpt., p. 24.
38. For a brief history of the growth of Nabadwip see Aniruddha Ray, 'Urbanization in Medieval Bengal, *c.* A.D. 1200-*c.*1600', in *The Proceedings of the Indian History Congress, 1992-93*, Warangal Session, pp. 147 ff.
39. *Voyage Dans les Deltas du Gange et de l'Irraouddy, 1521* (Texts in Portuguese French and English, tr. and ed. by G. Bouchon and L.F. Thomaz), Paris, 1988, pp. 323 ff.
40. Aniruddha Ray, 'Archaeological Reconnaissance of the City of Gaur: A Preliminary Report' in *Pratna Samiksha*, Calcutta, 1995, nos. 2-3, pp. 245-63.
41. Voyage, p. 327.
42. Ibid., pp. 330 ff.
43. See the account of Caeser Fredericki in *Puchas and His Pilgrimages*, Edinburgh, n.d., vol. V, pp. 410-11.
44. R.C. Majumdar, *History of Medieval Bengal*, Calcutta, 1973, pp. 247-8; A.C. Bannerjee, *Madhyayuge Bangla O Bangali* (Bengali), Calcutta, 1968, pp. 50-8.
45. Vipradas, pp. 67-8; Vijay Gupta, *Padma Puran* (Bengali), Calcutta, n.d., pp. 46-52.
46. Riyaz, pp. 126-7.
47. Vrindaban Das, *Chaitanya Bhagawat* (Bengali) written about 1563, pp. 789-804.
48. Krishnadas Kaviraj, *Chaitanya Charitamrita* (Bengali), ed. U. Mukhopadhyay, Calcutta, 1989, pp. 72-3.
49. Ibid., p. 82.
50. Mukhopadhyay, pp. 334-6.
51. Ibid., p. 363.
52. Ibid., p. 364.
53. Ibid., p. 363.
54. Ibid.
55. Ibid.
56. For the legend of Ismail Ghazi and his two tombs, see ibid., pp. 354-7.
57. Mukhopadhyay, pp. 373-4.
58. Ibid.
59. Sarkar, pp. 135-6.
60. Vijay Gupta, *Padma Puran* (Bengali) Calcutta, n.d., p. 4.
61. Mukhopadhyay, pp. 384-7.

62. Ibid., pp. 392-4.
63. Jayananda, op. cit., pp. 14-15.
64. Vrindaban Das, pp. 347 ff.
65. Mukhopadhyay, p. 403.
66. Abdul Karim thinks that Fateh Shah got the throne by forming a party of nobles that led to the troubles, see *Sultani Amal*, pp. 255-7.
67. M.R. Tarafdar, *Hussain Shahi Bengal, 1494-1538*, Dacca, 1999.
68. Krishnadas Kaviraj, pp. 82-3.
69. Mukhopadhyay, pp. 512-17.
70. Krishnadas Kaviraj, pp. 265-6. Abdul Karim mistakenly called him *Kotwal* of Gaur, see *Sultani Amal*, p. 315.
71. See Mukhopadhyay, pp. 520-1.
72. Krishnadas Kaviraj, p. 185.
73. A.B.M. Habibullah, 'Hussain Shahi Dynasty' in *History of Bengal*, pp. 151 post. For *Rajmala* see the entire text cited by in Mukhopadhay, pp. 467-81.
74. See, Habibullah, pp. 150-2; also Tarafdar, pp. 64-7; R.C. Majumdar, pp. 247-52; A.C. Bannerjee, pp. 50-8.
75. Mukhopadhyay, p. 551.
76. Ibid., p. 545.
77. Jayananda showed that the parents of Chaitanya migrated to Nabadwip from Sylhet due to famine prevailing there (Jayananda, pp. 10-11).
78. Vijay Gupta, p. 4.
79. Krishnadas Kaviraj, pp. 200-1.
80. Habibullah, pp. 164-5.
81. M.L. Dames (ed.), *The Book of Duarte Barbosa*, New Delhi, 1989, vol. II, pp. 135-48; A. Cortesao (ed.), *The Suma Oriental of Thome Pires*, 1990, 2 vols., I, pp. 88-94.
82. Surendranath Sen, 'An Early Portuguese Account of Bengal', in Surendranath Sen, *Early Career of Kanohji Angria and Other Papers*, Calcutta, 1941, pp. 88-95. It gives the description of the first visit of an accredited Portuguese agent to Bengal in 1517.

CHAPTER 6

Skilled Labour Migration in Pre-Colonial India from 16th to 18th Centuries

SHIREEN MOOSVI

'Internal migrations' began to constitute a special concern of the Indian censuses after it became clear that something more was desirable than mere head-count and community identification that had marked all census operations until and including the first all-India census of 1868-72 (generally cited as the 1872 census). Figures for internal migrations were furnished in particular detail in the report on the 1901 census.[1] It is to be remembered that since only places of birth were taken into account, the figures are confined to first-generation migrants. The further point to note is that the migrants are restricted to those born outside the 'province' or princely 'state'/'agency' (group of states) of their domicile. Inter-district migrations were not considered (each Indian province and large princely states being divided into 'districts', generally larger than English counties). Nor unfortunately were these figures cross-checked with those of occupations, so that while it is established as to how many migrated, the migrants are not classified by occupation (e.g. peasants/labourers/artisans, etc.).

These facts must be borne in mind when one considers the total number of migrants placed (immigrants only) at 7.02 million out of a total population, then, of 294.4 million. The internal migrants thus comprised 2.39 per cent of the total population. Given the fact that only migrants over large distances were being considered in the Indian census, the number of internal migrants, relative to the total population in India in 1901 was not small. The total internal migration within England and Wales counted only on inter-county basis was (counting immigrants) no more than 5.18 per cent over the 20-year period, 1781-1801, and 5.95 per cent over the 30-year period, 1801-31, as estimated by Dean and Cole.[2] The comparison is particularly instructive since England during the period concerned was in the throes of the great population shift of the Industrial Revolution while India in 1901 was at the tail-end of a long-drawn process of de-industrialization, though the newly built railways might be supposed to have facilitated long-distance migrations over some regions.

We might thus accept the 1901 census as indicative of the fact that migrations on some scale were a part of reality of pre-industrial India. Unluckily, as we have noted, the census does not give an occupational breakdown of the migrants, and so the extent to which the migrations in 1901 were those of skilled labour cannot be established. In some areas, like Assam, the bulk of immigrants were undoubtedly peasants and plantation labourers. Immigrants into Bombay Presidency were, on the other hand, in large part artisans and town labourers. But beyond such general statements we can hardly quantify occupational migrations, given the census data as they have been published.

If this is the case even well into the census period, one cannot hope at all to quantify migrations during the seventeenth and eighteenth centuries, with which we are concerned here. Our study is bound to be almost entirely qualitative.

Another problem is of source material. Much of the data about the migrations comes from official ethnographic surveys of the late nineteenth century, later collected together in the major official series of volumes on tribes and castes, covering the Presidencies of Bengal, Madras and Bombay, the North-West Provinces (now UP), the Punjab and the Central Provinces.[3] The information is uneven, as may be expected from such publications. What I have used in this paper is information relating to what these reports themselves describe as old migrations. Wherever possible this information is supplemented by material from earlier sources.

One may think that in a traditional society like India, to

which much rigidity has been assigned in modern sociological thought since Weber, migrations of craftsmen, bound by their castes and by local ties should have been a rare phenomena. This concept of social rigidity was well contested by Morris D. Morris, but he was concerned with caste adjustments rather with geographical mobility.[4] We have already seen from the 1901 census that at least a hundred years ago caste offered no barrier to migration, since internal migration over long distances involved fairly sizeable numbers. Indeed, I argue below that caste could also have provided a good motive to migrate. We must remember, besides, that pre-colonial India had large cities, markets, a system of banking, credit and insurance, and a large sector of commodity production.[5] Craft mobility would be an essential element for sustaining such a system.

For one, the establishment of cities, the primary centres of production for long-distance trade, could be established only by immigration of craftsmen. When a sixteenth-century poet of Bengal Mukunduram gave an imaginary account of the establishment of a mythical city, he particularly describes the settlement of Muslim migrants into this city. They included *Julahas* or weavers, *Kagozia* or papermakers and so on.[6] When Mahmud Beghra, Sultan of Gujarat (1459-1511) established Mahmudabad, it is stated by an eighteenth-century historian that large numbers of artisans and craftsmen came to settle there and made textile products of Ahmedabad and Mahmudabad famous all over the world, especially in 'Iran, Turkey and Syria'.[7]

According to Mughal regulations newcomers to a town were required to offer sureties, but this was done apparently to discourage thieves and undesirable elements. Any consideration of protecting local craftsmen against outsiders does not seem to lie behind the restriction.[8] Indeed, far from discouraging artisan immigration, local authorities always tended to encourage it. Everyone, we are told, was 'free to settle here (Ahmedabad) and live by his craft or his business without molestation or interference by anyone', so Geleynssen reported in 1629.[9] In 1672 an imperial order was issued to the officers of Gujarat prohibiting them from realizing unauthorized cesses from the cotton-dressers and oil-pressers who had recently come to Gujarat from other places and opened new shops there.[10]

The tastes of consumers of craft products also caused changes in demand which induced migrations of specialists in the crafts. Connected with this was the coming of new craft techniques, which would diffuse along with their practitioners, a phenomenon so common in early modern Europe too.[11]

In India a simple illustration of this comes from the reign of the Mughal Emperor Akbar (1556-1605). The Emperor was keenly interested in Kashmir shawls and over a thousand workshops of Kashmir shawls were, therefore, established in Lahore in Punjab.[12] Apparently, this could be done only by bringing a large number of Kashmiri shawl-weavers to Lahore. Similarly for manufacturing Persian carpets, weavers migrated from Iran to India. Such a community of Persians was found settled in the Godavari district of Andhra in 1679. They made high quality carpets, and claimed to have come over a hundred years earlier (i.e. in the sixteenth century).[13]

Although direct evidence for actual migrations of specialists in certain techniques is not always available, this is strongly suggested by the fact that wherever found, they were monopolized by Muslims.

Buchanan reports in 1810 that all the paper makers in Patna and Gaya as well as in Rangpur were 'Muhammedans'.[14] In 1820 William Erskine found a small town called 'Kaghizwera' (Kaghaziwara) near Daulatabad (Maharashtra) making paper that was sent to Hyderabad, Nagpur, Pune, and so on. His statement that in spite of it being the month of Ramazan, the manufacturers displayed the process to him, makes it evident that the paper-makers were Muslims.[15] It was reported from Patna (Bihar) in 1811-12 that to give a fine gloss and smoothness to paper, a particular technique of rubbing it with polished glass was practised. This technique was the monopoly of a class of Muslims called Muharahdars.[16]

The makers of glass-bangles or *Churihar* in the North-West Provinces were all Sunni Muslims while the *Manihar*, who made bangles of lac, comprised both Hindus and Muslims. But Muslims were even here 'much in excess' and invariably Sunnis.[17] In the Central Provinces the glass-bangle makers were in the early period only Muslims, but in early twentieth-century Hindus had also joined the profession. A tradition was produced to the effect that Goddess Parvati refused to put on bangles made by Muslims and so Mahadev (Lord Shiva) caught hold of a kshatriya (a member of the Hindu 'warrior' caste) and forced him to make glass bangles; his descendants thereupon followed the profession.[18]

The Atishbaz, makers of fireworks, formed a professional caste and uptil the nineteenth century, all of them in the North-West Province were Muslims.[19]

While dyers in the Central Provinces were both Hindus and Muslims the technique and the raw material used by the Hindu and Muslim castes of dyers were quite different. The Muslim dyers were called Rangrez, and used safflower and myrobalans and produced a variety of colours. The Hindu dyers of the caste known as Chhipa or Rangari practised a separate branch of dyeing.[20]

Tinning was another profession which the Muslims dominated. Buchanan in 1809-10 says that at Dinajpur as well as Rangpore the Muslim tinners who did not form a separate professional class introduced a technique of coating tin inside the vessels used in cookery but 'the Hindus have not yet had the sense to use vessels secured in this manner from the deterious effects of the copper'.[21]

If certain techniques remained confined to Muslims or to a particular caste, this was not owing to any official policy of the Mughal government, which generally seems to have been averse to the monopoly of any craft by any group. When in the Ahmedabad mint the Srimal caste of smelters and wire-drawers did not let others follow the profession an imperial order came that their monopoly should be disregarded since no one could stop anyone from following any profession, by law.[22] Naturally, this could encourage migration since artisans would know that they could establish themselves in any new place.

Textile-making having been particularly developed in India as a craft, weavers specialized in a number of different techniques. Specialists in a particular technique would therefore move to areas where their products became popular. This mobility most probably continued till the nineteenth century when Lancashire gravely devastated the entire profession in India. Before that time, however, there are various instances of weavers' migrations.

The migration of Saurashtras also known as Patnulkaran, to south India from Gujarat offers an interesting illustration. In the 1890s the Patnulkaran, 'a caste of foreign weavers' was found spread in all the Tamil districts but mainly in Madura town. They 'far-outnumbered' the Kaikolans, the main Tamil weaving caste. Their tradition was that they had first moved from Saurashtra in Gujarat to Mandesor (now in MP) and Devagiri (in Maharashtra) and finally to Vijaynagar (Karnataka). From here they migrated to Madura, from where they dispersed over what is now Tamil Nadu. There is a further tradition that the Nayaka rulers of Madura (seventeenth century) were not happy with the work of Kaikolan weavers and so invited the Patnulkarans from Gujarat.[23] The Patnulkaran, as their very name suggests, were silkweavers, while the Kaikolans were essentially cotton weavers. It was probably for the reason of their specialization in silk-weaving that they found a ready welcome in the areas of the extreme south. They claimed to be Brahmans. The Tamil Brahmans did not raise any objection to their claim though they did not accept them into their own fold.[24]

Their migrations did not come to an end still. *The Mysore Census Report*, 1891, records that Haider Ali, while returning from his expeditions against Madras in 1769, forcibly brought with him twenty-five families of these weavers, who were living in the Tanjore district, and established them at Ganjam near Seringapatam; in order to encourage silk and velvet weaving. He exempted them from certain taxes. The industry flourished till the fall of Seringapatam to the English in 1799 when most of the class fled the place.[25]

Besides the Patnulkarans, there were major concentrations of Telugu weavers called Devanga in the Tamil districts of Madura, Coimbatore and Salem.[26] The Koshthi weaving caste of Chhotanagpur (Madhya Pradesh), who made varieties of coarse cloth, migrated to Madras.[27]

The Chaliyan, a caste of cotton weavers from the east coast of Kerala were reported in Tamil districts in the 1891 census, when they were held to be relatively recent immigrants.[28] While weavers from different places migrated to Tamil districts the members of the main Tamil weaving caste, the Kaikolan, emigrated to the southern districts of Andhra and adopted Telugu as their language.[29] The famous Tanti weavers of Bengal, specializing in weaving muslins,[30] migrated to the south, though the date of their migration is not known. But at the time of the *Census of 1891*, they were considered quite old settlers in Ganjam, then in Madras Presidency.[31] The Karna Sale, the main caste of Telugu weavers, migrated to Tamil districts of Madura and Tanjore[32] and also to the Malabar districts of Kerala, where they were known as Saliyar and Seniyar. Members of this caste also emigrated to coastal Sri Lanka and were reported to have been absorbed into Sinhalese society under the name Salagama.[33]

But the geographical mobility was in no way restricted to weavers alone. Various other castes specializing in different crafts were also mobile. The Kevuto at Ganjam in Madras Presidency, according to the *Census of 1891*, were the descendants of the Kaibartas, the caste of boatmen and fishermen of Bengal.[34] They migrated to Ganjam and continued in the same profession.[35] The Kharvi, Marathi fishermen and boatmen, came to South Kanara from Maharashtra, and made good sailors.[36]

Chakkiliyans, the leather-workers in the Tamil districts, were held to be immigrants from either Kanara or the Telugu region.[37] Kamsalas, a Telugu caste of brass-smiths, carpenters, goldsmiths and stone-cutters, migrated to Behrampur in Ganjam district (Orissa), then in Madras Presidency. This, according to tradition, was an old migration dating back to the time when a Chola king got offended by their claim of being equal to Brahmans and ordered their destruction.[38]

The members of the *Pathinettan* caste of carpenters appear to have been still more enterprising and migrated to Sri Lanka.[39]

Painters too formed a class of immigrants. Of Iranian immigrants whose paintings have survived, there is now an authoritative record,[40] and one need not say more about it. There were specialists in the related arts, who also migrated from Iran to India. Such was Muhammad Amin, expert in margin and tabular presentation and tracing, who invented the technique of tracing in seven colours and the use of mica paper. He trained Mulla Muhammad Husain of Herat,[41] another immigrant.

A caste of dyers and tailors, the *Rangaris*, was reported from almost all the Telugu (Andhra) districts in 1891. They were from Maharashtra and spoke Marathi and claimed to be kshatriyas.[42] The Potias, the mat-makers, came to south India from Potia in Orissa.[43]

A Tamil artisanal caste, *Kammala*, was very similar to the Telugu *Kamasals*, members of which were gold and copper-smiths, stone-cutters and also carpenters. They apparently first migrated to Sri Lanka ('Izhuva land') and from there they came to Malabar. Some eighteen families of carpenters returned much afterwards, probably at the close of the eighteenth century.[44]

The *Chaptegaras* were a carpenter caste that came from Konkan country to Tamil areas but retained their language.[45] The *Charodi*, a Canarese carpenter caste, migrated to the Madras region.[46]

How skilled workers responded to inducements to migrate is illustrated by their reaction to the English and Dutch East India Companies' proposals for settling them in areas under their control. In 1661 the Company desired that weavers from Bengal should be induced to migrate to the English Company's settlement at Fort St. George (Madras). The Company's factors at Madras were initially quite hopeful of the success since earlier the Protuguese succeeded in bringing the weavers of taffetas (a type of silken cloth) from Bengal to Chaul (near Mumbai) and getting a very good quality of taffetas made thereby. However, the factors in Bengal found it difficult even to bring the taffeta makers from Qasimbazar to Hugly. They showed no hope of being able to persuade the weavers to go as far away as Madras particularly so because it involved crossing the salt water which they thought was bound to make them lose their caste.[47] The excuse if offered by the weavers might have been one that could have been removed if better terms had been offered. In 1669 the Surat factors reported that it would be difficult for them to induce washermen to go to Bombay because 'their employments are so full here that they have as little reason as inclination to remove . . . nor can they live at so cheap a rate as the people there'.[48] It is reported that the few bricklayers that the English took from Surat to Bombay also came back because they had greater employment available at Surat.[49] Earlier in 1632 the English were unable to persuade calico-washers to move from Masulipatam (Machhilipatnam) to Petapoli since at Masulipatam they had better employment opportunities provided by the Dutch, the Danes and Muslim merchants. The two packers who agreed to go to Petapoli were to be paid one month's salary in advance and the salary at two and a half pagodas a month appears not a low one by contemporary standards.[50]

The Dutch, however, had better luck. In January 1660 they succeeded in sending 37 weavers and chintz painters to Jaffna (Sri Lanka) from Nagapattanam[51] and again 500 weavers and painters with their wives and children in December 1660.[52] In 1673 they claimed that from the Coromandel as many weavers and calico painters as needed could be sent.[53]

In 1694 the English when establishing a mint at Bombay found it very difficult to get skilled mintmen for the work. They tried to take two *zarrabs* (coin-strikers) and two *chocksees* ('chaukasis', assayers) from Surat, but found that their terms were very high. The *chocksees* asked for Rs. 300 per annum while at the Surat imperial mint they received just Rs. 150 or Rs. 200. The *zarrabs* asked for Rs. 8 a month when there was no work and Rs. 6 per 1,000 coins struck, while at Surat they recieved only Rs. 5 per 1,000. They further asked for advance payment and charges for fuel, etc. Finally, the English managed to procure two *zarrabs* and two *chocksees* from Cambay but the Mughal Governor raised great objections and pressed for their return.[54] It is interesting to contrast this with the position within the Mughal Empire. When in 1694, there was need of more *zarrabs* at the Delhi mint these were readily secured from Surat, despite the much greater distance involved.[55]

Naturally, things would be different, if force was employed. Nadir Shah after his sack of Delhi (1739) took away a large number of artisans to Iran. He is reported to have 1,100 boats built in 1740, on the banks of the Oxus by Indian carpenters and shipwrights whom he had despatched there. He also engaged a large number of Indian carpenters, as well as stone-cutters, masons, goldsmiths and other craftsmen, since he intended to build in Iran a city on the model of Delhi.[56]

An interesting question is whether caste migration also involved a change in caste-status, that is, whether it was motivated by a desire for 'Sanskritization', which, according to the definition of M.N. Srinivas, means elevation in status through a shift to the ritual and customs of upper castes.[57] Such 'Sanskritization' might be thought easier by skilled craftsmen, if in a new place where their previous position was not known, they might use their relative affluence to get recognition of a higher position. We have already seen that the Saurashtras (*Patnulkarans*), immigrant weavers from Gujarat, proclaimed themselves Brahmans in south India, and that the *Kamsalas*, an artisan caste migrating from Andhra to Ganjam, had annoyed the Chola king by their pretensions to a Brahman status. The *Rangaris* were dyers and tailors originating from Maharashtra, of apparently low status. On coming to coastal Andhra they claimed to be Kshatriyas.[58] The *Kharvis*, who were Maratha fishermen and boatmen, upon migrating to South Kanara, started wearing the sacred thread, signifying a claim to belong to the 'twice-born', i.e. the three upper castes (Brahmans, Kshatriyas and Vaishyas) even though by their calling they were barred from such presumption. They compromised by wearing it only for seven days a year when they abstained from their profession.[59]

A carpenter caste, the *Chaptegaras*, who migrated from Konkan to the Madras Presidency, not only started putting on the sacred thread but also began to employ Brahman priests for their rituals![60] The analogous carpenter caste of *Charodi* from the Kanara districts followed the same practice on moving to Madurai.[61] These claims were seldom disputed in the immigrants' new homes, but they were generally not assimilated in the local caste hierarchy or treated socially at par as may be seen in the case with the Saurashtras.

The *Muchaveru* shoe-makers who in the seventeenth century came along with the Mughal noble Qasim Khan from Ajmer to Karnataka, pretended to be of the Kshatriya caste. They were not, however, allowed even to eat or inter-marry with the local painters and weavers who too had come from Rajputana to Karnataka. They were yet allowed the 'privilege' of the Rajput caste such as polygamy and domestic seclusion of women.[62]

Beyond all these factors inducing what may be called voluntary migrations were the vagaries of nature that left skilled labourers no option but to flee.

Indian agriculture, being dependent on the monsoons, the country has been particularly subject to famine and drought. Every famine became a source of forced migrations. Skilled workers, having themselves no direct access to food supply, used to be the worst victims of famines, and so were especially prone to distress and migrated when famines occurred. The severe famine of 1630-2 in Gujarat caused such an exodus of textile workers that even in 1634 the English reported that 'the artificers and mechaniques of all sorts were so miserably dead or fled from all parts of the kingdom of Gujarat' that they were unable to procure any calicoes whatsoever.[63] In 1664, when the rains failed in Gujarat, causing a local scarcity, 500 families of weavers fled from Surat, while the others were ready to leave.[64] The Dutch reported that as a result of the famine of 1686 that spread to the Deccan, the weavers and painters of world-famous south Indian chintz, had en-masse deserted the Coromandel coast.[65] In December 1687, the Dutch again reported that weavers and calico painters were still fleeing especially in northern Coromandel, due to a heavy rise in prices.[66]

The migrations would be long-distance ones, as well as over short distances, depending upon the range of famines. The *Daleras*, basket makers in Bareilly district, UP, were reported in 1901 to have migrated some hundred years earlier from the adjacent districts of Meerut and Bulandshahr.[67]

In this case the artisans emigrated for good. But these migrations being forced, often tended to be temporary and the emigrants could come back as soon the situation at the original places improved. In 1634 the English found weavers gradually returning to Gujarat, but still thought that it would take five years or so for the situation to get back to normal, provided no further calamities occurred and the Mughal officials refrained from acts of oppression.[68]

Migrations were sometimes, indeed, a form of protest or way of escape for the artisans against particular acts of oppression and tyranny. When in 1636, the Mughal 'governor' at Baroda resorted to a forcible procuring of cloth at prices dictated by him, the weavers refused and departed for Surat. They were well on their way, when the governor relented and persuaded them to return.[69] This incident confirms the fact, already noted, that the Mughal government did not generally impose any restrictions on the movement of the artisans and they could not be forced to stay at any particular place. But the English themselves when they obtained authority sought to exercise control on the movement of the artisans. Thus when in 1776, the weavers of Palaiyam villages near Cuddalore, having been reduced to the state of wage-labourers by the English East India Company, migrated to neighbouring districts under the Nawab of Arcot, the English compelled the Nawab to issue orders for their seizure and return. The Nawab, however, protested that 'it is contrary to the customs of the country'.[70] Only those who emigrated to Pondicherry, where the French were founding weaving settlements, could escape the English Company's clutches.

While the degree of mobility of labour is held to be an important test of the cohesion of an economy, the test is seldom applied by proponents of the thesis, fairly widespread these days, that only regional economies in precolonial times need to be studied, and an 'Indian economy' in those times is more or less a historians' illusion.[71] Our qualitative evidence shows that mobility of skilled labour in geographical terms was extensive enough to suggest that in a country as large as India (roughly equal in size and population to western Europe), its different parts were connected well enough to rectify imbalances in production through labour migrations. The caste system set a social framework for the whole country, which as we have shown, facilitated rather than obstructed migrations of communities of artisans. The administrative practices of the Mughal empire too imposed no restraints on migrations: the artisans of Mughal India could in no sense be described as 'semi-serfs', however appropriate this may be as a designation for the peasants of the period.[72] This does not imply, of course, that the Indian economy during the seventeenth and eighteenth centuries had modern characteristics, but it does show that it had far more flexibility and cohesiveness than it is now often credited with.

NOTES

1. H.H. Risley and E.A. Gait, *Census of 1901*, vol. I-A, part II, Tables, Calcutta, 1903, esp. Table XI, part III.
2. Phyllis Deane and W.A. Cole, *British Economic Growth*, Cambridge, 1962, pp. 103, 108-9.

3. H.H. Risley, *The Tribes and Castes of Bengal*, 2 vols., Calcutta, 1891; E. Thurston and K. Rangachari, *Caste and Tribes of Southern India*, 7 vols., Madras, 1909; W. Crooke, *The Tribes and Caste of North Western Provinces & Oudh*, 4 vols., Calcutta, 1896; D. Ibbeston, *Punjab Castes*, Lahore, 1916; R.V. Russell, *The Tribes and Castes of Central Provinces of India*, Indian reprint, Delhi, 1975.
4. 'Values as an Obstacle to Economic Growth in South Asia', *The Journal of Economic History*, XVIII, no. 4, 1967, pp. 588-607.
5. The main text on medieval Indian economy is still T. Raychaudhuri and Irfan Habib (eds.), *Cambridge Economic History of India*, Cambridge, 1982.
6. Mukundram's *Chandimangal* cited in J.N. Das Gupta, *Bengal in the Sixteenth Century* AD, Calcutta, 1914, pp. 91-2.
7. Ali Muhammad Khan, *Mirat-i Ahmadi* Supp. (1761), ed. Nawab Ali, Baroda, 1930, p. 7.
8. Abu'l Fazl, *A'in-i Akbari* (*c.* 1595), ed. H. Blochmann, Calcutta, 1867, p. 284. See especially Abu'l Fazl's explanation of the regulation (which he says he proposed to Akbar in 1582) in the *Akbarnama* (full translation of the passage, S. Moosvi, *Episodes in the Life of Akbar*, New Delhi, 1994, pp. 87-9). Those without sureties were not in any case to be turned away but put up in inns in an earmarked zone (*A'in*, I, p. 284, *Mirat-i Ahmadi*, I, p. 169).
9. W. Geleynssen, 'Verclaringe ende Bevinding', etc., extracts tr. W.H. Moreland, *Journal of Indian History*, IV (1925-6), p. 75.
10. *Mirat-i Ahmadi*, I, p. 287.
11. On this see C.M. Cipolla's insightful remarks, *Before the Industrial Revolution*, 2nd edn., London 1980, pp. 157-9.
12. *A'in*, I, p. 104.
13. Streynsham Master, *The Diaries of Streynsham Master, 1675-80 and Other Contemporary Papers Relating Thereto*, II, ed. R.C. Temple, London, 1911, p. 171.
14. F. Buchanan, *An Account of the District of Bihar & Patna in 1811-12*, II, Patna, n.d., p. 625.
15. 'Diaries of William Erskine', *Journal of the Bombay Branch of Royal Asiatic Society*, XXV, 1918-19, p. 383.
16. W.W. Hunter, *Statistical Account of Bengal*, London, 1875, XII, pp. 115-16.
17. Crooke, II, p. 232.
18. Russell, III, p. 281.
19. Crooke, I, p. 19.
20. Russell, IV, pp. 477-8.
21. Buchanan, *Purnea Report*, Patna, n.d. p. 533.
22. *Mirat-i Ahmadi*, I, pp. 292-3.
23. Thurston, VI, p. 159. There is no suggestion in their tradition that

their migration was a result of Muslim conquest of the places they came from, as suggested by Vijay Ramaswamy, *Textiles and Weavers in Medieval South India*, Delhi, 1985, p. 329.

24. Thurston, III, p. 31. They spoke a language called Patnuli which is a mixture of Gujarati and Tamil besides some other languages.
25. Sherring, *Tribes and Castes of the Madras Presidency*, vol. III, part II, London, 1909, p. 122.
26. Thurston, II, p. 154.
27. Ibid., IV, p. 3.
28. Ibid., II, p. 11.
29. Ibid., III, p. 252.
30. Risley, II, p. 295.
31. Thurston, VII, p. 175.
32. Ibid., III, p. 252.
33. S. Arasaratnam, 'Weavers, Merchants and Company, The Handloom Industry in South-eastern India, 1750-1790' in *Indian Economic and Social History Review*, XVII(3), 1980, pp. 261-2.
34. Risely, vol. I, p. 454.
35. Thurston, III, p. 279.
36. Ibid., III, p. 280.
37. Ibid., II, p. 2.
38. Ibid., III, p. 141.
39. Ibid., VI, p. 159.
40. S.P. Verma, *Mughal Painters and their Work: A Bibliographical Survey and Comprehensive Catalogue*, Delhi, 1994.
41. Abdul Baqi Nihawandi, *Maasir-i Rahimi*, ed. M. Hidayat Hosain, III, 1931, pp. 1679-80.
42. Thurston, VI, p. 242.
43. Ibid., p. 223.
44. Ibid., III, p. 280.
45. Ibid., II, p. 22.
46. Ibid., p. 23.
47. *English Factories in India (EFI), 1661-1664*, ed. W. Foster, Oxford, 1915, pp. 63-4.
48. *EFI, 1668-69*, pp. 229-30.
49. Ibid.
50. Ibid., *1630-33*, p. 235.
51. W. Ph. Coolhaas (ed.), *Generale Missiven van Gouverneurs-generaal en Raden aan Heren XVII der Verenigde Oostindische Compagnie, Deel III: 1655-1674*, Martinus Nijhoff, 's-Gravenhage, 1968, p. 390. I owe this reference to my colleague Dr. Ishrat Alam.
52. Ibid., p. 336.
53. Ibid., p. 859.

54. *Surat Factory Records*, India Office, MSS. G/36/94, ff. 28a, 34b, 39a, 58a. I owe this reference to Dr. Najaf Haider.
55. *Akhbarat*, no. 2361, dated 24th Shaaban, 37th R.Y. of Aurangzeb.
56. Lockhart, *Nadir Shah*, London, 1938, p. 187.
57. See M.N. Srinivas's essays on Sanskritization in his *Social Change in Modern India*, Indian edn., Hyderabad, 1972/1985.
58. Thurston, VI, p. 242.
59. Ibid., III, p. 282.
60. Ibid., II, p. 22.
61. Ibid., p. 23.
62. F. Buchanan, *A Journey from Madras through the Countries Mysore, Canara and Malabar* I, London, 1807, pp. 302-3.
63. *EFI, 1634-36*, p. 64.
64. Ibid., *1661-64*, pp. 320-1.
65. G.M. V, 23 September 1687, p. 100.
66. Ibid., 23 December, 1687, p. 137.
67. Crooke, II, p. 245.
68. *EFI, 1634-36*, p. 65.
69. Ibid., p. 290.
70. Madras Public Proceedings, 1778, 240/45, Nawab to Governor, 22 May 1778 quoted from S. Arasaratnam, 'Trade and Political Dominion in South India, 1750-1790: Changing British-Indian Relationships', *Modern Asian Studies*, 13, 1, Cambridge, February 1979, p. 35.
71. For an extreme statement of this view see Muzaffar Alam, 'Eastern India in the Early Eighteenth Century Crisis: Some Evidence from Bihar', *Indian Economic and Social History Review*, 28, 1(1991), p. 43*n*. He interestingly cites only non-Indian votaries of this genre.
72. On constraints upon movements of peasants, see Irfan Habib, *Agrarian System of Mughal India, 1556-1707*, 2nd rev. edn., New Delhi, 1999, pp. 130-3.

MODERN INDIA

CHAPTER 7

A Brief Encounter: The Mughals and the Renaissance Man

SABYASACHI BHATTACHARYA

It is somewhat surprising that the transactions between Rammohun Roy, the Mughals and the British authorities between 1829 and 1833 have attracted little attention from historians, except by way of recording them in Rammohun's biographies as an episode that led to his journey to England where he died in 1833. The episode merits attention for a number of reasons other than that. First, the various *shouqas* and documents issued from the Mughal court on Rammohun Roy's appointment as an agent or spokesman and the letters exchanged on the status of Akbar Shah II are illuminating in respect of the Mughal conceptions of treaty obligations incurred by the East India Company and the propriety of their political conduct *vis-à-vis* the Mughal court. In a larger sense, the correspondence enables us to recover, despite the negligence of colonial historiography, what was the Mughal notion of entitlements of the descendents of the chief 'native' power in India in the context of the British redefinition of those entitlements and indeed of the issue of sovereignty in India. The documents from the East India Company's servants, from the Resident in Delhi up to the Governor-General of India, offer a running commentary on the Mughal 'pretensions' in their correspondence with one another, and also in their communications to the Mughal court and to Rammohun. The British, the new claimant to sovereignty, in course of their ascendancy, began a process of delegitimation of their predecessors. In the construction of the colonial state, specially in building its theoretical underpinnings, the period 1829 to 1833 is vitally important.

Secondly, at this conjuncture in 1829-33 the contestation of the British representation of the theoretical position is equally interesting. The documents drafted by Rammohun Roy on behalf of the 'King of Delhi' contain his approach to the questions of equity and justice in relation to premier pre-British dynasty—an approach that anticipates later nationalist thinking on British dealings with the 'native' princely states. Rammohun's discourse of justice and equity uses notions which might have come from high political theory (British, of course, because he is addressing them for the redressal of injustice, and not necessarily because his entire discourse is borrowed from what he learned from the British masters of India), but his style of argumentation is strongly reminiscent of his training in Indian philosophy and logic. The challenge implicit in Rammohun's efforts on behalf of the Mughals forced the British authorities to conceptualize their relationship with the former ruling 'House of Tymur' at Delhi in new terms so as to clarify British self-conception as the sovereign power in India—a process that culminated later in the post-1857 trial of the last Mughal on grounds of treason against the State.

Apart from all that, there is a third reason why the contact between the Mughal court in Delhi and the *bhadralok* in Calcutta is of absorbing interest. It is a moment laden with dramatic interest—one of the last members of the fallen imperial dynasty at Delhi seeking the aid of a man who came to be known as the mentor of a new age in India. Did Rammohun's writings in Persian attract attention in the Mughal court? Or was he so well-known as a public figure in Calcutta that even Akbar Shah II at his isolated and dilapidated palace in Delhi heard of him? What accounted for the strong bond of loyalty (this will be evident from documents cited below) between the two despite persistent British efforts to persuade Akbar Shah to disown his envoy, Rammohun? Archival materials of the East India Company do not allow us to answer all these questions. All that can be established is that in 1829 Rammohun Roy was asked by the representatives of Akbar Shah II to be a spokesman on his behalf. Probably the king's *vakeel* or agent at Calcutta, Afzul

Beg, and the chief minister or *mukhtar* in the Mughal court, Sohan Lal, initiated the move with the approval of the king.[1] Rammohun Roy writes that 'in obedience to the orders of His Majesty, having attentively perused the Treaty between the Hon'ble Company and his late father' he found that the treaty had indeed been violated and when Akbar Shah 'condescended to require my services' he accepted the service 'to the end that the rightful might obtain justice and that this august family might live in contentment'.[2] Rammohun himself drafted an address in Persian on behalf of Akbar Shah to 'His Majesty the King of the British Empire' which Akbar Shah approved; Rammohun sent its English translation to England directly, and a copy to the Governor-General in India.[3] As we shall see later, Akbar Shah II greatly valued Rammohun Roy's services and thought that he was under an obligation to reward Roy's family even after Roy' failure in England and his death. What does all this tell us about what the Mughal Empire meant, even in its dying days, is a question we are unable to address now, nor do we know enough as to why Akbar Shah's men approached Rammohun. In this encounter between two eras of India's history there are many questions which remain unanswered.

II

To begin with, let us note that the effort of the Mughal court to appoint an agent to go to England took place despite strong resistance and explicit remonstrances from the British Indian government. First the Resident was instructed to confirm from Akbar Shah II whether indeed he acknowledged Roy as his agent.[4] Akbar Shah decisively acknowledged 'the intention of deputing Baboo Ram Mohan Rao to England as his Agent'.[5] Then the Calcutta government wrote to the Resident at Delhi to convey to Akbar Shah the government's displeasure with the communication from Akbar Shah through Rammohun Roy to the King in England, for it was 'against the forms of intercourse established'. Further, there was an admonition that 'if His Majesty (Akbar Shah) avows Rammohun Roy to be his agent for this appeal . . . you will give notice that His Lordship (the Governor-General) will be compelled to avoid an interview with His

Majesty, and to suspend further written correspondence until the issue of this appeal shall be known'.[6] Akbar Shah declined to disown his envoy, Rammohun.

Likewise he refused to oblige the Governor-General again in July 1833 when the latter offered a compromise—mainly in the form of increase in the amount payable by the Company to Akbar Shah. This offer was subject to a condition, laid down by the Governor-General, that Akbar Shah should 'refrain from prosecuting further the claims which Rammohun Roy is urging in England'.[7] Akbar Shah refused to accept the condition, rejected the compromise proposed and preferred to await advice from 'the Royal Agent I have sent' to prosecute claims against the Company in England.[8] A few weeks after this Rammohun Roy died in England and probably the news reached Akbar Shah some time in 1834. In September that year Akbar Shah accepted the financial compromise originally proposed, but he never disowned Rammohun despite much pressure from the government at Calcutta and its Resident at Delhi.[9] Even after Rammohun's death Akbar Shah continued to respect the claims that, as he conceived it, sons of Rammohun had acquired on the king's support and protection. Akbar Shah's *Khureeta* to the Governor-General in February 1837, observes 'Raja Rammohan Rai Bahadur confiding in my promises and favour undertook the distant journey to England and fell a sacrifice . . . the family of a man who has sacrificed his life in the service of the master, ought to be maintained by that master—especially Rao Radha Purshard and Rao Ram Purshard, sons of the late Raja Rammohun Rai, who are my devoted servants. . . .'[10] Akbar Shah proposed that out of the money payable to him by the Company a permanent allowance be paid to Rammohun's family. Among the papers connected with this proposal we also find a 'memorandum given by Dwarkeenath Thakoor on the distribution of the allowance to the king of Delhi' making a case for the grant of a monthly allowance for Rammohun's sons[11] in the event the Company refused to allow grant of money to any person other than the members of the royal family at Delhi.[12] The king refused to sign the *Razeenama*, the deed of agreement, to the end and it was left to his weak-kneed successor Bahadur Shah Zafar to do so.

The above account and the substantial number of *Shauqas*, *Khureetas*, responses to *arz-dashts* and records of personal conversations between the king of Delhi and the Resident allow us to form some impression of the system of political beliefs prevalent in the Mughal court in the first decades of the nineteenth century. In the value system a high place was accorded to reciprocal obligations between the Lord and those who served him. One is reminded of European feudal notions of the obligation of the Lord towards his vassal, to protect and support those who serve him in terms of an unspoken pledge: 'whatever the inequalities between the obligations of the respective parties, those obligations were none the less mutual'.[13] This is, of course, merely an analogous sentiment, neither institutionsalized nor verbalized in the fashion of western and central Europe.

Secondly, a notable feature is the vocabulary of the *Padshahi* regime as well as titles and ceremonies considered appropriate to the House of Tymur. The Mughals in their correspondence with the English used the term *peshkash* for what the English called his pension or stipend, the term *nazr* for inconsiderable gifts received from English officials, *arz-dasht* for letters received from the Resident and of course any Indian, and so forth. It was not merely a matter of the *mukhtar* or the chief minister at the court or the head *munshi* or clerk retaining an old style: it was a matter of serious importance in that these words carried a connotation which mattered to the king and the court and became subject of extensive correspondence when any departure from the language or style was mooted. As late as 1834 the term *peshkash* was being used—it meant a presentation from an inferior to a superior authority, not unlike a tribute for it was usually cash which thus changed hands. The Resident at Delhi reported to the Political Secretary in October 1834 that 'His Majesty at my request, communicated privately, has discontinued the use of the term *Pesh Cush*'.[14] Under the arrangements made by Wellesley in 1805 'territory assigned for the support of His Majesty' was specified and this combined with the ambiguity regarding *peshkash* kept alive in the Mughal court a notion of tributary relationship *in form*.[15]

The term *nazr* meant a gift to superior authority in all ranks of society; originally in Arabic it meant a 'vow', symbolizing allegiance, and when the English translated it as 'present, or gift' it failed to carry the import the *nazr* had in Mughal political vocabulary. We find in the records the Mughal king's complaint in 1825 that customary *nazr* was not paid to him; the decision of the Company's government was to refrain from such practice, which had been discountenanced by the Earl of Moira in 1813, particularly because it was 'desirable to seize every opportunity of discontinuing those observations which imply a recognition of the possessions in India'.[16] The Mughal court referred, with pathetic perseverance, all communications from the Resident who was the practical ruler of Delhi, as *arzdasht,* i.e. petition, the English style of addressing. His Majesty as a matter of form, lent some thin credibility to the pretence. In the first half of the nineteenth century these linguistic conundrums became increasingly matters of contention between the Mughal court and the Company's government. The Company's officials began to drop the conventions of older times and shortly after Rammohun was appointed as an Envoy, Lord Amherst decided to further abbreviate formal recognition of the Mughals' royal status. Akbar Shah complained bitterly: 'His Lordship . . . had recourse to the novel procedure of setting aside the ceremonials and forms of address (*ad ab wo alkab*) observed by his predecessors, thus lowering me even in respect of the style of correspondence adopted towards me'.[17] To sum it up, the Mughals, denuded of the reality of power, were clinging to some signifiers of authority traditionally established in their culture. These were symbols verbalized in concepts like *peshkash, nazr,* etc., and thus something more than niceties of language was involved.

III

To the conceptual framework established in the Mughal court described above on the basis of diplomatic correspondence, Rammohun Roy may not have been altogether a stranger for he was well-versed in the Persian language and culture. But he brought with him a new approach, a product of his knowledge of English law and politics. What was new about it?

The question is answered if one analyses the papers he drafted on behalf of Akbar Shah.[18] Firstly, Roy raises the issue of equality of states under international law, while conceding the inequality between the King of Delhi and the King of England in terms of political power they commanded. In the letter he drafted as an appeal from Akbar Shah to the English King, in the very first sentence it was stated that while 'the language of fraternal equality' was used between them, Akbar Shah was 'King only in name'. Secondly, Roy makes a distinction between the British Indian government and the government in England. The East India Company are the latter's subjects 'permitted to exercise the government' of India, but 'these very subjects, although elevated to the dignity of empire, are still amenable to your Majesty (i.e. King of England) for every part of their conduct'. Thirdly, Roy's familiarity with British Indian laws enabled him to strengthen Akbar Shah's claim in respect of his dues from the Company's revenue. For the first time in the protracted dispute on this question Roy points out that regulation XI of 1804, regulation VIII of 1805 and regulation X of 1807 distinctly recognize certain territories as 'assigned for the support of the Royal family at Dehlee'. Thus, 'the code of Regulations by which this branch of the British Indian empire is governed' clearly establish Akbar Shah's claims to the revenue of 'assigned *mahals*' or '*khalsa lands*', though in 1829 the British Indian government rejected such claims. This was a telling argument to which, judging by the correspondence, the Company seemed to have no answer. Fourthly, Roy emphasized the contractual obligations between the Company and the Mughal king, though he stopped short of posing the arrangement of 1805 as a Treaty. Roy claimed that it was a 'National Contract' and the Company could not evade 'mutual obligations of the contracting parties'. He wrote: 'I cherish the confident persuasion that your Majesty will not sanction the principle that in my case a National contract ought not or need not to be fulfilled because I am powerless to enforce its obligations'. Fifthly, while Akbar Shah and his predecessors harped on the greatness of the House of Tymur and their pitiful condition since 1805, Roy claimed on behalf of Akbar Shah a right and not a favour. 'I will not resort to such a plea. I will not condescend to accept and your Majesty (i.e. King of England) will disdain to confer as a favour that which is due as a right.' Finally, Roy chose to found his case on broad ethical and political principles. The incisive logic and language is clearly that of a metaphysician. For example, he wrote:

> The original articles of agreement are either binding or they are not. If they are binding, then any alteration . . . without the consent of the other to whom it is injurious must be null and void. If they are not binding, this must be either because they were never entered into which cannot be affirmed, or because some subsequent voluntary arrangement between the two contracting parties has superseded their obligation. But no arrangement tending to supersede the original articles of agreement has even been voluntarily recognised by my Royal predecessor or myself, and therefore the numerous and unauthorised deviations from the provisions which they contain constitute direct and systematic violations of truth, honour and justice.

A political argument was also put forward—that lack of observance of past engagements will impair the confidence of the surrounding states, 'naturally jealous of their independence' and cause anxiety to 'neighbouring Princes who have beheld with alarm the progress of your Majesty's arms'.

A weakness in the case Roy so carefully constructed lay in the status of the appeal made to the King of England. Was it to be linked to the plea of a subject to obtain justice from the highest authority? Evidently not. Was it an effort of one sovereign to recall another sovereign to his treaty obligations under international law? That could not be claimed, for there was no treaty between the Mughal and the British. Thus, the status of the appeal was ambiguous, for the Mughal king would not claim justice as a subject, and could not claim restitution of rights as a party to an international treaty. Roy might have been aware of this infirmity in the case and his language is ambivalent, but generally tending to take the second of the above positions. The fact was that Shah Alam in 1805 was thankful for whatever the victorious British provided to him. This provision of money for his maintenance was a negotiated administrative arrangement which constituted an undertaking by the Company, endorsed by the Commander-in-Chief and the Governor-General, but it did not have the status of a treaty.

Despite this weakness in Roy's case he was able to put together arguments which appeared to make a dent in the Company's hitherto inflexible position. The resultant compromise, an increase in the Mughal's *peshkash,* or pension in British officialese (offered to Akbar Shah long after Rammohun's death in England) is intrinsically not of great interest to us. To cite large portions of the long document we have cited above will be tedious. It is enough to note the major points Rammohun wanted to make and what is interesting is the way Rammohun situated in the document outlined above, the descendent of the great Mughals in a conceptual frame which combines the language of contemporary English political discourse and traditional Mughal cultural and political practice.

What is perhaps most remarkable is the way Rammohun conceived his role as a representative, answerable to not only the king of Delhi but *also* the people of India. This notion is probably totally external to the political culture of the Mughal court which he expounded in defence of Akbar Shah II. This new notion of responsibility is best illustrated in a somewhat extraordinary statement, coming from an Indian in those times. In a letter to Sir Charles Grant, Rammohun Roy wrote:

> Any just man feels desirous to be informed whether the powers entrusted to his servants, particularly those in a remote country, have been properly exercised, and to prove that when any injustice has been done by them he is anxious to afford redress—a course which is calculated to discourage future injustice. But with regard to the Court of Directors, I am sorry to find that in my humble opinion the case is quite the reverse. In the meantime I am here so situated as to be responsible not only to the King of Delhi but to the whole body of my countrymen for my exertions in his behalf and for their welfare.[19]

It is perhaps possible to read in Rammohun's statements of this kind his awareness of his role as a public spokesman, even though a public sphere was as yet in an inchoate and underdeveloped stage and the countrymen on whose behalf he spoke were more subjects than citizens.

IV

Let us now turn to the theory implicit in the British Indian government's pronouncements and actions in response to Rammohun Roy. This theory is confronted by the challenge of Roy's counter-positions and thus, the British Indian government now clarifies things left unspoken till now. First, the British Indian government would not allow Rammohun Roy to accept the title 'Raja' awarded by the Mughal king. They wrote to Roy refusing to 'acquiesce in His Majesty's grant of a title to you'.[20] Roy wrote to Bentinck that he was not 'anxious for titular honour' but in principle, the past usage and a resolution of the British Indian government in 1827 had recognized the King's power of conferring titles on his own servants.[21] Roy happened to be technically correct and his knowledge of the past actions of the British Indian government came useful.[22] In the meanwhile, the Governor-General had conveyed to the Court of Directors his refusal to acquiesce in the grant of the title 'Raja'.[23] However, the Indian authorities said no more about the matter, perhaps conceding the correctness of Roy's position in terms of their own earlier decision. From then on, however, the Governor-General decided to allow the power to grant titles, the prerogative of a sovereign, only in respect of the royal household and the Resident.

Another issue that touched upon the question of sovereignty was the right to communicate with the government in England and to send an envoy, Rammohun. Upon being informed by Roy that he was appointed Akbar Shah's '*elchee* (envoy) to the Court of Great Britain', the government in Calcutta wrote to him within a week refusing to recognize the appointment.[24] At the same time, as we have seen already, Akbar Shah was pressured to withdraw the appointment. In the event, these moves failed. Roy decided not to insist on his ambassadorial status, to divest himself 'of all public character' so as to be 'exempted from all jealousy of a political nature'.[25] That last phrase was a barbed reference to the British Indian authorities' reluctance to allow the natives direct communication with their 'Home authorities'. In their political theory 'protected' status meant denial of the protected monarch's right to communicate with foreign powers. It was essentially an abridgement of the native potentates' sovereignty in exchange for benefits of British protection. Communication with the government in England was not to be classified as 'foreign relations', but the British Indian government did not like being outflanked by Roy and Akbar Shah. Roy managed to reach the Court of Directors. In course of the next two decades a convention was formed that communications might be made to the Directors in London only through the British Indian government. Thus, we find that in 1844 when George Thompson was nominated an Agent by Bahadur Shah of Delhi, the Court of Directors refused to 'recognise any agent, or representative of that Prince in England, nor hold communication with His Majesty through any other channel than that of the Indian government'.[26] Thus, the Mughals were finally excluded from all direct communication with the international community of sovereign states. This was one of the final actions to delegitimize the pre-colonial sovereign power.

It is well known that when the British historian F.W. Buckler presented in 1922 at the Royal Historical Society a case in defence of the last Mughal, Shah Alam who was accused of 'treason' in his trial after the rebellion of 1857, his critics reverted to the position outlined above.[27] The critics, Douglas Dewar of the Indian Civil Service and H.L. Garrett, argued that (a) the nominal sovereignty of the Mughal king in Delhi had been terminated in 1803, after Lord Lake's victory in Delhi and the grant of a pension to the king, and (b) the *de facto* power in India belonged to the British and thus, no other claim to sovereignty was sustainable. Hence, Buckler was mistaken in questioning the validity of the charge of treason against Bahadur Shah in the post-Mutiny trial.[28] This did not quite meet the points made by Buckler who demonstrated with elaborate documentation (a) the ambiguities in the East India Company's transactions with the Mughal king, leaving it open for the latter to interpret British actions in the light of Mughal political culture and practices, as actions consistent with Mughal sovereignty, and (b) the fact that *de jure* sovereignty can be and indeed was undisturbed even if *de facto* power had ceased to rest in the hands of the Mughals. Unlike Buckler, Dewar and Garrett did take notice of Akbar Shah's letter to the King of England of 23 February 1829; they did not know or do not mention that Rammohun Roy drafted the letter and they apparently misread it in some ways. In their opinion the 'whining petition to King George IV is utterly inconsistent with Mr Buckler's assertion'. The reason, they say, is that Akbar Shah speaks of 'my fallen House', i.e. the Timur dynasty, of himself being 'bereft of power of dictating terms' and the reality of 'British rule in India'. This stout defence of the British imperial point of view completely misses the point made by Buckler. There being no question about the situation of the 'powerless House of Tymur' since 1803 nor about the superior coercive power exercised by the East India Company the point at issue was *de jure* sovereign rights. Dewar and Garrett conclude the story with the statement that eventually the Court of Directors enhanced the Mughal king's 'stipend' from twelve to fifteen lakhs but

> Akbar Shah died on 28 September 1837, so never received the additional stipend. It was offered to his successor, Bahadur Shah II, who in the typical Oriental manner, started trying for a bargain. On 20th February, 1838, he put forward ten requests none of which was granted. These related to various claims made by his father which had been disallowed.[29]

Dewar and Garrett are quite explicit that the basic question is, who has the power to make his will, or what he wants, effective? They write,

> If Akbar Shah was in fact the Mogul Emperor, he had but to issue an order to compel the British to leave India. No such order was issued by Akbar Shah. His failure to issue such an order must have been due to one of two reasons: either he was not the Mogul Emperor, or he was so happy and contented that he declined to give the Company notice to quit. . . . The fact is that no one knew better than Akbar Shah his utter helplessness and impotence.

Basically, we have here Dewar and Garrett in an irreconcilable debate with Buckler whose position was in part anticipated in

Rammohun Roy's arguments that the injustice had been done by the British to the descendents of the Mughals who had *de jure* entitlements.

The continuing efforts of the Mughal court in Delhi to assert its rights against infringements by the East India Company from 1833 to 1857 in respect of *peshkash*, *nazr*, *khilat*, titles, etc., culminating in the rebellion of 1857 and the irony of the subsequent trial of Bahadur Shah on the charge of 'High Treason' is another story which we cannot pursue now. The bottom line for the British position at that trial in 1857 (as in Dewar and Garrett's defence of the trial proceedings) was, who holds real power? Thus, it boiled down to coercion as the basis of the empire. This was in tune with Warren Hastings' famous statement: 'The sword which gave us the dominion of Bengal must be the means of its preservation; . . . the next proprietor will derive his right and possession from the same natural charter.'[30] It may be said in a general way that this faith in coercion as the basis of British sovereignty coexisted with a legal point of view which was asserted at certain other moments. At those moments the talk was about cession of sovereignty to the British by pre-existing claimants to sovereignty who entered into treaty or agreements. This was the reasoning developed by exponents like Sir Courtenay Ilbert and A.B. Keith from late eighteenth century to later twentieth century. Thus, there was on the one hand, the discourse of *coercion* which was the 'natural charter' of Imperialism, on the other the discourse of *reasons of law* which had a whole tradition of Enlightenment behind it. In the last years of his life, in his advocacy of the cause of the Mughal in Delhi from 1829 to 1833, Rammohun takes recourse to the discourse the British had brought to India, their discourse of law and legal entitlements and justice. His efforts meet with failure because the reality was that the British had superior powers of coercion. In the slice of history we have looked at, this encounter between the discourse of power and the discourse of reasons of law, both inherent in the construction of the colonial state, is as significant as the encounter between the old and the new era, between the Mughal Akbar Shah of Delhi and Rammohun Roy of Calcutta.

NOTES

1. From HRH the Heir Apparent at Delhi to Governor-General, through T. Metcalf, Magistrate In-charge of Palace Affairs, *c.* 17 April 1830, Pol. Proceedings of GOI, 23 July 1830, no. 98. All references to the Proceedings of the Govt. of India and of Bengal are from the National Archives of India, New Delhi, unless stated otherwise. I may add that this essay forms a part of my forthcoming book *The Colonial State in India: Theory and Practice*. Parts of the argument presented below also appeared in my address as the General President (2004) of the Indian History Congress, published in Indian History Congress Proceedings, Delhi, 2005. I am happy to be able to add to this volume my tribute to Prof. V.N. Datta from whom I have learned a great deal, as no doubt many others did in my generation.
2. Rammohun Roy's *arzee* to the Heir Apparent at Delhi, 10 November 1830, enclosure no. 2, in report from Resident at Delhi to Govt. of India, 30 December 1830, Pol. Progs. 21 January 1831, no. 16.
3. Ibid., and Rammohun Roy to Chief Secretary. At Calcutta, 23 February 1829, Political Consultations, 13 March 1829, no. 19.
4. Deputy Secretary to Resident at Delhi, 13 March 1829, Pol. Progs. 13 March 1829, no. 21.
5. Resident at Delhi to Deputy Secretary Calcutta, 2 April 1829, Pol. Progs. 22 May 1829, no. 2.
6. Secretary, Govt. of Calcutta, to Resident at Delhi, 20 November 1831, Pol. Progs. 13 January 1832, no. 4.
7. Agent/Resident at Delhi. to the King, 12 July 1833, Pol. Progs. 2 August 1833, no. 13.
8. Resident at Delhi to Political Secretary at Calcutta, 18 July 1833, Pol. Progs. 2 August 1833, no. 13.
9. *Shouqa* from King of Delhi to Resident at Delhi, 13 September 1834, Pol. Cons. 16 October 1834, no. 22.
10. King of Delhi to Governor-General of India, n.d., *c.* February 1837, Pol. Cons. 8 May 1837, no. 26.
11. Enclosure no. 5, Secretary Lt. Governor, NWP, to Political Secretary at Calcutta, 8 April 1837, Pol. Cons. 8 May 1837, no. 25.
12. Governor-General to King of Delhi, Pol. Cons. 8 May 1837, no. 27.
13. Marc Bloch, *Feudal Society*, London, 1961, vol. I, p. 228.
14. Resident to Political Secretary, 30 October 1834, Pol. Cons. 31 December 1834, no. 15.
15. Communication from Chief Secretary at Calcutta to Resident at Delhi and Commander-in-Chief, 23 May 1805, Secret Cons., 20 June 1805, no. 422.
16. Governor-General in Council to Court of Directors, Letters to Court, Pol., 14 September 1825.

17. *Shauqa* from H.M. King of Delhi to Resident, 26 January 1832, no. 5.
18. Rammohun Roy to Chief Secretary, enclosing a letter from King of Delhi to King of England, 23 February 1829, Pol. Cons. 13 March 1829, no. 19; Roy drafted Akbar Shah's letter in Persian and translated it into English, vide Roy to Heir Apparent at Delhi, 10 November 1830, Pol. Progs. 21 January 1831, no. 16.
19. Roy to Charles Grant, 11 October 1831, K. Nag and D. Burman (eds.), *The English Works of Raja Rammohun Roy*, Calcutta, 1947, part IV, p. 122.
20. Secretary to Government of Bengal to Roy, 15 January 1830, Pol. Cons. 22 January 1830, no. 52.
21. Roy to Governor-General, 8 January 1830, Pol. Cons. 22 January 1830, no. 51.
22. Deputy Secretary to Government in attendance on Governor-General to Chief Secretary, 5 October 1827, Pol. Progs. 1 February 1828, no. 2.
23. Governor-General in Council to Court of Directors, 14 October 1830, Letters to Court.
24. Pol. Cons. 22 January 1830, nos. 50 1.
25. Roy to Governor-General, n.d., *c.* September 1830, *English Works of Rammohun Roy*, part IV, p. 117.
26. Secretary, Court of Directors, to G. Thompson, 10 April 1844, Letters from Court, Pol., 1 May 1844.
27. F.W. Buckler, 'The Political Theory of the Indian Mutiny', *Royal Historical Society (London) Transactions*, 5, 4th series (1922), pp. 71-100.
28. D. Dewar and H.L. Garrett, 'A Reply to F.W. Buckler's Political Theory', ibid., 7, 1924, pp. 131-59. Garrett, a member of the Indian Education Service, is not to be confused with G.T. Garrett, the well-known co-author (with Edward Thompson) of *Rise and Fulfillment of British Rule in India*. H.L. Garrett had to his credit only one work of research, a history of the Lahore College, and Buckler wrote in his rejoinder that he found the above article wanting in scholarship.
29. Ibid. and F.W. Buckler's rejoinder printed along with the essay by Dewar and Garrett: 'My critics . . . proceed to attack my argument concerning the de jure source of the Company's authority in India by illustrations of its de facto power. The latter, I dispute not at all. The former, they do not touch. They fail to see that the greater the de facto power of a rebel, in the eyes of the de jure sovereign, the greater and more dangerous the rebel.'
30. Minute by Warren Hastings, Bengal Select Committee, 12 October 1772, cited in H.H. Dodwell, 'Development of Sovereignty', *Cambridge History of India,* vol. V, New Delhi, 1963, rpt., p. 597.

CHAPTER 8

'Seventy Times Seven': The Sin of 'Christian Manhood' in a Colonial Situation

SUDHIR CHANDRA

I can honestly say that I have observed the 'seventy times seven'[1] rule in my dealings with Ganpatrao.

REV. DOUGALD MACKICHAN

... But if the policy of our Mission Committee has changed and we must be degraded for our skin, I will resign ... I shall at least have kept my Christian manhood in tact.

REV. GANPATRAO R. NAVALKAR

I encountered Rev. Ganpatrao Raghunath Navalkar (1837-1912) during my as yet unfinished research on 'Upper Caste Converts to Christianity: Interpenetration of Religion, Culture and Nation'. There was a mention of him in the Free Church of Scotland papers' intimation of an out of the ordinary person. What emerged from the papers was a tragic figure driven to heroic defiance by the realization of his subjection and manhood. The realization was the same as that of a growing number of English educated Indians: the realization of oppression. But it was also different. His conversion to Christianity added an ecclesiastical subjection to the political subjection he shared with his non-Christian compatriots; and to the awakening of Indian manhood was added the stirring of 'Christian manhood'.

*My gratitude to the Maison des Sciences de l'Homme, Paris, the Institute for Advanced Study in the Humanities, University of Edinburgh, and the British Academy, whose generous support made this paper possible.

Reinstating this forgotten figure among the remembered is not the sole motive of this paper. His tragic defiance constituted more than an individual failure. It was part of the failure of his generation of public-spirited Indians. They laboured for their country in the knowledge that their efforts would bear fruit long after they would be gone.[2] Besides, his failure symptomatized the failure of what were designed—certainly projected—as grand civilizational interventions. Imperialism was one such intervention.[3] As a civilizing mission it was never wholly accepted by its subjects. Christianity, another of those interventions, was more successful. It was believed to be entirely a blessing by those thinking minds that accepted it. The belief survived even the experience of ecclesiastical subjection and the loss of the illusion that the Kingdom of Christ was 'one loving brotherhood'.[4]

For both the European proselytisers and the proselytised among the colonized, the political and the ecclesiastical were inextricably mixed. But while few proselytisers saw the hubris of power behind their compassion and service, no thinking convert missed it. Inevitably, serious tensions marked their relations. Usually, the tensions were on both sides contained by a pragmatique that held in tenuous balance a range of antagonistic sentiments. The balance was upset every once in a while, throwing the tensions into public view, when a Navalkar felt chafed to demand a semblance of justice and conformance with Christian ideals.

Focused on a figure that is both representative and extraordinary, this paper examines the play of subjection and resistance in the relationship of the more aware converts with their Missions.

I

Born in Bombay on 4 September 1837 in a Pathare-Prabhu family, Navalkar belonged to the second generation of educated Indians in western India who joined pioneers like Rev. Narayan Sheshadri (1820-91) and Rev. Dhanjibhai Nauroji (1821-1908) in the fold of Christ. Falling under Christian influence 'almost' from his 'early boyhood',[5] Navalkar was nineteen at the time of his baptism in 1856. This was at the Scottish Free Church Institution where he had drawn the attention of the famous missionary triumvirate, John Wilson, Robert Nisbet and Murray Mitchell. After completing his education, he was appointed a teacher at the Institution, and in that capacity also his brilliance was acknowledged.

At thirty-six Navalkar chose to become a minister, and was licensed to preach, leading the Foreign Missions Committee of the Free Church of Scotland, in Edinburgh, to record their 'gratification . . . that one so highly qualified has consecrated his talents to the Christian ministry'.[6]

During his Bombay years he directed his energies especially to converting the educated Indian youth.[7] By that time, compared to the 1830s through the 1860s when gifted individuals had shown greater receptivity to Christianity, proselytisation among the educated had become difficult. Navalkar explained the difficulty by quoting Max Mueller:[8]

> Natives of honest and independent character cannot afford at present to join the ranks of converts without losing that true caste which no man ought to lose—namely, self-respect. They are driven to keep up their tottering religions, rather than profess *a faith which seems dictated to them by their conquerors*. Such feelings ought to be respected. (Italics in the original.)

Nonetheless, Navalkar endeavoured to persuade his 'educated countrymen' not to 'feel jealous of Christianity because it is a foreign religion, or because its missionaries belong to the dominant race'. For, 'Christianity, as regards its origin, is entirely free from all political or national associations. Its founder was a despised peasant, who belonged to a conquered nation.' Patriotism itself, Navalkar turned the argument on its head, demanded acceptance of Christianity: 'Have you really been awakened to a sense of patriotism, and do you aspire to political freedom and influence?' 'If it is so,' he exhorted, 'I entreat you, my beloved fellow-countrymen, to . . . accept Christianity.'[9] In another appeal, combining patriotic and spiritual considerations, he said:[10]

> The true basis for a social and national union is not education, is not government, nor is it social enlightenment—it is emphatically religion. . .

and Christianity acts most powerfully on the spirits of men. When it shall have thoroughly cleansed and renovated the individual consciousness of both the races [Indian and Parsi], they will spontaneously seek a complete union. Hence the necessity of Christianity.

Able to preach and write in both English and Marathi—cultivated as well as colloquial Marathi—Navalkar could address a cross-section of the society like few missionaries, Indian or European, could. With equal facility he could preach in the town and also in the country, switching his idiom to attract the English educated youth as well as the unlettered villager. Even after discounting for the possessed preacher's faith in the magic of his word, the following description by Navalkar is worth considering. At a fair on top of a hill overlooking the sea—a 'most romantic scenery'—his assistants having collected a goodly crowd of 'men, women and children' by means of singing:

> . . . the missionary [Navalkar] spoke for nearly an hour . . . and the proud, handsome, learned, big Brahmans as well as the unsophisticated Shudras heard with deep attention, without a word or murmuring disapprobation, the women and the children in their holiday clothes, sitting or standing like statues, with their eyes fixed on the speaker . . . the crowning proof of the impression made was that the learned priest of the neighbouring town, who sat at the feet of the preacher, lifted both his hands to his head, and did the obeisance that Natives are in the habit of making.[11]

Navalkar was a complete missionary, a rare species among his Indian and European coevals. He was efficient in every aspect of his calling, be it educational, evangelical, literary or organizational. When the Bombay Mission opened a new station in Alibag, in the Konkan, he was chosen to head it. Still a licentiate, he had not yet been a full-time missionary for five years. Further recognition followed soon. He was given additional charge of Rewadanda in 1885, when the old mission station there was re-opened with a view to converting the local Beni-Israel Jews.[12]

Navalkar was ordained in 1882, soon after taking over the Alibag mission. For reasons that will engage us later, the Foreign Missions Committee sanctioned his ordination on condition that this should not entail any additional burden on them by way of an increase in his salary.

The authorities continued to value Navalkar's pastoral-missionary activities. George Smith, the secretary of the Foreign Missions Committee for a whole thirty years (1879-1910), congratulated him in 1887 'on the work you have done & are doing by God's blessings'. 'You are indeed', Smith wrote, 'Bishop of the town & district'. 'No one else', he continued, 'could do the work which you are doing there, among Jews and Heathens'. This was no routine epistolary encouragement from a boss who, drawing upon two decades of his Indian experience, kept from distant Edinburgh a hawk's eye on the Indian field. For, the praise ended: 'not even a European missionary . . . could do the work which you are doing'.[13]

The following year the Scottish Free Church sent out two Deputies from Edinburgh to report on its Indian field.[14] They, too, noted Navalkar's work favourably. Besides mentioning the reach of his preaching, they singled out his educational endeavours with which 'no other Mission schools' could be compared. They also appreciated his social concern, saying that he had 'brought forward and given education to the low-caste Kolis of the neighbourhood'.[15]

Meanwhile, Navalkar was nominated to the Western India Mission Council. Without formally excluding 'native' missionaries, the Mission Councils were designed to be European strongholds.[16] The Western India Missions Council was no exception. True, it had Dhanjibhai Nauroji as a life-member. But, rather than threaten it, his genial presence served to cover up the Council's exclusive character. Navalkar's nomination was in the circumstances a measure of the authorities' faith in him, besides being a recognition of his talent.

II

Smith's praise of 1887 was the high point of Navalkar's association with the Scottish Free Church Mission. The association had for the most part been uneventful. In contrast, his friend and contemporary, Rev. Baba Padmanji (1831-1906),[17] who had been baptised just about a year earlier than him, had made a reputation and resigned as the native pastor of Poona, the cultural capital of Maharashtra, even as Navalkar was entering the ministry.[18] For one so conscious of his own worth, dreaming of big things, and measuring himself against the best, Navalkar had achieved frustratingly little. Then came Alibag, and in five years he demonstrated what the missionaries could, but did not, do.

The year 1887 also marked the surfacing of a clash that in less than six years brought about his downfall. The incipience of this clash can be traced back, in hindsight, to the disenchantment that had set in during the early years of his conversion. Already in 1860, his *Thoughts on Indian Missions* had complained of the European missionaries' un-Christian attitude towards Indian Christians. As the feeling strengthened, Navalkar was persuaded that the moral ground won for Christianity by evangelizing pioneers like Duff and Wilson, was lost by their more pragmatically inclined successors. Christianity in India would best be served henceforth by her own inspired converts.[19]

Smith's praise confirmed Navalkar's belief of having inherited the burden of the pioneering fathers. This was reflective of a deep, pathetic irony. He vacillated between deference and defiance in relation to the Europeans. He wanted to be their equal, preferably superior; and both in their terms. His pride in being a 'black subject', we shall see below, needed the supporting thought of also being a Scotchman *par excellence*. The rulers' mastery over him was inviolate.

The urge to defy was temporarily mitigated by the elation, following Smith's epistle, of being a trusted agent of the Mission. That is when the Deputies came. They were to report on certain contentious issues, such as the importance of higher education and elite conversion. Given his sense of the criticality of the subject, Navalkar felt bound to try and convert the Deputies to his way of thinking.

Believing himself to be 'unskilled to flatter',[20] his mode of persuasion was to speak candidly and forcefully. His entry into the ministry, in fact, had begun with characteristic self-assertion. Assured that he deserved to work in the Presidency town of

Bombay, but asked by the Presbytery to labour away in a mofussil town, he had objected to the posting. Such had been 'the strength of his objection' that the Foreign Missions Committee had intervened to get him the desired posting.[21] That spirit underlay his dealings with the Deputies as well.

Of the two Deputies, the one who counted was Rev. Professor Thomas M. Lindsay, the convener of the Foreign Missions Committee. Navalkar interacted with him in varied situations, viz., at the Mission Council deliberations, on social occasions, and during the inspection of his twin pastorate. It was during a leisurely bullock-cart ride between Rewadanda and Alibag that Navalkar treated Lindsay to an exposition of what ailed the Mission. Recalling the pioneers under whom he was converted, Navalkar bemoaned that 'the Free Church Missionaries of today are by no means such good missionaries'. As a result, missionary educational institutions had ceased to be the effective agency for conversion 'they were in his young days'. Even the Gospel had lost its primacy for the Mission, which was erring 'greatly in not making more use of Christian literature'.[22]

Navalkar could hardly have said all this to Lindsay in measured terms. Their hierarchical divide, compounded by the divide between the rulers and the ruled, would have rendered difficult a relaxed exposition of his ideas by the small town 'native' pastor. Beginning hesitantly, one can visualize, he would have warmed to the passion of his ideas and ended up sounding much more strident than he must have planned during the endless rehearsals of the conversation in his mind.

Navalkar was also, perhaps, lured into a feeling of false accord with Lindsay. In order that his interlocutors were not put on their guard or tempted to say what they might imagine he wanted to hear, Lindsay had resolved not to speak his mind. Rather, he would feign an occasional agreement to lull them into intimacy. This is probably what happened during the bullock-cart conversation. Lindsay, Navalkar reminded him later, had then said 'repeatedly that our views coincided'.[23]

The Scottish Free Church papers at the National Library of Scotland record neither Navalkar's nor Lindsay's immediate assessment of each other. Lindsay's later recall suggests that he was quick to take a dim view of Navalkar. The latter, it appears, was too busy trying to convert the Deputies to detect the adverse effect of his well-intentioned naivety. Before the Deputies' visit was over, however, even he had an uncanny feeling that things had gone amiss.

The feeling was confirmed by a series of hurtful developments. The first was the rejection of Navalkar's request that his salary be paid in gold. The request had its roots in the vexation felt by most agents of at least the Free Church of Scotland. Adopting a 'Missionary economics' that worshipped frugality,[24] the Free Church paid its agents emoluments that rarely kept them above want, no matter whether they were 'native' or European. But the vexation of the 'native' agents was aggravated by their resentment against the comparatively better salaries, allowances and facilities of their European colleagues. Full of petitions for more money, the Church records reveal widespread frustration, discontent, even anger, among its agents.

Navalkar had had his share of such cheerlessness. Even his ordination, we noticed above, was sanctioned subject to the condition that it would entail for Edinburgh no additional financial commitment. Three years prior to that he had applied for an increase of salary and been exasperated by Edinburgh's dilatory tactics.[25] Domestic budget had in the meanwhile kept outstripping the monthly income. Navalkar badly needed a raise in his salary. A direct request to that effect, he realized, had little chance of success. Desperate to get past Edinburgh's high-minded economy, he requested that his salary be paid 'in gold'. This meant fixation of his salary in pounds sterling according to the exchange rate prevailing at the time of his joining the service. Besides immediate increase in proportion as the rupee had fallen in the intervening years, the arrangement would mean gain with every subsequent devaluation of the rupee. The rupee was worth 1 shilling and 9 pence around the time he took charge of the Alibag station. In 1889, when his request was turned down, the rupee had come down to 1s. 6d. In 1892, when he repeated the request, there had been a fall of another 2d. This last rate, Navalkar wistfully calculated, would have brought an increase of Rs. 100 per month.[26]

That remained a dream. He whose work 'not even a European missionary' could have equalled was told that 'our fixed principle for many years has been to pay nothing in gold but the salaries of European missionaries'. There were exceptions like Dhanjibhai Nauroji and Sidoba Misal. Their 'stipends had been fixed in gold before', and the 'bargains once made' could not be annulled. But the Committee would no more interfere 'with our principle'.[27] Let alone the Europeans and a 'native' stalwart like Dhanjibhai, to none of whom he considered himself inferior, Navalkar would not be treated at par even with a Sidoba Misal,[28] who was doing run-of-the-mill work and getting—in gold—a salary that was about half of his own.

That was mortifying. Navalkar had not flaunted his credentials while asking for salary in gold. But now he confronted Lindsay with extracts from Smith's letter, and demanded: '. . . why shd I be always told that I am not a European, and cannot be given this or that?' He claimed that his salary, too, was originally fixed '*in gold*, but Dr. MacKichan *without my knowledge and that of the Council* on his *own* responsibility had it paid me in Rupees, and *then afterwards* got the Committee's sanction for his arbitrary proceedings.' (Italics Navalkar's) When he—Navalkar—brought the matter before the Mission Council, MacKichan, its chief, justified his action on the ground that he had 'utilized the exchange for the benefit of the Mission'.[29]

Navalkar had protested to Lindsay. But the reply came from Smith. It opened with a reprimand: 'Your letter to the Convener . . . notwithstanding his to you of 4th April, leads me to inform you officially that no letters on the business of the Mission can be considered by the Committee unless they come through the Western India Mission Council of our Church.' Smith, 'nonetheless', had condescended to verify Navalkar's claim and found it without 'any justification'. Also unjustified was the charge against MacKichan: 'On the contrary, your salary, in silver, has been more than once increased, & that on the kindly recommendation of Rev. Dr. MacKichan.'[30]

The two parties had divergent perceptions. The authorities believed they had treated Navalkar generously, and expected him to be grateful. Navalkar, for his part, felt short-changed. If gratitude was wanting, as indeed it was, he detected the want elsewhere.

Perceptions apart, Smith had got his facts wrong. Navalkar's salary was increased only once. Worth Rs. 420 a year, that increase had come when he was given the additional charge of Rewadanda. However the authorities viewed it, Navalkar could not have seen the additional payment for additional work as a favour.[31]

The salary issue did not bring matters to a head, not with Smith at any rate.[32] *Vis-à-vis* Lindsay, however, the chasm began to widen. Lindsay was convinced that Navalkar had been pampered and deserved to be put in his place. The conviction, at one level, was part of the ecclesiastical bosses' commonly held belief that their 'native' subordinates tended to get spoiled by praise. At another level, it went back to Lindsay's personal interaction with Navalkar. Having suffered him as a Deputy in India, Lindsay, the Convener, was now anxious to discipline the pretentious pastor. So, when Navalkar asked for his salary in gold and grants for projects in Alibag, Lindsay responded, on 4 April 1889, with a barely concealed rebuke and reminder. A rebuke that Navalkar should have had the impudence to expect his salary in gold; and a reminder that Smith's testimonial had not changed him into a European.[33]

Navalkar could see the beginning of his fall from grace. Contemplating a quiet, respectable retreat, he asked Edinburgh if he could retire on his existing salary. That, he was told off, 'would be quite impossible'.[34]

Lindsay, meanwhile, followed his missive of April 1889 with one a year later that—saying 'I fear it is necessary to be quite plain and distinct'—wrote off Navalkar's intellectual pretensions. Referring to three letters in which Navalkar had propounded his ideas about education, Lindsay derisively remarked: 'Any one can see that.' The real question was: 'Is it worth while keeping up colleges not connected with the University System? and to this question I get no very practical answer from your self and other critics.' He added to this his 'own sincere opinion'—the sincere opinion of the convener of the Foreign Missions Committee—that 'too much' was being spent on Navalkar's station, Alibag.[35]

The signs were ominous. But it was hard for Navalkar to quit. He had family responsibilities, the most pressing being the education of his four children, the youngest of whom was only seven. He had before him the worrying example of the neglect suffered by Rev. Narayan Sheshadri's children.[36] He would save his children a similar fate. The problem was apparently aggravated by a heightened, and none-too-Christian, sensitivity about class and by the children's delicate health. 'We have', he agonized, 'not yet sent them to any school, and the Indian Boarding Schools—at least those on our side, are most injurious to the health of respectable children.[37]. . . And our children are always ailing, the least change in the weather affects them seriously. We must be with them, and suitable schools exist only in Bombay and Poona.'[38]

In a fit of desperation, realizing that the authorities would not oblige and transfer him to Bombay or Poona, Navalkar pleaded with Smith to recommend him for appointment by the rival Established Church of Scotland 'who have no missionary of theirs in Bombay'.[39] Sense prevailed within a week, and he wrote resignedly: 'I will remain where I am till I am pensioned. I cannot begin any work afresh.'[40] In yet another desperate move, he tried to please Lindsay, and dedicated to him his *Marathi Christian Literature*.

For the first time, subject to somatization, Navalkar started feeling old and feeble: 'You will see how both myself and my dear wife are getting very old, and the infirmities of age are telling upon us.'[41] 'My brain and heart are almost wasted by constant work', he lamented to Smith, and pleaded: 'I have worked for upwards of 36 years, and I may be allowed the pension I claim. It is not likely that I will survive long.'[42]

The pension he claimed was his full salary, Rs. 200 a month. The authorities had pronounced that 'impossible'. Navalkar thought otherwise. He explained to Smith why 'the Committee might deal liberally with me in my case of necessity'. His exceptional services had cost him dear. Ignoring 'all personal considerations', he had declined 'liberal offers of other Missions'. The Church Missionary Society, for instance, had wanted to engage him on a European's salary. Sir Charles Wodehouse, the Governor of Bombay (1872-77), had offered him a deputy collectorship.[43] He 'could have easily become a great landlord', while carrying on with his professional work. But he had 'not done so'.[44]

He had, moreover, meant savings for the Mission. Other missions employed 'two Europeans for a High School, one European for the English service, a Native Pastor for the Vernacular service, a European for evangelistic work, and other men for literary work'. 'But at Alibag one man does it all', unaided by a single European who would have cost three times the salary of this man![45]

But financial constraints did not weaken Navalkar's larger commitment. Characteristically enough, in the very letter of 2 January 1891 in which he had pleaded for retirement on full salary, he accused the European missionaries in general and the Mission authorities in particular of hindering the cause of Christianity. They did that by creating a wedge between Christian and non-Christian Indians and by discriminating against the Indian missionaries. They adopted an attitude of hostility towards non-Christians and encouraged the converts to consider themselves superior to their non-Christian compatriots. Indian Christians, as a result, were not 'loved and respected by the non-Christian classes'. This made difficult a dialogue with the non-Christian majority whose conversion was the Mission's *raison d'être*.

'Native' missionaries, Navalkar insisted, must be respected and freed from European domination. 'Who that knows anything of the Hindus', he asked, 'will despise our work, and propose to degrade us by putting us under Europeans?' Implicating Lindsay and the Foreign Missions Committee by name, he wrote:

> Whatever views Dr Lindsay might entertain of the competency of European workers, Europeans that have been in India will never, never displace Natives of experience and ability by Europeans, however great might be their scholarship and ability . . . why should our Committee despise us? Why should they create 'a middle wall of partition' between the Europeans and us?

Earlier, 'such unkind distinctions were never made; otherwise you would never have found me in the Mission now'.[46] Within less than twenty years of his joining it, the authorities had rendered the Mission incapable of attracting intelligent Indians.

To this grave charge Navalkar gave a theological twist. The authorities had forgotten the supreme power they were bound to obey:

> But whether the Committee despise or honour us, they ought to bear in mind that we are Christ's servants; and we shall seek His approval; and that He does not despise us is apparent from the amount of work He helps us do for Him, and the effects our labours have upon the people among [whom] we live and work.

Navalkar was at the time smarting under a gratuitous display of racial discrimination. In 1890 Edinburgh had sent out the Deputies' *Report* for distribution among 'their missionaries in India, for their opinion'.[47] But it was circulated only among European, to the exclusion of Indian missionaries. Navalkar had suspected such a thing while the Deputies were still in India, and obtained from Lindsay a promise 'to *let us* all' see the *Report* when it was ready.[48] Resenting the 'disgrace', he warned: 'Surely we who are veterans can give you better and more reliable counsel than the Europeans who have not been long in the country.'[49]

Exactly a week after expressing the above sentiments, Navalkar sent off another letter that announced:

> But if the policy of our Mission Committee has changed and we must be degraded for our *skin*, I will resign my connection with it no matter what be the temporal consequences of my resignation. I shall at least have kept my Christian manhood in tact, and there is no disgrace or sin to slave and starve with the retention of the priceless gift of God. (Emphasis Navalkar's)

In invoking his *Christian* manhood to resist being degraded for his *skin*, Navalkar was making a striking connection. That manhood—a new self—was God's gift to the convert. No Mission or Church could violate it. If they did, the convert must resist, to the point of severing connection with them. Here was an explication of the theological twist provided in the letter of 2 January. With it was ready the high moral ground for Navalkar to repulse the charge of disloyalty and insubordination at the height of the crisis: 'I do not understand what Dr. Smith means by using 'Mission discipline' . . . in reference to me.'[50]

Once related to the *skin*, the violation of Navalkar's *Christian* manhood also afflicted his *Indian* manhood, the one he shared with those who shared his skin. The protest against the twin violation completed his indictment of the authorities. The man desperate for a decent pension declared to Edinburgh:

> Although we are poor, black and subjugated by a foreign race, we have not lost our manhood yet, and may God help us to preserve it, though we may have to suffer from absolute want and injustice.[51]

Navalkar was seething, and being transformed. The personal was fusing into the public, prompting him towards martyrdom as he talked of 'we' *vis-à-vis* those responsible for 'our' subjugation; and of the duty of the subjugated to safeguard their manhood.

Rather than dissolve into the public, however, the personal tended to dominate it. Stated in terms of 'we' and 'us' in January 1891, the argument regarding divine signs had the first person looming large towards the end of the year: 'I may be a fool and a black man, but *still God has helped me to work*, and God cannot be said to have *erred*.'[52] (emphasis Navalkar's)

Navalkar was feeling hounded. Almost the whole of 1892 was spent in pestering Edinburgh with one proposal or another. Nothing came. A letter to Lindsay, written mid-way in 1892, conveys his desperation:[53]

> Considering my long and hard service, the Committee ought gladly to pay my present salary in gold, or give me a pension and allow me to retire. Give me anything that you in the Committee may please. I am old and feeble—my eyes are become diseased.

But the will to fight was not gone.

III

This sad, paranoid, proud Indian pastor was invited to speak at the Decennial Missionary Conference on 'Work Among the Educated Classes'. The subject in his view was crucial for

Christianizing India. He wanted to go and speak. But he also dreaded going. Differences on the subject had aggravated his relations with the authorities. His wife, knowing his views and lack of tact, pleaded with him to stay back. Why risk the family's daily bread and the children's education? What would his solitary endeavours achieve? Three times he tried to decline the invitation. Finally, the drive to speak prevailed. His name, he found, had appeared in the programme. That helped him quell his own foreboding and his wife's counsel.

The Conference was designed to have speeches and not written presentations. But fearing that his inner turmoil might erupt under the spell of the moment, Navalkar wrote out a speech that, without concealing his views,[54] contained little that was exceptionable. It mentioned his own Mission just once to say: 'Even the Free Church Mission Committee has determined to reduce their work among the educated Indians, if not totally to discontinue it.'

This related to his main argument that most missions had retarded evangelization by focusing away from 'the educated classes' on to 'what are called low castes'. *Even* his Mission had followed suit. Compressed into this 'even' was a whole history of missionary enterprise since Alexander Duff. Going against his instructions from Edinburgh, and the proselytising practice of the day, Duff had sought the conversion of the upcoming educated Indian elites. His idea was to trust the mechanism of downward filtration to Christianise India through its emergent leaders. However, because it operated slowly, though surely, and prepared the ground imperceptibly, the strategy required patience. Navalkar realized that '. . . we cannot altogether blame the good people in England and America who so liberally patronise our work. They expect perceptible results, and such results we who are chiefly labouring among the higher classes are not able to present.'

But that did not justify the rejection of the strategy. He issued a stirring call:

> The former Missionaries for the educated classes were men of strong and definite convictions, and their heart was ablaze; burning words and expressions came out of their lips that made the bosoms of their

auditors glow with intense ardour, while acts of self-abnegation and heroism, which are regarded as impossible at present . . . were performed with alacrity. . . . But such enthusiasm and courage cannot be produced in the heart by what is indefinite and uncertain. . . . They should dare to be alone and single in the cause of Righteousness, with the whole world in arms against them.

The call, it is clear, was marred by a self-righteousness that, missed by none, enraged his local bosses. No sooner was the address over than MacKichan rushed to dismiss it as the spleen of an embittered Mission agent. But while reporting it to Lindsay, MacKichan couched his outburst in the following decent language:[55]

I explained to the Conference that it appears to me that Mr Ganpatrao had been led to make his erroneous statements regarding our Free Church work on account of what the Mission had done [reduced its grant] in regard to . . . his own district. I repelled his assertions regarding the work done in our Institutions and protested against such statements being made by any one who had no knowledge of what was being done in the missionary institutions alluded to.

A European eyewitness better suggests what actually happened: 'His words uttered with great feeling were, "I repudiate such statements with scorn." These words do not become Dr MacKichan. I ask would he have used them to any of the English Ministers present? They are utterly unjustifiable.'[56] MacKichan, if Navalkar can be trusted, was even more vitriolic, and said: 'I scornfully repudiate the statements of this man.'[57] When Navalkar tried to accost MacKichan and clarify things, the latter 'cried out most insolently, Go away, Sir, go away, Sir, I have now done with you, Sir'. These words, 'addressed before a large crowd', made Navalkar feel 'as if I was a dog'.[58]

Immediately after MacKichan's onslaught, and on the second day as well, Navalkar was not permitted the right to reply.

IV

The official reaction was quick and sharp. The Western India Mission Council formally demanded Navalkar's expulsion:[59]

It was reported that several members of the Council had intimated that partly in consequence of the attack publicly made by Mr Ganpatrao[60] in the Decennial Conference on the work of the Free Church Mission and on missionaries generally and partly on account of his subsequent proceedings in connection therewith they declined to sit with him in Council.

In his letter forwarding the resolution, MacKichan was 'glad' that Lindsay did not need to be explained why 'such a necessity' had arisen, and that the resolution would 'at once recommend itself to your [Lindsay's] judgment in the light of your own experience'.

Foredoomed, Navalkar was charged with disloyalty. He had made a pre-meditated attack on 'his own Mission'.[61] Besides, he had accused 'a whole body of modern missionaries' of rendering 'their work ineffective' on account of their 'lax views of Christian truth'.

MacKichan further reported that when the Conference re-convened after sabbatizing the following day, Navalkar tried forcibly to speak after the chairman, pressed for time, had disallowed him. He 'was at last compelled to obey the ruling of the Chairman and returned from the meeting soon after'. Navalkar, further, had his address printed and circulated by young men, some of whom even drafted a memorial in his defence. Worse, he got published in the *Bombay Guardian* a 'mischievous'[62] account of the meeting, the students' memorial, and a letter by 'An Indian Christian' criticizing the Conference.

MacKichan bemoaned the expansion of the Council that had brought Navalkar in:

> It has worked unpleasantly, as you already know, in the past; but we have borne with these difficulties in the hope that our patience would lead to smoother working. The result has been, however, very different from what we hoped for and this public outbreak has gone beyond the limits that are consistent with the merest appearance of propriety.

He insinuated in the end an action more drastic than Navalkar's removal from the Council:[63]

> Missionaries of other Societies have expressed astonishment at Mr Ganpatrao's continuing in the service of our Mission. We have not felt it to be desirable to raise this question, although we do feel that his attitude is not one that is compatible with true loyalty to the Mission with which he is connected; but we feel that the question of his

relation to the Council is one which must be settled without delay.

Lindsay needed no hints that Navalkar must be out of the Mission, not just the Council. He prepared for the Foreign Missions Committee a detailed statement, telling 'what I know of the man and his relation to the brethren at Bombay'. Navalkar, Lindsay reported, 'appeared to me to be an earnest and devout Christian, with quite a literary gift' and reputation as a Marathi preacher. Then came the condemnation:

He was, however, excessively vain and irritable, resenting fiercely any criticism, *continually measuring himself against Europeans and contemplating his superiority to them*. He was prone to criticise others, *especially European missionaries*, and used very strong language and imputed bad motives very freely. (Emphasis added)

The vividness of Lindsay's portrayal came from a want of self-understanding. MacKichan put it unwittingly well while complimenting Lindsay: 'Your recollection of the details of Mr Ganpatrao's aberrations is marvellous.'[64] The vividness lay in the concentration on the subject's 'aberrations', especially his obsession with Europeans.

In terms redolent of the colonizers' identifying distinctions between themselves and their colonized subjects, Lindsay described the relationship between MacKichan and Navalkar:

Dr MacKichan has been a very warm and indulgent friend treating Ganpatrao as a good brother would a sick & querulous sister. My impression was that Dr MacKichan was too indulgent and that no European missionary would have been permitted to act in the way Mr Ganpatrao was allowed. He seemed to me to be indulged in like a spoilt child. I say this to make it plain how forbearing Dr MacKichan was in every possible way.

Lindsay cited three 'incidents' in evidence. The first occurred during the opening of the new building of the Wilson College, when Dr and Mrs MacKichan had 'invited the missionaries and the leading Christian natives to dinner at the mission house'. Informed that Sheshadri and Navalkar would not come for the opening, MacKichan had not invited them to dinner. Let us follow Lindsay's graphic account:

On the morning of the day however Dr MacKichan reproached himself incessantly with not having invited them & it was agreed that if we or I saw the two at the College we were to invite them verbally. I saw both pointed them out in separate parts of the Hall and we agreed that I should try & get hold of Mr Ganpatrao while Dr MacKichan should make for Dr Sheshadri. I missed my man; Dr MacKichan caught his. All the way home Dr MacKichan again tormented himself at not being able to find Ganpatrao. He made many fruitless enquiries and at last within an hour of dinner discovered where he was stopping. Then he was again worried whether Ganpatrao would be most offended to be asked to dine at such short notice, or at being asked to come in the evening. A note was written asking him to come in the evening. Ganpatrao came and found that the gentlemen were still in the dining room, tramped out of the house & went off next day to Alibag. Whence he wrote me a letter in which he called Dr MacKichan a liar and a hypocrite, and asked me to show this letter to people to let them see how Europeans trampled on native Christians. I replied telling him all the circumstances & saying that if I laid the letter before the Committee as he seemed to suggest the question would probably arise whether a man who could make so little allowance for neighbour & used such intemperate language towards one who was always going out of his way to serve him was fit to be entrusted with the care of a district as a Christian missionary. I must also add that Dr & especially Mrs MacKichan seemed to feel more sorrow at not having sent the invitation by post than anger at the man's intemperate petulance.

Lindsay's account of the second incident began snidely: 'Ganpatrao had what he called a Technical School at Alibag & applied for a grant.' The effect created, it finished off quickly:

The inspector was Professor Scorgie,[65] a life-long friend of Mr Small,[66] a Free Church member, a warm friend of and subscriber to our missions. He had to report honestly against the school, but to make matters as easy as possible for Ganpatrao he gave the grant for one year but refused to renew it. His report was read in the Bombay Council when I was present. Ganpatrao thereupon uttered very outrageous abuse of Prof. Scorgie—saying things so bad that two of the missionaries present said they must leave if he was allowed to proceed. His only argument if I can rightly recollect was that Professor Scorgie, who he said was a man of mean birth, could not understand his—Ganpatrao's methods.

In the third incident—the veracity of which Lindsay assumed—Navalkar had written:

> under a thinly disguised signature, a series of letters in one of the Bombay newspapers attacking some missionaries in Bombay (not our missionaries) accusing them of living in luxury on the cool heights of Malabar Hill (which was not true in fact) and doing nothing for the heathen of the city. Of course this was not merely very bad conduct, but it placed our missionaries in a most awkward position to have a member of their Council attacking brother missionaries in such a way.

'These things', Lindsay concluded, 'made me feel while in India that Mr Ganpatrao ought not to be on the Council, and that when we drafted rules for Councils we ought to see that *native missionaries should not be made life members*.' (Emphasis added)

Coming to the impugned speech, Lindsay admitted that it contained mostly opinions Navalkar had 'held for a long time'. Only its last portion was 'an attack in temperate language for *him* [Navalkar]—intemperate for most other people—on a Mr Slater whose paper he seems to have misunderstood and in which he contrives to insinuate that modern missionaries are half-hearted in their proclamation of the truth of the Gospel'. This, however, did not justify expulsion from the Council, let alone the Mission. Lindsay managed to contrive that:

> To us reading it quickly at a distance and too ignorant of local circumstances to understand the correct thrust contained in his general assertions, the paper though objectionable in many ways, seems scarcely worth the strong feelings it had called forth. Had we the local knowledge we should doubtless discover the allusion to his own mission—my slight knowledge made me discern one at least—which not merely caused great irritation but were [*sic*] utterly unworthy of a Christian missionary.

Lindsay ended his special pleading with the reiteration that 'it would be very much better for the Mission if Mr Ganpatrao were not on the Council'. Indeed, not removing him would seem 'want of loyalty to our missionaries' who had been 'cruelly attacked on this very matter by Indian newspapers', and the attacks had reverberated in the British press.[67]

Yet, Lindsay felt constrained in laying before the Committee a definite 'deliverance'.

That was Navalkar's doing. Shaken by the Conference fiasco, Navalkar sent off an undated letter to Lindsay that bore no trace of the fervent speech:

> I do not know if I have a right to write to you in the matter of my treatment by an agent of our Mission in a public meeting. But still I venture to write and enclose certain excerpts. Please excuse the trouble.
>
> If I had not my children to educate, I should have quickly retired from my present work; but it is impossible to do so now. Could you not separate me and my work altogether from the Mission Council? Or could you not fix my grant, so that I may use it as I like—as I have hitherto used?
>
> I am suffering from insomnia.
>
> You wrote to me to write through the Mission Council, but would you still insist on the same?

He wrote again on 3 February to press for a swift settlement of his retirement. Any delay would leave the work 'altogether wrecked', and the worker 'utterly ruined'. Even European dominance seemed to trouble him no more: 'You are so anxious to appoint a European in the district, and this will be a good opportunity.' (Which is what happened in the event.) Monetary security, too, seemed not to matter. 'If you cannot give a pension, please write to that effect', he despaired, 'and I shall then decide what to do. Anything might be given, and then I shall see how I must make up the deficiency.'

The man was ready to submit. There were, though, signs of retrieval as well. Instead of the timid query if he would still be required to write through the Council, there was the intimation to Lindsay: 'I can never write to you through the local Mission Council.' Further, that he had decided to 'simply sever' his connection with the Council, because it was in 'dread' of 'Dr. MacKichan, a comparatively young man, [who] openly abused me in a public meeting in a very ferocious and coarse way, without any provocation whatsoever, as my paper was a general statement of my views—views that I have openly asserted since 1861'.

Nevertheless, Navalkar felt defeated. 'I will not formally complain,' he wrote resignedly.[68]

Another six days and he had got back his manhood. This was,

ironically, a gift from the Mission Council.[69] Even as he was planning a dignified withdrawal, he got wind of the resolution for his removal. Leaving now would confirm the calumnious resolution. He would not let MacKichan 'and those combined with him'—all Europeans[70]—'dishonour and ruin' him. Reluctant on 3 February even to complain formally, he launched an offensive on 9 February. He demanded 'a searching inquiry into the matter'.[71] He sent Lindsay three extracts from the *Bombay Guardian* and a copy of his speech at the Conference, saying: 'you ought to rejoice at my fearless exposure of Missionary inactivity and indifference'. The same audacity led him to warn Lindsay, the supreme boss and an expert on Church history:

> Sir, you forget that I am a Freechurchman, and a Scotchman to boot, and a genuine Scotchman and Freechurchman will not flinch to declare the truth and the whole truth with the whole world in arms against him. Though not born a Scotchman, I am by taste and education and culture a Scotchman of Scotchmen, and will suffer disgrace, starvation and death rather than prove a coward and a traitor to truth, justice and religion, like the old *Disruptionists*.[72] (Italics in the original)

It was this offensive that obliged Lindsay to take the case to the Foreign Missions Committee without a deliverance. It forced him into 'a very painful dilemma'. The dilemma, however, was untouched by the justice or pathos of the case. It belonged to the higher reaches of legality. Navalkar, '*a member of Council*', had demanded 'a searching inquiry'. How could that demand be 'summarily' dismissed 'without formally calling for more evidence of fault', and 'without formally stating to him the accusation made against him, and asking what he has to say in his defence?' As *a member of Council* (stress Lindsay's), Navalkar had to be treated 'in the very same way' as any of his European counterparts. Whatever be the decision in the case, it would act as a precedent. There was one 'very dangerous precedent' that they must avoid. They should not remove 'unheard' a member 'from his seat on the Council'. After all, 'formally' they did not even have before them the speech on which rested the case against the man.[73]

The Committee considered the 'Ganpatrao question' on 21 March 1893. It put on record its 'sympathy' for, and 'unabated confidence' in its missionaries whom 'portions of the Press' in India and Britain had subjected to 'very unworthy attacks . . . in consequence of proceedings at the Decennial Conference'. For the rest, the Committee authorized Lindsay to settle the question.[74]

This time Lindsay acted with a decisiveness that was in marked contrast to his inability to offer a deliverance. His dilemma, for all its moral protestations, was procedural. He scrupled at Navalkar's removal, without due enquiry, from the Council. No analogous difficulty precluded the man's dismissal from service, provided the action was differently named. Even procedural propriety vanished within four months, and Navalkar was told that he could continue in service, 'but he must distinctly understand that he is no longer a member of the Western India Mission Council'.[75]

The name chosen for dismissal was retirement. Lindsay explained to his agents in Bombay that it was not possible to 'at once' remove Navalkar from the Council. But, if they agreed, the Committee would try and ease him out of the Mission.[76] Their response was quick, grateful and enthusiastic.[77] Promised what they had wanted but dared not demand, MacKichan and his men henceforth started complaining that Navalkar had lapsed into such 'obstinate disloyalty' that there was 'no prospect of his doing loyal and truly helpful service'.[78]

To precipitate the desired end, Lindsay wrote to Navalkar on 22 June 1893:

> The Committee are very much grieved to find a state of matters existing between yourself and *all* your colleagues of such a kind that they (your colleagues) unanimously ask for your withdrawal from the Council, while you declare that you can never write to the Committee through them, and that you ask to be freed from all connection with Dr MacKichan 'and those combined with him'.

The rule was clear: 'Every Missionary, whether European or Indian, must work under the superintendence of the Mission Council or leave the service of the Mission.'

Lindsay disposed of Navalkar's demand for an enquiry by insinuating his guilt and promising clemency. The Committee had no wish 'to begin an investigation which in the end might compel them to take some severe measure and place in a humiliating position an old and valued servant of the Mission'. Emphasizing the Committee's magnanimity and the danger of spurning it, Lindsay wrote: 'They therefore put aside all the causes of dispute in the hope that the arrangement they suggest may relieve them of all necessity of further investigation and judgment.' He then made an offer, and explained how it was more lucrative than might initially appear:

> . . . you ask leave to retire on a pension. The Committee have no Pension Fund, and they are not in the habit of giving pensions. But they are willing to allow you to retire from their service as you propose, and to guarantee a retiring allowance of Rs. 100 per month, being one half of your present stipend. As your time will be at your own disposal you will no doubt be able to earn enough money to make your income what it now is.

Lindsay concluded with an 'appeal' to Navalkar's 'personal honour to refrain from attacking either publicly in your own name or anonymously your own former colleagues'.[79]

This cleverly crafted letter followed the familiar formula of authority. Seeking variously to make its recipient malleable, it addressed his interests, his reason, and his honour, all at once. But the recipient was hard to crack. And the authorities would not protract. 'They must', Navalkar was told two months later, 'now press for an immediate decision.' In yet another display of authority to break the man, this message came from the secretary and not the convener, who would no more condescend to correspond with him. Also, this message was more minatory. It reminded Navalkar that the recommendation of the Mission Council was unanimous, 'agreed to by Indian as well as European Missionaries'. Still, the Committee had acted 'with great forbearance'. But 'mission discipline' required that:

> You must either retire as you have asked to do on an allowance of Rs. 100 a month, or you must consider yourself directly under the control of the Western India Mission Council & be prepared to obey its instruction. I must earnestly entreat you for your own sake to accept one or other of the two alternatives offered. If you do not the Committee will be obliged to act in a way which they have no desire to adopt.

The alternatives offered were not as reasonable as the letter suggested. Enclosed with the letter was a minute of the Foreign Missions Committee, containing the humiliating condition that if he chose to stay in service, Navalkar would cease to be a member of the Mission Council.

An ultimatum was issued a month later. Whether or not he accepted the Committee's terms, Navalkar would cease to be on the Mission's 'active service' 'from and after' 30 November 1893. The term 'valued', which Lindsay's earlier overture had used to describe Navalkar's services, was dropped from the ultimatum. Similarly, while the overture had trusted Navalkar's sense of 'honour', the ultimatum warned that the monthly allowance was subject to Navalkar refraining from attacking the Mission Council.[80]

V

The 'Ganpatrao question' was for the authorities a matter of disciplining an insubordinate native agent. The higher motive behind the 'insubordination' was beyond them, convinced as they were of having shown him great 'forbearance'. This is best articulated in Lindsay's reply to a letter Mrs Navalkar had, in sheer desperation, written him. 'And what shall I say to you?' is how, with appropriate delicacy, he came to the point after apologizing for replying late 'owing to pressure of work combined with lack of strength'. 'I am greatly grieved', he commiserated helplessly, 'at the situation in which you have been placed—placed solely from your husband's conduct. We had no alternative but to act as we did. And we took no action until after long and patient waiting'. When they did act, they acted 'with great generosity.' For, they might 'without injustice have dismissed him at once'. Such generosity was not shown when a European missionary 'manifested somewhat similar insubordination'. Even at the time of proposing his retirement on half his salary, he was offered the alternative of remaining in his position 'if only he would promise to be obedient to the Mission Council'. But, Lindsay regretted: 'He made no such promise. We can do nothing more.'[81] Likewise, believing that he had followed the 'seventy times seven' rule, MacKichan could only feel hurt and betrayed as he told Lindsay:[82]

> You came to your conclusion [about Navalkar] when things came to a climax during your visit. I came to the same conclusion then but for years I had striven against it at no small cost . . . had tried to see the best of him and ignore the worst.

So deep was the authorities' sense of forbearance and rightness that they believed themselves incapable of behaving otherwise. Smith, as we have seen, was convinced that Navalkar had received more than one increment. There at least differing interpretations of what increment meant were possible. Not so when the authorities disregarded their own principle about not removing a member from the Mission Council without trial. Much, similarly, was made of the unanimity in passing the resolution about Navalkar's expulsion from the Council, whereas it was not unanimous.[83]

Never shaken, the sense of forbearance permitted the 'other' to be seen, and shown, as unregenerate and sinning.

Navalkar felt equally right. Blind to his own cunning, jealousy, paranoia, and other personal factors—which a fuller study must highlight—he believed himself to be a martyr. Self-absorption apart, he was indeed an inspired Christian. His is the story of the awakening to his predicament of an unfree convert. It signifies the inseparability, in a colonial situation, of Christianity from the hubris—and exploitation—of power. It also signifies the innate beauty and power of Christianity, at least for those who felt drawn towards it. But for that beauty and power, Christianity in colonial India—in any colonial situation perhaps—could not have survived the very European missionaries who came out to bring the 'natives' to God through Christ.[84]

Navalkar's is not a unique story. There were many others, e.g. Rev. Krishna Mohan Banerji (1813-85), Rev. Lal Behari Day (1824-94), Kali Charan Banerji (1847-1907), Pandita Ramabai (1858-1922), and Rev. Narayan Vaman Tilak (1862-1919), who *as Christians*—and *Indians*—were driven into varying modes of resistance.

NOTES

1. 'Then Peter came up and said to him, "Lord, how often shall my brother sin against me, and I forgive him? As many as seven times?" Jesus said to him, "I do not say to you seven times, but seventy times seven." ' Matthew, 18: 22-3.
2. I have dealt with this tragic predicament of the nineteenth-century Indians, Christian and non-Christian alike, in *The Oppressive Present: Literature and Social Consciousness in Colonial India*, New Delhi, 1992.
3. Consider the following specimen: ' . . . impossible as it is to condemn adequately the arrogance and cruelty of those unprincipled Englishmen who sometimes come to this country, the English, as a nation, are the noblest people in the world, whose real and earnest desire is to effect our real regeneration. When they have accomplished this noble mission which God has assigned them, they will generously resign our country into our own hands, and withdraw to other parts of this wide world, to dispense the blessings of civilization and Christianity to other peoples. All this must appear Utopian to those who are strangers to the Divine loftiness of character which Christianity imparts.' Ganpatrao Raghunath Navalkar, '*The Intuitional Theory of Religion*', *a lecture delivered before the United Students' Association, on the 25 November 1876*, Bombay, 1877, p. 7.
4. Christianity, Navalkar believed, 'has produced peace and harmony wherever it has been established, bringing jarring nations into one loving brotherhood'. See his *An Inquiry into the Parsi Religion*, Bombay, 1879, p. 40.
5. Navalkar to (presumably) Convener, Foreign Missions Committee, 13 June 1902, MS. 7823, ff. 190-8. (All the manuscript materials cited in this paper belong to the National Library of Scotland, Edinburgh.)
6. MS. DEP. 298/110, p. 94.
7. Even before joining the ministry, he had written a little book of twenty-three pages entitled *Ratnagiri and its People, Viewed in Connection with Missionary Enterprise*, Bombay, 1872.
8. Navalkar also quoted Professor Wordsworth, Principal of the Elphinstone College: 'Whatever our enthusiastic Christian missionaries might say, impartial and calm reasoners amongst the professors of that religion have serious doubts as regards the claims of that faith to be considered as by far the best calculated to secure the spiritual salvation of the natives of India. The alleged superior claims of Christianity upon the natives of India are not of such a character as to command implicit and ready faith in their reasonableness and soundness.' *The Intuitional Theory of Religion*, Preface, p. 5.

9. Ibid., p. 7.
10. *An Inquiry into the Parsi Religion*, p. 40.
11. Navalkar to Smith, 2 January 1891, MS. 7820, ff. 22-7. Navalkar also mentioned an address 'chiefly for educated students, who were from Bombay and other places.'
12. Foreign Missions Committee minute of 20 October 1885, MS. DEP. 298/112, pp. 356-7.
13. Smith to Navalkar, 31 August 1887, MS. 7773, f. 105.
14. They were Rev. Prof. Thomas M. Lindsay and Rev. John Fairley Daly.
15. MS. DEP. 298/117, p. 85.
16. The Foreign Missions Committee proposed when first discussed the question: 'That there shall be a Mission Council at each of the Presidency seats composed of all the ordained European Missionaries in each Presidency respectively, and the European teacher sent by the Free Church.' Further: 'That the native Missionaries ordained at this date shall be members of the Mission Council, in their respective Presidencies, but that no additional native missionaries shall be added to the Council without the consent of the Committee on Foreign Missions first formally obtained upon application from the Council.' MS. DEP. 298/108, pp. 5-6. This proved a ticklish issue, and it took a while to frame the rules which, despite marginal changes, remained predominantly discriminatory. In the 1880s and 1890s, the times we are dealing with, the rule was fairly simple: 'The Council shall consist of the Principal and all the European missionarics, ordained or not.' 'Native' missionaries would be appointed only in exceptional circumstances. This caused a good deal of resentment among Indian converts and missionaries. Perhaps the earliest case of clash on this account occurred between Rev. Lal Behari Day and his spiritual mentor, Rev. Alexander Duff. Day has left behind a fascinating account of this encounter in his *Recollections of Alexander Duff, D.D., Ll.D.*, Edinburgh, 1879, pp. 214-15. To ensure European managerial control, the same policy was followed with regard to the College Councils. These councils—in Calcutta, Bombay, Madras and Nagpur—consisted of *all* ordained European missionaries and European lay professors 'together with such *Native Christian* Professors as the Foreign Missions Committee may be pleased to accept'. (italics added) MS. DEP. 298/112, p. 352.
17. Baba Padmanji had also made a name as the author of *Yamuna Paryatan*, a landmark Marathi novel. His autobiography has a poignant description of his first wife, a Hindu, visiting him in Bombay to reclaim her conjugal status. Baba had meanwhile married a Christian lady, under the Act of 1850 that enabled converts to annul their earlier marriage(s) and marry again on the refusal of their spouses to join them. This episode took place in Navalkar's house where Baba,

then posted in Poona, was staying. J. Murray Mitchell (ed.), *Once Hindu: Now Christian, The Early Life of Baba Padmanji: An Autobiography*, London, 1890, pp. 134-7.

18. The very meeting of the Foreign Missions Committee on 13 August 1873 that recorded its gratification at Navalkar's license, also recorded Padmanji's resignation on account of 'very unsatisfactory state of his health', hoping that 'he may be strengthened to prosecute those literary labours in connection with which he has already earned a high reputation, and otherwise to further the cause of India's enlightenment.' MS. DEP. 298/110, p. 94.
19. While, in theory, holding the same view about the efficacy of 'native' agency, European missionaries actually remained resistant to investing their Indian counterparts with increasing autonomy and decision-making powers.
20. This was stated in relation to Lindsay: 'I have done him no harm; but on the contrary I tried my best to please him as an honest man. Of course I am unskilled to flatter, but I did all that any honourable man might do for him.' Navalkar to Smith, 27 November (?) 1891, MS. 7820, ff. 128-30.
21. MS. DEP. 298/111, pp. 7-8.
22. See Lindsay's undated memorandum on Navalkar (probably written in March 1893). MS. 7825, ff. 265-72.
23. Navalkar to Lindsay, 14 April 1893, MS. 7820, ff. 249-53.
24. Lindsay laid particular stress on 'Missionary economics', and dwelt on the 'duty' of the Foreign Missions Committee, of which he was the convener, 'to administer with due economy—using that word in its noblest sense'. MS. DEP. 298/117, p. 17.
25. That was in 1879. After waiting expectantly for upward of a year, he had sent off an enquiry to Smith. The reply, sent not by Smith but by Robert Young, the Assistant Secretary of the Foreign Missions Committee, was an ambiguous bit of procedural information. The application, he was told, 'shd come to us officially thro' the Presbytery or rather perhaps thro' the Missions Council'. Robert Young to Navalkar, 3 April 1880, MS. 7750, f. 591.
26. Navalkar wrote to Lindsay on 19 February 1892: 'If my present salary be paid in gold, I shall not need any other increase to my salary. Can you oblige me? I wd then get Rs. 300.' MS. 7820, ff. 145-6. Exchange rates for different years along with individual missionaries' salaries can be seen in the minutes of the Foreign Missions Committee for April (occasionally March) of the relevant years in MS. DEP. 298.
27. Lindsay to Navalkar, 4 April 1889, MS. 7775, f. 85.
28. Sidoba Misal was at this time stationed in Amraoti. MS. 7774, f. 107. For a brief description of him, see C. Rainy, *A Visit to Our Indian Mission Field*, Edinburgh, n.d., pp. 299-301.

29. Navalkar to Lindsay, 13 May 1889, MS. 7820, ff. 166-9. MacKichan, then in Edinburgh on furlough, was shown this letter by Lindsay.
30. Smith to Navalkar, 16 June 1892, MS. 7775, f. 154.
31. Smith may have had in mind a technical increase of salary, in 1878, at the time of Navalkar's confirmation in the ministry. It was then decided, 'in view of the exceptional circumstances of the case, to allow him the same salary as he received when a teacher in the Mission Institution', i.e. Rs. 165 a month. Even this increase was, in fact, mere protection of salary. MS. DEP. 298/111, p. 100.
32. On 2 January 1890, Smith wished Navalkar 'a spiritually fruitful new year, in yourself, your family & the Mission'. He also favourably acknowledged a letter Navalkar had written on 11 December, and said he would 'make some use of it in a forthcoming No. of the *Monthly Record*'. MS. 7774, f. 65.
33. Not quite realizing what Lindsay thought of him and his work, Navalkar made 'a personal appeal' to the convener to raise money for the Alibag Technical School. Lindsay refused to oblige not only because his official position forbade his 'pleading the scheme of any individual missionary', but also because: 'I certainly have no intention of pleading for more money to be spent on schools, technical or high schools.' MS. 7775, f. 85.
34. Salary in gold was refused in early April 1889. Towards the end of the same year, on 17 December 1889, Navalkar was informed by the Foreign Missions Committee that they had 'at present no pension fund for native agents', and further that even if they had one, retirement on full salary was inconceivable. MS. DEP. 298/112, p. 215.
35. Lindsay to Navalkar, 22 April 1890, MS. 7774, ff. 145-6.
36. 'Dr Sheshadri spent all his time in the service of the Mission and the education of his children was neglected. The same will happen with mine.' Navalkar to Lindsay (?), 10 December 1891, MS. 7820, ff. 137-40.
37. Prone to exaggerate his fears, maybe also hoping to persuade Smith the better thereby, Navalkar added: 'Two or three of my wife's nieces have died in a boarding-school, which was the best managed in Bombay. . . .' 'Two or three' may sound callous, even unconvincing, in the context of reporting the deaths of one's nieces. Nonetheless Navalkar is earnest and concerned.
38. Navalkar to Smith, 2 January 1891, ibid., ff. 22-7.
39. Daydreaming, he asked for a salary of Rs. 250 plus house and carriage allowances worth Rs. 100 a month, and added by way of justifying his demand: 'They paid two European workers 1200 Rupees a month!' Ibid.
40. Navalkar to Smith, 9 January 1891, ibid., ff. 28-9.
41. Ibid., 2 January 1891, ibid., ff. 22-7.

42. Ibid., 10 December 1891, MS. 7820, ff. 137-40.
43. Eight months later, writing to Lindsay on 11 August 1894, Navalkar would recall the same offer as having been made by the Governor's son. MS. 7821, ff. 78-81.
44. See Navalkar to Smith, 2 January 1891, MS. 7820, ff. 22-7; and to Lindsay, 19 January 1894, MS. 7821, ff. 7-8.
45. Navalkar to Smith, 2 January 1891, MS. 7820, ff. 22-7. The exclamation mark figures in the letter. In a letter written after he had been eased out of the Mission, he complained: 'Bombay High School has employed a man to superintend at a salary of Rs. 300! I myself superintended my High School, and taught in it. I had my English and Marathi services. . . . I did evangelistic work; I did literary work, and also district work . . . and I was paid only Rs. 200!' Navalkar to Lindsay (?), 11 August 1894, MS. 7821, ff. 78-81.
46. Navalkar described how a Brahman deputy collector, who had been posted at various places, 'passed by my house, and stopped to have a talk with me. Then he told me that he was much surprised at the favourable impression we had made upon the people of the district.' He had found the Christians and the non-Christians 'hostile to each other, but it was just the reverse here.' Navalkar to Smith, 2 January 1891, MS. 7820, ff. 22-7.
47. The Foreign Missions Committee's minute of 22 April 1890, MS. DEP. 298/113, p. 234.
48. 'Dr Lindsay promised to *let us* all see it [the *Report*], and the European Missionaries remember the promise given in a meeting with Council in Bombay.' (emphasis in the original) Navalkar to Smith, 9 January 1891, MS. 7820, ff. 28-9.
49. Navalkar added tangentially that the Foreign Missions Committee lacked the sense and the nobility to value their 'native' agents: 'Miss Rainy showed herself to be a more sensible, nobler person than the members of the Committee; she consulted with us most freely and adopted our suggestions, as is evident from her book.' Navalkar to Smith, 2 January 1891, ibid. ff. 22-7. The reference is to C. Rainy, *A Visit to Our Indian Mission Field.*
50. Navalkar to Lindsay, 31 August 1893, MS. 7820, ff. 302-3.
51. Navalkar to Smith, 9 January 1891, ibid., ff. 28-9.
52. Ibid., 27 November (?) 1891, ibid., ff. 128-30.
53. Navalkar to Lindsay, 13 May 1892, ibid., ff. 166-9.
54. 'I would not play the coward and the hypocrite because I would displease some men and women.' Navalkar to Lindsay, 14 April 1893, ibid, ff. 249-53.
55. MacKichan to Lindsay, 3 February 1893, ibid, ff. 209-12.
56. Report in the *Bombay Guardian*, sent along with Navalkar's letter of 9 February 1893 to Lindsay, ibid., ff. 265-72.

57. Ibid.
58. Ibid.
59. Western India Mission Council Resolution of 20 January 1893, ibid., f. 213.
60. Following a subtle formal distinction, but rarely disregarded, Europeans were mentioned by their family names and the 'natives' by their personal names.
61. MacKichan to Lindsay, 3 February 1893, ibid., ff. 209-12. In a subsequent letter he wrote: 'The paper contributed nothing really to the discussion of the subject before the Conference and gave the impression of an opportunity snatched for the purpose of attack. It was not a spoken address . . . but a paper deliberately planned and delivered with vehemence and acrimony.' MacKichan to Lindsay, 21 April 1893, ibid., ff. 262-3.
62. MacKichan to Lindsay, 24 February 1893, ibid., ff. 230-2.
63. Unless indicated otherwise, the account of what MacKichan wrote to Lindsay is based on the covering letter of 3 February 1893. Ibid., ff. 209-12.
64. MacKichan to Lindsay, 21 April 1893, ibid., ff. 262-3.
65. James Scorgie was Professor of Mechanism and Applied Science, Civil Engineering College, Poona.
66. John Small, missionary in Poona.
67. Lindsay's undated statement about Navalkar, MS. 7825, ff. 265-72.
68. Navalkar to Lindsay, 3 February 1893, MS. 7820, ff. 207-8.
69. His letter of 3 February betrays no inkling of the Council resolution, which had been passed two weeks earlier. It is possible that the resolution was kept a closely guarded secret until it was finally despatched to the Committee.
70. Even Lindsay, in his undated statement, was constrained to notice with regard to the resolution against Navalkar: 'Mr Dhunjibhai is conspicuous by his absence.' MS. 7825, ff. 265
71. Navalkar to Lindsay, 9 February 1893, MS. 7820, ff. 215-16.
72. Ibid., 14 April 1893, ibid., ff. 249-53.
73. Undated statement, MS. 7825, ff. 265-72.
74. MS. DEP. 298/114, p. 71.
75. Ibid., p. 114.
76. To assure them of his solid support to them, he forwarded for their perusal the statement that sealed Navalkar's fate.
77. 'The Members of the Council are deeply grateful to you and the Committee for the very thoughtful care which you have bestowed on the subject and for your sympathy with the Council in the whole matter. . . . You have done full justice to the significance of our act.' MacKichan to Lindsay, 22 April 1893, MS. 7820, f. 267.
78. Ibid., f. 268.

79. Lindsay to Navalkar, 22 June 1893, MS. 7775, ff. 561-2. Another condition that related to the allowance was: ' . . . should you obtain fairly remunerative employment making your income larger than it was while in their service, they shall be at liberty to withdraw or reduce the allowance'. The Committee had approved the draft of this letter two days earlier. MS. DEP. 298/114, p. 110. A copy of the letter was sent to MacKichan. MS. 7758, f. 600.
80. Foreign Missions Committee minute of 19 September 1893, MS. DEP. 298/114, p. 122.
81. Lindsay to Mrs Navalkar, 23 December 1893, MS. 7775, ff. 727-8. In his confidential statement on Navalkar, Lindsay mentions Mrs Navalkar as 'a gentle, good, helpless woman' suffering on account of her husband's false notions of dignity and position. She was the sister of Runga Rao of Bhandara, described by Lindsay as 'one of the finest most devoted & most self-sacrificing native Christians I have seen in India.' MS. 7825, ff. 265-72.
82. MacKichan to Lindsay, 21 April 1893, MS. 7820, ff. 262-3.
83. See R. Scott (a member of the Western India Mission Council) to Smith, 29 April 1893, ibid., f. 270.
84. This statement is made in full acknowledgment of what a 'renegade'—Verrier Elwin—described as 'the spirit of adventure and dedication' that the European missionaries brought to India: 'Hundreds of them have gone to live in the remotest places, denying themselves the comforts and amenities of life for many years. They have been the pioneers in the treatment of leprosy, championed the underdog, befriended the untouchables and taken a leading part in sponsoring the cause of the tribal people. They have done much for the languages of India, especially the tribal languages. In the fields of education and medicine their work has been distinguished by professional competence and human affection for children and the sick.' *The Tribal World of Verrier Elwin: An Autobiography*, New Delhi, 1999, p. 95.

CHAPTER 9

Questions of Public Health and Foreign Philanthropy: Rockefeller Foundation in India, 1915-1945

DEEPAK KUMAR

Almost every European nation has been the recipient of Rockefeller Charities, even such ones as are piling up armaments for offence and defence. . . . We have grave doubts whether the spirit of the Donor looks with approval upon such large endowments to countries which have surplus enough to manufacture armaments for the destruction of mankind. However, it is for the present administration of the Foundation to satisfy their conscience. To us the policy appears to illustrate, apart from anything else, the well known adage of 'carrying coal to New-castle'. The endowments will be justified if the receipients are men who are carrying on useful work, but probably, owing to their views, may not be in favour of their respective Governments.

In the long and impressive list of the endowments we are sorry to note that 'India occurs nowhere'. We may be permitted to observe in this connection that neglect of India does not appear to be consistent with the motto of the foundation 'to promote the well-being of mankind throughout the world', when one fifth of the human race—inheritors of the most ancient civilization of the world—are left out altogether from the operation of the Great Charity especially when considerable scientific investigation is being carried on in this country under very discouraging circumstances.

Editorial, *Science and Culture,* IV(2), 1938, 101

*This work was made possible through a study grant from the Rockefeller Archive Centre, and the author is grateful for the excellent facilities provided by its staff and its director, Dr. Stapleton. Mr. Sirish N. Kavadi of FRCH, Pune and Dr. J.N. Sinha of Rajdhani College, Delhi, shared their collection from the RAC and this help is gratefully acknowledged.

Right from the late nineteenth-century questions relating to public health engaged both the official and public mind in India and the debates gradually became more intense in the wake of major cholera and plague epidemics. It ranged from assertions of imperial altruism to allegations of colonial callousness.[1] The questions asked were: What was the nature of colonial medical intervention? Was it merely enclavist or could it transcend certain geo-cultural boundaries? How effective it was and what more could have been done? In the end, it left several questions unanswered and several quarters dissatisfied.

I

Here one may also ask, how 'public' was public health? At present it is defined as 'a grand social intervention' and also as 'a historical, self-conscious social and scientific movement'. Can this definition be applied to a colonial situation? In Britain, Edwin Chadwick had attempted an administrative and engineering solution to the problem of high urban death rates. For funding, he coaxed Britain's towns to raise taxes, and this led to a political storm which ended his career. Could there be a Chadwick in colonial India?

Public health usually refers to organized efforts made under the direction of medical experts for preventing disease and improving the health of the people. Contemporary medical opinion, however, had different perceptions. Some thought excessive reliance on medical intervention as 'one-sided' and 'dangerous'. For example, J.D. Megaw who in the early 1930s was the Director General of the Indian Medical Service (IMS), argued:

> Suppose for a moment that the public health services of India were to achieve complete success in stamping out malaria, cholera, small-pox, tuberculosis, and all other great killing diseases of India, and suppose that nothing was done to increase the production of food or to restrict the growth of population, the inevitable result would be the replacement of the tragedy of death from disease by the greater tragedy of death from starvation.[2]

Medical intervention was thus clearly no panacea. But at the same time many thought that the control of disease would promptly raise the standards of life and would gradually induce decline in fertility. Yet in the final analysis the situation in India was always found too dismal to warrant such optimism. So the standard official argument would be that public health does not depend only on the control of preventable disease but also on the state of nutrition and general economic conditions. To quote Megaw again, 'a public health policy must be worked out in terms of agricultural and industrial production; it must look ahead and take into account the maintenance of a proper relation between the number of the people and the available supply of the necessities of life'.[3] This indeed was a tall order. The colonial government had neither the intention nor the wherewithal. To the growing demands for greater indigenization of the services, the government responded with a retrenchment policy (vide Inchape Committee Report, 1923). To this were later added severe economy measures in the wake of the Great Depression. Agriculture and public health were obviously the early casualties.

Under these circumstances the government looked for private support. Within the Indian municipal system, it was not easy to raise finance for public health through higher taxation. In some places like Madras the taxes were already very high. In a detailed study of the Calcutta Municipal Corporation, it has been found that the *rentier* class was extremely reluctant to pay higher taxes for public health purpose.[4] In some places there was very little or no surplus revenue. The nascent Indian bourgeoisie would put all responsibility (or blame) on the government which they argued had sucked every little surplus that the Indian economy could generate. The situation was complex, dismal, and in many ways pathetic. This was duly reflected at different national and international sanitary conferences and other forums. Though everyone tried to fix responsibility on the state, there were sporadic instances of private philanthropy. In 1903, for example, an American gentleman Mr. Phipps donated $100,000 to the Government of India to be used for health or agriculture purpose. This money was promptly utilized to create an agricultural college-cum-research institute at Pusa which would furnish a complete course of agricultural instruction from the elementary to an advanced stage.[5] In the name of public health, government had maintained apart from dispensaries, cinchona plantations, and vaccine/serum production centres at Bombay, Kasauli and Coonoor. But given the vast areas and huge population, these were awfully inadequate. It is against this background that one needs to see the Rockefeller Foundation's (RF) philanthropic interventions in public health in different parts of the world.[6]

II

The sole purpose of the Foundation, as stated in its Charter, is 'to promote the welfare of mankind throughout the world'. No restriction, no perpetual endowments and no fixed guidelines. But in practice the resources were devoted to combating what its founder considered to be the two chief scourges of mankind—hunger and disease. Thus, agriculture and public health assumed utmost importance. The focus first fell on the plantations in different parts of Asia and Latin America which needed to be made lucrative through greater scientific input and the control of diseases which impaired labour productivity. So hookworm was initially picked for all attention in the farm areas of Malaya, Ceylon and Madras.

Commercial and economic motives were definitely there but this need not cloud the underlying humanitarian concerns. Decades before the Foundation's effort, socio-medical activities had called for strong sanitary measures, even a 'sanitary despotism'.[7] This gave birth to the concept of 'sanitary engineering' which gradually developed to denote 'environmental health' rather than the limited original concept of 'plumbing'.[8] Environmental health included not only water, sewage, refuge, and so on. but also equally important subjects like ventilation, lighting, safety, housing, town-planning, and rural sanitation.

The concept of public health had thus become virtually all-embracing. To quote J.B. Grant, an important RF functionary in India,

> Public Health is the science and art of social utilisation of scientific knowledge for medical protection by maintaining health, preventing disease, and curing disease through organised community efforts for (a) the hygiene of the environment, (b) the control of the community

infections, (c) the education of the individual in principles of personal hygiene, (d) the organisation of medical and nursing service for the early diagnosis and preventive treatment of disease, and (e) the development of the social machinery which will ensure to every individual in the community a standard of living adequate for the maintenance of health. As such public health becomes social medicine and is primarily a field of social activity, applying practically every basic science directed towards a comprehensive programme of community service.[9]

The RF's involvement in India reflected these larger concerns and it is also possible that this broadening of the canvas was facilitated by its experiences in China and India. However, its work in India lacked the intensity and thrust that it enjoyed in China or Eastern Europe.[10]

III

In India RF's involvement began with the visit of Dr. V.G. Heiser (RF Director for the East) to Madras in late 1915. He surveyed the then existing medical institutions in Madras and probed into the prevalence of hookworm disease.[11] He was impressed with the activities of Indian Research Fund Association (IRFA, established in 1911), and felt that enormous amount of work could be done under IRFA at a comparatively small cost. He impressed upon the foundation to initiate works on hookworm control, at least in Madras Presidency.

Hookworm infection was found in all parts of India but appeared most acute in the provinces of Bengal, Assam and Madras. It was supposed to have infected 75 per cent of the native population, 80 per cent of the rural population in plains, and 75 to 90 per cent of the labouring classes.

The disease was first noticed in 1879 when McConnell discovered the *Ankylostomum duodenale* while making necropsies in Calcutta. In 1887 the parasite was again found in necropsies made in Madras. But these observations received very limited notice and were altogether forgotten. It was only around 1910 that both the government and plantation employers realized the economic necessity of clearing up the situation.[12] An anti-hookworm campaign was started in Madras in early

1920 and the RF lent the services of Dr. G.P. Paul and Dr. J.F. Kendrick for this purpose. This campaign had two parts: (1) investigational, and (2) educational. RF and the government shared the expenses (Rs. 26,000) and the programme involved, publicity, examination and treatment.[13]

1. Publicity

1922: 124 lectures to audiences aggregating 26,000 persons were given.
1923: 2,866 lectures were given to audience aggregating 2,65,000 persons.

2. Examinations

1922: 6,741 persons were examined of whom 4,676 were found infected.
1923: 26,700 persons were examined of whom 16,563 were found positive.

3. Treatment

1922: 49,916 treatment were administered.
1923: 93,469 treatments were given.

During his residence in India (1921-34), Dr. Kendrick developed control of hookworm by means of travelling treatment units and latrine building. He made several important studies on the species of hookworm and the flow of ground water in connection with board hole latrines.[14] The most important component of this campaign was the emphasis on creating public awareness. This was done through lectures, pamphlets, and lantern-shows. An exceptionally interesting mode was the use of local story-telling method. One such pamphlet used the popular *Baital* stories to create awareness. In one such story the demon manifested itself in the form of millions of worms hooked in the intestines, creating sickness in the body and the only solution lay not in religious rituals but in taking purgative medicines and adoption of clean ablution methods.[15] This method proved exceptionally successful.[16] The government soon realized that the loss in efficiency due to this disease, if expressed in terms of cash, must be enormous. Dr. Clayton Lanes who examined about 46,000 persons in the tea-gardens of Assam and the jails of Bengal, showed that the entire war-debt of India could be paid by the wages lost by hookworm-ridden employees in India through sheer physical inability to keep at work. He wrote, 'the disease is a menace and an obstacle to all that makes for civilization. As a handmaiden of poverty, a handicap of youth, an associate of crime and degeneracy, a destroyer of energy and vitality, it stands in very forefront of diseases'.[17] The usual government excuse of 'want of funds' was considered lame. One thousand patients could be cured for a trifling sum of Rs. 125, it was argued.

IV

The RF was also engaged in several other works in India.[18] In 1927, Dr. W. Cary Sweet was assigned to Mysore State at the request of its government to serve as their consultant on public health policy, and to advise and assist in setting up their public health organization and in developing a sound programme. In addition to helping in the organization of the Mysore Public Health Department, Dr. Sweet had a special interest in malaria and made several important studies in that field, as well as developing a programme for control of hookworm. Most of the senior personnel in Mysore State were trained during Dr. Sweet's time through a cooperative programme with the government for foreign fellowships and local training. In 1939 Dr. Sweet set up an office in Calcutta but a year later left for China. In April 1940, Dr. J.L. Hydrick arrived in India to take Dr. Sweet's place, having under his supervision the work in Bengal, Orissa, Bihar and Assam. Dr. Hydrick remained in India until 1942.

Dr. W.P. Jacocks was assigned to Travancore State from March 1929 to September 1930, where he assisted the government in developing a public health programme and rural health unit. The RF had maintained frequent contacts with the Travancore health services through visits from Dr. Jacocks and other staff members stationed in Ceylon and in India. They showed considerable interest in the development of the new medical college and medical centre in Trivandrum.

In 1934, Dr. Jacocks moved from Ceylone to Madras, where he remained till February 1935 when he went to Delhi to set up a permanent office. He remained in charge of the Delhi office until 1942. One of the main activities of Dr. Jacocks, during his period of contact and residence in India was the development of local health units, an activity in which he was assisted by other staff members. The first of these was set up at Mandya, in Mysore state in 1928 under the direction of a former RF fellow. Other health units developed with RF assistance included Nevtyyattinkara (Travancore) in 1931; Partapgarh (UP) in 1932; Poonamalle (Madras) in 1935; Closepet (Mysore) in 1936; Najafgarh (Delhi) in 1938; Singur (Bengal) in 1939 and Sirur (Bombay) in 1940.

All these units were supported for a period of five years by RF assistance on a decreasing scale and were later turned over to the respective governments. In general, they served as the main public health field training centres for the respective states, and in later years had served with some modification as models for extension of public health work to other areas. This was particularly true in Mysore State.

In September 1934, Dr. Paul F. Russell arrived from the Phillippines, and during 1934 and 1935 toured India to study malaria in various localities. He selected Madras Presidency for permanent studies, and in 1938 set up a laboratory at the King Institute, Guindy, and field studies at Ennore and at Pattukkottai. In 1940 he moved the laboratory to Coonoor, largely for the purpose of studying foothill malaria, the field station continuing at Pattukkottai. In December 1937, Mr. Fred W. Knipe, sanitary engineer, arrived to work with Dr. Russell in the control of malaria in the Pattukkottai irrigated area and in the development of spraying techniques for control of malaria by killing adult mosquitoes. Both Dr. Russell and Mr. Knipe left India early in 1942. In February 1937, Dr. M.A. Barber and Dr. J.B. Rice studied malaria for six months in and around the city of Poona. Since both the doctor's had to return to the United States before the end of the year, this work closed in July but the studies revealed the mosquito vector and its habits. Early in 1938 Mr. B.R. Dyer, sanitary engineer, arrived in Delhi to study ground water but found that conditions and facilities for this purpose were better in the Punjab and moved to Lahore in October, where he worked and later published several papers on the movement of ground water. In October 1939 he moved to Calcutta, where in addition to research on soil pollution, he acted as professor of sanitary engineering at the All India Institute of Hygiene and Public Health (AIIHPH) from January 1940. He left India in November 1943.

V

The largest single investment of the RF in India lay in the establishment of the AIIHPH in Calcutta. In 1927, following a visit by Dr. W.S. Carter, Associate Director of the Division of Medical Education, the formation of this institute was recommended in association with the Calcutta Medical College and the School of Tropical Medicine for the purpose of providing graduate training in public health on an all India basis. In 1928 the proposal was approved and the RF agreed to contribute to land, building, equipment and salaries to the tune of US $6,04,000. The Government of India agreed to pay for future staff and maintenance.[19] The institute was formally opened in December 1932. In 1939, Dr. J.B. Grant arrived in India as director of the institute and continued till 1945. During this period the institute was thoroughly reorganized. In addition a blood bank was started and Dr. Grant advised the government on several occasions including the Bhore Committee on Health.

The AIIHPH was expected to undertake applied research and instruction in branches such as public health, (a) vital statistics and statistical methods, (b) epidemiology, sanitary engineering, biochemistry and nutritional diseases, rural hygiene including veneriology and tuberculosis and, maternal and child welfare.

Research at AIIHPH was to take the form of investigating the best ways of applying the results of pure research to the requirements of large units of population, both rural and urban.[20] Dr. W.S. Carter laid out these plans in consultation with Dr. Megaw,

Dr. Baptist, R.M. Pearce, Col. Stewart, and G.S. Bajpai. Carter records an interesting conversation with Bajpai, a senior official with the Government of India:

We had agreed upon a suitable building which will be adequate for present and future needs. When he was arguing for assistance in the matter of personnel, I stated that the proposal for a school of hygiene in India is the same as that made by the RF concerning the London School of Hygiene. He replied that Great Britain is a country of great wealth while India is not. I then said that the London School is for the entire British Empire and not for Great Britain alone. He replied that India has a population of 320 millions or more than three-fourths of the entire British Empire. This was sort of a solar plexus blow, statistically speaking, for I had to remain silent and could not say that quality sometimes counts far more than quantity, even when population are concerned.[21]

Probably the opening of the institute was preceded by a great deal of bargaining between the Government of India and the RF. Carter himself thought of Bajpai as 'a clever Indian politician who is endeavouring to get all that he can for nothing'. Government of India, on the other hand, was advised not to easily give in to the RF pressures. In a confidential minute, an official wrote,

I am strongly against the Government of India demeaning itself by going on its knees and holding out its hands for alms in America. It has to be borne in mind that the Rockefeller Fund in China have been lavishly dispensed in the founding of an immense University. What is this University? It is simply a trade development for the propagation of American Commerce throughout China.[22]

Apart from these suspicions, the spectre of the Retrenchment Committee and deep financial cut were always there. Earlier in 1920, the Strahan Committee had recommended the establishment of an all-India institute for medical research but it was shelved. In 1928, the Fletcher Committee revived this idea but then the Great Depression had set in and the idea was shelved again and could be opened only when A.V. Hill and Bhore re-emphasized its need in 1944. Under such circumstances, the establishment of AIIHPH seems astonishing and a tribute to the RF.

Another major difficulty was the process of Indianization that was taking place in the medical department. Senior European medical officers like L. Rogers, Megaw, Graham, and others were opposed to it and thought it would lower the medical standards. But in the wake of growing nationalist feelings nothing could be done to retain the 'pristine purity' of IMS. The IRFA under which AIIHPH functioned had a 13-member governing body, 7 of whom were Indians. This the senior IMS official resented but could do little to stem the tide.[23]

These teething troubles were over by the time Dr. J.B. Grant took over the institute. He went for a thorough reorganization of both syllabi and its departments. More emphasis now was to be put on (1) microbiology, (2) parasitalogy, (3) physiological hygiene, (4) nutrition and (5) public health chemistry. He did not want the institute to be run as an ordinary administrative government department 'without any real academic status or procedures'. He regretted that Delhi's consideration of the syllabus was 'based much more upon financial-political relationship than on technical considerations. Naturally one's reaction is to provide the institute with the same academic status and control as obtains in London or Johns Hopkins'.[24]

A comparative statement on the syllabi followed in London School of Tropical Medicine and Calcutta School of Tropical Medicine bears out Grant's resolve to fill the gaps and provide the best possible curriculum. Meanwhile the Second World War intervened. Several development works stopped but in a sense the war proved a boon. It led not only to the intensification of freedom struggle but also made people think what shape the country would take after independence. So the questions of planned development and post-war reconstruction came to the forefront.[25] In view of these developments, the Government of India invited Professor A.V. Hill to report on the state of scientific research in India and Joseph Bhore was asked to report on health issues.[26] In both these reports, the questions relating to public health, medical education and research were discussed, and their recommendations formed the bedrock for future work. The RF representative in India held consultation with both these committees.[27] In February 1944, J.B. Grant informed the Bhore Committee that public health in Bengal would not improve until the health services were provincialized for a period of sufficient duration to develop a public consciousness and efficient administration, after which they might and should be returned to local municipal authorities. Secondly, the administration had to be revamped and the communal ratio must be relaxed if necessary in the selection of personnel. Thirdly, refresher courses be introduced to train the lower level of administrative personnel.[28]

Needless to add that such advice remained on paper. However, it does show the genuine concern of the RF personnel.

VI

What did India gain from the RF? Well, the RF worked under certain policy guidelines and it simply could not have assumed the role of a government in any country. In India its objectives were fairly limited right from the beginning. But going through the Rockefeller Archive Centre (RAC) records one does not get a picture that commercial interests dominated its Indian activities. No such evidence could be found. J.B. Grant claimed that RF's object and success was that it aroused in both China and India 'a medical-technical consciousness' which they earlier lacked. According to Frank,

> There was almost complete ignorance on the part of governments as to what constituted adequate standards either in training of doctors or nurses or in public health organisation and administration. The RF pre-war policy consequently aimed at removing this defect and was directed through two channels, namely the training of personnel for key positions and assistance in demonstration of modern standards in teaching institutions and in administrations. In the case of China, this policy went so far as to undertake the entire responsibility for a complete demonstration of modern level of professional training. . . . The consequent development of technical consciousness has resulted in public health post-war reconstruction plans for India-China, which on paper may be considered abreast of modern trends and therefore satisfactory.[29]

In post-war world the RF found its role changing. In India, it moved towards agriculture. Indian health was now left entirely in the hands of Indians!

The Foundation's work nevertheless won accolades from the

chiefs of Travancore, Mysore and public figures like Patrick Geddes and Rabindranath Tagore.[30]

Sometimes it appeared that the RF personnel worked in collusion with the IMS. They were not opposed to Indianization but were definitely concerned about any consequent fall in medical standards. Megaw advocated a rather slow pace of Indianization leading to the creation of 'a real progressive indigenous school of public health'.[31] Both Megaw and Heiser (representing IMS and RF) argued that health work had to move hand in hand with better agriculture and control over human fertility. The former could be achieved (which later did happen as Green Revolution) but the population control would 'draw the fire of religious prejudice both native and Catholic. The first step should be to confront the leaders with actual facts ascertained by careful survey'.[32]

The diagnosis was fine, but the remedy given was much less than the required dose. Mutual suspicions ran high. The Indian leaders blamed the government for not undertaking adequate health measures in the name of economy and depression. The IMS, on the other hand, felt that the Indian politicians were using the depression and financial difficulties 'to get rid of all Britishers and replace them by incompetent Indians'.[33] RF personnel preferred a safe course. A recent piece on RF's involvement in South America criticizes the RF for not having appreciated the need for 'appropriate technology' and having overlooked local conditions.[34] In India this was not the case. They understood the local conditions and contemporary politics rather too well and consciously opted for a cautious lukewarm approach.

NOTES

1. For details see, Anil Kumar, *Medicine and The Raj*, New Delhi, 1988; Mark Harrison, *Public Health in British India*, Cambridge, 1994; David Arnold, *Colonizing the Body*, Delhi, 1993; Kabita Ray, *History of Public Health in Colonial Bengal*, Calcutta, 1998; P. Bala, *Imperialism and Medicine in Bengal*, New Delhi, 1991; R. Ramasubban, *Public Health and Medical Research in India*, SAREC Report,

Stockholm, 1982; Deepak Kumar, *Science and the Raj*, Delhi, 1995.

2. D.J. Megaw, 'Medicine and Public Health', in E. Blunt (ed.), *Social Service in India*, London, 1938, p. 186.
3. Ibid., p. 187. Megaw continued, 'If the masses of India were subservient to the orders of a dictator, he would frame the necessary plan in the fields both of production and reproduction, and compel the people to carry it out. . . .' How true!
4. Mark Harrison, pp. 166-226.
5. Home. Education, Nos. 36-7, December 1963, Pt. B. (preserved at National Archives of India).
6. Marcos Cueto, *Missionaries of Science: The Rockefeller Foundation and Latin America*, Bloomington, 1994.
7. Justice Cunningham, 'The Public Health in India', *Journal of the Society of Arts,* XXXVI, February 1888, pp. 241-65.
8. J.B. Grant, Director, AIIHPH, to DG, IMS, dt. 26.9.39; Rockefeller Archive Centre (RAC), IHB, 1.1, 464, Box 6, f. 40.
9. General Address by J.B. Grant on 6 January 1940 at the Indian Science Congress, Madras, printed in *Science and Culture*, VI, 8, 1940, pp. 480-6.
10. Indian commentators took note of the 'soft corner' RF had for China. *Science and Culture*, IV, 2, 1938, p. 100.
11. RAC, IHB, 5/2/Sp. Report, Box 49, f. 304a.
12. Ibid., 5, 464, 49, f. 303.
13. Ibid., 5/2/Sp. Report, Box 46, f. 306.
14. Ibid., 6.7, I, 6, f. 35.
15. Ibid., 5, 464, Box 49, f. 306.
16. As Dr. Megaw later noted, 'propaganda can never be successful in India unless it is administered as a sugar-coated pill—large amounts of sugar and only a little pill. Prosy talks about disease will never catch the attention of the people; music, witty dialogues, and stories must be used as ear-openers; then only will it be possible to 'put over' a few scraps of useful knowledge'. J.D. Megaw, n. 2.
17. G.O. No. 755, P.H. dt. 1 June 1992; RAC, IHB, 5/3/Rep. Box 24, Hookworm Report, 1923.
18. This section is derived from RAC, IHB, 6.7, I, Box 6, f. 35 titled 'Historical Notes'.
19. RAC, IHB, 1.1, 464, Box 6, f. 37.
20. Letter from Government of India to Under Secretary of State, 23 August 1928, RAC, IHB, 1.1., 464, Box 5, f. 32.
21. W.B. Carter to R.M. Pearce, 4.3.1928, RAC, IHB, 1.1, 5., f. 32.
22. Note by B.G. Charles, dt. 15.5.1923, India Office Library and Records L/E/7/1156.
23. RAC, R.G. 12.1, Heiser Diary, 1930-1, f. 198. See also L. Rogers to Heiser, n.d., RAC, 1.1, 464A, 6, f. 37.

24. J.B. Grant W.P. Jococks, 31, October 1939, RAC, IHB, 1.1, 464, Box 6, f. 40.
25. J.N. Sinha, 'National Planning Committee and Technology for Reconstruction', in R. Macleod and Deepak Kumar (eds.), *Technology and the Raj*, New Delhi, 1995.
26. A.V. Hill, *Report on Scientific Research in India*, London, 1944; and J. Bhore, *Report on Health*, Delhi, 1945.
27. RAC, IHB, 12.1, Grant's Diary, Box 20, 1944.
28. Ibid.
29. J.B. Grant to H.C. Balfour, 20 November 1944, RAC, IHB, 2-1944/464, Box 275, f. 1884.
30. RAC, IHB, 5/1/2, Box 171, f. 2201.
31. Megaw wrote, 'we are trying to keep communal consideration out of the picture but the tendency at the moment is very much in the direction of insisting on proportional representation of the Indian communities and of course the introduction of this policy would be fatal to the scientific departments'. J.D. Megaw to Carter, 27 July 1932, RAC, IHB, 1.11.644, Box 6, f. 37.
32. Heiser's Diary, 21 April 1931, RAC, 1.1, 464 A, Box 5, f. 36.
33. 'It does not matter to them how much institutions suffer; of course they are so blinded by intense nationalism and hatred that they can not think or act in terms of efficiency.'
    W.S. Carter to Lambert, 12 July 1934, RAC, 1.1, 464 A, Box 6, f. 38.
34. Marcos Cueto, 'Science under Adversity: Latin American Medical Research and American Private Philanthropy, 1920-1960', *Minerva*, 35, 1997, pp. 233-45.

CHAPTER 10

Forests, People and the State in India: Pre-History of Modern Resource Management Regime

SATPAL SANGWAN

The value of land is what man makes of it.

Arthashastra: 7.11.9

The last quarter of the twentieth century has seen a fundamental shift in historical research. After having the spotlight on ideas and institutions emerging from the grass-root level for nearly half a century, professional historians turned their attention to issues hitherto considered too technical to be handled by their breed. History of science and environmental history, the two emerging sub-plots, are two strings of a larger canvas which mirror the making of human ideas, their applications and resulting changes in the social and natural worlds. However, history of science and environmental history differ on a fundamental issue. While the former is primarily a success story of human genius, the latter largely deals with the negative aspects of human interaction with nature. As a result of its resolve to understand man's role and responsibility in changing the physical environment, environmental history is further burdened with controversies.

At the popular level history defines human society as a progressive march of humans from food gatherers to modern industrial producers, passing, in the process, through hunting-gathering, herding, agricultural and industrial stages.[1] This progressive ascendancy of man is closely followed by a corresponding decline of environmental ethics.[2] The moral of the story is that compared to the insatiable demands and penetrating capabilities of the modern man, our primitive ancestors were obliged to live in harmony with nature by their limited demands and ineffective extractive capabilities.

Forests, being the most visible organ of nature on the earth, act as benchmark for judging the limits of human interference with nature. Their (mis)handling by man in different locations and at different intervals of history not only idealizes basic human skills but also explains the cultural constructs of resource management strategies and moral patrimony. Forest history written with a moralizing agenda (of restoring the 'rights' of forest peoples) ends up blaming the colonial resource management practices and the increasing influence of market capital for all the woody ills.[3] A critique of the capitalist and colonial mishandling of nature ends up in a further endeavour to search for natural systems in equilibrium and a harmonious human relationship with the natural world. This has often led to romanticization of pre-capitalist and pre-colonial societies and their environment across the world as self-sustaining and in equilibrium.[4]

Colonial forest policy, however, was not created in a social or ecological vacuum. Neither was market economy the only mode of resource use with marks of a corrupting influence. There is a long pre-history of human extraction of the forests and forest resources, marginalization of the forest peoples and corresponding environmental debasement. Their cultural and technological differences notwithstanding, each human group and production system establishes a defined relationship with the forests. It may sound unreasonable or otherwise to persons with different priorities and capabilities. Therefore, concepts like sustainability and degradation, development and deforestation change over time and between different social and cultural identities.[5] A more sustained understanding would require conceptualization of the traditional mode of forest use in the given social and cultural context. Similarly a more critical reading of the colonial/capitalistic mode of forest use would require an evaluation of its contents not only in relation to existing practices but also in the light of the sustained yield model and utilitarian principles which came into place following the scientific and industrial revolutions of the eighteenth and nineteenth centuries.

Taking note of the current debate on the role of pre-colonial societies and pre-capitalist modes of production in defacing the face of the earth, this paper retraces the missing links of a long historical continuity of forest use in Indian history.

I

Human interaction with nature is shaped by various factors. Religious beliefs, cultural values, economic demands, and technological capabilities (not necessarily in this order) are at the root of man's use and misuse of nature. While some religious beliefs teach their followers to adopt self-restraint *vis-à-vis* other living and non-living species, some economic systems are less extractive than others. Being part of the nature, the primitive man, for example, did not have much effect on the eco-system.[6] It is a simple and plain truth of accumulated human experience. This unambiguous statement of man-nature relations is, however, often used by activist historians to brow-beat their political opponents. Environmental historians betraying sympathy for colonized societies of the South Asian region and the aboriginals of the Pacific Islands and the Americas often aim their guns at the extractive forces unleashed by colonialism. A general view is that pre-colonial regimes had limited capacity to extract wealth from agricultural and forested land.[7] At the same time modern day 'anti-developmentalists' are agitated against the capitalist sweep, which, they argue, has completely marginalized the traditional, simple resource use patterns.[8] Capitalist economy was, however, far from an exception. Recent studies question the 'environment friendly' image of the socialist ideology.[9] The forests in Soviet Russia, for example, were subjected to reckless clearing during the Stalinist regime, inviting the displeasure of some more serious comrades.[10]

The fact that man-nature relationship before 1492 and the industrial revolution was far from 'harmonious' is staring at our face in the form of the numerous deserted sites of old towns and villages, now represented by ruins of walls of mounds either buried in the sand of a desert or overgrown by dense jungle which indicate that the areas were once more or less densely populated.[11] There is a close interconnection between ruined cities and ruined land. Common results of deforestation around the sites of ancient civilizations, both in the Mediterranean regions and the river valley civilizations in the Indian subcontinent, are soil erosion of the hillsides and flooding, disruption of water supply and siltation of lowlands and coastlands.[12]

Foresters hobnobbing with forest history would explain that the desertion of these sites has not been due mainly to depopulation owing to invasion and extermination. The whole disappearing process was mainly brought about by the reckless, continuous and wholesale burning of forests which led to the gradual decrease in river waters, to the drying up of springs, small streams and rivers, the lowering of water-table in the soil and to a decrease in the rainfall of the country. Therefore, the war against the forests is spread over many centuries, probably 3,500 years or more.[13] In the Mediterranean region, when the peasant settlers went to look for new cultivable land in the middle of the thirteenth century they found that large amount of the original open forest of evergreen oaks and pines had already been cleared many centuries earlier by transhumance and sedentary sheep and the cloven-hoofed goat.[14] Falling in the same soil pool India could not escape similar environmental tragedies.

Professional historians now question the conventional obsession with colonialism. Such over-emphasis on a single factor, it is argued, obscures the role of regional and national variation, including the resiliency of local eco-systems, the coerciveness of the State, or the character of political culture.[15] There is a greater need to put colonialism into broader temporal, geographical, processual perspectives, and to explore contemporary environmental concerns in a wider context.[16]

A recent ruling on the subject is that all historical societies have transformed their relation with the environment. This is the very definition of their historicity.[17] The era of European imperialism was only a brief period in the history of human interaction with tropical and sub-tropical ecologies. There is a continuity of colonization of the landscape and resulting deforestation.[18]

Dissenting notes are also coming to the surface in India. Sumit Guha questions the assumption that indigenous, small communities by their nature had a sustainable and harmonious approach to environment management. Citing contrary evidence from eighteenth-century Maratha records, he questions the veracity of such 'sweeping endorsements' of little studied traditional institutions by non-historians.[19] M. Rangarajan questions if there ever was an equilibrium between all pre-colonial, pre-capitalist societies and their environment.[20] In a survey of agriculture economy of Gorakhpur in early nineteenth century, Meena Bhargava could hardly trace any remnants of an ecological equilibrium. The landholders and cultivators, she concluded, were not 'natural conservators' of their environment. For them forests were as ordinary a resource for their daily chores as any other natural resource, hence they treated it with the same amount of care and carelessness as any other human groups have dealt with. Even the small time forest users had hardly any concern for the sustainable use of forest trees. Rather some of their practices betrayed a tendency of wasteful extraction.[21] Moral of the story is that the indigenous peoples are neither helpless victims nor ecological saints.[22]

II

Recent researches in genetic palaeontology have clearly established the fact that Africa was the birth place of our ancestors and that human movements out of Africa were determined by the climate cycle and the availability of resources.[23] The first chain of humans coming to India was through the coastline about 70,000 years ago. The oldest settlers followed the ancient beachcombing route right round the coast, from India through Indo-China and up north to Japan and Korea, leaving colonies as they went.[24] Living a nomadic life of hunter-gatherers, this Upper Palaeolithic life pattern continued up to the Last Glacial Maximum (LGM), 18,000 years ago. The LGM had far-reaching effects on world population. Some believe that it caused 'a near total abandonment of the once vast Central Asian steppe formerly inhabited by Upper Palaeolithic mammoth-hunters'.[25] Next great opportunity came with the great warming episode of 13,000-11,000 BC. Warm temperatures changed the vegetation and plant foods became more abundant and the obvious key to survival. Around this time man also began cereal cultivation and domesticated goat and sheep, the two most social animals.[26] With these two sedentary practices, man became more and more dependent on natural resources like water and pasture.

Pre-historical sedentary human settlement in the Indian subcontinent is traced at Mehrgarh on the north-western edge of the Indus plains in Baluchistan *c.* 7000 BC.[27] Archaeological excavations at Mehrgarh reveal a progressive increase in food producing and storage capacity of the people as well as the expansion of the settlement.[28] While samples of food storage indicate a conscious effort to face the challenge of drought, expansion of the settlement and increased domestication of animals indicate an increase in human capacity to interfere in the world of nature. Given their technological limitations and food producing innovations, the inhabitants of Mehrgarh betray basic human tendency to innovate with the available resources, using their technological capabilities to draw bare minimum for survival, building up a mechanism for intensive resource utilization, and ultimately abandoning the site once it has exhausted its resource limit.[29]

Settlement history of the Indian subcontinent since the time of Mehrgarh has not been one of uniform progression. Parallel settlements have existed at a given historical time period, independent of each other until the beginning of the historical time. A more or less similar settlement and resource use pattern emerges from the archaeological sites in the Kaimur hills, south-east of Allahabad. People living here hunted game and collected wild rice in the eighth millennium BCE, and subsequently introduced domesticated rice and tamed animals into their diet by the fifth millennium. Presence of domesticated dogs, cattle, buffaloes, sheep, goats and pigs is also reported around sixth millennium BCE from archaeological sites in the upper Narmada Valley (present-day Hoshangabad district).[30] Farming spread to Malwa and western Deccan in the third-second millennium BCE.[31]

While the Mehrgarhians were on the verge of disintegration, a new culture was in the making further down along the Indus

River. The earliest site of the Indus Valley civilization (also known as Harappan culture) is traced at Balakot, near Karachi *c*. 4000-3500 BC. Subsequent Harappan sites betray continuity of human settlements. Spread over an area of more than 1 million sq km (though separated by time as well as the landscape) from the Indo-Baluchistan border on the north-western edge to Alamgirpur on the banks of the Hindan, near Delhi, and from the foothills of the Pir Panjal range to just short of the Ganges in the south-east, the Harappan culture was a watershed in the ecological history of India.[32]

The issue of Harappan ecology and the use of natural resources by the Harappan people is a contested yet crucial issue. The enigmatic Harappan civilization still 'wears a haunted look, where we can see the cities and the artefacts', but we know much less of environment and 'nothing of the people'. Conventional image of the Indus Valley landscape flashes a marshy environment covered by thick jungles, which would have impeded the early growth of agriculture.[33] Polynological investigations of the Indus basin suggested a more favourable climate than the present arid conditions.[34] Some studies have shown that the rainfall was particularly heavy in the period *c*. 4000-3000 BC, followed by a long drought lasting a few hundred years around 2000 BC.[35] Archaeological evidence also points to increased rainfall. The use of kiln-fired bricks, for example, implies that the climate demanded something more durable than the mud bricks universally used in the empires of the ancient east. Besides, reference to elaborate systems of paved drains and the presence of rhinoceros postulates that rainfall was more frequent as well as more considerable. That the Indus Valley was a flood prone area is also reinforced by the fact that Mohenjo-Daro is built on a brick platform. Whether the river flood was caused by large scale wood-cutting in the catchment area or heavy rainfall is a matter of conjuncture. In a further run-up climatic determinant historians have often concluded that the collapse of Mohenjo-Daro and Harappa was caused by the return of more arid conditions.[36]

Recent investigations of the climate data and extant woody remains, however, suggest that the Indus civilization flourished under essentially modern climatic conditions. Pollen recovered at Kalibangan, a Harappan city situated on the left bank of Ghaggar River, suggests the existence of riverine forests along with extensive areas of cultivation.[37] Given the state of the climate, technology and the flatness of the earth's surface, it would be safe to argue that the Harappan civilization, much like late Stone Age agriculture settlements at Mesopotamia (Iraq), Egypt, highland plains in Iran, Turkey and Palestine and some loess areas of China, had flourished in a loose alluvial soil dotted with thorny *acacia* species.[38] This is more or less true of all the Neolithic settlements (of polished stone tools) which could flourish only in forest free or lightly forested loess regions.[39] The presence of rhinoceros and other wild animals in the Indus does not confirm heavy rain for longer duration. The rhinoceros was known and hunted in the Punjab even in the sixteenth century.[40] Finally, therefore, a vegetation of scrub with bamboo and tall grass growing in pockets of marshy land, and supported by a climate with somewhat heavier rainfall for a few months in the year will satisfactorily account for the known facts.[41]

Environmental uncertainty of the Harappan civilization continues with historians falling short of a conclusive explanation for its disintegration. Conventionally, the disappearance of the Harappan people is attributed to the 'invading Aryans' who demolished the Harappan dam system, thus ruining the agriculture of the region and the cities.[42] A rigorous research would require critical assessment of climatic factors and tectonic shifts as well. Recently excavated archaeological sites in Maharashtra, for example, show a clear pattern of climatic change at the beginning of the second millennium BC. What had until that time been prosperous farming settlements with permanent houses rapidly declined into the camping places of nomadic groups. The cause was a general deterioration of the climate and the onset of drier conditions no longer suitable for growing cereals.[43] Kalibangan in north-east Rajasthan also appears to have declined primarily due to the partial capture of the Ghaggar-Hakra River's head waters by the Jamuna, following tectonic disturbances in the Himalayan foothills and northern plains.[44] Another tectonic uplift generated a dam about 90 miles down stream from Mohenjo-Daro in the area near Sehwan. This sudden change caused the normal discharge of the Indus to accumulate in a growing reservoir, which over time caused the flooding of Mohenjo-Daro.[45]

Although major climatic changes were caused by natural processes, human factor cannot be wished away. Indus Valley civilization represents the first watershed in man-and-nature relationship in general and man and forests in particular. It was spread over a huge geographical area (1.3 million sq km), larger than the influence area of ancient Egypt or Mesopotamia.[46] Although a major portion of the population was concentrated in the two magnificent cities of Mohenjo-Daro and Harappa,[47] there were around one hundred other permanent settlements belonging to the same cultural unit. The Indus economy was based on agriculture produce and livestock, supplemented by fishing and hunting.[48] Yet, people's engagement with productive activities was not uniform. In the cities, less than half of the population was part of productive workforce. The large number of non-productive workforce meant intensive use of natural resources, particularly agriculture. Such concentration would have required extensive outflow from the surrounding areas.[49] Although a passage in the *Rigveda* (X. 101-3-7) refers to a well with a stone wheel and wooden pails securely fastened with straps, and a trough,[50] technology was not really a barrier to such intensive use of agriculture resources. At a more familiar level, agriculture expansion would have involved clearing of large areas of jungle, and converting the same into cultivable fields. An equal pressure on natural resources was built up by the fodder needs. It is estimated that Mohenjo-Daro grew only about one-fourth of its fodder needs. Remaining three-quarters had to be obtained by foraging in the surrounding forests and grasslands.[51]

Increased outflow of resources from the countryside led to enormous population growth thereby making a revolutionary impact on the economy, which went far beyond the fulfilment of basic human needs.[52] While appearance of the bull in Harappan seals indicates a synthesis of a cattle-keeping tribe with one having agricultural economy, the oxen-drawn plough was a great landmark in the history of land utilization. Besides, Harappan metallurgists were also aware of the existence of iron.[53] Even if used at a localized level, the use of energy-intensive implements made possible the production of a greater quantity of food than was necessary for subsistence.[54]

Concentration of population in urban centres also entailed heavy pressure on cultivable soil and forest land of the surrounding areas. The farmers were not only feeding themselves but also a mushrooming urban population, a majority of which lived with urban luxuries. A heavy use of burnt bricks in house making confirm large-scale use of timber fuel. About five million fired bricks have been excavated from the ruins of Mohenjo-Daro. A mature *Kandi* tree provides fuel to fire about 1,000 bricks in modern kilns in Sind. It is estimated that 400 acres of gallery forest would have been felled for the building of Mohenjo-Daro at intervals of about 140 years.[55] Absence of any remains of brick-kilns in the main Indus area suggests that (i) Indus region had already exhausted its fuel timber, (ii) they were made at some distant place where some wood was still standing. Wood was also required in various aspects of human activities: in the production of commodities for exchange, as a form of energy (charcoal), for further extraction of other resources of production processes (such as wood required for mine shafts). The heating of the carnelian, copper casting and steatite glazing, for example, must have required a high volume of fuel.[56] Beside local requirements, there was a further pressure on natural resources on account of export quantities. Forest wood from Harappa was exported to other Bronze Age centres. Indian wood is reported to have been found in early Sumerian cities. An inscription indicates the importation of wood from India as early as 2000 BC.[57]

Ecological effects of an elaborate production system like that of the mature Harappan system would have been intensive as well as extensive. Removal of forest caused regular flooding. The accumulated silt thus elevated the ground level of Indus cities.[58] Part of the burden was also passed on to the areas lying outside the epicentre. The local, regional and export demands for timber, for example, would have entailed pressure on the forested areas in the foothills of the Sivaliks.[59] A similar use pattern might have settled on the copper mines of Khetri in the Aravalis and the Tosham area in Bhiwani district of Haryana. Ultimately it was the over-utilization of vegetation and mineral resources, which triggered the process of desiccation. This might have resulted in lowered productivity, decrease in surface water supply in springs, streams and wells, and diminution in underground water resources associated with a sinking water-table. Since the recovery of natural vegetation was rather slow in dry land, the immovable urban civilization of Harappa gradually began shrinking and finally disintegrated by the middle of the second millenium BC.

III

Disintegration of the Harappan civilization coincided with the colonization of land in the area south of the Satluj down to the south-eastern edge of the Gangetic plains by a different, yet more aggressive, ethnic group. Familiar with metal, horse and wheeled vehicle, the Indic speakers had travelled through Central Asia, Iran and Afghanistan under compelling environmental conditions. Radio carbon-dated tree rings and lake bed cores from South-Western Asia reveal that about 3800 BC, the solar insulation declined throughout the world, followed by weakening of the south-western monsoon. Repeated environmental shocks devastated small settlements anchored to capricious river channels and a constantly changing landscape. Archaeological surveys tell us that many people simply abandoned their villages, desperately fanning out in all possible directions.[60] Two main Aryan trails started off from Central Asia (most probably from modern Uzbekistan) in the second millennium: the first at the beginning and the second towards the end of the millennia. Their eastward movement continued as they moved on to the east of middle Indus towards the Punjab plains *c.* 1400 BC. Primarily pastoral nomads, the new migrants displaced the food-gatherers living east of the Indus basin.[61] However, land settlement pattern of the invaders was anything but permanent. The *Rigveda* (referring to events of 1500-1200 BC) says nothing of fixed settlements, let alone brick-built cities, or of reading, writing, art or architecture. On the contrary, there is a specific term, *Armah*, denoting the remnants of an abandoned *grama*.[62] Early Vedic people were a cluster of nomads shuffling across a large extent of the plains. A large population with fixed settlements was not possible without some form of food storage. Pastoral groups like the Aryans were not good at grains storing. However, as the Vedic people settled in the fertile plains, accumulation of food grains for periods of scarcity became a survival instinct. So much so that a man who stored away food sufficient to support his dependents for three years or more was entitled to drink *soma*.[63]

Vedic settlement pattern was demarcated by ecology and technology. Vedic people defined their geography in functional terms. The country lying between the two divine rivers, the Sarasvati and the Drsadvati was known as the land of the Veda. Its eastern and southern fringes were demarcated by the fields of the Kurus, the Matsyas, Pancalas, and Surasenakas. The same area was known as *Brahamarsidesha*, country of the priestly sages. The country to the east of the 'Disappearance' (*Vinashana*) of the Sarasvati, i.e. the Gujarat–Rajasthan border, up to Prayaga, was known as the *Madhyadesha*, Middle Country.[64] The use of cattle, horse-chariot and ox-carts enabled the pastoral Vedic people to move from one resource pool to another. Climatic instabilities remained a dominant cause of peoples' movement.[65] Depending on slash-and-burn for clearing the land, the early Vedic people moved eastward in a chain, a thin line along the Himalayan foothills and southern Nepal, touching south through the Champaran district of Bihar until they met the Gangetic riparian jungle. The Aryans had little difficulty in penetrating to within 50 miles of the Yamuna River. The thinner jungle here could be burnt down. Mere knowledge of metallurgy and metals would not help. Access to metal resources lying in the Gangetic basin would later enable them to colonize the heavy soil.

One critical question associated with the colonization of the plains by the Vedic people is the state of the landscape, vegetation type (of the area of their settlement) and the extent to which it was affected by their resource use patterns, technology and rituals. Repetitive occurrence of the term *jangal* or *vana*[66] in the epic literature has led to a serious misreading of the landscape. In popular imagery, fed on the Anglicized version of the Sanskrit term *jangal*[67] (denoting dry, cereal-bearing lands), *jangal* or *vana* typifies an uninhabited land area covered with large timber trees and natural grass in between. Plant geographers reject such a mythical reading of natural vegetation. Vegetation type, they argue, depends upon the quality of the soil, rainfall pattern and climatic conditions. On all the three accounts vegetation in the plains of north India was never, not in historical times at least, inclusive of evergreen large timber trees. A large part of the northern plains was, on the contrary, an expanse of unoccupied and unsettled land mass covered with thorny bushwood and tropical deciduous trees, essentially of the modern vegetation type.[68]

In the Vedic medical texts three distinct types of soil come to the notice: *jangal* (the dry lands), *anupa* (the marshy lands), and *sadharna* (the middle region).[69] *Jangal* is a flat and sparse terrain scattered with thorny trees. According to Caraka it is a land where 'trees and waters are scarce, it is swept by the winds, heat abounds, and the diseases are very few'. The opposite landscape is *anupa,* the marshy land where 'trees and waters abound, it is sheltered from winds, heat is hard to find, and it is full of troubles'.[70] Compared to the heavier impervious soils which carried great stretches of wood, the *jangal* thrived on lighter soils.[71] Salubrious and fertile, 'bursting with cereals', the loess *jangal* regions could easily be cleared by fire. Naturally, therefore, the seat of early Vedic settlements was in a somewhat drier Sarasvati-Ghaghra corridor.[72] Their movement into the Gangetic plains became possible only after iron came into their possession.

Given this broad background of the vegetation cover certain environmental mechanism backed by the troika of ecology, technology and social systems had evolved over a period of time. In the Vedic texts, for example, there is a clear demarcation of land to be occupied for human habitation and land to be left vacant, e.g. *jangal*. The *jangal* land itself was of two types, defined by the vegetation cover and its proximity to the settled area. The one near the *grama* (settled area) was available for regular chores: grazing, fodder and fuel.[73] The *jangal* also sheltered the sinners banished from the society who lived on begging.[74]

Although the colonization of the Punjab and the middle Gangetic plains by the Vedic people had a definite edge over the existing occupants in terms of material, equipment and mobility,[75] early Vedic economy and society was predominantly pastoral.

Prosperity of a clan was indicated by the size of their livestock: cows, goats, sheep, cultivable land and grain. In some cases, the size of cattle stock was as large as a thousand heads of cattle.[76] During the later Vedic times, pastoralism gave way to agriculture, which facilitated accumulation of food grains. Even then their wooden ploughshare-based cultivation allowed only marginal surplus. Their unplanned settlement patterns and technological limitations also put restrictions on the optimum use of natural resources. Shortage of iron meant the persistence of a subsistence *grama* economy.[77] The use of iron in productive activity, including agriculture, did not come until about 800 BC when rich iron deposits in south-east Bihar had been opened up.[78]

With a gradual shift in favour of semi-settled agriculture, the Vedic society also evolved into a neat division of labour and a defined use of the environment. A prayer in the *Yajurveda* (1000-800 BC) lays stress upon settled agriculture and metals. The same prayer divides land into two functional categories: ploughed and unploughed land.[79] Refinement of human relations called for State intervention in matters like land settlements and the use of non-timber forest resources. The king was desired to create settlements in dry, open country with plenty of grain for his people.[80] He could also take 'a sixth part of trees, meat, honey, medicinal herbs, spices, flowers, roots, and fruits'.[81] Access to resources was, however, controlled by community and individual privileges were conspicuous by their absence.[82] Certain occupational classes using forest produce (basket weavers, hunters, dyers, carpenter, roots-diggers, bird-catchers) are also reported in Vedic literature.[83]

Environmental implications of Vedic settlement pattern, their economic systems, social networking and rituals are not difficult to discern. Early Vedic economy and value system did not call for an intensive use of agricultural resources. Rather, the early Vedic people lived with minimum interference with nature. Elaborate farming was called a 'deadly (*pramrta*) mode of life', despised by 'good people' because the wooden plough with the iron mouth injures the earth and the creatures that live in the earth.[84]

Land clearance had little effect on trees as grassy areas were cleared first. However, it did not really minimize their impact on local environment. The predominantly herding life pattern of the Vedic people had no less lasting effects on the landscape than the agricultural economy of the Harappans.[85] In pockets under intensive cultivation pulling up of 'weeds' by the reaper[86] indicates increasing human capacity to guide vegetation cover. The Vedic people also indulged in forest cutting for non-agricultural purposes. They brought down timber from the foot-hills of Himalayas to build their ships for inland navigation.[87] As a result deforestation in the catchment area of River Yamuna caused flooding in the plains down. The fourth chief in the line of the Kurus after the battle of Mahabharata had to shift his capital due to regular flooding of the Hastinapur region.[88]

Besides, the Vedic people had left a mark on the forest, forest people and wildlife on account of their rituals, their wars with the non-Aryans, and inter-tribe infightings. As per the Vedic rituals defined in *Yajurveda* and *Brahmanas,* every beast and bird was sacrificed in the Vedic *yajna* to gain returns in the form of cattle, food and prosperity. The Vedic people, therefore, sacrificed one resource to gain the other. The accumulated result of all this was devastating in contemporary terms.[89]

Patriarchal Aryans living on cattle rearing and plough agriculture were at war against the matrilineal non-Aryans engaged in hunting and hoe-cultivation. Nature and natural resources remained the first victims of battles among the tribes. Egged on by their rule books, the Vedic people often set fire to the settlements of the dark-hued people (*asiknivisah*), who deserted their possessions without fighting.[90] The grazing forays of the Vedic clans led to a further divide between the dominant Aryans and the unassuming forest people.[91] Dispossession of the unassuming forest tribes by the Vedic people continued through the practice of establishing *ashrama* in forward areas.[92] Scramble for good pasturage often ended into pitched battles not only between the Vedic and the forest people but also between the two competing *gramas* leading to *samgrama*, literally the meeting of *gramas*.[93]

Scarcity calls for conservation. Formulations of certain restrictions could only be natural follow-up of the continuous misuse of natural resources and wildlife. *Manusmriti* ruled against eating carnivorous birds or any birds that live in villages.[94]

There were different kinds of remorse for killings birds, reptiles and animals, including wild carnivorous and non-carnivorous animals.[95] Injuring medicinal plants and cutting down green trees for firewood fall in the category of minor crimes.[96] Any one pulling up medicinal herbs grown by tillage or growing by themselves in the forest was required to follow a cow for one day, living on nothing but milk.[97] Injuring fruit trees, shrubs, vines, creepers, or flowering plants was also a criminal offence.[98] Damaging ponds could invite death penalty by drowning or by simple killing. Even if one repairs the damage he could not escape paying heavy fine.[99] The Vedic concern for the natural selection of food grains was also noteworthy as was selling of spurious seed, liable for mutilation.[100] Human concern for wildlife continued during the next few centuries as India witnessed the ascendancy of more tolerant tenets of Buddhism and Jainism.[101]

IV

Locked in the alluvial soils of the Punjab plains for about a millennia the Vedic people, like their predecessors in the Indus Valley, had reached a saturation level in terms of commodity production, land settlement and technological capacities. Further opportunities lay in areas of heavy, forested soils of the Gangetic basin. Iron ores of the modern Bihar region offered opportunities for a technological shift. Around 800 BC, the Vedic people moved into the Benares region. In next two centuries they were able to scatter a vast expanse of land up to south Bihar. The expanse was caused both by interregional demographic shifts and continuous intrusion from outside. Under such circumstances, the ecological disruption in the area of their intrusion was not uniform. It remained in a fissured form, intensive in a few pockets near centres of political authorities and sparse at other locales.[102] Shifting demography also implied the recovery of soil fertility and forest cover at the abandoned sites.

Clearing the fertile, yet heavy soil with the help of iron tools they soon developed sound production systems. As social relations became more and more defined and stringent and state formation began taking a concrete shape, human relations with nature in general and natural resources like forests in particular, outstepped the informal boundaries of a community control model.[103] Territorial expansion being the guiding principal of the Mauryan state,[104] land settlement in the newly conquered territories came under the direct control of state, resulting in large-scale land clearance in the Gangetic basin. Working on an elaborate settlement plan *Arthashastra* decreed that villages, consisting of 100-500 families each, consisting preferably of people belonging to shudra peasants, herders and traders, the three lower *varna* of the society, should be set up at the interval of 1 or 2 *krosas* (3 miles or so).[105] In addition to the political *mantra* of expansion, a greater use of iron for agriculture purposes led to large-scale settlements in the thickly forested and heavy-soil areas of the middle Ganga basin.[106]

Revenue from the cultivated land being the main source of national income,[107] cultivation of the fields was a duty towards the state and the society. Failure to cultivate farm plots led to the confiscation of the land from the assignee.[108] Intensive cultivation of land continued uninterrupted. Farmers worked on their fields unmindful even of 'two fighting armies within sight'.[109] However, new rulers did interfere in re-assignment of wasteland to their favourite clans, nobles and Brahmins, especially from the second to the seventh century AD.[110] Initially, the assignees in such cases acted as development pioneers, brought plough agriculture to replace the slash-and-burn cultivation. However, as the assignees preferred living in towns close to the seat of power, the land, in some cases, lapsed into the hands of the relaxed landlords.[111]

The expansion of agriculture was followed by a corresponding increase in the population of livestock which had a direct bearing on the local environment. Kautilya disapproved the reclamation of pasture land for agriculture saying that it (pasture land) enriches the treasury and produces animals for transport.[112] Rather, the state took a proactive role and appointed a Chief Superintendent of Pasture (*Vivitadhyaksha*), making him responsible for organizing pastures in the regions between villages by clearing land and providing watering facilities.[113] On their part, the rural people augmented their income by cattle rearing, especially the milch cattle. Herds of cows were so big that they were given away in hundreds and thousands as sacrificial fees.[114]

Enormous increase in livestock and the presence of elephants in the imperial armies meant a greater pressure on fodder reserves.[115] During next few centuries the raising of cavalry by the imperial power as well as local chieftains brought additional pressure on common lands.[116]

Post-Vedic economy also marked the consolidation of urban life pattern, at least in areas near the heart of the emerging political authority. Northern Black Polished Ware (*c.* 600-250 BC) marks the beginning of urban life and the rise of trade and commerce. The *Arthashastra* state engaged itself in large-scale commodity production, especially in metallurgy and forest-based products.[117] With an underlined philosophy of maximization of material wealth through agriculture, trade and metal work, the Mauryan state was able to turn its near subsistence economy into a surplus economy. During next few centuries, trade with the Roman cities flourished. The main export items from India included wood, iron objects, crude glass, lead, tin, red coral and steel, all drawing upon natural resources in one or the other way.[118] Flourishing trade postulates intensive use of natural resources and added impact on the environment, much to the discomfort of the learned class.[119]

The urban growth was, however, far from a uniform upward movement. Instead, it was marked by a forward and backward movement over the one and a half millennia of the historical times, recording urban growth at certain historical junctures and return of rural life pattern thereafter. In ecological terms this overlapping of the intensive and expansive use of land resources helped to restore soil fertility and vegetation. A long spell of material prosperity beginning with the Mauryan state up to the Gupta period was followed by an equally long spell of 'productive crisis', running through a couple of centuries. It was rooted in the exhaustion of soil fertility due to over-ploughing, receding water resources, increase in population and over-taxation by the state. Repeated occurrences of famines and droughts resulted in the desertion of urban and rural sites.[120] In the Puranic literature the period is known as *Kaliyuga* (The Dark Age), indicating a break in traditional mode of production.[121] In ecological terms such cyclical productive crisis helped the soil to regain its lost natural vegetation and fertility.

The assimilation of forests and forest resources, both timber and non-timber, in the overall economic system remained the dividing line between the Vedic and post-Vedic phases of Indian history. The assimilation of forests in the national economy was also due to the fact that compared to the Vedic settlements of the arid and scarcely wooded areas, land expansion at this stage was in the real timber forest of the mid-Ganga valley.[122] Forest land was further categorized on account of its functional utility: *pashuvana* (forest for the wild animals), *mrigavana* (forest for domesticated animals), *dravyavana* (economic forest), and *hastivana* (elephant forest). The Magadha state's exploitation of forests and metal resources of the country was comparable only with that of the British colonial state. Forest timber was heavily used in construction work. Reliefs at Karle, Kondane and other cave monasteries show that the many storied houses were built mostly of wood. The late Mauryan audience hall in the Kumrahar suburb of Patna, had flooring, ceiling, roof, substructure and even drains made of heavy timber. The fortifications of Patna were all of timber covered with earth. Even roads built of corduroy or trimmed logs ran for miles through Bihar as late as the seventh century AD.[123] It is perhaps for the first time that forests were assessed as a source of revenue from their non-timber resources like roots, fruits, flowers, medicinal herbs, honey, meat, and firewood.[124] At the local level, forests between villages of the same *janapada* continued to supply fuel, timber, hay, game, edible produce and grazing.[125] Besides, in the prevailing geo-political conditions, forests were also maintained as a buffer against approaching enemy and a cover to raiding parties.[126]

With forest resources emerging as a distinct source of revenue, the state began taking initiatives to reserve and develop forests, especially those featuring particular kinds of forest produce and animal species.[127] Contemporary literary texts provide an elaborate description of forest management plans which were in place during the Mauryan empire. *Arthashastra* speaks of *Kupyadaksha* (Superintendent of Forests) who was assisted by a number of forest guards. In the Jataka literature (primarily denoting the north-western regions) forest administration further emerges with a high standard of efficiency. Here the *vana-*

pacara (forest lands) were in abundance, looked after by the *vanacarakas* (the foresters). Another ancient treatise on state policy, *Shukra-Nitisara* of Shukracarya gives ample information about the forestry of the day. It says that a forest of 6 *yojanas* (48 miles) should have a good royal path (*rajmarg*). *Sumantra* (finance minister) should keep the king informed about the number of forests, villages and cities to enable him for preparing budgets and land settlements. It further informs that a Superintendent, who was an expert in plant science and had full knowledge of how to administer timely soil and water to the trees, was kept in charge of parks and forests. *Shukraniti* suggests that the dung of goat and sheep, the powders of *yava* (barley), *tila* (sesamum) and water kept together for seven nights would act as good fertilizers to the trees. There is a well laid out plan for tree-planting: the good ones should be planted at a distance of 20 cubits, the middling at a distance of 15 cubits and the ordinary ones at a distance of 10 cubits from one another.[128] One may trace the roots of modern silvicultural practices in the ancient Indian tradition of plant sciences and forestry practices.

The duty of forest guards was not much different from the duties laid out by the British colonial administration. Protecting the forests from external encroachers was what they could be employed for. People who damaged forest produce were severely fined and at times were asked to compensate for the loss.[129] In the protected forests, hunting of certain species of animals was forbidden.[130] When hunting was allowed a levy was taken on the products of the hunt.[131] Felling of trees for timber and other commercial uses was selective. 'Straight trees', Chankaya noted, 'are cut down, the crooked ones are left standing'.[132]

Another notable feature of the Mauryan tradition of forest management was restrictions on forest fires. Before the time of *Arthashastra* burning forest for land reclamation was the main feature of land settlement.[133] But once forest land became an economic sphere under the Crown, burning was restricted. *Arthashastra* clearly states that 'one who sets on fire a pasture, a field, a thrashing ground, a house, a produce forest or an elephant forest shall be burnt in fire'.[134] In the beginning the ban on forest burning was purely on economic rationale. Later, Ashoka added the dimension of non-violence to it.[135]

V

As a result of continuous shuffling of agro-pastoral communities, most of the northern plains region of India was already dotted with villages at a distance of 20 to 30 miles from each other when a new wave of intrusion began in the eleventh century AD.[136] But given the fact that the overall population of India at the turn of the tenth century was not more than 150 million[137] these villages were only small clusters of human groups scattered on a vast extant of scrub land. Besides, in the given economic and ecological cycles, the agro-pastoral communities preferred a slash-and-burn cycle of cultivation: settling at a given tract for few decades, exhausting the soil fertility through some decades of intensive farming and moving on to new land with their herds. When rains failed, they switched over to herding. Livestock provided a cushion against falling agricultural productivity. In such situations they had neither the energy nor any incentive to penetrate the heavy forested soils.

In ecological terms the coming of the Turks, Pathans and the Mughals did not make much of a difference on the landscape. In fact, initially their presence was hardly noticed by the local agro-pastoral communities who continued their chores unmindful of the political changes. The informal, unorganized process of land settlement in unoccupied shrub land continued uninterrupted throughout the medieval and early modern period. One can imagine destitute, desperate contingents of people wandering aimlessly across the landscape in search of food and fodder. Mobility was the classic response of herders and farmers to famine and climatic pressure. Babar noted in his memoirs that in 'Hindustan hamlets and villages, towns indeed, are depopulated and set-up in a moment. A group collects together, they make a tank or dig a well. They need not dig water-courses or construct dams because their crops are all rain-grown. They need not build houses or set up walls. *Khas* grass abounds, trees (are) innumerable, and straight away there is a village.'[138]

In such situations forests co-existed along with cultivated fields and pastures. In the eleventh century AD, Mahmud Ghazni found the banks of the Yamuna (near Mathura) covered with thick forests.[139] Evidence of the thirteenth and fourteenth centuries suggests that large tracts of the Gangetic plains were still under forest cover as rebellious peasants (*mawasat*) took shelter there. These territories stretched from the middle of the Doab, across the Ganges to Katehar (modern Rohilkhand) and then to Awadh and Bihar.[140] In the Delhi region, large a tracts of forest existed in the Mewat, territory, where rebellious elements took shelter.[141]

Agriculture being the mainstay of pre-British Indian economy, the medieval state pursued a policy of agricultural expansion and provided incentives to farmers for bringing new land under the plough. Taking a leaf out of *Arthashastra,* Mohammad Tughluq provided *sondhar* (*taccavi*) loans to peasants, to enable them to extend cultivation (to new areas) and for digging wells.[142] During the Mughal rule jagirdars and zamindars employed professional wood-cutters to clear jungles for new settlements.[143] A Mughal document belonging to the reign of Shahjahan clearly states that 'wood-cutters and ploughmen used to accompany his troops', so that forest may be cleared and land cultivated. *chaudhuris* (*pargana* headmen) were appointed to populate the country. There was a general order that whosoever cleared a forest and brought land under cultivation, would get the *zamindari* rights of such land. It is estimated that between 1660 and 1760, a total of 288 known tax-free grants (*madad-i-ma'ash)* in *jangal* land were given to pioneers by Mughal authorities in the Chittagong area for the purpose of clearing forests and establishing permanent agriculture settlements.[144] Elsewhere, in Maharashtra, when Shahji entrusted his desolate *jagir* of Poona to Dadaji Kandadev, the latter offered *istava* assessment (minimum revenue rates to be increased over 7 to 8 years) to the hill people of the Western Ghats to clear the *jangals* and settle down on the lands. In the eighteenth century the Peshwa government vigorously promoted the cultivation of wasteland.[145] Settlement was not always on unoccupied 'waste' lands. In some cases more enterprising human groups dislodged weaker tribes to create their own settlements. Their rationale was unambiguous: 'those who do not cultivate land have no right to stop others from doing so'.[146]

Another compulsive reason for the peasants' encroachment upon the wasteland area was the high revenue demands of the successive political dynasties and the aversion of peasants to permanent land titles.[147] Beginning with early Muslim political authority in India, *Ria'iyat-i zor talab* (peasants from whom revenue had to be collected by force) was a common entry in the revenue records. Even the method of calculating land revenue was based more on assumed rather than real yields. *Amils* measured the fields and took officially decreed yields (*wafa-ha-i-farmani*) and calculated with decreed prices (*nirkh-ha-i-farmani*).[148] In times of scarcity, peasants were unable to pay the rent. To avoid further coercion from the *amils* they would abandon their fields and move on to another piece of land at some distant place.[149]

VI

The practice of settlement-abandonment-resettlement continued well into the nineteenth century. A ruler of a handful of tribal hamlets in central India informed a visiting British official in the 1820s that his ancestor Nilakantha came from the north to Chapa and found 'much jungle here; he cut down the trees and made a settlement'. In the legend of Lingo, the Gond hero, Lingo was depicted as cutting the trees, building a city, establishing a market and introducing settled agriculture and the use of carts and axes.[150] The swiftness with which villages were settled and abandoned in India had also impressed the British officials. Writing from south India Thomas Munro noted: 'Their (natives) own labour, for two or three days, is the price of their house, which is built of mud and covered with straw or leaves. Firewood cost them nothing, and dress very little.'[151]

However, at the political level, the ascendancy of British colonial rule 'marked the beginning of a new charter of man-nature relationship in India'. Compared to earlier settlers in India, the British intruders represented different ideals, values and priorities. This difference was even sharper in terms of natural resource use patterns. A dominant view among the European scientific elite up to the end of the eighteenth century was that unattended nature produced worse forms and lapsed into degenerated state.[152] Forests and forest people were seen as last impediments in the march of civilization.[153] Agriculture reclamation, Europe's intellectuals believed, marked the chasm between the primitive and the progressive. The land of the non-agricultural people was declared *terra nullius*, available by legal and moral right to anyone who could use it.[154] 'The improvement of the ground', wrote Francis Bacon, 'is the most natural obtaining of riches, for it is our great mother's blessing, the earth's. . . .'[155] Elsewhere in Germany, Frederick the Great, announced that 'of all the arts farming is the greatest; without it there would be no businessmen, no poets and no philosophers'. He is reported to have employed Dutch hydraulic engineer van Haarlem to drain over four thousand acres of marshland in Brandenburg between 1773 and 1776. In all Frederick the Great is reputed to have reclaimed over 2,50,000 acres of land and settled 3,00,000 colonists from other parts of Germany.[156] Late eighteenth century saw a growing interest in the agricultural pursuits among European revolutionaries, philosophers and aristocrats. Contemporary engravings depict ladies of the court dressing up as milkmaids.[157]

The Europeans looking for fortunes in India viewed the Indian climate as a bigger enemy. Forests and tropicality, they argued, connoted lethargy, disease, and corruption. Hence it was viewed as inimical to progress.[158] Removal of forests, clearing the landscape and application of European knowledge would relieve the besieged culture.[159] Improvement became nostalgic—to make the landscape look like 'the old country'. It often meant settlement of an idealized yeomanry, hence clearing.[160] The clearing of the forest was initially viewed as an unmixed good by the British officials. When the issue of conservation began to be aired in official circles, R.K. Pringle, collector of Khandesh, informed the revenue commissioner that the 'destruction of the Jungle, so far from being looked as an evil, has been considered as a benefit and measures have been proposed to accelerate it'.[161] As late as 1862, L.R. Ashburner, collector of Khandesh, thought that destruction of the forests was worth some sacrifice of revenue. He suggested that Bhils be given land at a nominal rate for the next twenty years to attract them from neighbouring princely states so that 'the jungle would gradually disappear and the country become more healthy'.[162]

Riding high on 'progressive ethos' the colonists constructed terms like 'waste' to disparage the resource-use-patterns of local agriculturists. Waste was not only a category of land created for tax records (for the Revenue Department 'waste' was nothing but 'revenue waste'), it was a colonial commentary on native society. With productivity as the ordering criterion, waste was seen as a synonymous of idle, unproductive land on the one hand and the cultural inferiority and physical infirmity of Indians on the other.[163] Wasteland implied an 'inappropriate' use of human energy, thus a reflection on 'idleness, extravagance, and oriental despotism'. John Shore debunked Bengali zamindars, branding them as 'useless, idle, oppressive race, practicing every species of extortion, or countenancing it by their inactivity and ignorance'.[164] Colonial construction of 'waste' replaced the Mughal category of unmeasured and uncultivated land.

British plan in India was to extend cultivation to 'wasteland' and increase land revenue on existing estates. Although human settlement of the Indo-Gangetic region was complete by the time the British took over, a large area was still under forest cover, scrub and minor bushes. In the colonial imagery it was all waste, to be reclaimed only by good governance and human genius. Lord Cornwallis had noted that 'one third of the Company's territories (in Bengal) lay waste'.[165] Even some parts of the fertile plains in the Karnal area, the rice bowl of modern India, were also found to be unattended in 1803, with not less than fourth-fifth of it covered with useless forest. Further north-west, almost the whole of the Sirsa was an 'uncultivated prairie with few permanent villages'.[166]

Further up, M.L. Darling was confronted by 150 miles of waste tract between Jhelum and Sutlej. It was, as the settlement officer had recorded, 'some of the ugliest and dreariest countr(ies) in the world . . . , an endless waste of bush and scrub, with little sign of life beyond the uncertain foot-mark of camel, buffalo, and goat'. Similar reports came from the Jhang region which was found to be 'unrivalled in the world for its combination of the most disagreeable features'. Darling quotes a local peasant settler having found the Lyallpur area (the newly settled village named after Malcolm Lyall Darling himself, renamed as Faislabad by the present political regime in Pakistan) 'all waste but dotted with *jand* trees (a species found in extreme arid areas), snakes lifting angry heads, enormous scorpions and not a bird to be seen'.[167]

Claiming wasteland for agriculture was one thing and clearing customary forests for agriculture another. In the Gorakhpur region the colonial state pursued a policy of reclamation of wasteland, including forestland, for agriculture purposes. In 1801-2, the East India Company invoked earlier Mughal pattern of inviting proposals from the landholders for farming wastelands and grass jungles on a five year *junglebari patta* (a conditional *sanad*) at very low rate of Rs. 5 to 200 per 100 *bighas*. The Company also promised to bestow proprietary rights of wastelands on the farmers at the end of two years, subject to the improvement of the land. It was obligatory for the assignees to cultivate one-third of the assigned land at the end of five years and another one-third at the end of nine years, failing which the land would be transferred to another farmer. The Company hired the services of migrant labour from Butwal (a hill state to the north of Gorakhpur), and the *raiyat* who had fled from Awadh.[168]

During the first half of the nineteenth century, the British interests in India were dominated by a strong agriculturist lobby led by peasant sympathizers like William Sleeman and Thomas Munro and their collaborators in the revenue department.[169] Therefore, in many districts large tracts were completely cleared, the forest rooted out, and the land brought under cultivation. Where forests were left, most of the accessible timber was cut and brought away to be used as fuel and charcoal, for shipbuilding, for railway sleepers, for bridges and other buildings. We have this chilling account from the Central Provinces where railway contractors, 'went into the jungles with bags of rupees in their hands and spread them broadcast among the wild tribes with instructions to fell, fell and spare not'! The ensuing assault on forest resulted 'in every teak tree larger than a sapling being laid low and marked with the contractors' own mark'. Nothing except scrub escaped the axe. Captain Forsyth found the forest-covered hills on the blue horizon 'as an agreeable vanishing point in the landscape'.[170]

However, by the end of the nineteenth century, there was a complete reversal of land policy in favour of forest conservation.

Although climatic rhetoric played some role in legitimizing the save-the-forests call, commercial interests in the logs acted as counter-argument against the whims of the revenue department. The issue of forest conservancy was first raised during the closing years of the eighteenth century by British shipping interests (alarmed by the depletion of oak timber in England)[171] and later by a lobby of professional botanists and naturalists who linked the deteriorating environment of India with the disappearing wood land.[172] By the middle of the nineteenth century some thinkers had begun thinking deforestation as disaster rather than destiny. But until the arrival of Dietrich Brandis, a professional forester from Germany on the scene in 1855, forest management remained a peripheral issue in British resource management plans. Brandis founded the Indian Forest Department, arranged professional training for forest recruits in the forestry schools of France, and clearly laid down the principles of 'scientific' forestry in India.[173] Wading successfully through the roadblocks created by the agriculturists' lobby and rolling over the traditional rights of forest peoples, the Indian Forest Department went on to become the biggest landlord of the country. In the process it has earned the ill-repute of being an anti-people encroaching agency which has completely reversed the resource use pattern the people of India had shaped through their cumulative experience.[174]

VII

Changes in the environment are both natural and human induced. Both differ on a temporal and spatial scale. Before global climate settled to present conditions some 7,000 years ago, man's impact on environment was non-existent. Stabilization of global climatic conditions and sea levels was followed by sedentary herding and cultivation. Initially, some odd group of hundred would clear a patch of land, demarcate their living, herding and cultivating boundaries. Gradually their size would expand and so would their area of influence. A few generations of intensive exploitation of the natural resources would lead to soil exhaustion, decreasing productivity, and receding water supplies. Unable to sustain their expanding material needs, the group would leave the place, segregate itself into smaller groups and move in different directions in search of new habitat. This was the first stamp of human-induced environmental change. But man escaped the catastrophe because of mobility and abundance of natural resource elsewhere.

This game of hide-and-seek between man and the natural environment continued until the establishment of more permanent city-states. Settlements of urban life patterns exposed man to the vagaries of depleting resources. To feed the unproductive class of affluent, the cultivators had to grow more food, the herders to supply more milk and butter, and the wood-cutters had to fell more trees. All this meant a near ruin of the natural resources and the ultimate annihilation of the civilization living on the threshold of environmental catastrophes. This is the sum total of global human history.

In India, the trail of critical human impact on natural resources like water and forests begins with the establishment of first sedentary herding and cereal growing settlement some seven thousand years ago. The Indus valley people, with the highly intensive resource use practices, were first to deform the face of the landscape, ultimately ruining themselves. The coming of the Indic speaking Vedic people opened the plains of the Indo-Gangetic forested areas and in less than a millennia they penetrated deep into the eastern frontiers of the continent, clearing the standing woods and pushing or marginalizing the forest people. In economic terms, the Mauryan state and the *Arthashastra* economy brought the forests and forest products in the over-all economic game-plan. Therefore, the war against the forests is not necessarily a colonial phenomenon. In fact, most of the cultivable plains of India had already been divested of its woodland when the British established their political authority. At the same time the elaborate forest management system of the Mauryans almost pre-dated the colonial forest use model.

The British colonial rule in India, however, did mark a departure from the existing land use practices in general and forest use in particular. Riding on the wagon of progressivism, backed by a strong administrative and technological cartel, and with heavy commercial and infrastructural demands, the British stand above everyone else in the ascending pyramid of forest exploiters. But theirs was a historical reality which cannot be separated from its prehistory. More micro-level studies and a holistic approach to environmental changes under different political, economic and cultural systems are required to place the whole issue in a proper perspective.

NOTES

1. Richard T. Ely, *An Introduction to Political Economy*, New York, 1889, pp. 49-50, quoted in W. Coleman, 'Science and Symbol in the Turner Frontier Hypothesis', *American Historical Review*, 72, pp. 22-49.
2. Sing C. Chew, *World Ecological Degradation: Accumulation, Urbanisation, and Deforestation 3000* BC-AD *2000*, Altamira, 2001, p. 1.
3. M. Gadgil and R. Guha, *This Fissured Land: An Ecological History of India*, Delhi, 1992; Vandana Shiva, *Staying Alive: Women, Ecology and Survival in India*, New Delhi, 1988; R.P. Tucker, 'The Depletion of India's Forests under British Imperialism: Planters, Foresters and Peasants in Assam and Kerala', in D. Worster (ed.), *The Ends of the Earth: Perspectives on Modern Environmental History*, Cambridge, 1988.
4. Peter Coates, 'Clio's New Greenhouse', *History Today*, 46(8), August 1996, pp. 15-22.
5. Anja Nygren, 'Development Discourse and Peasant–Forest Relations: Natural Resource Utilization as Social Process', *Development and Change*, 31, 2000, pp. 11-34.
6. Victor Shelford (1933) referred to by Dan Flores in his review of Thomas Yale (ed.), *Fire, Nature Peoples and the Natural Landscape*, Washington D.C., 2002, in *Environment and History*, 9(2), 2004, pp. 313-14.
7. K. Sivaramakrishnan, *Modern Forests: Statemaking and Environmental Change in Colonial Eastern India*, New Delhi, 1999.
8. Vandana Shiva, *Violence in the Green Revolution: Third World Agriculture Ecology and Politics*, London, 1991, p. 14.
9. Dominique Moran, 'Lesniki and Leskhozy: Life and Work in Russia's Northern Forests', *Environment and History*, 10(1), 2005, p. 106; Judith Shapiro, *Mao's War on Nature*, New York, 2001.
10. Brian Bonhomme, 'A Revolution in the Forests/Forest Conservation in Soviet Russia, 1917-1925', *Environment and History*, 7(3), 2002, pp. 411-34.
11. Robert Pague Harrison, *Forests: The Shadow of Civilisation*, Chicago, 1992, p. 57.

12. D. Hughes, 'Deforestation, Erosion and Forest Management in Ancient Greece and Rome', *Journal of Forest History*, 26(2), April 1982, p. 67.
13. E. Stebbing, 'Forest Catchment Areas and Water Supplies', *Indian Forester*, April 1951, pp. 216-46.
14. Frank E. Huggett, *The Land Question and European Society*, London, 1975, p. 23.
15. John Mackenzie calls for 'deimperialisation of scapegoatting'. John M. Mackenzie, 'Editorial', *Environment and History*, 10(1), 2005, pp. 1-2.
16. Tamara Giles-Vermick, 'Beyond Colonialism', *Environment and History*, 10(1), 2005, pp. 34-6.
17. A. Touraine, *The Voice and the Eye: An Analysis of Social Movements*, tr. A. Duff, Cambridge, 1981; Libby Robin and Tom Griffiths, 'Environmental History of Australasia', *Environment and History*, 10(4), 2004, pp. 439-74.
18. John M. Mackenzie, 'Empire and the Ecological Apocalypse: The Historiography of the Imperial Environment', in Tom Griffiths and Libby Robin (eds.), *Ecology and Empire: Environmental Histories of Settler Societies*, Edinburgh, 1997, pp. 215-28.
19. S. Guha, 'Economic Rents and Natural Resources: Commons and Conflicts in Pre-modern India', in A. Agrawal and K. Shivarama-krishana (eds.), *Social Nature: Resources, Representations and Rule in India*, Delhi, 2001, pp. 132-53.
20. M. Rangarajan, 'Environmental Histories of South Asia: A Review Essay', *Environment and History*, 2(2), 1996, pp. 129-44.
21. See Meena Bhargava, 'Forests, People and State: Continuities and Changes', *Economic and Political Weekly*, 26 October 2002, pp. 4440-6.
22. J.F. Richards, *The Unending Frontiers: An Environmental History of the Early Modern World*, Berkeley, 2003.
23. Stephen Oppenheimer, *Out of Eden: The Peopling of the World*, London, 2003, pp. 345-7.
24. Along the coastline of the Indian Ocean we still find small colonies of so-called aboriginal peoples who may have descended locally from those first beachcombers. Stephen Oppenheimer, pp. 156, 243.
25. Ibid., pp. 349-50.
26. Brian Fagan, *The Long Summer: How Climate Changed Civilization*, London, 2004, pp. 86-92.
27. Discovery of granaries with charred remains of cereals (barley and wheat) dating from the sixth to seventh millennium BC at Mehrgarh indicate the existence of a somewhat regular settlement, defined by some as the 'early food producing era' *c.* 6500-5000 BC. J.M. Kenoyer,

Ancient Cities of the Indus Valley Civilization, Oxford, 1998, p. 26. Around the same time another wave of migrants moved further north-west populating the European landscape.

28. By *c.* 3900-3500 BC the size of Mehrgarh increased to 50 ha, Rajesh Kochhar, *The Vedic People: Their History and Geography*, New Delhi, 2000, pp. 60-3.
29. Mehrgarh was finally abandoned *c.* 2300 BC.
30. B.K. Thapar, *Recent Archaeological Discoveries in India*, Paris, 1985, pp. 39-41, 51.
31. Sumit Guha, *Environment and Ethnicity in India, 1200-1991*, Cambridge, 1999, p. 23.
32. B.B. Lal and S. Gupta (eds.), *Frontiers of India's Civilisation*, New Delhi, 1984, pp. 521, 523-6.
33. J.F. Jarrige and M. Lechevallier, 'The Excavations at Mehrgarh and Their Significance in the Context of the Prehistory of the Indo-Iranian Borderlands', in M. Taddes (ed.), *South Asian Archaeology*, 1977, Naples, 1979, p. 464.
34. G. Singh, 'Indus Valley Culture Seen in the Context of Postglacial Climatic and Ecological Studies in North-West India', *Archaeology and Physical Anthropology in Oceania*, 6: 2(1971), pp. 177-89; G. Singh et. al., 'The Quarternary History of Vegetation and Climate of the Rajasthan Desert, India', *Phil. Trans. of the Royal Society*, London, B, 267, (1974), pp. 467-501.
35. A.K. Singhvi and A. Kar (eds.), *Thar Desert in Rajasthan: Land, Man and Environment*, Bangalore, 1992, pp. 26-9.
36. H.T. Lambrick, *Sind: A General Introduction*, Hyderabad (Sind), 1964.
37. George Erdosy, 'Deforestation in Pre- and Protohistoric South Asia', in Richard H. Grove, Vinita Damodaran and Satpal Sangwan (eds.), *Nature and the Orient: The Environmental History of South and Southeast Asia*, New Delhi, 1998, p. 60.
38. The wooden plough-share of the Harappans could be effective on light alluvial soil than heavier impervious soil.
39. Earliest traces of agriculture emerge from areas devoid of thick forests: Mesopotamia (Iraq), Egypt, Indus Valley, highland plains in Iran, Turkey and Palestine and some loess areas of China (Yellow River Valley). William L. Thomas, Jr. (ed.), *Man's Role in Changing the Face of Earth*, Chicago, 1956, p. 416.
40. D.D. Kosambi, *An Introduction to the Study of Indian History*, 2nd edn., Bombay, 1975, p. 60.
41. K.A. Chowdhury and S.S. Ghosh, 'Plant Remains from Harappa', *Ancient India*, no. 7, 1946, New Delhi, 1951; M.B. McKean, 'The Polynology of Balakot: A Pre-Harappan and Harappan Age Site in

Las Bela, Pakistan', Ph.D. thesis, Southern Methodist University, 1983.

42. Kosambi, p. 74. Archaeological evidence and the Vedic description do not substantiate the thesis of Aryan invasion.
43. Bridget Allchin, 'Early Man and Environment in South Asia, 10,000 BC-AD 500', in *Nature and the Orient*, pp. 47-8.
44. Robert Raikes, 'Kalibangan: Death from Natural Causes', *Antiquity*, 1969.
45. Sing C. Chew, p. 35.
46. D. Agrawal and R.K. Sood, 'Ecological Factors and Harappan Civilization', in G. Possehl (ed.), *Harappan Civilization: A Contemporary Perspective*, New Delhi, 1982.
47. The Mohenjo-Daro alone was spread over 3 miles in circuit with a population density of 800 sq. ft. per person.
48. Jonathan Mark Kenoyer, 'Uncovering the Keys to the Lost Indus Cities', *Scientific American*, July 2003, pp. 66-75.
49. Kosambi, p. 62.
50. Shereen Ratnagar, 'An Aspect of Harappan Agriculture Production', *Studies in History*, 2(2), 1986, p. 146.
51. Walter A. Fairservis Jr., 'The Origin, Character and Decline of an Early Civilization', in N. Lahiri, *The Decline and Fall of the Indus Civilization*, New Delhi, 2002, pp. 251-63.
52. Population of Mohenjo-Daro and Harappa was estimated at 41,000 and 37,155 respectively around 2500 BC. Shereen Ratnagar, *Encounters: The Westerly Trade of the Harappan Civilization*, New Delhi, 1987; J. Marshall, *Mohenjo-Daro and the Indus Civilization*, London, 1931; H.T. Lambrick, *Sind: A General Introduction*, Hyderabad (Sind), 1964.
53. D.K. Chakrabarti and N. Lahiri, 'The Iron Age in India: The Beginning and Consequences', *Puratattva*, 1993-4, pp. 12-13.
54. Discovery of large granaries (some measuring 15 by 6 m), which could store many hundred metric tons of grain, indicates surplus production often achieved with the intensification of the culture-nature relations. Kosambi, p. 69.
55. R.L. Raikes and R. Dyson, 'The Prehistoric Climate of Baluchistan and the Indus Valley', *American Anthropologist*, 63, 1961, pp. 265-81.
56. Jonathan Kenoyer, 'Trade and Technology of the Indus Valley: New Insights from Harappa, Pakistan', *World Archaeology*, 29(2), 1997, pp. 262-80.
57. G.R. Tibbetts, 'Pre-Islamic Arabia and Southeast Asia', *Journal of Malayan Branch of the Royal Asiatic Society*, 29(3), 1956, pp. 182-208. Indian wood was still imported in Central Asia in the ninth century AD. A mosque in Shushtar, an ancient Persian town on the

borders of modern-day Iran and Iraq was built in the year 868 of *shisham* wood brought from India by medieval Shushtari traders. William Dalrymple, *White Mughals: Love and Betrayal in Eighteenth Century India*, New Delhi, 2002, p. 160.

58. Archaeologists have found the ground stories filled with silt. Koṣambi, pp. 62-3.
59. Two Harappan sites of Kotla Nihang Khan and Ropar on the left bank of Sutlej were the centres for the supply of forest wood to settlers lower down. Teak came from the Gir forests or from Panch Mahals, Surat and the Dangs. B.B. Lal, *The Earliest Civilization of South Asia: Rise, Maturity and Decline*, New Delhi, 1997.
60. Fagan, pp. 134-5.
61. Kosambi, p. 41.
62. Rajesh Kochhar, *The Vedic People: Their History and Geography*, New Delhi, 2000, pp. 201-2.
63. *The Laws of Manu*, tr. Wendy Doniger and Brian K. Smith, New Delhi, 1991, 11: 7 (hereafter cited as *Manusmriti*).
64. *Manusmrti*, 2: 17, 2: 19, 2: 21. The country around Kanauj was still known as Madhyadesa when it was visited by Alberuni in AD 1030. C. Sachau, *Alberuni's India*, p. 187.
65. D.A. Washbrook, 'Progress and Problems: South Asian Economic and Social History *c.* 1720-1860', *Modern Asian Studies*, 22(1), 1988, pp. 57-96.
66. In the epic literature many forests are mentioned by name: the Dvaitavana extending up to Saharanpur-Dehradun region where the Kuru clan grazed their herds; Khandava vana in the vicinity of Delhi which was cleared by the Pandavas for establishing their capital of Indraprastha; the Kurujangla in the Ghaggar River basin. The Delhi Doab was also known as *Jangal Des* (Jungle Country).
67. Francis Zimmerman, *The Jungle and the Aroma of Meats: An Ecological Theme in Hindu Medicine*, New Delhi, 1999; Mark Harrison, *Climates & Constitutions: Health, Race, Environment and British Imperialism in India 1600-1850*, New Delhi, 1999, p. 60.
68. K.A. Chaudhuri, *Ancient Agriculture and Forestry in Northern India*, Bombay, 1977.
69. In the Mediterranean literature also three land types are mentioned: *ager* (the cultivated field), *saltus* (the rough pasturage or fallow), and *silva* (the wood), all three interchangeable. Stephen J. Pyne, *Vestal Fire: An Environmental History, Told Through Fire, of Europe and Europe's Encounter with the World*, Seattle, 1997.
70. Zimmermann, *Jungle and the Aroma of Meats*, p. 39.
71. Pollen analysis has, however, revealed that even the lightest soils were not devoid of the wood. The pollen of forest trees in many localities is abruptly replaced by that of other vegetation, and the light soils are

revealed not as treeless steppes but as areas of vigorous tree growth. A. Garnett, 'The Loess Regions of Central Europe in Pre-Historic Times', *Geographical Journal*, CVI, 1945, pp. 132-43, quoted in H.C. Darby, 'The Clearing of the Woodland in Europe', in William L. Thomas, Jr. (ed.), *Man's Role in Changing the Face of Earth*, Chicago, 1956, pp. 188-9.

72. Chinese culture had originated in the Yellow River Valley, whose loess lands were not densely wooded. The more heavily wooded areas of central and southern China were only gradually opened up.
73. The Dvaitavana extending up to Saharanpur-Dehradun region, for example, was a grazing ground with huts where the Kuru clan grazed their herds.
74. *Manusmriti*, 11: 73.
75. R.S. Sharma, *Sudras in Ancient India: A Social History of the Lower Order Down to circa* AD *600*, New Delhi, 2002, pp. 332-3.
76. *Manusmriti*, 3: 6; 11: 14.
77. There were few cities worth the name up to 800 BC. Taxila was hardly more than a village before the fourth century BC. Kosambi, p. 87.
78. Ibid., 89. The *Yajurveda* (1000-800 BC) refers to plough drawn by twelve oxen. First settlement in the Benares region was also reported around this time. Ibid., p. 115.
79. Ibid., 83.
80. *Manusmriti*, 7: 69.
81. Ibid., 7: 131.
82. Certain occupational classes like *karmara* (smith), *taksan* (carpenter), and *carmamna* (the tanner) had access to specific natural resources. Sharma, p. 32
83. *Manusmriti*, 8: 260.
84. Manu advised priest and ruler to avoid farming. *Manusmriti*, 4: 5; 10: 84. A similar preference of pasture was in practice in classical Greece and Egypt. According to Cicero, when Cato, the classical agronomist, was asked what is the most profitable thing in the management of one's estate, he answered 'Good Pasturage'. What is the next best? 'Fairly good pasturage'. What is the third best? 'Bad pasturage'. What is the fourth best? 'Tilling the soil'. D. Hughes, *Pan's Travail: Environmental Problems of the Ancient Greeks and Roman*, Baltimore, 1994, p. 146.
85. From environmental point of view agriculture was found to be 'creative' while grazing was termed as 'extractive'.
86. *Manusmriti*, 7: 110.
87. There are passing references in the Rigveda to ships with a hundred oars and voyages on water three days from the nearest land. Kosambi, p. 90.
88. Ibid.

89. *Manusmriti* refers to environmental hazards like 'dust storms' (4: 115) and 'famines' (10: 105-8). The Upanishads speak of a famished Brahmin accepting soiled food from a low-caste elephant driver. Ibid., p. 104.
90. Manu advised the king to 'spoil the fodder, food, water and fuel of his besieged enemy' and also to 'break the tanks, ramparts, and ditches'. *Manusmriti*, 7:195-6.
91. There is a reference to a bloody contest between the Kurus and the *gandharvas* (forest dwellers), seemingly over access to forest territories. T. Parkhill, *The Forest Setting in Hindu Epics: Sages, Demons, Princes*, Lewiston, 1995, quoted in Romila Thapar, 'Perceiving the Forest: Early India', *Studies in History*, 17(1), 2001, pp. 1-16.
92. Thapar, 'Perceiving the Forest:', pp. 1-16.
93. The dark skinned Yadu pastoralists had driven out the more advanced and technologically superior cult belonging to Indra out of the Punjab plains. Krishna's brother Balrama then promoted settled agriculture among his tribesmen. Kosambi, pp. 88, 118.
94. *Manusmriti*, 5: 11.
95. Ibid., 11: 132-8.
96. Ibid., 11: 64-5.
97. Ibid., 11: 145.
98. Ibid., 11: 143; 8: 285.
99. Ibid., 9: 279.
100. Ibid., 9: 228.
101. *Chankayasutra* underlined that a 'ruler addicted to hunting of antelope/blackbuck loses his righteousness and wealth'. V.K. Subramanian, *Maxims of Chankaya*, New Delhi, 2000, p. 29.
102. Kosambi, p. 140.
103. The Magadha state was first of its kind in the entire history of India with an open aim to bring all cultivable wasteland under the plough and also to control the forest and metal resources of the country.
104. According to Kautilya's *Arthashastra* which broadly refers to the state of society of the fourth century BC with some interpolations relating to later period (up to AD 150), the ultimate objective of conquest is *Chakravartikshetram*, the area of operation of the King-Emperor. *The Arthashastra*, ed., tr. and introduced by L.N. Rangarajan, New Delhi, 1987 (hereafter *Arthashastra*).
105. *Markandeya Purana* defines the village as a settlement where Shudras are numerous and cultivators thrive. Quoted in N. Bandyopadhyaya, *Economic Life and Progress in Ancient India*, Calcutta, 1945, p. 329.
106. Erdosy, p. 64.
107. *Arthashastra*, 15.1.1.

108. *Apastamba Dharmasutra*, II, 11, 28, 1, in Ram Gopal, *India of Vedic Kalpasutra*, Delhi, 1959, p. 133.
109. Kosambi, p. 151.
110. *Arthashastra*, 7.16.16. Almost all extant copper plates discovered all over the country are charters which, from the fourth century onward, record land grants to Brahmins. D.D. Kosambi, p. 174.
111. In the early nineteenth century North Canara, the land still belonged to the landlord though it was endowed to a particular pagoda. The 'Sunnud' (land grant documents), clearly stating that 'the government rent of such and such estates is granted to the Brahmans'. Thomas Munro traced some 'Sunnuds' in Madras Presidency, the oldest belonging to the eighth century. Munro to Colonel Alexander Read, 16 June 1801, in P.R. Krishnaswami, *Tom Munro Saheb, Governor of Madras: A portrait with a Selection of his Letters*, Madras, 1947, pp. 158-64.
112. *Arthashastra*, 8.4, 37-40.
113. Ibid., 2.34.7.
114. According to *Katyayana Shrautasutra* (XV, 4, 430) one hundred thousand cows were given away as sacrificial fees at the Rajasuya. Quoted in Ram Gopal, p. 135.
115. The army of the Nandas, according to Greek writers, consisted of 20,000 cavalry, 200,000 infantry, 2,000 chariots, and 3,000 elephants. The Mauryan standing army was much larger. Pliny quotes the figures of 9,000 elephants, 30,000 cavalry and 600,000 infantry. Romila Thapar, *A History of India*, New Delhi, 1966, pp. I, 57, 79.
116. The Mughal imperial army moved with a large contingent of elephants, horses, camels, ponies and sheep (sometime around 20,000 to supply meat for the contingent). Such large movement of animals required a continuous supply of fodder which came from standing crops and village common lands, causing serious social and environmental crisis.
117. In fact, in *Arthashastra*'s schema of a state, mining was only next to agriculture in commodity production. *Arthashastra*, 2.12.37. Besides, *Arthashastra* laid emphasis on extensive rather than intensive use of mining thereby bringing more and more mines under state operation. *Arthashastra*, 7.12.13-16.
118. Sharma, p. 237.
119. Baudhayana disparaged urban life more on account of the environmental risks than any thing else. Even a virtuous person of subdued senses, he cautioned, cannot attain salvation by residing in a town, for his whole body is soiled and eyes and mouth filled with dust of the town. Quoted in Ram Gopal, *India of Vedic Kalpasutra*, Delhi, 1959, p. 150.
120. By AD 600 Patna was reduced to a miserable village.

121. Sharma, pp. 193, 195.
122. Rita Ghosh Ray, 'The Attitude of Kautilya to Aranya', *Environment and History*, 2(2), 1996, pp. 221-30.
123. Kosambi, p. 160.
124. *Gautama Dharmasutra*, X, 26 quoted in Ram Gopal, pp. 181-2; *Manusmriti*, 7: 131.
125. Kosambi, p. 147. One may also notice the evolution of forest-related occupational classes: *Vanakamma* (dealing with wood and tree felling), *Inglakamma* (dealing with charcoal prepared out of wood), *Kallaharaga* (wood-gatherers), *Puttaharaga* (leaf-gatherers), and *Lanaharaga* (grass-cutters). K. Krishna Murthy, 'References to Trees, Herbs and Forests in Ancient Indian Literature', *Indian Forester*, December 1965, pp. 858-61.
126. A.R. Saraswati, 'Political Maxims of the Emperor Poet, Krishnadeva Raya', *Journal of Indian History*, 4, 1926, p. 65.
127. *Mrigavana*, forested area where antelope was found in abundance, was reserved forest for royal hunt. Zimmermann, p. 183.
128. *Shukranitisara*, ll. 528-9, ch. I, 35; ll. 207-8, ch. II, 73; ll. 115, 122, ch. 4, l. 166, quoted in K. Krishna Murthy, pp. 858-61.
129. K.T. Shah, *Ancient Foundations of Economics in India*, pp. 87f. However, access to forests was allowed in the time of epidemics and natural calamity.
130. Thapar, 'Perceiving the Forest . . .', pp. 1-16.
131. *Arthashastra*, 2. 26. 1.
132. Relating the fate of straight timber with human relations Chankaya noted that 'straightforward' people always become first victims of their detractors. *Chankayarajanitisastra*, 124, quoted in V.K. Subramanian, p. 112.
133. *Satapatha Brahmana* (eighth century BC) refers to the journey of Videgha Mathava from the banks of the Sarasvati (in modern day Haryana) to north Bihar (Videha), carrying fire, burning the scrub and forests in the process. The episode symbolizes the expansion of the Brahminical culture into the eastern part of the Ganga Valley.
134. *Arthashastra*, 4. 11. 20.
135. Ashoka lists those animals that were inviolate, and some were inviolate on particular days. In the Fifth Pillar Edict (Delhi-Topra version) Ashoka states that forests must not be burnt either uselessly or in order to destroy (living beings). E. Hutznch, *Corpus Inscriptionum Indicarum*, vol. 1, 126.1.10; D.C. Sircar (tr. and ed.), *Inscriptions of Ashoka*, p. 71.
136. In Alberuni's time the area between Mathura and Ujjain was dotted with villages at 5 *farsakh* (I *farsakh* = 4 miles) and less from each other. Edward Sachau (ed.), *Alberuni's India: An Account of the Religion, Philosophy, Literature, Geography, Chronology, Astrology,*

Astronomy, Customs, Laws and Astrology of India about AD *1030*, New Delhi, 2002, p. 190.

137. Broad surveys of India's population under the Mughals (AD 1595) has placed it around 160 million, which, by the end of the eighteenth century rose to 200 million. In the year 1860 it rose to 245 million and then almost doubled during next hundred years. Morris D. Morris, 'The Population of All–India, 1800-1951', *Indian Economic and Social History Review*, 11, 1974, pp. 309-13.
138. *Babar Nama*, tr. A.S. Beveridge, London, 1921, pp. 487-8.
139. O.H.K. Spate and A.T.A. Learmonth, *India and Pakistan: A General Regional Geography*, London, 1967, p. 7.
140. Minhaj refers to several raids by the Sultans of Delhi to flush them out. Minhaj Siraj (1259) *Tabaqat-i-Nasiri*, ed. Habibi, Kabul, 1963 & 1964, Eng. tr. H.B. Raverty, Calcutta, 1873-81, pp. 11, 17-18, 26, 27-8, 29, 53, 7-58, 71-2, 77; Z. Barani (1357), *Tarkh-i Firoz Shahi*, ed. Saiyid Ahmad Khan, Calcutta, 1872, pp. 492-3, in *Cambridge Economic History of India*, I, p. 48. At the beginning of the fourteenth century tigers harassed travellers between Badaun and Delhi. *Fawa'id u'l fu'ad*, 1307-22, in *Cambridge Economic History of India*, I, p. 48.
141. It was finally divested of its forests during the reign of Balban and Firoz-Shah Tughluq. Ziauddin Barani, *Tarikh-i-Firoz Shahi*, p. 56. By the end of the sixteenth century most of this tract was under cultivation. W.H. Moreland, 'The Agricultural Statistics of Akbar's Empire', *Journal of United Provinces Historical Society*, vol. II (1), 1922.
142. Barani, *Tarkh-i Firoz Shahi*, ed. Saiyid Ahmad Khan, pp. 484, 498-9; *The Travels of Ibn Battuta* (d. 1377), tr. H.A.R. Gibb, Cambridge, 1956, pp. 88-9; Shams Siraj Afif, *Tarikh-i- Firoz Shahi*, Calcutta, 1890, pp. 91-2.
143. Satish Chandra, 'Role of Local Community, the Zamindars and the State in Providing Capital Inputs for the Improvement and Expansion of Cultivation', in Satish Chandra, *Medieval India: Society, Jagirdari Crisis and the Village*, Delhi, 1982, p. 175.
144. Richard Eaton, *The Rise of Islam and the Bengal Frontier, 1204-1760*, Delhi, 1994, pp. 228, 239.
145. Tapan Raychaudhuri and Irfan Habib (eds.), *The Cambridge Economic History of India*, vol. 1, *c. 1200-c. 1750*, New Delhi, 1984, p. 201(hereafter *CEHI*).
146. In the local chronicles of north Konkan the founder King Pratapbimba had conquered the country, then mostly a desolate forest extending for 28 *pukka kos* (70-80 miles), from Vinaji Ghodel, a raja of low birth. The enterprising raja and his people had the forest cleared. Sumit Guha, p. 154. A more or less similar enterprising settlements

was made by the Jat peasants in the Aligarh region in the middle Gangetic plains during the mid-seventeenth century. William H. Sleeman, *Rambles and Recollections of an Indian Official*, rpt., New Delhi, 2003, p. 386.

147. Thomas Munro noted in 1807 that Indian peasant 'is so far from asserting either a proprietary or possessory right that he is always ready to relinquish his land and take some other'. Munro, 1807, III, p. 510.
148. Yahya bin Ahmad Sirhindi (1434), *Tarikh-i-Mubaruk Shahi*, ed. M. Hidayat Husain, Calcutta, 1931, tr. K.K. Basu, Baroda, 1932, pp. 101-2.
149. Bernier reported that out of the seventeen villages of the *pargana* of Fatehpur two villages were completely deserted. Francois Bernier, *Travels in the Mogul Empire, 1656-68*, London, 1914, pp. 205, 226-7. Aurangzeb's *farmans* to Rasikdas Muhammad Hashim also speak of decline in cultivation and the flight of peasants from land. *CEHI*, p. 225.
150. Guha, pp. 126, 154.
151. Munro to his Father, Wamlere, 10 May 1796, in *Tom Munro Sahib*, p. 131.
152. Buffon declared that 'wild nature is hideous, and dying; it is I, I alone who can make it agreeable and living'. Marcus Hall, 'The Provincial Nature of George Perkins Marsh', *Environment and History*, 10(2), 2004, pp. 191-204.
153. Keith Thomas, *Man and the Natural World: Changing Attitudes in England, 1500-1800*, Penguin, 1987, p. 195.
154. Pyne, p. 40.
155. Francis Bacon, *The Essays*, London, 1902, p. 88.
156. Quoted in Alan Mayhew, *Rural Settlement and Farming in Germany*, London, 1973, pp. 121-2. See also Huggett, pp. 92-3.
157. Huggett, pp. 86-7.
158. Harrison, *Climate & Constitution . . .*, pp. 204-5.
159. James Ronald Martin, *Medical Topography of Calcutta*, 1837, pp. 43, 55-60.
160. Libby Robin and Tom Griffiths, 'Environmental History of Australasis', *Environment and History*, 10(4), 2004, pp. 439-74.
161. Quoted in Guha, p. 136.
162. *Annual Report on the Administration of the Bombay Presidency 1862-63*, p. 93, quoted in S. Guha, 52, 136.
163. V.K. Gidwani, 'Waste and the Permanent Settlement in Bengal', *Economic and Political Weekly*, 25 January 1992, pp. 39-42.
164. Minute by John Shore, 18 June 1789, in Fifth Report, vol. II, 40. paras 168-9.
165. W.K. Firminger (ed.), *The Fifth Report from the Select Committee of*

the House of Commons on the Affairs of the East India Company, Calcutta, 1917-18, 512.

166. See Shereen Ratnagar, 'An Aspect of Harappan Agriculture Production', *Studies in History*, vol. 2(2), 1986, p. 146.
167. M.L. Darling, *Punjab Peasant in Prosperity and Debt*, Oxford, 1947, p. 112.
168. Meena Bhargava. 'Forest, People and State: Continuities and Changes', *Economic and Political Weekly*, 26 October 2002, pp. 4440-6.
169. Thomas Munro, who opposed the early conservation measures on the western coast of India, had found the forests impeding the march of civilization. T. Munro, 'Timber Monopoly in Malabar and Canara', in A.J. Arbuthnot (ed.), *Major-General Sir Thomas Munro: Selections from his Official Minutes and Other Writings*, vol. 1, London, 1881, pp. 178-87.
170. 'Early History of Forestry in India', *Indian Forester*, xvii, 1891, pp. 101-2.
171. In 1806 Captain Watson was appointed Conservator of Forests in Malabar and Captain Johnson in the same post in Canara.
172. Richard H. Grove, *Green Imperialism: Colonial Expansion Tropical Island Edens and the Origins of Environmentalism, 1600-1860*, Delhi, 1985.
173. Satpal Sangwan, 'Making of a Popular Debate: The Indian Forester and the Emerging Agenda of State Forestry in India, 1875-1904', *Indian Economic and Social History Review,* 36(2), 1999, pp. 187-237.
174. M. Gadgil and R. Guha, *This Fissured Land: An Ecological History of India*, Delhi, 1992; Vandana Shiva, *Staying Alive: Women, Ecology and Survival in India*, New Delhi, 1988.

CHAPTER 11

'Abolish Indenture' and the Indian Nationalist Discourse in the Early Twentieth Century

RADICA MAHASE

> Sir, I rise to move:
>
> That this Council recommends to the Governor-General-in-Council that the Government of India should now take the necessary steps to prohibit the recruitment of Indian labourers under contract of indenture, whether for employment at home or in any British Colony.
>
> India is the only country, which supplies indentured labour at the present moment. Why should India be marked out for this degradation? The conscience of our people unfortunately asleep too long, is now waking up to the enormity of this question, and I have no doubt that it will not rest till it has asserted itself.

On 4 March 1912, Gopal Krishna Gokhale moved a resolution in the Imperial Legislative Council calling for the prohibition of Indian indentured labour. Only twelve years prior to this, Indian emigration in general was not given any substantial amount of attention in the discourse of the Indian nationalists and the indentureship system did not exist as a subject matter. By 1915 however, there was a cry to 'abolish indenture' which could be heard quite distinctly in the Indian nationalist discourse. This paper will attempt to raise certain questions regarding Indian emigration and the nationalist discourse. What was the structural background to the inclusion of Indian indentured labourers in the nationalist discourse? How strong was the 'abolish indenture' cry, which was raised by the Indian nationalists? What was its impact on the system of indentured labour and the emigration of Indians in general? These are some of the questions for which tentative answers will be given here.

This paper will show that the development of Indian nationalism was part of a prolonged historical process and the nature of nationalism changed over time. In its early stages a contradictory situation existed where the Indian nationalists criticized certain aspects of British imperialism but yet were collaborators with the British Imperial Government. The issue of discrimination faced by Indians in other parts of the world was a major point of contestation by Indian nationalists and Indian emigration in general came under this subject of discrimination. Later on as nationalism grew in intensity, the position of Indians in the British Empire and the equality of all Indians with British citizens became one of its principal concerns. It was felt that the status of Indians would only be boosted when India achieved independence. In the beginning the emigration factor was just a minor part of the wider objectives of the Indian national movement. However, by 1915 Indian emigration occupied a major space in the nationalist discourse and the dehumanizing aspects of the system were used to illustrate the iniquitous character of British rule.

The inclusion of the emigration issue in the Indian nationalist discourse may not have led to the actual termination of the indentureship system *per se* but was indeed instrumental in keeping a check on the system. This had important implications for the system of indentured labour as it created a scenario whereby the British Imperial Government and the Government of India were aware that Indian nationalists were monitoring the system so that they adopted protective measures regarding the system. The delegation of various commissions to investigate the conditions of the emigrants and the working of the system is one example of this. The mere fact that doubt was cast on the system was sufficient to throw a shadow over it and most important of all, the inclusion of this subject matter in the Indian nationalist discourse helped to accelerate the actual date at which the system was terminated.

I

As mentioned above Indian nationalism was part of a historical process. Throughout its period of development it showed the tendency to be anti-imperialist. But the extent to which this occurred and the manner in which this was done varied and changed according to the shifting demands of the Indian nationalists. In its initial stages, it existed as a critique of the British Imperial Government and was not so much an organized political movement against the British rulers. It was dominated by the middle class intelligentsia and was largely concentrated in the Presidencies of Bombay, Madras and Bengal until about 1914. By the 1890s, the Indian middle class which had operated as 'collaborators' with the British Imperial Government were demanding certain 'moderate' concessions from the British rulers which appeared to be more beneficial to their class rather than to Indians in general.[1] For example, in its initial stages, that is the period approximately from 1885 to 1905, the Indian National Congress (hereafter referred to as the Congress) declared its loyalty to the British crown and its demands did not extend further than the desire for a reduction in taxation and military expenditure, a need to assist Indian industries; to expand the foundation of the representative bodies and to raise the number of Indians in the privileged administrative offices.[2] At this stage nationalism developed as a reaction only to certain aspects of British rule in India—aspects which were in the interests of the higher classes, English-educated Indians rather than Indians all over India.

In the beginning of the development of nationalism, the Indian intelligentsia acknowledged that the interests of Indians differed from the interests of the British as Indians perceived themselves in relation to the British. Certain economic aspects of British rule were criticized as the basis of India's poverty and the cause of economic stagnation. Publications such as *Poverty and Un-British Rule in India* by Dadabhai Naoroji (1876) and the two volumes of *Economic History of India* by R.C. Dutt (1901 and 1903) that attempted to show the extent to which British rule was draining the resources of India, gave stimulus to this aspect of Indian nationalism.[3] By the beginning of the twentieth century, the desire for certain concessions was changed to the aspiration of self-dominion status like that in Australia, South Africa, New Zealand and Canada. Later on there were more changes, most important of which was a call for complete home-rule.

It is important to note that the development of nationalism is merely one of the ways in which imperialism and colonialism have been contested. Edward Said has noted that

> It is a historical fact that nationalism—restoration of community, assertion of identity, emergence of new cultural practices—as a mobilized political force instigated and then advanced the struggle against Western domination everywhere in the non-European world . . . (and) the first intellectual stirrings against injustice included attention to the abused rights of the oppressed classes.[4]

Eric Hobsbawm has stated with regards to India that, 'In this subcontinent of almost 300 million inhabitants, an influential bourgeoisie—both commercial, financial, industrial and professional—and an important cadre of educated officials who administered it for the British were increasingly resentful of economic exploitation, political impotence and social inferiority.'[5] While the common notion is that nationalism developed as a reaction to the repressive and exploitative policies of the colonial state, it is important to distinguish between the developments of nationalism as a political movement which challenges the colonial state, and as a cultural construct which enables the colonized people to posit their differences and autonomy.[6]

Although the main idea is that the development of nationalism came as a reaction to imperialism, this should not be interpreted as a complete non-existence of any type of nationalist sentiments in India preceding this. Partha Chatterjee has shown that prior to the stage where nationalism launched itself against the colonial state in India, there were anti-colonial feelings that attempted to create their own domain of sovereignty within the colonial state itself. Consequently the space was separated into two—one was the external material world, which was represented by Western supremacy, and the other was the inner space or the spiritual world that represented the national culture, which was to be protected and defended.[7] The fact is there was the development of sentiments in India, which was in opposition to the hegemonic power of the British Imperial Government—whether these sentiments were constructed as cultural or political is beside the point. This anti-colonial consciousness indeed developed and was expressed as both political and cultural consciousness, but this paper will deal with only the political aspects of the national movement in India.

With regards to India, the growth of nationalist sentiments was both a product of colonialism and a reaction to colonialism. The idea is that the colonial rulers were the ones who introduced an English system of education that was perpetuated by both English and Indians. The proliferation of English-medium educational institutions in Calcutta and Bombay are a good example of this. This system of scientific education brought ideas of liberalism and rationalism; notions of self-government; ideas of freedom of speech; the proliferation of the press and social reforms, and these in turn gave rise to Indian nationalism. According to Bipin Chandra,

> During the decades immediately following the Revolt of 1857, there was general belief among the educated Indians—the rising leaders of the growing nationalism—that British rule in India was productive of considerable benefits to its people. But with the lapse of time and as a result of increasing political activity and consciousness doubts began to arise about the value and material content of such benefits, though the positive aspects of the legal, constitutional and other non-material consequences of British impact were recognized and acknowledged by a section of the Indian national leadership.[8]

Another historian has noted that the central idea regarding the Indian national movement is that of 'an English-educated "middle class" reared by British rule, engaging in various renaissance activities, and eventually turning against their masters and so giving birth to modern nationalism—out of frustrated selfish ambitions, ideas of patriotism and democracy derived from western culture, or natural revulsion against foreign rule'.[9]

Thus, one can see that while Indian nationalism was mainly engaged in a process of contestation, its form and expression changed over time to incorporate new ideas and develop new ideologies. The changing nature of Indian nationalism is especially visible with respect to the situation of Indian emigration and specifically the Indian indentured labourers and the way in which Indian emigration was adopted and included in the Indian nationalist discourse.

II

When analysing Indian emigration and the Indian indentureship system it is possible to distinguish three phases in the manner in which these issues were incorporated into the Indian nationalist discourse. While the concerns and issues of these phases often overlapped, there were some distinctions in the way in which the Indian nationalists adopted Indian emigration and the indentureship system. Till about the end of the nineteenth century the development of Indian nationalist sentiments had not yet evolved to a stage of mass mobilization or agitation against Indian emigration. In fact, Indian emigration generally did not occupy any place of importance in the Indian nationalist discourse and the Indian indentureship system was referred to only sparingly.

The main references made to Indians abroad were related to Indians in South Africa. This was due mainly to the work of Mohandas Karamchand Gandhi in South Africa. Gandhi was concerned about Indians who were discriminated there on the basis of race. Gandhi himself had been a victim of racial discrimination in South Africa and had already begun his agitation for changes in the system, as it existed there. However, Gandhi started off his campaign against the indentureship system as a liberal rather than as a nationalist. His campaigning was centered on the fight against discrimination rather than on any political aspiration at this point in time. In fact by 1900, while Gandhi was agitating for an improvement in the political status of Indians in South Africa, Gandhi's concepts were now taking shape and these were closely related to the issues dealt with by the nationalists in India.

In South Africa, Gandhi's work gave special attention to the inequality that Indians were faced with in the Transvaal and the Orange Free State. His protests were focused on the laws, which prevented Indians from obtaining employment other than in the menial tasks, and the poll tax of £3 for entry into Transvaal. Gandhi sought the aid of the Congress in bringing the indentured labour problem to the notice of the Government of India and even when he attempted to do this initially he was only permitted a limited time to speak about it.[10]

The topic of the Indian indentured labourers in the British West Indies in particular was not included in any substantial way in the Indian nationalist discourse at this point in time. In 1890, Indian emigration to foreign territories in general was the topic of a lecture delivered by Mahadev Govind Ranade at an industrial conference in Poona. According to Hugh Tinker, Ranade said that, 'the modernization of India could not yet be achieved by the expansion of trade and industry—which he saw as the long term solution; instead, inland and overland emigration . . . can alone afford the sorely needed present relief'.[11] In 1892, Ranade again mentioned Indian emigration when he presented a paper entitled 'Indian Foreign Emigration' at another industrial conference in Poona. In this presentation he gave, 'A Summary of the History and Progress of Indian Foreign Emigration' and noted the, 'practical utility of this great movement and its close relations to the social, economic and political development of the country'.[12] Ranade also noted that, 'the rise in numbers of population could not only be solved, for the time being, by migration to the thinly populated parts of India and overseas; though industrialization was the eventual alternative'.[13]

Ranade's views suggest that Indian emigration was probably not considered a topic of discussion, as Indian nationalists did not see the negative aspects of the system at this time. It was in fact seen as one way of alleviating the problems associated with an increasing population, namely the pressure for land space and employment opportunities. In addition to this, the indentureship system was seen as another form of contract labour and hence as a system with measures in place to protect the Indian immigrants. At this stage the stipulations of the contract itself were not questioned and the dehumanizing conditions of this system were not emphasized. This was probably due to the general lack of information on the system and on the conditions of the immigrants in the British West Indies. The emigration of Indians to South Africa occupies much space in the Indian nationalist discourse because of the work of Gandhi in South Africa who was mainly responsible for communicating to India and to Gokhale and Naoroji in particular, about the conditions of Indians there.[14]

The direct reference to Indians in the British West Indies was not evident in the Indian nationalist discourse possibly because of the distance factor as well. The remote distance of the colonies from India meant that it took a longer time for information to be disseminated from the West Indies to India and vice versa than from closer settlements. For this reason perhaps the relationship between India and the British West Indies was not as strong as that between India and South Africa, for example. This meant that many Indian nationalists simply were unacquainted with the circumstances of Indian immigrants in the West Indies.

Also, up to 1900 only two major reports on emigration had been completed. John Geoghegan conducted an investigation in 1873, which was recorded as a 'Note on Emigration from India'. The second was by Major D.W.D. Comins in 1893.[15] These reports painted a favourable picture of emigration in general. Comins' report was one of the first to deal with indentured labourers in the British West Indies specifically and it reassured the Government of India that the Indian immigrants were generally doing well in the colonies and that cases of neglect and ill treatment were the exceptions and not so much the norm. From the inception of the system of indentured labour, the local governments of Madras and Bengal—the ports from where the emigrants departed—kept annual reports on the emigration of Indians. However, these also painted a positive picture of the system. Given the framework in which the system was introduced, that is as a replacement to African slave labour which had existed up to 1834 and the fact that the Anti-Slavery and Aborigines Protection Society and other humanitarian groups in Britain were closely monitoring the system,[16] it should come as no surprise that the British officials in charge of the system emphasized more the positive aspects of the system. Hence, on the one hand not much information on the Indians in the British West Indies was available and on the other hand, those records that were in fact kept were written to reflect the affirmative aspects of indentureship and to assist in justifying the introduction and perpetuation of the scheme. Perhaps this was one reason why the Indian nationalists did not pay any particular attention to these emigrants.

It could also have been that the Indian immigrants in the

West Indian colonies were just a small minority in relation to the total population of India and hence may have been seen as insignificant. For example, from 1842 to 1870, while approximately 3,51,400 Indians immigrated to Mauritius only about 42,500 were indentured labourers in Trinidad, 79,000 in British Guiana and 15,000 in Jamaica.[17] In 1906 while Natal and Fiji had a total of 1,46,000 persons of Indian nationality residing there and Mauritius had about 2,64,000 there were only approximately 1,03,000 persons of Indian nationality in Trinidad, 1,27,000 in British Guiana and 13,000 in Jamaica.[18]

It may have also been that the Indian nationalists belonged to the privileged strata of the Indian social order and were more concerned with obtaining certain concessions that were beneficial only to the Western educated, middle classes at this time. The Indian immigrants in the British West Indies were simply not needed in this effort and thus, there may have been no motive to include them in the struggle against British rule. Indeed, later on Indian nationalists were criticized for not recognizing the importance of the problems of Indian emigration because 'educated men have not turned their thoughts to it or they are unwilling to extend their sympathy to the Emigrants who till now belonged to a class, by no means rich or educated, but who still form the major portion of the Emigrant population'.[19]

In the first decade of the twentieth century one can see the topic of overseas Indians creeping into the nationalist discourse. The period 1900 to 1910 can be referred to as the 'formative phase' for Indian emigration in the Indian nationalist discourse. It was at this stage that emigration entered the Indian nationalist discourse in a more distinct manner and the Indian indentureship system became a point of interest. The racial discrimination of Indians in South Africa continued to dominate the nationalist discourse and when Indians in other colonies were admitted to the discourse, this was done in comparison to the situation of the Indians in South Africa. Hence, one can see where the circumstances of Indians in other areas were assessed or analysed with reference to the situation in South Africa. A good example of this is seen in 1904 when reference was made to the British Guiana Ordinance. This ordinance was seen as comparatively better than an ordinance enforced in Natal regarding Asiatics, specifically the Chinese. It was noted that, 'the British Guiana Ordinance does not deprive the indentured man of the use of his intelligence. It does not insist upon the indentured labourer leaving the country on the termination of his indenture, nor does it reduce the immigrant merely to the status of an unskilled labourer by prohibiting him from doing anything else, or by prohibiting others from making use of him as anything else than an unskilled labourer'. It was also noted that, 'the labourer in British Guiana is free to settle in the country after the termination of his indenture and work as an independent man'.[20] These statements also reinforce the idea mentioned above, that Indian emigration and the indentureship system in the British West Indies was seen as something positive or that sufficient information to question the system was not available.

It is important to note that Indian emigration and indentureship system was assessed and mentioned as one small entity in the political aspirations of the Indian nationalists. In this phase the concept of *swaraj* was one of the subjects of the Indian nationalists. *Swaraj* at this time represented a movement towards self-governing status within the British Empire. Indian nationalists were agitating for the same rights and privileges of British citizens on the basis that Indians were British subjects and therefore should not be discriminated against in any part of the British Empire. Thus, the subject of racial discrimination of Indians was expanded to incorporate Indians in other territories, namely Canada and Australia. By the end of the decade it extended to include Indians who had emigrated to other parts of the British Empire, as information was now available regarding the conditions of Indians there. The Sanderson Committee presented the information in 1909 in the form of a report. This committee had been appointed to consider the general question of emigration from India to the Crown Colonies, the particular colonies in which Indian immigration may be usefully encouraged and the general advantages to be reaped by India itself and by each particular colony.[21] The report noted that in Trinidad, Ceylon, British Guiana, Jamaica and Seychelles, the system was working to the advantage of the Indians and the respective colony. It did not recommend the re-introduction of the system to the Windward Islands where emigration had been stopped. It questioned whether or not the system should be ended in the Straits Settlement and the Federated Malay States. The report did not recommend of the continuation of the system in Mauritius. It further noted that it was necessary to make changes in the system for it to operate to the benefit of all in Uganda, British East Africa and Fiji. However, this committee gave its blessings to the system of Indian indentured labour and to emigration in general. As the committee comprised mainly retired bureaucrats, this should not appear as a surprise. In fact, the delegate selected by and representing the Government of India, S.H. Fremantle, himself advocated for the continuance of the system and defended the system of indenture on the basis that immigrants were able to earn much more in these colonies than was possible in India.[22]

In the first place, as the report of the Sanderson Committee provided information regarding the situation of Indians in far off places like the British West Indies, the Indian nationalists were now more aware of these Indians than they were in the decade prior to this. Secondly, by this time the India Office was conscious of the fact that Indian nationalists and other groups were monitoring the conditions of Indians abroad (probably because of the work of Gandhi in South Africa) and hence the intention was to publish this report to 'allay the rising opposition to oversea emigration which is beginning to manifest itself in India . . .'.[23]

By the end of this phase, one can also see the emigration of Indians becoming a topic at public meetings presided over by Indian nationalists, such as the one that was held under the auspices of Annie Besant in Benares in 1910 where a resolution was passed protesting the treatment of Indians in South Africa.[24] Hence one can see that the topic of Indian emigration, though still largely restricted to Indians in South Africa, was not only included in the nationalist discourse but was now occupying a greater space in the public sphere.

The years 1911 to 1915 can be referred to as the 'definitive phase' of anti-emigration agitation as well as the inclusion of Indian emigration in the nationalist discourse. It was during this phase that Indian emigration and the Indian indentureship system was clearly defined in the Indian nationalist discourse. This occurred in a variety of ways and for a number of reasons. Firstly, it was at this stage that the demand for *swaraj* was fully consolidated and its advocacy reinforced. Most clearly discernible was the notion that patriotism went contrary to empire and that Indians could not be patriotic to the British Empire when they were regarded as inferior. This was a drastic change from the attitude that existed prior to 1900 when the 'collaborators' were patriotic to the British Empire. One author noted in 1914 that '. . . patriotism and empire were two inconsistent terms; that Empire carried with it the idea of subject peoples and that subject peoples could never be "patriotic" towards an Empire which meant to them only political subordination'.[25]

At the same time the Indian nationalists were evaluating the position of India in relation to the self-governing dominions and the status of India itself as a Crown Colony. There was a conspicuous distinction between a colony and a self-governing dominion. Whereas the dominions were permitted to implement regulations and laws in their interest, it was felt that policies in India were solely geared towards the interests of the British Imperial Government at the expense of the Indian people. Also, it was felt that India was contributing most to the British Empire and yet, was treated as secondary and inferior when compared to the self-governing dominions. India was not receiving the same, 'claims and rights of the self-governing Dominions' although. 'India has been contributing to the wealth of the British Empire and to the United Kingdom before and far much more than these dominions'.[26]

Indian nationalists also had problems dealing with what they perceived as the inability of Indians to travel freely within the British Empire. It was felt that Indians were discriminated against on the basis of colour, as mentioned previously with respect to Gandhi in South Africa. The protests of the nationalists now continued to extend outside of the South African context but with a more calculated view to situate India within the British Empire and not just deal with concerns about racial discrimination. The fact that Indian nationalists took up the issue of the Canadian Immigration Law is a good case in point.[27] Many nationalists protested against the Canadian Immigration Law that was found to be not only discriminatory against Indians but that Indians should be allowed to emigrate freely to any other territories, self-dominions or others. One such response was by Besant who noted that 'complete freedom of movement between the habitants of all countries is desirable. In a civilized world all persons, who are healthy and who are not criminals or paupers, should have complete freedom of movement and of settling. Still more should this be the case within an Empire.'[28]

Inadvertently Indians abroad were drawn into this discourse, not just those who emigrated as free labourers but also those who went under the indentureship system. In the first place the freedom of Indians to emigrate was a major point of discussion and in the second instance it was felt that *swaraj* was the only solution to the kind of discrimination that Indians were faced with. If India were given self-governing status, it would be able to promote its own interests. In the case of emigration of Indians, there was the rising conviction that 'unless they secured Self-Government on a much more national basis in India, the emigration problems would never be solved satisfactorily'.[29] Also, the fact that India occupied a subordinate status in the British Empire was reflected in the category given to Indian emigrants abroad, free or indentured. This was seen by the mere fact that all Indians were referred to as *coolies*. Besant, noted that,

> India, the granary of the world, is unable to maintain her surplus population and thousands of her children like her raw materials, are sent away to other countries for employment for the bare necessaries of life. The immigrants, so absolutely necessary for the development of the resources of South Africa, Australia and Canada, are treated there as helots and India is regarded to-day throughout the civilized world as the recruiting ground for coolies necessary for manual labour. I do not hesitate to denounce this degrading system as the last relic of slavery within the British Empire.[30]

In a resolution moved in the Imperial Legislative Council, Gokhale too noted that one of his objections to the system of indentured labour was that; 'it is degrading to the people of India from a national point of view. . . . Wherever the system exists, there the Indians are only known as coolies, no matter what their position may be.'[31] Hence, with notions of *swaraj* on the rise, Indian nationalists were now uneasy about the status of

Indians all over the British Empire and Indian emigration was included in their discourse as a matter of concern. By the end of 1914, the Congress reiterated the point that emigration was detrimental to the self-respect of Indians in the colonies and to India as a whole. It passed a resolution which advocated for 'its abolition as early as possible, the system being a form of slavery which socially and politically, debases the labourers and is seriously detrimental to the economic and moral interest of the country'.[32]

During the period from about 1910 to 1915 the emigration of Indians overseas, particularly to far off colonies like the British West Indies, entered the Indian nationalist discourse very clearly as an attack on British imperialist policies. That is, emphasis was placed on Indian emigration and specifically the indentureship system as indicative of the negative aspects of British rule in India. It was during this period that Gokhale raised the question of Indian emigration in the Imperial Legislative Council[33] and that a call was made to prohibit the emigration of Indian indentured labour—again by Gokhale in the Imperial Legislative Council.[34] A number of points can be used to illustrate this quite clearly.

Firstly, some amount of attention was given to the economic aspect of emigration. It was felt that economically the system of indentured labour was fully geared towards the promotion of British imperialist interests at the expense of India. Nationalists saw Indian labour on British West Indian plantations as necessary in maintaining low wages since it provided competition for the labour of the free African population. Hence, by permitting the system of indentured labour to continue, the Indians were also condoning British imperialism. However, it was impossible to overlook the imperialist actions of the British Imperial Government on the one hand, and on the other hand demand self-rule. At the same time India needed to maintain its labour supply if it was to progress in agriculture and industries. As early as 1905, the India and Ceylon Chambers of Commerce had held a conference at which they passed a resolution asking for a government committee to investigate the inadequacy of labour for organized industries and noted that the difficulty had become more acute every year. This conference and the subsequent resolution that had been ignored then, was now brought into the nationalist discussion and used as 'proof' that there was an increasing labour problem in India.[35] It was at this point that 'economic nationalists' added fuel to the debate and the structural basis of emigration was emphasized, that is British rule was the main cause of the intensification of poverty in India and the impoverished population may have sought emigration as an option in order to survive.[36]

Secondly, the dehumanizing aspects of indentured labour now occupied much more space in the Indian nationalist discourse than previously and free labour to Ceylon and the Malaya states was condemned because of the bad conditions of the labourers there. By this time the Indian nationalists were provided with information by the reports completed (as mentioned earlier) about Indians abroad. In 1913, yet another investigation was conducted by James McNeill and Lala Chimmanlal. It was published as the 'Report to the Government of India on the Conditions of the Indian Immigrants in four British Colonies and Surinam'.[37] McNeill himself was inexperienced regarding the issue of emigration and only qualified for the task in terms of his senior position. Chimmanlal on the other hand was specially chosen by the Government of India as the 'Indian delegate' to accompany McNeill, as he was the manager of some tea plantations in the north-east and therefore had some idea of conditions and terms of labour on plantations.[38] Their report outlined quite clearly the situation of Indians—indentured and free in Trinidad, British Guiana, Jamaica and Fiji as well as the Dutch territory of Surinam and like those before, generally gave a favourable impression of the indentureship system in these colonies.

What is important to note though, is that the general conclusions of the reports were de-emphasized and the negative aspects of the system were used by nationalists as further evidence of the inability of the British Imperial Government to take care of its subjects properly. In the first instance, the report itself was withheld from the Indian public for a short while and the nationalists thought this was done as the report contained evidence detrimental to the continuance of the system. This resulted in continued criticism of the system. In the second instance, by this time both arms of government—British Imperial and Indian, acknowledged the increase of nationalist agitation against the indentureship system and were attempting to dispel some of the apprehensions associated with the system. The fact that there was more interaction with Indian emigrants also worked against the British Imperial and Indian Government. By 1915 some Indian emigrants had been repatriated to India, some nationalists had visited South Africa, Fiji, Mauritius and other colonies and generally direct interaction between India and the colonies had opened up a great deal. Hence, information was disseminated much faster from colonies to India and within India itself, especially with the rise of the press.

Thirdly, it was at this point of time that the status and position of female Indian emigrants also entered the Indian nationalist discourse. The circumstances of those Indian women who emigrated under the indentureship system were projected as one of the most negative facets of British imperialism and propagated by nationalists to the extent that it dominated the press and public forums. Cases of sexual abuse and female abduction were projected as the norm more than as exceptions. The Indian woman, more so the female indentured emigrant, was seen as the 'Mother' and the struggle against British rule was equated to that of the worship of the 'Motherland'. The case of Kunti, a female indentured labourer in Fiji who was accosted by an overseer and punished for not responding to his advances, received widespread coverage. In 1913, Kunti herself, along with her husband, was present at a public meeting in Calcutta, presided over by Baba Bupendra Nath Basu.[39] Nationalists conveniently used Kunti's case and the case of all female indentured labourers in order to emphasize the inability of the British government and the Government of India to protect Indian women.

Interestingly, not only the British Imperial Government was under attack by Indian nationalists at this point of time but also the Government of India. It was attacked for the neutral stance that it had adopted at the commencement of the Indian indentureship system and then for its lack of protection offered to Indians abroad. Indian nationalists also called for the Government of India to adopt a more pro-active attitude towards the system of indentured labour. The nationalists also gained some encouragement and the anti-agitation movement was further stimulated when Lord Hardinge expressed his sympathy towards the Indian emigrants and promised that the system will be abolished as soon as a scheme of free migration was developed to replace it.

The years 1915 to 1917 can be seen as the 'phase of consolidation' of the indentureship issue into the nationalist discourse. Indeed, Indian emigration was given precedence in the nationalist discourse. Anti-emigration agitation itself had gained momentum and specifically the issue of Indian indentured labour occupied a central place in the nationalist agenda. According to one writer in 1916, 'a subject which was once considered worthy of discussion only at the Annual Session of the Indian National Congress now finds a prominent place in the Provincial and District Conferences and even at Public Meetings'.[40] Karen Ray also noted that by March 1917 'almost every group had rallied around the anti-indenture banner: Muslims and Hindus, Brahmins and non-Brahmins, Bishops and Theosophists, Swarajists and Moderates, "the best" and the not-so-good Indians, Marwaris and villagers. Each group for whatever reason wanted indenture to end: most groups were eager to take the credit for ending it. The situation was critical.'[41]

By 1915 there was a general feeling that it was time for the indentured system to be abolished. Emigration had stopped during the inter-war years for practical purposes, that is, the unavailability of ships to transport Indians and the danger involved in travelling, especially as far as the British West Indies. Whereas previously the steamers of Nourse and Company were mainly used, now they were not available due to engagement in the war.[42] At one point, the debate even included whether or not recruitment of Indians for the colonies was not actually affecting recruitment of Indians for the war effort. The Indian nationalists had hoped that emigration would not be re-started but in 1915 emigration was re-commenced to British Guiana as the Panama Canal was opened and ships were able to use that route rather than the Cape of Good Hope. This showed that the emigration issue was still alive and brought a fresh spirit of agitation.[43]

The nationalist discourse continued to emphasize the dehumanizing conditions of Indian indentured labourers as the negative aspects of British rule in India. The idea that continued to prevail was that British rule was the cause of Indians emigrating from India in the first place and for the duration of the period of indentureship, British rule was unable to keep the Indians in suitable conditions. Therefore, British rule was detrimental to the Indians and to India, and the moment had come when the system of emigration as well as British rule should be eradicated. By 1915 the emphasis was on the punishments Indians received while in the colonies and the need to include a clause in the terms of conditions of the Emigration Act, so that it would become mandatory for Indian emigrants to be informed about the penalties they would incur for breach of contract while in the colonies. The condition of women continued to be used by the nationalists in their attempts to end the system. In this year Reverend Charles Freer Andrews and William Pearson visited Fiji and conducted an enquiry there as well. They showed especially how the male-female sex ratio forced Indian women into a situation similar to that of legalized prostitution. This brought a fresh spate of agitation.

One of the major differences in the nationalist discourse at this time was that from a demand of the abolition of indentured labour, it now changed to demanding an *immediate* end to the indentureship system. In 1916 a motion for the abolition of the system of Indian indentured labour was delivered by Madan Mohan Malaviya and was accepted by Lord Hardinge. It was felt that it was a matter of time before the system was ended legally and that the British Imperial Government and the Government of India were unnecessarily prolonging that moment. Hence, both arms of government came under considerable criticism from the Indian nationalists. In 1917 an Inter-Departmental Conference on Emigration was held in London to consider proposals for a new assisted system of emigration to British Guiana, Trinidad, Jamaica and Fiji.[44] In the first place, the Government of India was again criticized for its choice of representatives, as neither Gandhi nor Andrews were included in the delegation when they were the ones most familiar with the issue of Indian emigration. Secondly, the new scheme, which was proposed—'A scheme of Aided Colonization for Indians in British Guiana, Trinidad, Jamaica and Fiji'—was seen by Indian nationalists as another system of coercion with the tendency to be abused. It was felt that the system demonstrated too closely, the imperialist nature of British rule.[45]

In 1917 N.E. Majoribanks and Ahmad Tambi Marakkaya were delegated to Ceylon and Malaya to study the methods of recruiting and the conditions of Indians there. Their report entitled 'Report on Indian Labour Emigration to Ceylon and Malaya' did not pronounce any judgement on the system but provided additional information for the Indian nationalists to use in their agitation. It was during this period that the Congress progressively intensified its stance against the emigration of Indians. At the thirtieth session of the Indian National Congress in 1915, it re-affirmed a resolution passed at the previous session and urged for the abolition of indentured labour as soon as possible.[46] In 1916, it urged that Indian emigration should be *immediately* stopped and that recruitment of such a form of labour be prohibited during the ensuing years.[47] By 1917 the Congress noted that, 'nothing short of complete abolition of indentured labour, whether described as such or otherwise, can effectively meet the evils which have been admitted by all concerned to have done irreparable harm to the labourers'.[48] In 1917 Gandhi threatened to call for a *satyagraha* if the indentured emigration system was not abolished by the end of March of that year.[49] The years 1915 to 1917 were not only the years when the emigration issue dominated the Indian nationalists' discourse but they were also the last two years of the indentureship system itself—recruitment of persons for labour under the system was abolished on 20 March 1917.

III

While ultimately the decision to abolish the indentureship system rested in the hands of the British Imperial Government it must be noted that both arms of the government—British Imperial and Indian—were forced to recognize the agitation of the Indian nationalists and to implement certain policies although these were geared towards appeasing public opinion rather than making structural changes in the system *per se*. As early as 1911 the Government of India noted that,

> There is one matter to which we think that attention should be called, viz., the change that is coming over public opinion in this country in connection with indentured emigration in general. There is no doubt that this feeling has gathered much strength in recent years and expression has been forcibly given to it in both the press and at public meetings. . . . The fact remains that a not inconsiderable portion of Indian opinion is more and more coming to believe that the system is objectionable and should be discontinued.[50]

With this in mind, the Government of India therefore suggested that the report of the Sanderson Committee should be published as it, 'may do something towards preventing the agitation from coming to a head'. It also suggested that colonies which imported Indian indentured labourers should be informed of this agitation so that measures could be implemented to alleviate the conditions of the Indian labourers there. With respect to these colonies it noted that,

> If their indentured labourers have grievances which remain unredressed, capital is certain to be made out of the fact, the Government of India will be appealed to, and the continuance of the indentureship system will be seriously threatened. In view of the existence of the feeling to which we have referred, it behooves the Colonies, if they value the continuance of imported Indian labour, to take prompt action on the recommendations which have been made by the committee. . . .[51]

The British Imperial Government supported the proposal of the Sanderson Committee that Indian officials should be delegated to the colonies at periodic intervals to report on the conditions of Indians there. The Colonial Office emphasized the fact that it could not see any 'objection from the Colonial standpoint, to the proposal that officers in the service of the Indian Government should pay periodical visits of inspection to the Colonies' and that, 'these visits will not be found to provoke opposition to the policy of encouraging emigration'.[52] The Government of India on the other hand did not think that, 'there is a case for sending inspecting officers at the expense of the Indian taxpayer except when special circumstances arise' and grudgingly submitted that although 'a charge on the Indian taxpayer may enhance the rising opposition to Indian emigration' it will, '. . . risk that and readily fall in with quinquennial visits or any other arrangement that the India Office may decide on' as the India Office, 'however favour systematic visits . . . and think such a scheme may help to forestall criticism'.[53]

Interestingly, the Government of India acknowledged that agitation by Indian nationalists was important in emphasizing the conditions of Indians abroad and therefore kept the Government of India abreast of what was happening regarding these Indians.[54] The Government of India was also forced to adopt a more proactive attitude towards emigration in general and the indentured labourers in particular because of the rising agitation by Indian nationalists. It noted that, 'the agitation has been steadily growing for many years past and has now attained to the status of a national movement in the face of which the Government of India are finding it increasingly difficult to maintain their avowed attitude of neutrality'.[55]

While it may be true to say that Indian emigration was not abolished entirely due to the work of the Indian nationalists, it is indeed important to note that the pressure placed on the Government of India forced it to accelerate its communication with the India Office and was therefore, instrumental in bringing forward the actual date for the end to the system of indentured labour. Agitation by the Indian nationalists combined with other pressure points such as the work of social reformers in India and anti-emigration organizations in Britain created such a massive wave of opposition that the British Imperial Government was forced to prohibit further recruitment in 1917. The end of the system of indentureship finally came in 1920.

NOTES

1. Anil Seal, *The Emergence of Indian Nationalism: Competition and Collaboration in the Later Nineteenth Century*, Cambridge, 1971, p. 9.
2. Surjit Mansingh, *Historical Dictionary of India*, Bombay, 2003, p. 189.
3. Dadabhai Naoroji was president of the Congress in 1886 and 1893.

He expounded on the 'economic drain' theory and concluded that India's poverty was a consequence of the continuous exploitation of British rule. Romesh Chander Dutt was president of the Congress in 1899. His publication also elaborated on the 'economic drain' theory of colonial rule.

4. Edward Said, *Culture and Imperialism*, London, 1994.
5. Eric Hobsbawm, *The Age of Empire 1875-1914*, New York, 1989, p. 287.
6. This idea is taken from Partha Chatterjee, *Nationalist Thought and the Colonial World: A Derivative Discourse*, London, 1986.
7. Ibid.
8. Bipan Chandra, *The Rise and Growth of Economic Nationalism in India: Economic Policies of Indian National Leadership, 1880-1905*, Delhi, 1977.
9. Sumit Sarkar, *Modern India 1885-1947*, Delhi, 2001, p. 5.
10. *The Collected Works of Mahatma Gandhi,* vols. 1-3, Delhi, 1999.
11. Hugh Tinker, *A New System of Slavery*, London, 1993, p. 279.
12. *The Indian Emigrant,* vol. 1, no. 5, 21 December 1915. *The Indian Emigrant* was a monthly journal published from 1914. It was a record of the status and doings of Indians in British colonies and in foreign countries as well as an advocate of equal rights of British citizenship within the empire. Its main objectives according to its first volume, were to give the Indian public a clear account of the relations which existed between Indians at home and abroad; to end the emigration of ignorant and uneducated labourers to distant colonies; and to highlight cases of cruelties and injustices and to encourage voluntary emigration of educated Indians to places where there was a need for them.
13. Tinker, p. 279.
14. *Collected Works,* vols. 2 to 10 show quite clearly the extent to which Gandhi corresponded with these two Indian nationalists. Gandhi regarded Gokhale as a 'Rajguru' or 'prince of teachers' and was deeply influenced by him. From 1904 Gandhi sent copies of *Indian Opinion* to Naoroji on a regular basis.
15. John M. Geoghegan was the Under-Secretary of the Department of Agriculture, Revenue and Commerce in 1871. As was the case with many of the government officials at this time, he was a supporter of the emigration system. He was one of the first officials to compile a statistical account of the emigration of Indians overseas. D.W.D. Comins was a Surgeon-Major who was sent to the West Indies to report on the conditions of Indian immigrants there. He acted at intervals as Protector of Emigrants in Calcutta. He visited the British West Indian colonies of Jamaica, Trinidad and Demerara. He also

visited the smaller island of St. Lucia and Dutch Surinam. The bibliographic details of these two reports are: (a) J. Geoghegan, 'Note on Emigration from India', Calcutta, 1873, House of Commons Paper 134 of 1874 and (b) D.W.D. Comins, Note on Emigration from India to Trinidad, Calcutta, 1873. Comins had separate reports on British Guiana and St. Lucia as well.

16. In 1910 this society communicated its disapproval of the indentureship system and commented on various parts of the report of the Sanderson Committee, such as the recruitment of Indian women. See CO 885/21, Letter to the Earl of Crewe from Travers Buxton, 9 November 1910.
17. CD 5192, report of the Committee on Emigration from India to the Crown Colonies and Protectorates, Great Britain. June 1910. Referred to as the Sanderson Report. The Minutes of Evidence (CD 5193) and the papers laid before the Committee (CD 5194) were printed separately.
18. CD 5192. The Sanderson Committee did not specify whether persons of Indian nationality included those Indians born in the colony or only those who had emigrated from India.
19. *The Indian Emigrant*, vol. 1, no. 5, 21 December 1915.
20. *Indian Opinion*, 11 June 1904. Also cited in Mahatma Gandhi, *The Collected Works*, vol. 4, p. 20.
21. CD 5192, Sanderson Report.
22. Fremantle was supposed to be the authority on labour problems in northern India and in 1906 he had prepared a 'Report on the Supply of Labour in the United Provinces'. In fact, in 1912 when Gokhale moved his resolution in the Legislative Council calling for the prohibition of emigration, Fremantle was the spokesman of the government and he reiterated his support for the system.
23. CO 885/21, India Office to Colonial Office, no. 30 of 1911.
24. Annie Besant Papers, No. R-4799, 1 February 1910, NMML, Delhi.
25. 'Indians and British Citizens', *The Indian Emigrant*, vol. 1, no. 1, August 1914, p. 40.
26. 'Position of Indians in the Empire', *The Indian Emigrant*, vol. 1, no. 3, 31 October 1914, p. 71. This article was the summary of a lecture delivered by Mr. B.G. Horniman to the Students' Brotherhood in January 1914.
27. H.E. Hardinge, *The Indian Emigrant*, 30 September 1914. Canada had implemented laws that forbade the entry of Asians into the country as free and skilled labourers. For further information refer to Hugh Johnston, *The Voyage of the Komagata Maru—The Sikh Challenge to Canada's Colour Bar*, Delhi, 1970.
28. *The Indian Emigrant*, vol. 1, no. 2, 30 September 1914. Also recorded in Annie Besant Papers, No. R-4799, NMML, Delhi.

29. *The Indian Emigrant*, vol. 1, no. 1, August 1914, p. 5.
30. Address at the 31st Indian National Congress, Lucknow, December 1916, Annie Besant Papers, NMML, Delhi.
31. Gokhale, 'Prohibition of Indentured Labour', *Proceeding of Imperial Legislative Council*, vol. 4, p. 370, 4 March 1912.
32. Resolution proposed by the Honorable Mr. V.S. Srinivasa Sastri at the 30th Indian National Congress, 27 December 1915. Annie Besant Papers, NMML, Delhi.
33. CO 885/21, No. 30 of 1911. Gokhale asked a number of questions regarding Indians in Mauritius. Specifically he questioned the non-validity of marriages in Mauritius under Hindu and Muslim rites; asked for information on the annual emigration of Indians to this colony; reiterated the recommendation of the Sanderson Committee that emigration to Mauritius should be terminated and questioned the government on the steps to be taken regarding this recommendation.
34. Gokhale, 'Prohibition of Indentured Labour', 4 March 1912.
35. The debate started with an article written in the *The Times* (London), which alluded to the shortage of Indian labour. Comments and responses to this article can be found in various volumes of *The Indian Emigrant*, 1915.
36. I have shown the structural effects of British economic policies on India's economic development and its relationship to the emigration of Indians overseas in a previous paper which was presented at the Staff/Graduate Seminar, Department of History, University of West Indies, 6 February 2003.
37. This report was published by the Indian Commerce and Industry Department, Government of India, 1915.
38. CO 885/21, No. 67 of 1912.
39. 'The Wails of a Woman', *Bharat Mitra,* 1 August 1913.
40. *Bharat Mitra*, vol. 11, nos. 11-12, May-July 1916, p. 43.
41. Karen A. Ray, 'The Abolition of Indentured Emigration 1916-1917. The Race for the Spoils'. Paper presented at ISER–NCIC Conference on Challenge and Change: The Indian Diaspora in its Historical and Contemporary Contexts, The University of the West Indies, Trinidad, August 1995.
42. CO 571/3, Colonial Office to India Office, 26 February 1915.
43. Ibid.
44. 'Proceedings of the Government of India', no. 10294, Government of India, Department of Commerce and Industry, 1 September 1917, Simla.
45. 'Proceedings of the Government of India', Colonial Office to India Office, 4 September 1916.

46. 'Proceedings of the 30th Indian National Congress, Bombay, 27 December 1915. Annie Besant Papers, NMML, Delhi.
47. The 31st Indian National Congress—Draft Resolutions, Lucknow, December 1916, ibid.
48. The 32nd Indian National Congress—Draft Resolutions, 1917, ibid.
49. Ray, 'The Abolition of Indentured Emigration'.
50. CO 885/21, No. 30 of 1911, Department of Commerce and Industry, Government of India.
51. Ibid.
52. CO 885/21, Colonial Office to India Office, 21 March 1912.
53. CO 885/21, 'Indian Emigration Memorandum—Minor Questions Affecting all the Colonies', December 1911, p. 104.
54. CO 885/21, Department of Commerce and Industry, Government of India, 1912, p. 60.
55. CO 571/3, Government Emigration Agent for British Guiana, 26 February 1915.

CONTEMPORARY INDIA

CHAPTER 12

Naga Ethnicity: Historical Roots and Contemporary Ramifications

SURANJAN DAS

This paper explores ethnic assertion of the Nagas in its historical context. Naga ethnic politics is largely an outcome of 'entangled territorial identities'. Colonialism had subjected the Nagas and other tribal population in north-east India to a circumscribed territorial existence. What followed was a process of 'human territoriality', which entailed a mixture of 'territorial awareness with collective identity'.[1] This generated amongst the Nagas, like other hill tribes, a feeling of separatism from the Indian mainstream. Neither the Indian national movement nor the nation-building process in the aftermath of independence could effectively break the Naga isolation. The roots of the current Naga ethnic imbroglio lie in this. An understanding of the Naga ethnic politics thus requires a contextualization of the construction of ethnic identities in the region and the identification of historical conjunctures, which have determined the nature of their articulation. Examining the construction and assertion of Naga ethnic identity can also be an important entry point for a study of the challenge posed to Indian federalism by the politics of ethnicity of the north-east.

*This is a slightly revised version of my Sectional Presidential Address to the Indian History Congress, 2003. I am grateful to Mushirul Hasan, Atluri Murali, Basudeb Chattopadhyay, Bhaskar Chakrabarti, Rakhahari Chatterjee, Ramkrishna Chatterjee and Suparna Gooptu for their valuable comments on the first draft of the paper. Errors, if any, are entirely mine.

I

Naga is a generic term applied to denote at least 36 tribal groups.[2] According to one estimate the total Naga population approximates 2 million, of which 800,000 live in the Indian state of Nagaland, while the rest are scattered in Assam, Brahmaputra Valley, Manipur, Tirag and Changlong of Arunachal Pradesh and across the frontier in parts of Myanmar. Contrary to some Western perceptions,[3] these Nagas in India had close interactions with the plains people during the pre-colonial period. While the Nagas relied on the plains to barter their products, the plains people secured from them salt, herbs, medicinal plants, elephant tusks, rhino horns, rubber and other forest items. The Angamis were efficient rice cultivators; the Semas developed an expertise to prepare salt from brine springs; cotton was widely cultivated and weaving was well known in the region; iron smelting was also an established skill in the Naga Hills.[4] The Brahmaputra, Barak, Surma Valleys and the Himalayan foothills were regular centres for trade between the Nagas and plains people. What is of crucial significance was the fact that the Hill tribes were neither completely subjugated by outsiders, nor did they experience the process of Sanskritization or Hinduization, to which the tribals of Manipur or Tripura had been exposed. It was the British who in the 1820s brought the Nagas for the first time under alien control, and English colonialism rudely shattered the traditional Naga political economy.[5]

The intrusion of colonialism into the Naga Hills can be dated from the end of the first Anglo-Burmese War of 1825, especially in the wake of the British search for a route from Assam to Manipur. British interest in the region was initially dictated by a need to use it as a buffer between Assam tea plantations and the plains. But faced with an 'excessive' cost of administration, lack of local economic resources and continuous Naga recalcitrance, the British decided to retreat from the Hills in 1850. Nevertheless, the recurring Naga raids on the plains—19 by Angami Nagas alone between 1852 and 1865 causing a toll of 232 British subjects[6]—once again brought the British back to the region in 1867. The 1872 Proclamation notified the Naga

Hills as a British Agency. Once the six month long Angami rebellion of 1879—popularly known as the Naga War of Independence—was brutally suppressed, British domination over the Hills was consolidated.[7] By 1888 centres of British administration for the Hills were established in Kohima, Wokha and Mokokchung. Nevertheless, at the popular level the acceptance of British hegemony over the Naga Hills was never unquestioned. This was clearly evident from a millenarian uprising of the followers of the Haraka cult, initially led by Jadunang and then by his seventeen-year daughter Gaidiliu.[8]

In conformity with the Ahom tradition of claiming sovereignty over the Hills without undermining the independence of Naga villages, the British chose not to impose its direct administration over the Naga Hills. But unlike the Ahoms, the British introduced for the Hills a regulated tax structure and created for the Nagas new geographic, political and administrative boundaries, of course, without the 'consent and knowledge of concerned Nagas'.[9] Moreover, this demarcated region was considered as a 'protected area' from outside influence which led to a snapping of its economic ties with the plains. The Simon Commission, in its recommendations for constitutional reforms in British India, proposed a 'separate status' for the Naga Hills. Subsequently, the 1935 Government of India Act categorized the Naga Hills as 'excluded' and 'partially excluded area' that was placed under the direct administration of Assam governor and kept outside the ambit of either the federal or Assam legislature. The British 'made it an unwritten rule, observed until the last years of the Raj, that no Indian official should be posted in the Hill districts; and by regulation they made sure that traders and speculators from the plains ... would not be allowed to infiltrate and exploit the Naga areas'.[10] The only formal channel of contact with the outside world was the local officer, responsible to the governor of Assam. Duties of daily administration were left to *dobashis*—originally appointed as interpreters but then entrusted with resolving disputes—and *gaonburasu* or headmen.[11] The Criminal and Civil Procedure Codes were inapplicable in the district; Calcutta High Court's jurisdiction extended to the district in criminal cases which only involved Europeans. Administrative cost was kept to a minimum and the sole colonial concern was maintenance of peace and taxation. No developmental measures were undertaken.

At the same time, growth of tea plantation and the construction of the Assam-Bengal Railway in the late 1890s caused an alienation of the forest land of tribals.[12] The British did encourage tea plantation, in the hope that 'tea culture' would 'see . . . our (British) supremacy gradually, extended over the hills, without which, . . . there seems to be little hope of effecting any great change in the habits of the people, or our being able to avail ourselves of the great natural resources of this fine tract of mountainous country'.[13] In fact, the delineation of ethnic boundary of the Nagas became coterminous with colonization which imposed an insular existence upon the Nagas.

The British—civil servants, missionaries and anthropologists—were unsure of how to define the Naga community. But all of them shared a common perception that socially, culturally and ethnographically the Nagas were non-Indians and much closer to people in Borneo or Melanesia. Mongoloid physical features of the Nagas and their Indo-Tibetan language, culture, food and dress were believed to have no synonymity with Indo-Aryan socio-cultural ethos of the plains.[14] The Nagas were also told that their acceptance of Christianity had further alienated them from the Indian way of life. Colonial anthropologists even documented how the Nagas were supposedly unique in attaching meanings to their dreams.[15]

Cadogan, a member of the House of Commons, claiming to have Naga connections emphatically stated during a parliamentary debate on the Simon Commission the 'separateness' of the Nagas who were always suspicious of being deprived of their 'immemorial rights and customs' by the outsiders.[16] V. Elwin, a British anthropologist, was strongly disposed to the maintenance of the cultural integrity for the Hill tribes, even to the extent of preserving for them the right to head-hunting.[17] Interestingly, the initial British derison for the Nagas as 'savage, distrustful head-hunters' was gradually replaced by a feeling of paternalism. The British civilian Pawsey recalled how

> their (Nagas') courage and cheerfulness, magnificent physique, truthfulness, their independence, absence of servility and lack of caste,

soon endeared them to the British. . . . British officials laboured for a hundred years to ensure that Nagas should retain their racial characteristics and should not be reduced to the status of tribals in the Plains, regarded as untouchables to be exploited by moneylenders and all of higher caste.[18]

The colonial discourse on the Naga incompatibility with mainstream Indian identity increasingly made the tribal leaders visualize the Indians as 'babus' of the plains. Underlining the non-Indianness of the Naga society, a Naga commentator had once noted:

Possessing his own house, built on his own land, no family ever pays tax. Forests, woodlands and rivers belong to the people for their exploitation without paying taxes. We cultivate as much land as we need and there is no one to question our rights. We have food to eat and drinks to drink exceedingly above our needs. . . . We have no beggars (and) . . . no landlords to harass. . . . We do not arrest nor ever imprison anyone. Our civil authority is God in the matter of life and death. We fear nobody, individually and collectively. . . . What peace we have. No police, no CID. We have no locks. Our granaries are kept outside the village and no guard is needed for there is no one to steal from them. . . . If by ill-fortune a man falls sick or dies, he is brought home to his family without counting the costs. We talk freely, live freely and often fight freely too. There is order in this chaos.[19]

This feeling of Naga uniqueness was imparted a political content when colonial sociology understood all Naga tribes as belonging to one administrative structure. The origin of the term 'Naga' is still shrouded in mystery.[20] Traditionally, the Nagas did not constitute a united people. The primary referral point for the Nagas was their village (*lim*) or local group, which the British mistook as some larger combination into which villages could be classified.[21] But the British categorized as tribes, which were essentially clans, villages and *khels* (territorial divisions within a village, usually containing several clans). Thus although a Naga viewed himself or herself as a member of a particular group rather than being a Naga[22] and the pattern of governance varied from group to group—from hereditary chieftainship to councils, autocracy and clan democracy[23]—the colonial officials clubbed together these different groups in official communications and private tour diaries under the broad generic term 'Nagas', presuming they constituted a single homogeneous coherent group. As early as May 1846 an official of north-east thus, wrote to G.A. Bushby, Officiating Secretary to the Government of India (Foreign Department), of the need 'to encourage homogeneity among the various Naga groups'.[24] Later colonial officials like Hutton tended to consider 'the Nagas as a people rather than an assortment of tribes or even of villages (who) had something in common which has made them recognizable as a people'.[25]

Other colonial observers also stipulated the Naga society to be 'one society, an aggregate of communities who share a set of structures or principles in common, but who emphasize them differently'.[26] Once the census reports classified the different tribes as sub-tribes of one generic tribe—the Nagas—there occurred for the Nagas a transmutation of village and sub-tribe-based identity to a generic identity.[27]

The process of imparting an administrative notion to the term 'Nagas' has been characterized by many scholars as 'detribalization'.[28] Increasing monetization of the Hill economy, an offshoot of colonialism, led to a concentration of wealth amongst the tribals, causing considerable indebtedness and rise of a landless class. Reflecting on this process Hutton, an anthropologist and at one time Deputy Commissioner of Naga Hills himself admitted:

> Loans in former days were given in grain or in cattle and to repay them the debtor must till the land and grow rice or breed cattle, but to repay a loan in cash he must sell something—and it is generally his land, and after the sale of that he can rarely if ever recover his old independence.[29]

Colonial rule thus, destroyed the 'traditional moorings' of the Naga society and imposed upon it 'an identity from without' which generated amongst the Nagas both a spirit of separateness from the Indian mainstream and encouraged loyalty to their new-found British patrons. Certainly neither this separatist spirit nor this British loyalty was total amongst the Nagas. But this political trend provided a convenient backdrop to the 'crises of identity and autonomy, unification and confrontation, fear and apprehensions, hopes and aspirations'[30] amongst the Nagas during the prelude to the transfer of power from British to Indian hands in August 1947.

The colonial administrative policy of imposing an 'isolationist identity' upon the Nagas was reinforced by activities of Christian missionaries, the most active group among them being the American Baptists.[31] The American Baptists began effectively functioning in the Naga Hills in 1876 and by 1894 succeeded in intruding into the tribal society. Despite initial opposition, the Christian conversion movement in Naga Hills ended as 'one of the large mass movements to Christianity in Asia'.[32] The number of Christian converts rose from 0.18 per cent of the total Naga population in 1901 to 17.9 per cent in 1941, 45.7 per cent in 1951 and 66.76 per cent in 1971.[33]

The social impact of Christian missionary activities in Nagaland was significant. Missionaries considered the Nagas 'uncivilized, barbaric and savage' who were to be made 'worthy' and 'civilized' through Christianity.[34]

In this process social changes amongst the Nagas which would have normally taken centuries were pushed through within a couple of decades.[35] Missionaries condemned Naga customs like headhunting or feasts of merit through which the wealthy sections of the community customarily improved their social position. Simultaneously, medical work of the missionaries sought to substitute the 'essentially supernaturalistic'[36] tribal healing practices with western medicine. Missionaries were also involved with spreading education in the Naga Hills. They introduced Roman script for the unwritten tribal languages, primarily to enable the tribals read the Bible. Village primary schools emerged as an important nucleus of missionary activity. By 1923 the American Baptist Mission alone had organized 208 such schools with 5,438 students.[37] The importance of these schools in the proselytising mission was admitted by a leading missionary in Kohima.[38]

But the standard of knowledge imparted in missionary schools was 'quite low'. This was largely because the missionaries were primarily interested 'to train and employ good preachers', and hence the curriculum was loaded in favour of religion and literature. Nevertheless, Christian missionaries in the Naga Hills assumed the status of 'official educationists', the government having realized that the gospel had the ability to transform a tribe from 'a liability' to 'an asset'.[39]

Such missionary activities, however, eroded the traditional code of conduct in the Naga tribal world. Personal status in Naga society was traditionally determined by headhunting, feasts of merit and sexual prowess.[40] But interference with these customs deprived the Naga life of its vibrancy and dynamism. Even contemporary western observers commented on how colonial attempts to suppress status-feasting became coinstantaneous with increasing inequalities within Naga villages.[41] Feasts occasioned distribution of surplus food and drink held by the prosperous, but the colonial undermining of this custom resulted in the accumulation of stocks in storehouses of the rich, while the poorer sections of the village remained hungry.[42]

Besides, exposure to Western knowledge through missionary education resulted in the emergence of a first generation of educated elite amongst the Nagas, who not only questioned the hitherto undisputed authority of tribal chieftains by refusing to pay taxes for village festivals or challenging customary methods of resolving property disputes, but also became carriers of modern politics.[43] The acceptance of an alien religion even tended to create a distance between the Naga Christian converts and the plains people, most of whom were either Hindus or Muslims. Romanization of tribal dialects made the tribals forget the plains languages—Assamese in the case of the Nagas and Bengali for the Khasis and Garos. This estrangement of the Nagas from the plains in turn generated a 'sense of groupness' amongst the Christian Nagas.[44]

Many commentators stress a subtle difference between the perceptions of missionaries and colonial officials. The former are believed to have been driven by a zeal to transform the Naga society, but the latter were supposedly only interested in reforming some of the customs of the Nagas without disturbing their tribal existence so that they could be presented to the outer world as anthropological or museum wonders.[45] The Naga leader Aliba Imti thus recollected how the Deputy Commissioner of Naga Hills would ensure that

> no tribal student could dress in the western way and to have his hair

cut in western mode. They were to dress in plain cloth as that was the dress of the tribal and to have their hair cut in the tribal way—round the head and anyone found not in the attire was to be fined Rs. 2, a big sum those days.[46]

In other words, while the British government sought to ensure political stability through minimum interference with tribal customs, the missionaries were motivated by a drive to convert the Hill people from animism to Christianity. If missionaries are believed to have pinned their hopes on the newly educated tribals, the colonial administrators are thought to have relied on traditional tribal chieftains who felt that their moral authority was being threatened by proselytising missions. Missionaries are also thought to have faced a combined opposition from the British government and local tribal chieftains.[47]

It is, however, difficult to draw a clear dividing line between the activities or concerns of missionaries and of colonial officials. Both were interested to promote western notions of civilization, and the missionaries could not have worked without the support or sanction of the colonial administration. In many instances the initial encouragement for missionary activities in the Naga Hills came from local colonial officials. Frustrated by their failure of early military ventures against the Nagas, they felt that the Bible could be more effective in 'taming the recalcitrant tribes'.[48] Captain John Butler, Private Assistant to the Agent of Governor-General in North-East, wrote to Major Jenkins, Agent of the Governor-General in North-East on 13 May 1847:

> I am strongly impressed with the idea that the schoolmaster (missionary) with the Police will do more to bring these tribes into submission and make them peaceable subjects than frequent military expeditions into their country.[49]

We have evidence of the local government paying teachers' salaries in missionary village schools and providing financial help in printing school texts.[50] Even in the economic exploitation of the Hills the missionaries rendered a helping hand. For instance, the missionary Rev. Bronson had a lengthy correspondence with Major Jenkins, the Agent of the Governor-General in the Naga Hills, about the 'Naga workers in brass and copper'.[51]

The missionaries themselves looked for help from local officials. A leading missionary of the nineteenth century thus solicited 'the assistance of government for the support of the Naga school, which the missionaries have succeeded in establishing in the Naga country'.[52]

Recent studies have stressed how Christianization and the 'selfless' social world of missionaries had a 'soothing' effect on the Hill people which facilitated the extension of colonial political control over the region'.[53] In other words, Christianity proved to be an effective tool for attaching the turbulent north-eastern tribes to the colonial Raj.[54]

II

Colonialism thus constructed a Naga ethnic identity based on a dichotomy between the Mongoloid Hill tribes and Aryan Indians of the plains. The beginning of the assertion of this identity along organized political lines is usually traced to the period following the return of the survivors of the 2000 odd Nagas—mostly from the Sema clan—who went to France to work as labourers during the First World War. One of the first Naga groups to be exposed to the outer world, these returnees helped Charles Pawsey, the British Deputy Commissioner of Naga Hills, to establish in 1918 the Naga Club in Kohima, the British administrative centre for the Naga Hill District. Modelled on Western lines, the club's primary agenda was twofold: (a) to assist the British rulers to understand social and administrative problems of the Naga tribes and (b) to consolidate a distinct Naga nationality. It also ran cooperative stores in at least two Naga villages. The club was not a nationalist body like the Indian National Congress, propounding headlong collision with imperialism. Instead, it was to be a tribal pressure group within the colonial administrative framework, acting 'as a counterpoint to popular independence movement'.[55] The club's separatist stance from mainstream nationalism was demonstrated when it submitted a memorandum, with the support of local colonial officials, to the Simon Commission demanding non-incorporation of Naga Hills within the province of Assam and proposed that: 'when or if the British actually left (India), the Nagas should revert to the independence they enjoyed before the British came'.[56]

The memorandum further asserted:

> Our languages are quite different from those of the Indians and we have no social affinities with either the Hindus or Muslims. We are looked down upon by one for our beef and by the other for our pork and by other for our education which is not due to any fault of ours.[57]

The Simon Commission itself took a favourable view of the dictum of 'independent rights of Nagas'.[58]

Another important step in the colonial process of facilitating the articulation of the Naga identity was taken in 1939 when Charles Pawsey organized the Naga Hills District Tribal Council, designed to integrate under one roof the tribal councils of various Naga tribes. The administrative project to represent the Nagas as one tribe and not numerous sub-tribes came to be soon internalized by the emerging Naga middle class. Instead of the earlier practice to have political associations along sub-tribal lines like the Ao Student Association, Angami Students Association, Lushai Student Association, Paite Student Association, the new middle class leadership tended to consider themselves as representing one generic tribe. The internalization of a constructed separatist Naga identity by the Naga leadership was again evident when it demanded exclusion of the Hills from the ambit of the Government of India Act of 1935. One would not perhaps be wrong to suspect a British inducement to the Naga elite to insist on this constitutional segregation. This supposition gains ground from the schemes of British officials like Sir Reginald Coupland to create a British Trust Territory consisting of what today is Nagaland and Arunachal Pradesh.

The Second World War proved to be the next turning point in the articulation of a separate Naga ethnic identity under colonialism. Although some Nagas, including the future leader of the Naga ethnic politics A. Zapu Phizo, joined Subhas Chandra Bose's Indian National Army, a considerable number of Naga tribes rallied around the British war-effort primarily 'as intelligence behind the Japanese lines, (and) as interpreters, scouts and porters'.[59] The Naga assistance was crucial for the British to ward off the Japanese advance upon Kohima in 1944.[60]

If, however, the British benefited militarily from Naga loyalty during the war, the Nagas, too, gained from their participation in it. It accustomed the Nagas with modern armaments and the rapid improvement of communication between India and Burma removed much of the traditional isolation of the Nagas from the Indian mainstream. Besides, the Naga leadership now came to hope that their loyalty would be rewarded by the British support for Naga autonomy or independence in a decolonized South Asia.[61]

In fact, during the war itself British officials of the Hill Districts like J.P. Mills had endorsed the Naga demand for separation from the successor state of India. Their encouragement was certainly crucial in the transformation in March 1946 of the Naga Hills District Tribal Council to the Naga National Council (hereafter NNC) for representing Naga interests and providing support to British civilians 'working for the uplift of the Nagas'.[62] Beginning with 29 representatives of different Naga groups and a monthly newspaper *Naga Nation*, the NNC, was a 'territorial organization' which opposed the Cabinet Mission 'Grouping Plan'.[63] Emphasizing the importance of the formation of the Naga National Council for the politics of Naga ethnic identity, a leading figure of Naga politics remarked:

> Our people were yearning for a change in our way of life because we were aware of the changes that were taking place near and around us but we were still chained to the old way of life and this was the reason why the whole Naga people welcomed the starting of the Naga National Council and freely exchanged our individual views and problems. When the common people saw that the Naga National Council could be their mouthpiece, the spontaneous response was most encouraging.[64]

The legacy left behind by the British rule over the Naga Hills was twofold: (a) disruption of the traditional tribal moral economy and insulation of the Nagas from the Indian mainstream, and (b) introduction of modern political ideas and institutions, although for its own administrative interest. What, however, most disturbed the Naga leadership during the crucial days leading to the transfer of power was the failure of the departing Raj to ensure self-determination for the tribal areas.[65] Throughout the constitutional negotiations of the 1940s, a section of British officials projected the Hills as a separate state and adopted a patronizing attitude to Naga separatist feelings.[66] Mention may, for example, be made of the idea of converting the North-East Frontier Province into a Crown Colony or a separate state under colonial governance. The advisor to the Assam governor, Adams, urged the Naga and Mizo leaders to accept whatever terms came from the Indian nationalists, since the Indian nation state was bound to wither away within five years when they could have their own nation state.[67] As late as 8 August 1947—only seven days prior to Indian independence—J.P. Mills wrote:

> . . . The tribal areas have not, and cannot engage, lawyers to examine the matter from their point of view and it is, therefore, I would submit, all the more important that we do it for them. If the tribal areas have . . . the right of deciding whether or not they will accede to the Indian Dominion, they should be informed of that right and allowed to exercise it.[68]

However when the transfer of power actually occurred no provision was made either for Naga independence or autonomy.

Unfortunately, the Congress leaders failed to dispel the political confusion afflicting the Naga leadership. The 1936 Faizpur Session of the Indian National Congress had unequivocally rejected the system of Excluded and Partially Excluded Areas for the Hills as:

> another attempt to divide the people of India into different groups . . . to obstruct the growth of uniform democratic institutions in the country . . . and keep the inhabitants of those areas apart from the rest of India for their easier exploitation and suppression.[69]

But the Congress failed to formulate an alternative blueprint to protect the distinct Naga identity that had had been constructed under British colonialism. While in prison in 1944 Jawaharlal Nehru preferred to be flexible on the question of Naga autonomy. He wrote:

> The right of any well-constituted area to secede from the Indian federation or union has often been put forward. . . . Before any such right of secession is exercised there must be a properly constituted, functioning, free India. It may be possible then . . . to consider such questions objectively . . . far removed from the emotionalism of today

. . . (It) may be desirable to fix a period, say ten years later after the establishment of the free Indian State, at the end of which the right to secede may be exercised through proper constitutional process and in accordance with the clearly expressed will of the inhabitants of the area concerned.[70]

But on 1 Augsut 1946, Jawaharlal Nehru wrote to T. Sakhrie, secretary, NNC that 'Naga territory in eastern Assam is much too small to stand by itself, politically or economically. . . . Inevitably, therefore, the Naga territory must form part of India'.[71] Once he assumed the mantle of premiership, Jawaharlal's response to the Naga issue turned particularly rigid:

You can never hope to be independent. No state, big or small, in India will be allowed to remain independent. We will use all our influence and power to suppress such tendencies.[72]

Nehru seems to have insulted Naga sentiments when he referred to Assamese or Hindustani as the most helpful languages for the Hills, advising the Nagas to learn Hindustani for greater integration with mainstream Indian life. Such integrationist feelings and a general failure to identify ways for the preservation of Naga identity made the Naga politicians lose faith in the Congress as a protector of the Naga ethnic cause.

It would be, however, wrong to contend that organized Naga political opinion had from the beginning favoured an 'outright severance' of ties with an independent India.[73] For instance, Rev. J.J.M. Nichols Roy questioned the viability of the British Protectorate scheme for the Hills saying 'When the whole of India will get independence the hill people of Assam should also get their own share of independence and they should be connected with the Province of Assam.'[74]

On 19 June 1946, the NNC accepted the retention of Naga Hills within Assam, although with local autonomy and proper safeguards for Naga interests. Even as late as 6 December 1946 the secretary of the NNC reconciled himself at a public rally in Kohima with the idea of the Hill Districts becoming a part of the Indian Union.[75]

Yet, by the beginning of 1947, the NNC's political stance tended to change. Many commentators feel that encouraged by movements for a Sikh homeland and an Independent United

Bengal as well as the imminent realization of Muslim League's Pakistan dream, the NNC adopted the dictum for self-rule for safeguarding the interests of its constituency.[76] It is difficult to document with direct evidence the possibility of any British encouragement for this changed stance of the NNC. But Sir Andrew Clow, the governor of Assam, did visit Mokokchung in January 1947 where he appreciated the Naga claim for local authority and advised the tribal leaders to think about their political future and 'form their own conclusions'.[77] Even Mountbatten reportedly apprehended that the future Indian government would remain 'unaware of Naga aspirations and conditions'.[78] But it is doubtful if even at this stage the NNC was prepared for an instant separation from India. Otherwise, its memorandum to the Government of India on 20 February 1947 would not have proposed an interim arrangement by which Nagaland was to be a part of India for ten years, at the end of which the Nagas were to be given the right to decide their future political status.[79]

In this context Akbar Hydari, the first Indian governor of Assam, was entrusted with the responsibility of opening negotiations with the Naga leadership. A compromise settlement was arrived at on 29 June 1947. Known as the Hydari Agreement, it contained nine clauses. It acknowledged the Naga right to have autonomy for their own development. The Naga government was to be entitled to full legislative, executive and judicial powers as far as the Naga people were concerned. Central and Provincial Acts were not to be automatically applicable to Naga people; land and other natural resources in the Hills could not be alienated to non-Nagas. The ninth clause stipulated that the agreement would be reviewed after ten years.[80]

The conclusion of the agreement brought immediate satisfaction to both contracting parties. Reflecting upon the NNC's sense of achievement, Aliba Imti noted:

> The foundation stone of our cherished goal is already laid down. Let the spirit of difference, if there be any, be taken away from your hearts. Come forward with a united spirit. Let us build a new Nagaland based on the spirit of goodwill and understanding.[81]

At the same time Hydari could be content that at least for the moment the opting out scheme of Naga leaders had become inoperative. Unfortunately, the Constituent Assembly refused to ratify the ninth clause which reduced the agreement for the Nagas to nothing but a piece of paper.

The breakdown of the Hydari Agreement directly contributed to the rise of an extremist section within the NNC. Led by Zapu Phizo they considered the ninth clause of the Pact as a 'sell out' by the established leadership of the NNC. But when he failed to make his voice felt within the organization against the moderates like Aliba Imti and T. Sakhrie, Phizo left the NNC to form the People's Independence League that was to struggle for a sovereign Nagaland.[82] Despite concentrated efforts for popular mobilization, Phizo could not, however, win much public support. A frustrated Phizo rejoined the NNC.

At this juncture when the Naga leadership was envisaging a range of political options from outright independence to autonomy, both the Indian National Congress and the Muslim League preferred to keep themselves aloof from such Naga exercises. A seven-member Naga delegation did, however, have a favourable audience with Mahatma Gandhi on 19 July 1947. In his own characteristic way, Gandhi promised that an independent India, based on the principles of love, fraternity and non-violence, would treat the Nagas with honour. To quote Gandhi:

> Nagas have every right to be independent. We did not want to live under the domination of the British and they are leaving us. I want you to feel that India is yours. I feel that the Naga Hills are mine, the matter must stop there. I believe in brotherhood of man but do not believe in force or forced union.[83]

When the Naga leaders voiced their apprehension that the Nagas were likely to be intimidated by the Assam governor Sir Akbar Hydari to join the Indian Union, Gandhiji had exclaimed 'Sir Akbar is wrong. . . . I will come to the Naga Hills. I will ask them to shoot me first before one Naga is shot.'[84] Despite apprehensions the Naga leaders continued to draw solace from their interview with Gandhi.[85]

The construction and initial articulation of Naga ethnicity—as the above discussion has hopefully demonstrated—had occurred in the context of and within the framework of colonialism. In post-independent India, the Nagas became victims of a dual process: commercialization of their resources, and the hegemonizing dictum of 'one state, one nation'.[86] The retort from the Nagas was natural. Perhaps as a foretaste for the future, on the eve of Indian Independence Day, Kohima was literally covered with such inciting posters as: 'outsiders (Indians) let us separate as friends and live like good neighbours', 'Indians, it is better to go from Nagaland without delay' and 'Nagaland is for the Nagas'.[87] In fact, the NNC informed the UNO that it did not accept the Indian constitution and had resolved to boycott the celebration of the transfer of power.

It is significant to note here that some American Baptist missionaries like G.W. Supplee, headmaster of Kohima High School, had also dissuaded their Naga students from celebrating the Indian Independence Day.[88]

In the aftermath of independence the economy of the Hills—so long kept insulated by the Raj—was thrown open to the plains people, threatening the livelihood of Nagas. The British Deputy Commissioner of Naga Hills was not wide off the mark when in a note dated 9 April 1947 to the secretary to the government he feared:

> . . . that without adequate safeguards all the Angami terraced rice fields will pass into the hands of Hindu moneylenders. I have seen this happen to the Plains tribals in all the four plains districts of the Assam Valley in which I have served as district officer. . . .[89]

Besides, the partition of the subcontinent in 1947 resulted in the region's loss of access to Chittagong port and cutting off of crucial inland, water, road and railway communications. This abrupt severance of link with the mainland had a crippling economic impact for the north-east, causing increase in the cost of commodities and imposing further economic insularity. Sino-Indian hostilities of the 1960s also caused a virtual closure of an 'hitherto virtual open border with Myanmar'.[90]

At the same time the Nehruvian strategy of imposing a pan-Indian unity from the top failed to reconcile the Naga ethnic aspirations within the centrist federal framework of the post-colonial Indian state. Jawaharlal Nehru himself had emphasized before Independence the need to provide the tribal areas with 'as much freedom and autonomy as possible so that they can live their own lives according to their customs and desires'.[91] But as the first prime minister of India, he chose not to extend the principle of linguistic states to the north-east. Instead, the Naga Hills, along with other parts of the region, except the princely states of Manipur and Tripura, were made a part of the province of Assam. The tribal areas were to be administered in accordance with the Sixth Schedule of the Constitution, that envisaged a system of autonomous hill councils to assuage tribal feelings. It appeared that New Delhi was retaining the British policy of avoiding a direct rule over a 'fierce area' by making 'Assamese politicians and bureaucrats . . . as the last outpost of political India in a region where the process of Sanskritization was weak and the impact of the *Ramayana-Mahabharata* traditions marginal'.[92] The autonomy of the Hill Councils, however, proved to be a myth. Except for specific subjects like forest management and social customs, the Councils were made subordinate either to the authority of the Parliament or Assam provincial legislature. Even the management of mineral deposits was handed over to the provincial government on the pretext of sound management.

This centrist posture of the Indian state undermined the position of the moderates within the NNC and the Phizo-led extremist section gained ascendancy. In July 1948 the Naga National Council supremo Zapu Phizo was imprisoned for 'anti-Indian manoeuvres'. The threat of Indian domination that now rattled the psyche of the Naga leaders was amply expressed in a letter that Phizo wrote from jail to the country's first governor-general, C. Rajagopalachari:

> Since we endured a life together as British-conquered subjects along with the Indians, we sincerely believed India would not interfere in our liberty and freedom. . . . But the possibility of India's annexation of Nagaland and domination over unwilling Nagas has become a more fearful problem than the British imperialism whose home and country was at least several thousand miles away.[93]

The response of the Naga leadership to India becoming a Republic was equally symptomatic of their disenchantment with the ruling Indian establishment:

The Nagas will become a free nation. The Indian constitution cannot bind the Nagas. An appeal is made to India to declare to the world on Republic Day (26 January) that the Nagas will be given the freedom of choice to become independent.[94]

The strength of Naga animosity to the ruling regime in New Delhi was evident from a plebiscite organized on 16 May 1951 by the Naga National Council in which 99 per cent of the Nagas endorsed the demand of independence. Nehru, however, retorted that the Nagas would not be granted independence even if 'heaven fell and India went to pieces'.[95] In a major speech of July 1952 before the lower house of the Indian Parliament (Lok Sabha), Nehru snubbed the Naga demand for independence as 'completely unwise, impracticable and unacceptable' and firmly believed that the strength of the Naga separatist movement was rapidly eroding.[96] Subsequently, the Nagas overwhelmingly boycotted the first Indian general election of 1952.

Meanwhile, the Assam administration was found to be at unease in administrating the Naga territory. This was partly because of the differential experience of colonial rule for the different Naga groups.[97] At the time of decolonization while some Nagas had experienced British contact for 80-90 years, others like the Eastern Rengma or Konyaks were incorporated into the colonial administration only in the 1920s and 1930s. This implied that some Nagas had more exposure to Western contact than others. Besides, the strength of British hegemony over the Naga tribes varied greatly. For instance, the Angamis, despite their acceptance of British suzerainty, retained a voice in their territory in a manner which other Nagas could not enjoy. Faced with such a variegated situation, the Assam government looked at the Naga Hills as an area that required tough administration. The adoption of repressive measures that followed accelerated the Naga alienation from the Indian state. The Assam Maintenance of Public Order (Autonomous District) Act, 1953 enabled the Assam government to impose collective fines in disturbed areas, control meetings and processions, and requisition the services of porters from Naga Hills in an emergency. In reality the Act was designed for a large-scale deployment of military in that region. In 1955 the Assam Disturbed Act was promulgated that granted the Assam Armed Police and Asssm Rifles with extraordinary powers to 'contain any insurgency'. Again, when in 1962 the Assam legislature proposed Assamese as the province's official language, the Nagas, who had primarily gained literacy through English and had about 30 languages and innumerable dialects, found themselves disadvantaged in the race for joining schools, universities and government jobs of the state. The Nagas widely suspected that while the British had severely regulated the intrusion of outsiders into the Hills, the Assam administration now basically represented the interests of the plains people.

The line of division between New Delhi and the NNC formally surfaced in March 1953 when Jawaharlal Nehru refused an audience with NNC leaders whilst he was on a visit to the Naga Hills accompanied by his daughter Indira Gandhi and U Nu of Burma. During this visit the Indian premier, however, received a taste of Naga dissension when virtually the entire gathering walked out of a mass meeting upon his arrival. This incident initiated a period of Naga non-cooperation with the Indian state in the form of non-payment of taxes, non-participation in elections and local administration. Yet, another expression of Naga dissent was protest against the continuous alienation of their customary rights over the commons.[98] In March 1956 the NNC announced the formation of a Federal Government of Nagaland and its standing army, signaling the first powerful insurgency in post-colonial India.

The Indian state's response to this situation was fast and brutal. The Naga Hills was characterized as 'disturbed area' which virtually brought the region under martial rule. The size of Indian security forces in the Naga Hills rose in 1956 to two divisions of the Indian Army and thirty-five battalions of the Assam Rifles.[99] According to a Naga estimate the 'Indian Army' by the end of 1950s far-exceeded 'in number than British troops needed to keep down the whole of the Indian subcontinent' in the pre-Second World War period.[100] 'Curfew Raj' was the order of the day. According to one estimate, by 1955 'over 10,000 Nagas had been beaten and tortured, 1562 women were beaten and assaulted, 515 granaries were destroyed or burned down, 1811 men were maimed through torture. . . .'[101] Between January 1955 and July 1957, the Indian troops had allegedly burnt down 79,794 Naga houses, ransacked 612 villages and burnt 26,550,000 maunds of paddy.[102]

The *Newsweek* of 22 April 1957 alleged that 98,000 Nagas were being kept in concentration camps like conditions and provided with only 400 ozs of rice a day. Between 1956 and 1958 while 1,400 Naga insurgents were killed, 162 Indian soldiers lost their lives in these operations.[103] Even Naga Human Rights activists like Luingam Luithui of the Naga People's Movement for Human Rights (NPMHR) were subjected to persecutions of all sorts.[104]

The adoption of strong arm methods by the Indian government could not, however, stem the tide of violence in the Hills. The federalist Nagas stuck to their demand for a sovereign state, condemning the Nagas cooperating with the Indians as 'quislings'. It was left to the Baptist Council of Nagaland to take the initiative in 1964 to form a three-member Peace Commission comprising Rev. Michael Scott, Jayaprakash Narayan and Bimala Prasad Chaliha. The commission brokered a ceasefire between the Indian State and the Nagas.[105] But the peace process suffered a setback when the commission was dissolved in 1966 following the deportation of Rev. Michael Scott on charges of complicity with the Naga militants and resignation of the other two Indians from the body. In 1973, New Delhi unilaterally terminated the ceasefire on the pretext of violation of peace by the militants, symbolized through an assassination attempt on the Nagaland chief minister Hokishe Sema. The NNC was banned and security forces were unleashed on Nagaland to flush out the militants.[106] The Indian State's counter-insurgency operation now also included psychological warfare which sought to foment defections amongst the rebels, create a discord between civilians and rebels and win popular support for security forces.

A split within the Naga rebels, however, facilitated the Indian state's handling of the Naga outburst. Some analysts believe that factionalism within Naga politicians was rooted in the inherent tribalism in Naga politics, which was utilized by the

Indian government like its colonial predecessor. Perhaps the first sign of intra-Naga tensions became evident in 1956 when the moderate NNC leader T.N. Sakhrie was murdered by the extremists, apparently for his stand that insurgency could not be the only means for realizing Naga demands. This incident presaged the formation at Kohima in August 1957 of the Naga People's Convention to act as an intermediary between the Indian state and the underground Naga Federal Government. This overground organization preferred to work within the Indian Union and demanded the formation of a separate province of Nagaland. New Delhi readily rallied around these moderates, adopting, what a commentator calls, the policy of 'subsuming the rebellious communities in its ideology of territoriality'.[107] Nehru announced in 1960 the plan for a separate province of Nagaland that was actually implemented in December 1963.[108] Encompassing an approximate area of 6,366 sq miles with an aggregate population of 3.7 lakh in 700 villages, the new state has as its inhabitants fifteen major Naga tribes like the Konyak, Ao, Semaa, Angami, Chakhasang, Lotha, Chang, Phom, Sangtam, Khinmungan, Imchungar, Rengma and Zelieng.[109]

At the same time the Indian State won rapid success in subduing the outlawed Naga Federal Government which was in 1975 made to sign with New Delhi the Shillong Accord by which the former ratified the formation of the state of Nagaland, undertook to surrender its arms and agreed to enter into a dialogue with the Indian government for a political resolution of the Naga issue. Significantly, the accord was concluded when a national Emergency had been clamped on the country, abrogating all democratic rights of citizens. The Shillong Accord was, however, not an unmitigated success. For, it injected a new life into Naga militancy. The extremists within the Naga Federal Government refused to accept the accord and formed in June 1980, the National Socialist Council of Nagaland or Naga National Socialist Council (NSCN, later named Naga National Socialist Council of Nagalim) with S.S. Khaplang as chairman, Isaak Chisi Swu as vice-chairman and Thiungelang Muivah as general secretary.

Meanwhile, the Church continued to be a rallying point for Naga dissident politics. The American evangelist Billy Graham's visit to the Hills in 1972 is taken as a turning point in this respect.[110] Some Naga rebels, particularly on the Burmese side of the frontier, formed their own gospel groups.[111] At one point a section of Naga 'insurgents aimed to have a sovereign, Christian Socialist country'.[112] The interest of the international Church in Naga politics was seen even in the 1990s.

III

As in Kashmir and Sindh, the ethnic politics in Nagaland has also experienced external ramification. North-east India, having frontiers with Bhutan, China, Myanmar and Bangladesh, has international borders which far exceed those with rest of India. This geographical situation has enabled north-east Indian rebels to have easy refuge in Bhutan, Bangladesh and Myanmar. Not unnaturally, Nehru suspected a 'foreign hand' behind the Naga imbroglio whose main concern was to separate the Naga Hills from the Indian Union and convert it into an imperial base. Besides, a non-convergence between state and ethnic identity left the Nagas on both sides of the Indo-Burmese border with divided loyalties to the two successor states. This colonial legacy in Nagaland significantly contributed to the creation of conditions for the utilization of Naga insurgency in a proxy war against India by some of its neighbours.

The external radiation of Naga ethnic politics was first felt in 1956 when the self-styled Director of Intelligence of the Naga Federal Government visited Pakistan to explore possibilities of receiving support in their war of independence. Through Pakistan, Phizo himself reached London in 1960, from where he tried to internationalize the Naga question by lobbying in the United Nations and other international forums. Pakistan also used its eastern wing—the erstwhile East Pakistan and now Bangladesh—to grant the Naga rebels a safe sanctuary for shelter and military training.[113] In early 1965, the Pakistan Army even set up a 'Coordinating Bureau' to monitor anti-Indian subversive activities in the Naga Hills. A blueprint was also drawn to cement links between the Kashmiri militants and Naga insurgents. The Muivah-Swu faction of NSCN was reportedly linked to the ISI. In recent years Pakistan's intelligence agency—the ISI—has been found to be operating in the Hills, using the Bangladesh borders as its base.[114]

Externalization of the Naga issue was also seen through Chinese support for the Naga cause. Sections amongst the Naga rebels have hardly been secretive of their 'China connection'. On 29 May 1963, the Prime Minister of the Federal Government of Nagaland Kughato Sukhai openly requested the then Chinese Premier Zhou-en-Lai to 'recognize the territorial rights of Nagaland, her people, now and forever', and copies of this communication were endorsed to Indian and British prime ministers.[115] In soliciting Chinese support the Naga leadership did not even hesitate to use racial overtones. Sukhai thus implored the Chinese leadership to 'honour and follow their principles of safeguarding and upholding the cause of any suppressed nation of Mongoloid stock'.[116] Many scholars believe that the Chinese tilt of the Naga insurgents was dictated by their failure to evoke Western response to their cause. Mao Ze Dong himself reportedly 'urged Naga tribesmen to launch a full-scale revolt against Indian occupiers'.[117]

Chinese support to the Naga insurgents is usually dated from 1966 when Muivah led about 100 Nagas across jungles of northern Burma to Kunming in Yunan province.[118] While these Nagas were the first men to receive Chinese military and political training, Muivah stayed on for four years and had the opportunity of meeting the then Chinese Premier Zhou-en-Lai. Muivah's trusted comrade Swu, too, reached China in 1968. But this Chinese-inspired Naga insurgency had not yielded much fruit. Instead, the question of retaining Chinese alliance caused a split amongst the Naga insurgents. General Kaito, for example, broke away from the Phizo camp and entered into a political truce with New Delhi. Most observers believe that the Chinese support to Naga insurgents has now effectively ended.

The United Kingdom also proved to be a safe haven for the Naga politicians waging a war against the Indian State. Phizo himself was granted British citizenship under the British Nationality Act of 1948.[119] London became a site of a publication drive to expose the torture, repression and atrocities perpetrated by the Indian army upon the Nagas.[120] There remains a lurking or patronizing sympathy for the Naga separatist cause amongst those English, who as civilians or otherwise, had some connections with the region.[121]

Within the United States political establishment, and the CIA too, some were favourably disposed towards the Naga insurgent cause. Former US ambassador to India Kenneth Keating, for instance, allegedly suggested that the Hill tribes should form a United Mongolian States.[122]

IV

What was necessary in the aftermath of Independence was, to quote Verrier Elwin:

> . . . first . . . to preserve, strengthen and develop all that is best in tribal society, culture, art and language. The second is to protect tribal economic rights. The third is to unite and integrate the tribes in a true heart unity with India as a whole so that they may play a full part in her life. And the last is to develop welfare and educational facilities so that every tribesman may have an equal opportunity with his fellow-citizens of the open country and the plains. . . . The great problem is how to develop the synthesis without destroying the rare and precious values of tribal life.[123]

But this, as has been demonstrated above, did not happen. As late as November 1948, A.Z. Phizo wrote to C. Rajagopalchari:

> In the first place let me clearly state Nagas are not hostile to Indian Union. Some interested people try to create the impression that Nagas are bent to do mischief. I want to assure your Excellency here and now that there is no danger in Naga Hills. There is no danger in Indo-Burma Border. Anybody who talks against the Nagas (are) but enemy to India as well. Anybody whoever he may be, who talks as if there is danger in Indo-Burma border is a liar.[124]

Even after Phizo was imprisoned shortly after the transfer of power, he assured the Indian government that 'there was no question of break in talk on the part of the Nagas'.[125] Such sentiments, however, went unreciprocated by the Indian government. Instead, a centrist perception of the new Indian ruling authority, as noted in the stances of Prime Minister Nehru, was clearly evident. Home Minister Sardar Vallabhbhai Patel even suspected 'loyalty or devotion to India' of the people in the north-east.[126] Personalities like Sir Akbar Hydari, initially entrusted with the resolution of the Naga question, were likewise unaccommodating:

> They (Nagas) have got to come in. . . . If they revolt, we shall shoot them up. It will be a pity but it will be their fault. We cannot give the Nagas residual powers.[127]

This attitude to the Naga question was manifest even in the thinking of the country's first non-Congress Prime Minister Morarji Desai. One may recall here the meeting that Desai had with A.N. Phizo in 1977 in London when he retorted:

> The Nagas are not suffering. And if you talk about Nagaland, I shall not talk with you. . . . I am prepared to meet you as a person but not about Nagaland.[128]

Nagaland also did not derive much advantage from Indian economic planning. While the First and Second Five Year Plans for Nagaland were substantially shelved because of insurgency, lack of adequate economic growth made the Nagas victims of 'relative underdevelopment'. Still now the Nagas predominantly earn their living from agriculture which again relies on the traditional *jhum* method. The Naga Hills are rich in such mineral resources as petroleum, gas, copper, coal, iron ore and lime. But they unfortunately lie untapped. The high quality of oil discovered in Wokha remains largely unexplored. The north-east as a region contributes only a little more than 2 per cent to the country's GNP, and Nagaland's share in the national industrial investment is only 0.01 per cent.[129] The Scheduled Commercial Banks' credit for Nagaland at the beginning of the present century was only Rs. 120.2 crore, considerably lower than states with roughly similar size like Pondicherry (Rs. 540.8 crore) and Goa (Rs. 1,654.3 crore).[130] The proportion of people below the poverty line in Nagaland is slightly lower than the national average—37.9 per cent as against 36 per cent.[131] What is, however, disturbing is the fact that while at the national level the proportion of rural population subsisting below poverty line has declined to 37.3 per cent, the figure for Nagaland is 45 per cent.[132] This is especially significant because Nagaland shares the general regional trend of 80 per cent of the population subsisting on agriculture. Only 6 million of the 25.5 million hectare of the land mass in the north-east is available for cultivation. But the Indian State has not undertaken sufficient measures for increasing productivity on this limited agricultural land.[133] Nor have schemes been adopted for adequate cultivation of commercial crops. Meanwhile, indiscriminate deforestation has deprived the tribals of Nagaland of their traditional means of sustenance.[134] The purchasing power in the north-east is also lower than the national average—the estimated per capita expenditure per month being Rs. 260.3 in the north-east compared to the national figure of Rs. 287.1.[135] We do not have separate data for Nagaland, but it surely follows the general regional pattern. Although Nagaland had been traditionally ahead of other states in the realm of literacy, it unfortunately recorded between 1991 and 2001 an increase of 1.8 million in the number of illiterates at a time when in the national scene the number of illiterates declined by 32 million.[136] Public health facilities are extremely inadequate. Drinking water is in short supply.[137] Significantly, the proportion of child population in the age group 0-6 in Nagaland has declined from 17.15 per cent in 1991 to 14.09 per cent in 2001. This figure is still slightly higher than the national average, but the declining ratio of child population in Nagaland may be taken to suggest rising incidence of child mortality. In recent years Nagaland has been afflicted by AIDS and other sex-related diseases—as is evident from the fact that 55.148 per thousand were recorded as seropositive, a figure alarmingly higher than the national aggregate of 20.82.[138]

In recent years, New Delhi has been introducing special economic packages for the north-east,[139] For example Rs. 1,060 crore for a population of 20 lakh people was announced by the Prime Minister Vajpayee during his trip to the state in October–November 2003. But such packages have not yielded rich dividends. Studies by the Centre for Monitoring of the Indian Economy show that much of the developmental fund pumped into the area went astray to create a *nouveau riche* consisting of politicians, contractors, bureaucrats and police officers.[140] Thus, while the region remains economically underdeveloped, the concentration of economic power goes on increasing. Nagaland does not remain free of this economic scenario. But at the same time national policy planners have generally failed to appreciate regional specificities and necessities which has denied the Naga society the benefits of public investment. For instance, technical developments introduced at the behest of New Delhi are proving to be out of tune with the region's 'consumption habits and management practices' since the production process in Nagaland is still largely dependent on communal ownership and management.[141] Unfortunately instead of rectifying its mistaken economic policy, New Delhi still appears to be more interested in disseminating the ideology of pan-Indianism. This evidently motivated the Union Ministry of Information and Broadcasting to announce a Rs. 700 crore package for spreading the State-run television and radio transmission to remote areas of the north-east.

New opportunities were created for a possible resolution of the Naga issue in Indian politics once the Indian State successfully took advantage of the discord between the Khaplang and Swu-Muivah factions within the NSCN and first made the Swu-Muivah faction accept a ceasefire agreement in 1997 and then persuaded the Khaplang group to reconcile itself with a formal truce in April 2001. The province has received a respite from continuous doses of almost fifty years of violence[142] that has reportedly taken a toll of more than one lakh Naga lives.[143] In the words of Udayan Misra:

> (While) the government's perceptions about the Naga struggle have undergone a sea-change and it has shown a large degree of flexibility in trying to work out a political settlement . . . those who have been fighting for an independent Nagalim have also become aware of the inherent complexities involved in their struggle and the impossibility of a military solution.[144]

The changed stance of the Naga leadership became evident from the following comment of Muivah to a leading Indian journalist:

> We are convinced that we cannot solve the problem by ourselves. In order to solve the problem, India must cease the use of force against all groups. . . . The differences should be settled through talks and peaceful means. . . . Talks have to be unconditional from both sides. We should be prepared to understand the difficulties of the people of India. India

should understand the difficulties on our part. Until we have the authority to decide our own future, how can we think of the future?.[145]

On another occasion Muivah emphasized:

We do not insist that they recognise our sovereignty for a start. . . . We will not do anything that is detrimental to India's security. Naturally, we would not remain inimical to India. If the Indians come forward honestly (with proposals), then the Nagas will be available to seek together the way toward a solution.[146]

Yet another manifestation of the new mood was seen when the Indian prime minister Vajpayee during his visit to Nagaland in October 2003 was reportedly offered a 'security cover' by the Issak-Muviah faction of the NSCN.[147]

There are also indications that the new generation of educated Naga elite has developed a stake in the modern political system and prefer to 'be an integral part of India while retaining their identity and control over their livelihood'.[148] Their political perception seems to be different from earlier tribal leaders who had a vested interest in the traditional system and remained inimical to the idea of union with India.[149] Increasing participation in general elections also demonstrate a growing reconciliation of the Nagas with the reality of the Indian Union.

In this transformed scenario the Indian State needs to abandon its hitherto statist approach towards settlements in Nagaland. All the three accords signed between the Indian State and Naga representatives—the Nine-Point Hydari Agreement of June 1947; the Sixteen Point Agreement of July 1960; the Shillong Accord of November 1975—were instances of what has been called securing 'domination through negotiation'.[150] The guiding aim of India for all these agreements was stronger integration of the Hills with Indian Union through gradual marginalization of Naga political voice. For instance, while the Hydari Accord acknowledged the Naga right 'to their freely expressed views', the Sixteen Point Agreement limited this right within the ambit of the Indian Constitution and the Shillong Accord hardly mentioned the political rights and demands of the Nagas.[151] Not unnaturally, these accords were contemporaneous with state repression of Naga rebel groups. But the Indian government has now a new opening to pursue a politics of cooperation with the new generation of Naga leadership and introduce structural reforms for satisfying the basic needs of the Nagas, 93.8 per cent of whom still feel that the government has failed miserably in this realm.[152] The new package can, for instance, include reorientation of tribal handicraft production in tune with modern commercial requirements, improvement of the existing state of animal husbandry, alternative and sustainable farming, integration of farming with pisiculture, horticulture and sericulture, and empowerment of indigenous people through greater involvement in the matter of governance. New Delhi should also utilize the present ceasefire to provide a platform for dialogue with various political forces in Nagaland. The Naga civil society groups like the Naga Students' Federation, Naga Peoples' Movement for Human Rights, Naga Mothers' Association, Naga Women's Union of Manipur and Naga Hoho also need to use the ceasefire as a political entry point in search of new democratic alternatives.[153]

At the same time in cultural terms Naga Christian eclecticism has also to be recognized in India's nation-building agenda. While interacting with Christianity the Nagas did not necessarily compromise with their cultural identity. For instance, Naga Christian converts continued with their traditional rituals like Feasts of Merit. Christian missionaries, too, respected Naga customs and sought a 'synthesis of beliefs'. Again, the Ao Nagas considered *tsungrem* as the High God, and in translations of Bible in Ao language the missionaries substituted the word 'God' or 'Jehovah' with *tsungerm*. But this Naga syncretic cultural past is being endangered by the current Hindu fundamentalist project of bringing all tribal identities within the Hindu fold.[154] Such cultural chauvinism needs to be confronted if Naga confidence in Indian State has to be secured.

The distinguished parliamentarian, late Minoo Masani was perhaps not wide off the mark when he commented as early as 1965 that the Naga problem involved 'a conflict not between right and wrong but between one right and another'.[155] An English observer had aptly assessed the Naga predicament:

> Would India . . . slowly reduce them (the Nagas) to a depressed unhappy case? Or would the Government swiftly reach some sensible settlement,

which would allow them to remain Nagas and preserve their way of life.[156]

A resolution of the Naga question surely requires the fulfilment of the second option. But unless New Delhi takes immediate initiatives in this direction peace in the north-east will remain illusive.

NOTES

1. For an explication of the notion of human territoriality, see J.J. Adney, 'Human Territoriality', *Psychological Bulletin*, 81, 1974, pp. 959-75; B.B. Brown, 'Territoriality', in D. Skols and I. Atman (eds.), *Handbook of Environmental Psychology*, New York, 1987, pp. 505-29; R.D. Sacks, 'Territorial Bases of Power', in A.K. Burnett and P.J. Taylor (eds.), *Political Studies from Spatial Perspectives*, New York, 1981, pp. 53-71.
2. These are: Anal, Angami, Ao, Chakhesang, Chang, Chothe, Chiru, Lamkang, Kharam, Khiamungan, Koireng, Konyak, Lotha, Mao, Maram, Maring, Monsang, Moyon, Nocte, Phom, Pochury, Poumai, Puimei, Rengma, Sangtam, Sema, Tangkhul, Tarao, Thangal, Wancho, Yimchunger, Zeliangrong, Lainung, Pangmi, Tangkhul Somara, Yimchunger Mukhori. The Naga tribes constitute 'marginal groups', in both India and Myanmar. See A. West, *The Most Dangerous Legacy: The Development of Identity, Power and Marginality in the British Transfer to India and the Nagas*, The University of Hull, Centre for South-East Asian Studies, Occasional Paper No. 34, 1999.
3. Take, for example, the following observation of Christoph von Furer-Haimendorf: 'To the Naga mankind appears as sharply divided between the small circle of his co-villagers and clansmen . . . and the entire outward consisting of the people of his own tribe living in other villages as well as the people of neighbouring tribes, who are his potential enemies and also potential victims of headhunting'. See his 'Morality and Prestige among the Nagas', in M.C. Pradhan (ed.), *Anthropology and Archaeology: Essays in Commemoration of Verrier Elwin, 1902-64*, London, 1969, p. 156.
4. David Syiemlieh, 'Socio-Cultural Background of the Peoples of North-East India (19-20 Centuries)', in J. Puthenpurakal (ed.), *The Impact of Christianity in North East India*, Shillong, 1996.
5. See, C. von Furer-Haimendorf, *Tribes of India: The Struggle for Survival*, New Delhi, 1985.
6. S. Ghosh, *Frontier Travails , Northeast: The Politics of a Mess*, Delhi, 2001, p. 30.

7. For details of the suppression of the revolt see Neville Maxwell, *India, The Nagas and the North-East*, Minority Rights Group, Report no. 17, London, and Asoso Yonuo, *The Rising Nagas: A Historical and Political Study*, Delhi, 1974.
8. J. Jacobs et al., *The Nagas: Society, Culture and the Colonial Encounter*, Stuttgart, 1990. The rebels were convinced that enemy bullets would be transformed into water if those were targeted against them.
9. Asoso Yonuo, *The Rising Nagas: A Historical and Political Study*, Delhi, 1914.
10. N. Maxwell, *India, The Nagas and the North-East*, London, 1980.
11. Even in the late 1930s, as Furer-Haimendorf noted: 'The entire administration of the Naga Hills District . . . was in the hands of one deputy commissioner stationed at Kohima and one subdivisional officer, whose headquarters was Mokokchung. With the help of a few clerks and a small force of Assam Rifles, these two officers maintained peace and order in a large hill region where bridle paths were the only means of communication'. See C. von Furer-Haimendorf, *Tribes of India: The Struggle for Survival*, Oxford, p. 35.
12. West, *The Most Dangerous Legacy*, p. 38.
13. Captain Jenkins to the Secretary, Government of India, Poll Department, 14 April 1840, para 3 incorporating a suggestion from Rev. Brownson, Foreign Political, 1840, 11 May, no. 128, National Archives of India (hereafter NAI).
14. J.P. Mills, 'A Sanctuary of Savages', PPMS 68/11-14, School of Oriental and African Studies, London.
15. See Henry Balfour, Pitt Rivers Museum, Oxford, to J.H. Hutton, 11 October 1925, Hutton Papers, Centre for South Asian Studies, Cambridge, Microfilm No. 47B. Also see, S. Ghosh, *Frontier Travails* p. 35.
16. V. Elwin, *Nagaland*, Shillong: 1961, pp. 36-7; S. Nag, *India and North-East India: Mind, Politics and the Process of Integration 1946-1950*, New Delhi, 1998, p. 58.
17. V. Elwin, *The Nagas in the Nineteenth Century India*, Bombay, 1969. The motive behind a headhunting raid was quite simple. Strength and force of a person was believed to remain concentrated in the head and that it was transferable. The Nagas reportedly felt that this soul-force guides the functions of human body and any variation in the sum-total of the entire community's soul-force had its impact on the prosperity of the race. See Major V.K. Anand, *Nagaland in Transition*, New Delhi, 1967, pp. 101-2.
18. Charles Pawsey, 'The Naga Problem', *Pawsey Papers*, Centre for South Asian Studies, Cambridge, Box I, 1965.
19. Cited in Verrier Elwin, *Nagaland*, Shillong, 1961, pp. 36-7.
20. Generally it is believed that the word Naga owes its origin to Nangta,

meaning naked to the plains people. See A. West, *The Most Dangerous Legacy*, p. 12.

21. Ibid., p. 10.
22. A. Yonuo, *The Rising Nagas*. Also see W. Robinson, *Descriptive Account of Assam*, London, 1841.
23. Jacobs et al., *The Nagas*, Chapter 7.
24. Foreign Political, Progs. May 1846, no. 30, NAI.
25. J.H. Hutton, 'The Mixed Culture of the Naga Tribes', *Journal of the Royal Anthropological Institute*, 95, 1965, p. 16.
26. Cited in Jacobs, et al., *The Nagas*, p. 64.
27. Captain Brodie, 'Narrative of a Tour Over that Part of the Naga Hills Lying Between the Diko and Dyang River', *Journal of the Asiatic Society of Bengal,* 1845, 167, pp. 828-44; J. Avery, 'The Ao Naga Language of Southern Assam', *American Journal of Philology,* 1886, 8, pp. 334-6.
28. S. Nag, *India and North East India,* p. 120.
29. J.H. Hutton, 'Anthropology as an Imperial Study', lecture delivered in 1938, Hutton Papers, Centre For South Asian Studies, Cambridge, Microfilm no. 47B.
30. Nag, *India and North East India*, p. 5.
31. Other missionary groups in the North-East were Welsh Calvinistic Methodists' Foreign Mission Society, Baptist Missionary Society, London Missionary Society, American Baptist Foreign Mission Society.
32. Richard M. Eaton, 'Conversion to Christianity among the Nagas, 1876-1971', *Indian Economic and Social History Review* (hereafter *IESHR*) 21, 1, 1984, p. 7.
33. Ibid.
34. Cited in Asoso Yonuo, *The Rising Nagas,* p. 116. Many company officials thought in a similar vein. See Captain John Butler to Major Jenkins, 13 May 1847, *Foreign Political Progs,* 5 June 1847, no. 24, NAI.
35. B. Pakem, 'Separatist Movement in North East India', in T.L. Bose (ed.), *Indian Federation: Problem and Issues,* Calcutta, 1987; M. Horam, *Thirty Years of Naga Insurgency,* New Delhi, 1990.
36. Lal Dena, *Christian Missions and Colonialism: A Study of Missionary Movement in Northeast India with Particular Reference to Manipur and Lushai Hills 1894-1947*, Shillong, 1988, pp. 105-6.
37. American Baptist Mission Society, *109th Annual Report*, 1923, 113. Cited in Richard M. Eaton, p. 43.
38. Ibid., p. 12.
39. *Missionary Herald,* 1935, p. 268. Cited in Lal Dena, *Christian Missions and Colonialism,* p. 98.
40. West, p. 17.
41. J.P. Mills, *The Ao Nagas*, Bombay, 1973.

42. West, p. 18.
43. See Lal Dena, pp. 111-12.
44. P. Moasosang, 'The Naga Search for Self-Identity', in Rathin Mitra and Barun Dasgupta (eds.), *A Common Perspective for North East India,* Calcutta, 1969.
45. Nag, *India and North East India,* p. 9.
46. T. Aliba Imti, *Reminiscences: From Inpur to Naga National Council,* Mokokchung, 1988, pp. 35-6.
47. W. Fernandes, 'Conflict in North-East: A Historical Perspective', *Economic and Political Weekly,* 18 December 1999.
48. S.K. Barpujari, 'Early Christian Missions in the Naga Hills: An Assessment of Their Activities', *Journal of Indian History*, vol. 48, 1970; N.K. Barooh, *David Scott in the North-East India 1802-1831: A Study in British Paternalism,* New Delhi, 1970.
49. *Foreign Political Progs.*, 5 June 1847, no. 24, NAI.
50. Richard M. Eaton, p. 12.
51. *Foreign Political Progs.*, 9 November 1840, no. 82, NAI.
52. Ibid., 11 May 1840, no. 128, NAI, para 5.
53. Lal Dena, see Chapter 1.
54. In this context James Johnstone, the political agent of Manipur, suggested 'a large number of Christian hillmen between Assam and Burma would be a valuable prop to the British'. See James Johnstone, *Manipur and Naga Hills,* New Delhi, 1971. J. Shakespeare, the Superintendent of North Lushai Hills, admitted when the government failed, the missionaries 'materially assisted in the pacification of the Lushais', Lal Dena, p. 44.
55. West, p. 21.
56. See N. Maxwell, *India, the Nagas and the North East,* 1980.
57. Cited in Nag, *India and North East India,* p. 14.
58. L. Richards, *A Journey into Nagaland,* Oxford, 1995, p. 7.
59. Ibid., p. 5.
60. Asoso Yonuo, *The Rising Nagas,* p. 148.
61. Ibid., p. 150.
62. Nag, p. 23.
63. This Plan of 1946 proposed the formation of a federation with British-ruled area and native principalities on the basis of grouping of provinces into (a) Hindu provinces; (b) Muslim provinces; and (c) Bengal and Assam.
64. T. Aliba Imti, p. 6.
65. Typescript of Hutton's analysis of Simon Commission's impact on the Nagas, *Hutton Papers,* Centre for South Asian Studies, Cambridge, Microfilm no. 47B.
66. See the note prepared by J.P. Mills, 1 June 1946, Mss. Eur. F. 236/78, India Office Library and Records (hereafter IOR).

67. A.Z. Phizo to Rajagopalachari, 22 November 1948, cited in Nag, p. 18.
68. J.P. Mills, Advisor to the Governor of Assam, to the Governor's Secretary, U.O. no. A.11/46 dt. 8.7.47, para 2, MSS. Eur. F. 236/78, IOR.
69. Cited in Nag, p. 21.
70. Cited in Maxwell, p. 4.
71. *National Herald*, 6 August 1946.
72. Ibid.
73. Nag, p. 11.
74. Cited D.R. Syiemlieh, 'Responses of the North Eastern Tribals of India towards India's Partition', *Indo-British Review: A Journal of History*, vol. XVII, nos. 1 & 2, September-December 1989.
75. T. Aliba Imti, pp. 164-5.
76. Yonuo, p. 166.
77. Cited in Asoso Yonuo, p. 169; V. Venkata Rao et al., *Century of Government and Politics in North-East India*, vol. III, New Delhi, 1987, pp. 38-9.
78. Mountbatten to Earl of Listowel, 24 April 1947, letter no. 210 in N. Mansergh (ed.), *Transfer of Power*, vol. 10, London, 1981, p. 70.
79. *Naga Nation*, February 1947.
80. Nag, p. 74.
81. T. Aliba Imti, *Reminisences*, pp. 66-8.
82. Yonuo, pp. 200-1.
83. *Collected Works of Mahatma Gandhi*, vol. LXXXVIII, 25 May 1947 to 31 July 1947, New Delhi, 1983, p. 373.
84. Ibid.
85. See Phizo's communication to the president of India of 1 November 1957; Girija Kumar and V.K. Arora (eds.), *Documents on Indian Affairs*, New Delhi, 1965, p. 108.
86. B. Datta, 'Ethnicity, Nationalism and Sub-Nationalism with Reference to North-East India', in D. Pakem (ed.), *Nationality, Ethnicity and Cultural Identity in North East India*, New Delhi, 1990.
87. T. Aliba Imti, p. 70.
88. Yonuo, p. 314.
89. Memo no. 262G of 9/4/47, para 6, Mss. Eur. F. 236/76, IOR.
90. B.G. Verghese, *India's Northeast Resurgent: Ethnicity, Insurgency, Governance and Development*, New Delhi, 1996, p. 2.
91. See the record of Nehru's meeting with a delegation of Naga Hills National Council, 4 August 1946, Mss. Eur. F. 236/76, IOR.
92. S. Bhaumik, *Insurgent Crossfire: North-East India*, New Delhi, 1996, p. 41.
93. Ibid., pp. 41-2.
94. Cited in N. Maxwell, p. 5.

95. Ghosh, p. 209.
96. Maxwell, p. 5.
97. West, pp. 35-6.
98. This protest reached a climactic point in 1979 with Naga raid on a forest reserve, resulting in 60 deaths and destruction of a number of houses. See N. Rustomji, p. 69.
99. Bhaumik, p. 42.
100. *Naga Vigil Bulletin,* no. 47, Mss. Eur. F. 236/426, IOR.
101. *The Naga Chronicle*, p. 148.
102. Ibid., p. 181.
103. Maxwell, p. 6.
104. For a graphic account of the encounters between Indian security forces and Naga rebels see N. Nibedon, *Nagaland: The Night of the Guerillas,* New Delhi, 1978; on violation of human rights in Nagaland, See Luingam Luithui and N. Haksar, *Nagaland File,* New Delhi, 1984.
105. For peace efforts of this group see M. Aram, *Peace in Nagaland: Eight Year Story 1964-72,* Delhi, 1974.
106. See the note by A.R. Dutt, Major General, General Officer Commanding and R. Zopinga, Chief Secretary, Government of Nagaland, March 1973, *The Naga Legacy*, p. 167.
107. Samaddar, *A Biography of the Indian Nation*, p. 265.
108. The new province of Nagaland comprised only the old Naga Hills District and did not incorporate all those who called themselves Nagas.
109. Anand, *Nagaland in Transition*, p. 13.
110. Hokishe Sema, *Emergence of Nagaland,* Delhi, 1986.
111. Jacobs, et al., *The Nagas,* p. 177.
112. B. Lintner, 'The Turbulent Tribes', *Far Eastern Economic Review,* 133/34, pp. 22-25.
113. Bhaumik, pp. 42-4.
114. See P.G. Rajamohan, 'Fundamentalism and the ISI in Northeast Insurgency', unpublished paper of Institute for Conflict Management.
115. Bhaumik, p. 45.
116. Ibid.
117. *Pawsey Papers,* Centre For South Asian Studies, Cambridge, Boxes V & VI.
118. Bhaumik, p. 44.
119. Yonuo, p. 307.
120. The first of such pamphlets was Phizo's 'The Fate of the Naga People and Appeal to the World', ibid., p. 308.
121. Richards, *A Journey into Nagaland,* p. 7.
122. Ibid., p. 318.
123. Cited in Anand, *Nagaland in Transition,* p. 133.

124. A.Z. Phizo to C. Rajagopalchari, Governor-General of India, 22 November 1948, cited in V.K. Nuh compiled and Westshokhrolo Lasuh, eds., *The Naga Chronicle*, New Delhi, 2002, p. 5.
125. Ibid., p. 53.
126. See Patel's letter to Nehru in 1950, cited in N.S. Narahari, *Security Threats to North-East India: Socio-Ethnic Tension*, New Delhi, 2002, p. 9.
127. Note from Sir Akbar Hydari dt. 6/6/47, Mss. Eur. F. 236/78, IOR.
128. *The Naga Chronicle*, p. 325.
129. Ministry of Industry, Government of India, SIA Statistics, April 2001.
130. Reserve Bank of India, *Basic Statistical Returns of Scheduled Commercial Banks in India*, 2001.
131. Tata Services Ltd., *Statistical Outline of India 2000-2001*.
132. Ibid.
133. Only 20 per cent of the net cultivable area has been irrigated. See the paper by K.P.C. Rao, the director of National Institute of Agricultural Research Management, Hyderabad, at a seminar in Jorhat on 24 and 25 February 1997, as reported in *The North East Age*, 4 March 1997.
134. *The North East Times*, 15 May 1998.
135. A. Shariff, *India Human Development Report: A Profile of Indian States in the 1990s*, Delhi, 1999, p. 257.
136. The decadal increase in illiterates in Nagaland during the period was from 3.8 million to 5.6 million, while the all-India figure registered a decline of illiterates from 328.2 million to 296.2 million. See the census data for 2001.
137. Unfortunately we do not have data for individual states in the north-east, but the percentage of households having access to protected water in the region is 61.9 as against the national average of 72 per cent. See A. Shariff, *India Human Development Report*, p. 239.
138. S. Parasuraman and P.V. Unnikrishnan (eds.), *India Disasters Report: Towards a Policy Initiative*, Delhi, 2000, p. 295.
139. The process started in 1995 when the Congress government in New Delhi created the North-East Development Bank with an authorized capital of Rs.500 crore. See the editorial in *The Statesman* (Calcutta), 24 October 2001.
140. A. Shariff, *India Human Development Report*, p. 229. The following is the percentage distribution of housholds in the north-east: 34.0 for income group Rs. 20,001-40,000, 16.9 for Rs. 40,001-62,000, 3.7 for Rs. 62,001-86,000. The corresponding national average is: 26.8, 8.9, 3.3 respectively.
141. Many commentators had indicated as early as the 1980s the pitfalls of introducing modern production system in the north-east without

changing the pattern of land ownership. See for instance B.K. Ray Burman, 'Points and Counter-points in North-East India', in A.D. Pant and Shiva K. Gupta (eds.), *Multi-ethnicity and National Integration: A Politico-Anthropological View,* Allahabad, 1985.

142. But a crisis ensued when New Delhi accepted the Naga demand not to limit the ambit of the ceasefire to Nagaland alone but to bring within it those Nagas living outside Nagaland. This step generated a hostile reaction in states like Manipur having a sizeable Naga population since they feared it would be a booster for the slogan of Greater Nagaland. Faced with the angry outburst, New Delhi abandoned its project of extending the territorial limits of the cease-fire.
143. The estimated figure varies between 1,50,000 to 3 lakh lives. See *Naga Resistance and the Peace Process,* Delhi, 2001, p. 23.
144. *Economic and Political Weekly,* 15 February 2003.
145. Cited in S. Hazarika, 'Nagas: The Long March', *The Asian Age,* 8 May 2001.
146. Cited in S. Hazarika, 'Do not blackmail the Nagas: Muivah and Swu', *The Asian Age,* 9 May 2001.
147. N. Dholabhai, 'How to Improve a State of the Mind', *The Telegraph,* 3 November 2003.
148. W. Fernandes, 'Conflict in North-East: A Historical Perspective', in *Economic and Political Weekly,* 18 December 1999, p. 3581.
149. See B.K. Roy Burman's 'Foreword' in Gangmumei Kabui, *Annal: A Transborder Tribe of Manipur,* Delhi, 1985.
150. K.S. Singh, 'Naga Accords: An Instance of Domination through Negotiation', ibid., pp. 32-51.
151. Ibid., p. 38.
152. See the opinion survey 'Seeking Truth' conducted by the Naga People's Movement for Human Rights, January 2000, cited in ibid., p. 21.
153. For an argument along this line see Ranabir Samaddar, 'Ceasefire in Nagaland, But What Worth is it', ibid., pp. 57-9.
154. Mention may be made of the RSS' Vanwani campaign. The RSS idea of 'authentic/pure Indian excludes Christian Nagas'.
155. M.R. Masani, 'Nagaland Problem: A Constructive Approach', *Times of India,* 19 February 1965.
156. Note by Archer of 4 December 1948, Mss. Eur. F. 236/75, IOR.

CHAPTER 13

Understanding Change in the Lives of Dalits of Punjab After 1947

HARISH K. PURI

Our struggle is not for wealth or for power but for freedom. Our struggle is for the reclamation of Human Personality!

B.R. AMBEDKAR

There was a time when we were treated like animals. Now we live like human beings. It is all because of Ambedkar.

NAMDEO DHASAL

The present study is related to the nature of change in the lives of the Dalits (Scheduled Castes) of Punjab since the Independence of India and the Partition of Punjab in 1947. Not many are aware that the Scheduled Castes (SC) constitute a very substantial segment of population in Punjab state—28.9 per cent, as per census 2001. This is the highest level of concentration of Dalits in any one state of India. The Dalits have been for ages the most deprived and oppressed and the most humiliated section of our society. The purpose of this article is to have a sense of the change that has come both in the external conditions of their living—demographic, economic, political and social—and also the change in the subjective dimension. The latter, in other words, refers to mental change or change in perception, i.e. the way persons belonging to the SC communities view themselves

*Revised version of the paper presented at the seminar on 'Social Transformations in North Western India During the Twentieth Century', organized by Institute of Punjab Studies at Chandigarh, 7-9 September 2005. The author is thankful to John Webster and W.H. McLeod for their comments and suggestions.

and the manner in which they are viewed and treated by others.

The focus of this study is more on the ground reality of the change and the dynamics of change on the basis of common sense knowledge. For that purpose the author went about observing their lives; talking and listening at some length to a large number of Dalits of different castes, age-groups and areas, many in their homes; participating in their celebrations; securing access to their recollections, experiences and observations, particularly from the elderly, including written responses to broad questions from a number of eminent Dalit leaders.[1] The autobiographical and literary writings of Dalits as well as the Punjabi fiction and folklore in general depicting the situations of the Dalits have also been taken into account. An attempt has been made to take note of the distinction between 'physical facts' and 'mental facts'.[2] The first part of the paper attempts to present a broad picture of the conditions of life of the SCs, their living as well as ideas and beliefs, around the time India became independent. The second part refers to an overview of the character of change that has taken place in their material conditions as well as the shift in their perception of social change, their present status and what it means to them, including their hopes and fears. The observations of the non-SCs about the changes in caste relations are also relevant.

I

The conventional writings on the Partition of Punjab and the violence that followed have generally tended to ignore the fate of Dalits, then called Harijans or Untouchables. However, recent works like *Borders and Boundaries: Women in India's Partition* by Ritu Menon and Kamla Bhasin and then Urvashi Butalia's *The Other Side of Silence: Voices from the Partition of India* have drawn attention to this neglect.[3] It occurred to the author that one needed to look for the fate of the Dalits in the Partition violence. Butalia observes: 'The fact that Harijans were, to some extent, rendered invisible in Partition violence had led to another kind of invisibility; that of history itself.'[4]

The first story recounted here, the only one of its kind available to us, in Butalia's book is of a Harijan girl, Maya Rani of

Dinanagar in Gurdaspur district. Butalia interviewed her some 40 years after the event in Batala town of that district. Maya was a child witness to the killings and looting, first of the Hindus and Sikhs by Muslims of the place in mid-August 1947 when rumours prevailed that the district of Gurdaspur had become a part of Pakistan. There was a dispute as to whether Gurdaspur was a Muslim or a non-Muslim majority district. A few days later, when the news spread that the area remained within India, Maya Rani witnessed widespread killings of Muslims by the 'others'.

Maya was among a group of about eleven girls of her age who viewed the anarchy and mayhem as an 'opportunity'. They jumped over roofs into the deserted or burning Muslim houses, searching, collecting and bringing home all kinds of available goods. These included a variety of household goods including *patilas, parats* and *hamams*—bales of cloth, clothes, *razais* (quilts), *atta* (wheat flour), even *desi ghee* (clarified butter) and almonds. This adventurous pillage continued for several days without any fear. Stated Maya:

> No, we weren't frightened, everyone tried to scare us, even our parents. But all children of *that area*, none of us was scared. . . . Our parents were worried, saying we would get killed. But we thought, who is going to take us away, who is going to kill us? We call ourselves Harijans. Hindus, Christians, no one can take us away . . . there was no danger for us. *Because we were Harijans*. Whether it had become Pakistan or Hindustan, it made no difference to us.

In this regard Butalia further observes that the Harijans 'did not see themselves as Hindus or Christians (or indeed any one else). Rather they had their own distinct identity; that in the mainstream Hindu society their *customary invisibility* was based on their being outside the pale of caste Hindu society. . . .'[5]

Perhaps there was another factor. In a society where the worth of a person was measured by the size of the land owned by his family, the outcastes without land or any other kind of property—'nothing to be looted, nothing to lose'—seemed to enjoy *a bizarre kind of immunity* during such violent times. The few references to the *Kamins* in the memoranda submitted by groups, and the proceedings relating to the Partition provides an eloquent evidence of the prevalent rationale for '*rejecting their personhood* but claiming their labour'.[6]

In this regard, it may be pertinent to refer to the testimony given by Sardar Harnam Singh before the Punjab Boundary Commission, pleading for the claim of the Sikhs to demarcate the central Punjab districts as a Sikh 'Homeland'. The argument was that only the Sikhs were the true 'sons of the soil', i.e. peasant proprietors—or at least, occupancy tenants, 'rooted in the soil of the districts'. Most of the Muslims, Harnam Singh argued, were a population of 'fakirs, beggars, weavers, herdsmen, cobblers, *kumhars* or potters, *musallis*, carpenters, oilmen, bards, barbers, blacksmiths, washermen, butchers, and *mirasis*—people who are described in the settlement reports as landless people and menials'.[7] Paul Brass underlines that whereas the Sikh spokesman counted the low caste Mazhabis (and other low caste Sikhs) as a part of their own total, it was argued that the people belonging to the above listed communities 'should not be counted in the total Muslim population. In other words, they were "non-persons". Leaving out these non-persons, the Muslims in the districts, whose Census population in 1941 constituted a majority in all of them, would be reduced to a minority.' [8]

It was reported, on the other hand, that M.A. Jinnah made a suggestion that the *kamins* (who were regarded neither Muslim nor Hindu/Sikh) may be divided 50-50 between India and Pakistan. After all both the dominions required scavengers, sweepers and leather workers.[9] B.R. Ambedkar and Jawaharlal Nehru had to personally intervene to secure the release of the SC people who were prohibited from leaving Pakistan for India by the Government of Pakistan through an order under a special Essential Services Ordinance.[10] That was in line with the prevailing rationale that 'rejected their personhood' but claimed their labour.[11]

The arrangements made for relief and rehabilitation of about 2,50,000 (50,000 families) of the 'untouchable' refugees pointed to similar kind of problems. The officers in charge of the relief camps did not allow them in the refugee camps. On 18 December 1947, Ambedkar complained to Nehru that 'the Scheduled Caste evacuees were not able to take shelter in refugee camps' and were not getting relief.[12] Rameshwari Nehru also wrote to Pandit

Nehru, drawing his attention to the rules regarding rehabilitation which left the 'Harijan refugees' out of reckoning. According to the rules, compensatory land was available only to the agriculturists, i.e. those who had owned land before migration. The Harijans were agriculturists but only tillers, and not landowners.[13] Lal Singh Dil, one of the foremost Dalit Punjabi poets, expressed his resentment that following the Partition, 'Sikhs grabbed all the land; not even a patch of *shamlat* (commons) land was left in the village.'[14] The *kamins* were divided and further weakened.

The second story the author wishes to share is his personal recollection. This was around 1948, when I was about 10 years of age. I vividly recall a Harijan woman scavenger, who used to come daily to clean our dry latrine located on the roof of the two-storey house at Jaito Mandi, a part of the then native state of Nabha. The lady must have been quite young and my memories of her are of a rather dark and fairly healthy lady, perhaps in her late twenties, who was fond of talking some sweet nothings with us children. On her afternoon round for collecting two *rotis*, she would often sit down to share some local gossip or her personal problems with my mother. She would often giggle and occasionally burst into a hearty laugh. But I had also seen that she was quite capable of showing her temper when feeling insulted.

One dimension of the recollections relating to her morning round to clean the dry latrine impressed its meaning on my mind much later in life. As occasionally we children were running up and down the stairs, playing some games, she would usually enter the *deodhi* shouting from outside, '*Kaka ji, Beeba ji, parey reho ji* (*mere nal lagg ke*) *bhitt na jayoji*' (O good lads! gentle lads! keep at a distance please, lest you are polluted [by contact, touch]. In her voice one suspected a trepidation. Once earlier she was rebuked profusely for not taking care to keep at a distance from the children. Perhaps more painful to her was the fact that she was a witness to the thrashing I had received from my mother for getting polluted and then running into and polluting the kitchen. It was hell that broke loose in our home; a nightmare for me. That lady had cried and begged of my mother not to hurt me, and apologized for her alleged 'carelessness'. That may have been the reason for her daily cry to keep the children away from her. I remember it as an instance of a marked acceptance and internalization of the polluting character of her touch and low status, as her fate. It could be that she considered that to be totally unjustified, yet upheld it as a fact of life that she and others like her must live with. There was no alternative. Untouchability was an ubiquitous reality of social life at that time and till much later.

The author's exchanges with the Dalits about life as it was lived at that time made him acutely conscious of the fact that looking back in time was, for all of them, an extremely painful experience—one of reliving the physical suffering, shame, ignorance, indignity and anger.[15]

A tour of the Vehra, Thathi or Chamarhli, back in time, where these people lived, brought one to a crowded colony wrapped in a mixture of stinks—from putrefying skeletons of dead animals, raw skins spread out for drying and cleaning, overflowing open drains that brought the sewers of the village to their low-lying *basti*, rotting manure and much more.[16] The one *kuchcha kotha* (mud house) per family was raised on *Mauroosi*, i.e. *shamlat* (village commons) land that belonged to the village. The family did not own the land; building a brick structure on that land was out of question. Custom and law prescribed obligatory *begaar* (unpaid customary labour) services for all the Untouchable or low caste men and women. That law was repealed only in 1957, a few years after the then Union Law Minister B.R. Ambedkar, managed to get another law repealed—the Alienation of Land Act of 1900—which excluded the 'non-agricultural castes' from buying agricultural land.

The established rules of untouchability prescribed everything—the occupation, the person's name, the manner in which one was to be addressed by others (expletives, curses and all) and the way the SCs were required to address the others. The SCs' dress, social and physical distance from the others, place and posture for walking, posture for standing and sitting in the presence of upper-caste people, the kind of food accessible to them and a whole range of social taboos were determined by rules of untouchability. Poverty was an essential component of that life. One present-day Class 1 officer of the Union

Government recalled that in his house the buffalo meat was dried and then cooked for several days and the fat stored in tins for cooking. ' "*Mail khaney log*" (dirt-eating people) was an epithet we were known by.'[17] Personal cleanliness was not a high priority. Soap cake, as a Mazhabi leader of Dehati Mazdoor Sabha disclosed, became an item of purchase towards the end of 1960s when the Green Revolution placed 'cash in our hands for the first time'.[18] The time of a brief break from labour was the time for picking lice from the hair and clothes and of self-deprecating abuse. The repertoire of threats, stares and gestures, folk sayings and names *kutti zat, kamzat, kujat, kutir, bhitt, chumm, dhed, vaddhi-tukki zat, jooth* and reference to human excreta, were regular reminders of their beings as filth. A theft or any other crime in the village was often blamed on the low caste people, who were the first to be hauled up and thrashed by the police.

Their recollections of social exchange or conversation had a significant element of lying and swearing which seemed a normal part of learning in their homes and colonies. Low self-esteem and self-hate found expression in curses, violence and variety of, what others described as, 'unsocial behaviour'. The *jajmani* system that maintained a custom-bound generational relationship of attached labour at the beck and call of the zamindar patron, was somewhat redeemed by an ambivalent kind of master-subject belongingness. 'Dignity', of course, had relevance only for the zamindars.

But there were obvious ambiguities and contradictions. The mid-wives who helped the high-caste women during child-birth were all Dalit. So the exceptional physical contact with the mother and the new-born was accepted as normal. Ironically, maternal and infant mortality was the highest in the community of these mid-wives. As described in Gurcharan Singh Rao's novel *Mashaalchi*, '*Sade Surtu da athwan munda masan magar lagaya ai . . . pehle sarey siley vich ye marde rahey*' (our Surtu's eighth one survived with difficulty; all the earlier ones died during delivery or soon after).[19] This kind of grief was peculiar to the Untouchable families. Ignorance drove the sick and the weak to the corridors of the quacks and sorcerers to satiate the evil spirits whose annoyance was commonly believed to be the cause of all kinds of sickness and suffering. The strictly imposed pollution yardstick did not, however, protect Dalit women from sexual exploitation or rape by people of the upper castes. Pre-marital adventure of a zamindar's young son was a part of folklore.[20] One 25-year-old Mazhabi student of the author's university told him that the children in their families grew up with the knowledge of the violation of one or the other of their women relatives. 'Just stay silent; this is our fate,' the elders would advise as 'nothing will come out of complaint to the police.' Strong protest could sometimes facilitate a *razinama* (compromise) with some material compensation to the victim's family.[21] The women of the Jat-zamindar household, as it appeared in Punjabi fiction, generally blamed Dalit women for enticing the masculine Jat males through some mysterious power or *jadoo-tona* (black magic). The uncommon fair skin of a Dalit new-born commonly invited the whispers about the probable father of the child. Bhagtu, the Mazhabi attached labourer, in *mashaalchi,* when rebuked by the *zaildar* for alleged arrogance of his school-going son Kattu pleads:

> Sardarji! such boys can only be your progeny; must have entered the women's wombs when they went to work in the field. Had they been ours they could not have breathed in your presence! . . . Have you ever seen us opening our mouths in front of you . . . so old have we grown in age ![22]

'Notified Criminal Tribes', a legally demarcated category under British colonial construction included members of at least seven of the presently listed SCs in Punjab. Alongside the creation of the 'loyal' and 'martial' castes, there was a construction of its obverse, i.e. not loyal, not trustworthy and thus dangerous 'predatory castes'.[23] All of these 'Notified Criminal Tribes'—Sansi, Bangali, Banjara, Nat, Bauria, Brara, Gandhila, Mahatams of Dharamkot—were from the lowest castes. Landless and without a permanent settlement, these vagrant poor were listed as communities of 'hereditary criminals'. A crime in their case was regarded not as an individual activity but an intrinsic feature of those belonging to a caste or tribe by birth and occupation.[24] It was in 1952 that an order for denotification and abolition of the above categorization was issued and these caste communities came to be known as *vimukta jatis*'.

Except in schools established by the Arya Samaj and the Singh Sabha, sending a Dalit child to school during those days was generally unthinkable for most Untouchable rural families. Viewed as an affront to the status of upper castes, the Harijan child often invited the wrath of the school teacher and the village elders. Even decades after Independence, a few Dalit children in the schools were routinely reminded that they were not fit for education and were ordered to sweep and clean the school ground and the rooms. In the words of Lal Singh Dil, 'If the school was meant mainly to remind you of your low-caste status every day, there was little meaning in going to school.'[25]

II

In last fifty years or so after Independence one witnessed the working of a complex and multi-dimensional process of change. A major difference was made by the demographic change following the Partition and the later reorganization of the Punjab state. According to Lal Singh Dil, '*Musalmanan de jaan naal shudran dian bahwan bhajj gayyian*' (the going away of the Muslims left the Shudras disabled). The large-scale presence of poor Muslim artisans in the villages of the present Punjab seemed to have been a factor of social and moral support for the 'untouchables' in a situation of cruel oppression by Jat landowners. He recalls the opening of a shop in his village by his people that was made possible because of the presence and support of the Muslims. Another incident in his village was remembered when the two socially oppressed groups—the Muslims and the Untouchables—had together fought a battle with a gang of the landlords, making the latter run for cover.[26]

The rehabilitation of the refugees and consolidation of holdings after Partition further empowered the Sikh Jat landlords. Their social and political dominance became more formidable with the reorganization of Punjab state in 1966 and the Green Revolution. 'The Sikhs grabbed all the lands . . . even a patch of the *Shamlaat*—the Commons, open to use by the untouchables—

was not left.'[27] While Punjab became a Sikh majority state (62 per cent of total population), Sikhism came to be dominated by the caste-class of Sikh Jat landlords. In the first serious anthropological study of a Sikh village, Indera Paul Singh discovered that 'most of the Sikh values are Jat values and Jats assert that they occupy the highest position among the Sikh castes'.[28] It was no longer possible to sustain the impression that the Sikh community was free from the canker of caste hierarchy and caste discrimination. In fact, the first successful political struggle of Shiromani Akali Dal after Independence related to the legal recognition that like the Hindu SCs the Sikhs had their own low castes—Mazhabi, Ramdasia, Kabirpanthi, Sikligar, and so on—which must be included in the list of the SCs.[29] A recent discussion among Punjabi writers underlined the recognition of an existing reality that caste is entrenched in the sub-consciousness of Punjabi society.[30] The Jat landlord's power and kinship connections in the state bureaucracy were able to defeat the government's policy of land reforms. *Jattvaad*, signifying a Jat hauteur or crude arrogance of power and oppression of the Jats, became for the rural Dalits the keyword of their oppression and humiliation.[31] On the other hand, the concentration and rise in the proportion of the SCs made a difference. In the pre-Partition Punjab when the Muslims constituted a majority of 53 per cent and Hindus and Sikhs were only 30 per cent and 14 per cent respectively, the 'Exterior Castes', according to the Census of 1931, constituted about 5 per cent of the population.[32] The Partition in 1947 and then the reorganization of Punjab in 1966 altered the caste configuration. By 1991 the SC population in the truncated Punjab state had gone up to 28.3 per cent, rising to 28.9 per cent in 2001. The rural population was composed mainly of Sikh Jats and SCs. The fact that in more than 3,000 villages their proportion of Dalits was over 40 per cent and in some villages like Talhan, it was more than 65 per cent, it became for the Dalits a measure of strength. It also underlined the potential for resistance and conflict.

A series of post-Independence developments together contributed to a noticeable transformation in the status and living conditions of the SCs of Punjab. The constitutional and legal measures for social justice, particularly those relating to abolition of 'untouchability'—making its practice in any form a crime punishable by law—proved to be significant. These included measures such as the Protection of Civil Rights Act, 1955 and a comprehensive Scheduled Castes and Scheduled Tribes (Prevention of Atrocities) Act, 1989; the abolition of *begaar* and the repeal of laws like the Land Alienation Act, 1901. Reservations, affirmative actions for social welfare by the government, the operation of the democratic system through universal adult franchise and regular elections made a difference for the better. Looking at the scenario at present, most of the Dalits feel that '*Par wadda farak chonan ne paya—lokan nun nazdeek liyanda*' (But the big difference was made by the elections that brought the people closer).[33] Another kind of difference was made by changes in the economy—such as the Green Revolution, urbanization, spread of education, new avenues of employment, and the beginning of the human rights movement. The Dalit activists believed that no less significant was the impact of the organized political and cultural assertion among them and the rising influence of Ambedkar as the messiah of SCs. No aspect of Dalit life remained untouched.

The impact of the changes was however uneven between regions, the rural and the urban segments, between the people of one SC community and another and between men and women. The situation in urban areas is vastly different and better today for them than in the rural areas. The Ad Dharmi, or Megh communities in the Doaba region are more urbanized, more upwardly mobile, more self-confident and politically assertive than the Balmikis, Mazhabis and the other communities. It is pertinent to recall that Ambedkar had advised his people to move to urban areas as there was no hope for them in villages which he regarded as 'dens of ignorance'. However, that was not easy. The urban population of the SCs in Punjab in 2001 was only 20.70 per cent and about 80 per cent of them still lived in the villages.

As of now, the belief in untouchability has practically come to an end in the Punjab, particularly in the urban areas. Studies conducted by a number of scholars and the author's specific inquiries and observations at various levels confirmed that the question of ritual pollution and purification ceases to be an issue.[34] There are practically no instances of separate cups or utensils. None would dare to offer left-over food to the Dalits. Dalit respondents routinely appreciated the change of times and that 'the previous isolation and segregation has also narrowed down'. Barring Hindu temples and occasional incidents in Sikh gurdwaras and *deras*, one does not notice any restriction on their entry to religious places. Conversely, many pointed to the presence of a fairly large number of SCs among the Sikh religious priests and religious singers (*raagis*) and even in *langars* and kitchens at gurdwaras. '*Mazhabi sikhan da laangri lagna aam hai*' (Recruitment of Mazhabi Sikhs as servers of food at *langar* is common).[35]

A conscious effort was made by a large number of SCs to move away from such traditional occupations that carried an alleged stigma. According to a recent field study of 51 villages by S.S. Jodhka, covering three regions of Punjab, not more than 20 per cent of them were presently involved in their traditional occupations. It was described as a phenomenon of 'Dissociation, Distancing and Autonomy'.[36] Only about 15 per cent of them work now as agricultural labourers. The secretary of the Amritsar District Khet Mazdoor Sabha—himself a Mazhabi—is convinced that 'no dalit now stayed to work with a zamindar if he was not treated well'.[37] Most Dalits appeared to hail the fact that a very large number of them had shifted to other callings such as trade, goldsmithy, shopping, construction-work or working as carpenters, masons, hawkers, and so on. A good number of them in the villages of Amritsar district were into dairy farming and selling of milk. The work of Dalit women as domestic helps in upper caste homes, including kitchens, came to be viewed as more or less normal in a village community. There was appreciation for the deliberate effort for personal cleanliness and hygienic living. As the author observed at several wedding parties of the 'upper castes', nobody seemed to bother that most of the waiters serving food (including cooks in many cases) were from the SCs. Practically all the members of the music bands at weddings in Amritsar were found to be Balmikis or other lower caste men. That meant a less noticed severing of the link between caste and its material base.

According to present estimates, over 2,00,000 Dalits in Punjab are in jobs in government departments and public sector undertakings including senior official positions. That includes IAS, IPS and PCS officers, doctors, engineers and many in business and trade. Jalandhar's Boota Mandi locality alone may well boast of over 100 SC millionaire industrialists and traders. Once the material base of caste was undermined, their reference to caste or consciousness of caste appeared to have become formal, or somewhat like membership in civic associations. The author found a fairly large number who are, not any more, shy of introducing themselves as Ad Dharmi, Ravidasi, Kabirpanthi and Mazhabi, even in villages.

The fact that over 90 per cent of the SCs have a brick house today was, for older men, not a small improvement. '*Kuchcha kotha ghatt hi labhda hai*' (mud house is scarcely noticed). Nearly half of the Dalit families have houses within the village proper.[38] A noticeable number in the urban areas have moved into posh localities. However, a majority of the people of one caste live in their separate colonies or clusters in the towns and villages. Discussions on that count reveal that such preference is related to the needs of emotional well being and social security.

'*Parhai kar ke zat badalni*' (acquiring education for going up the caste ladder)—education as 'the key to liberation from caste backwardness'—is another strikingly distinctive feature of Dalit aspirations. '*Putt dab ke parh lai, daliddar chukk ho joo; jattan di gulami na karni paoo*' (son, work hard for education, our scourge of wretchedness will be lifted). 'You will not have to suffer slavery of Jats' is a commonly repeated advice of the parents.[39] Making sacrifice and working harder for that purpose became, for the parents and children, an honourable struggle. For instance in 1961 the female literacy was just about 2 per cent. It rose to 31 per cent by 1991; and 51.8 per cent in the district Hoshiarpur.[40]

Emigration of SC men to foreign countries from the mid-1960s, particularly from the Doaba districts of Jalandhar, Hoshiarpur and Nawanshahr, proved to be a boon for them and their kinsmen. Remittances from abroad contributed to a conspicuous change in the living and aspirations of these families. It was believed that every fourth family of the Ad Dharmi in

Hoshiarpur, Nawanshahar, Nakodar and Jalandhar has at least one member living abroad. Construction of big houses is one way of announcing their success. Events like the honouring of the first Punjabi Dalit millionaire at the International Dalit Conference at Vancouver in 2003, contribution of Rs.1 crore by one Dalit NRI to Sant Sarwan Das Dera of Sachkhand Ballan, near Jalandhar for construction of an eye hospital, the building of 21 Ravidas temples in UK alone—or putting up gold sheeting on the domes of their temples emerged as a measure of the community's upward mobility and pride.

'*Sade vee din badal rahe ney*' (our days are also changing for the better) often conveyed in public and private, often with a glow of well-being, exuding optimism and hope. In fact, their social mobility appears striking in the face of decline in the fortunes of a large section of the Jat landowners, i.e. their socially dominant 'other', whose holdings have become smaller; many of whom are burdened with heavy debts and some even pushed into committing suicides.[41] A shared sense of their political importance among all sections of the SCs can be widely noticed. They appear to recognize the value of their voting power and the share of reserved seats. Not only that they are wooed by all the political parties at the time of elections; there is a confidence that no sensible political leader dares make a comment or observation which could be taken amiss by the SCs. In fact, the urge for registering their presence in public space—flaunting the importance of their votes in different elections—participation in political protests and demonstrations, large-scale gatherings and processions to celebrate the birthdays of Ambedkar, Ravidas, Balmiki and Kabir; installation of statues of Ambedkar, the struggle for naming colonies, roads, universities, colleges, etc., after their heroes, has become a prominent aspect of their aspirations. One of the significant gains of democracy in India, as some of the social scientists have noted, is that the excluded and the marginalized sections of society are keen to take advantage of it, in order 'to gain a voice, a foothold, a sign of status, a measure of effective power'.[42] The constitution of India drafted by Babasaheb Ambedkar is viewed by a number of Dalit elite as the instrument for constructing a new political order. When the NDA government led by A.B. Vajpayee appointed a

Commission to Review the Working of the Constitution in the year 2000, no distinct social segment felt as outraged as the SCs. Scores of organizations of Dalits in Punjab organized seminars and demonstrations to defend 'Babasaheb Ambedkar's Constitution' against the suspected anti-Dalit design of the BJP. It was felt that the weakest people had a high stake in the working of the constitutional political order.

Accordingly, one notices a striking shift in their attitude regarding their rights and needs and of resistance to protect those rights. They refuse to accept the upper-caste dominance as Karma or fate, or the 'other'—touted lowness of their status. The dominance of the Jat-zamindar routinely described as *Jattvaad* in the villages was viewed as a consequence of their ownership of practically all the agricultural land. Earlier, the resistance of the lower caste people against insult or unwelcome commands by the Jats meant inviting trouble. Therefore, their preferred course used to be concealment of anger and reaction, telling of lies and an affected show of submission or deference. Now the younger generation of the SCs lets it be known that caste insult would meet with instant retaliation; they make a show of self-confidence, even arrogance and readiness to physically strike back. Comments such as, 'the SCs wanted to behave as the Jats do', or '*ik din ehnan ney Jattan nun kuttna shuru kar dena hai*' (one day they will start beating the Jats), as a character observes in a novel, were commonly heard.[43] The difference between the older generation and the new generation of SCs in that regard comes out prominently in practically all creative literature by the Dalit writers.[44] It is interesting to note the rise of a fairly large number of Dalits as creative writers in Punjabi language.[45]

However, the picture of the social transformation and the existing reality of social life with reference to the SCs is rather complex and highly differentiated for different sections and *jati* segments. There is, on the one hand, a fairly visible section of the urbanized and educated—many of them second and third generation literates—and economically well-to-do, who are some time described as 'Dalit bourgeoisie'. A prominent tendency among them is to behave like the better-off upper-caste people. Their problem is related to the continued reference to their low caste status by their non-SC colleagues or contempt expressed through body language, if not through words.

A section of the SC elite is acutely sensitive about insult and shame. A most quoted expression is: 'When the other one says "I am a Jat" his chest expands. When we have to say "Chamar", we are reduced to nothing.' *They* refer to the popular songs of Jat superiority like *'Putt Jattan de bulaonde bakkarey'* (sons of Jats raise shouts of challenge), which appear to Dalits as a means to humiliate them. In Punjabi fiction, Jat characters are routinely portrayed as bragging '*Asin Jat hunde aan, asin zamindar hunde aan, asin koi nikki-sukki jaat nahin*' (we are Jats; we are landlords; we are no small mean caste).[46] That usually comes up as a sore point. Many of the SC employees appear to be inclined to hide their caste or avoid a particular company or a situation where there is apprehension of insult or humiliation. They feel vulnerable. Dalit writers, on the other hand, portrays Dalit character tending to avoid their less fortunate kin or deny their relationship to them.[47] Kanshi Ram, the founder president of the Backward and Minority Community Employees Federation (BAMCEF) and later also of the Bahujan Samaj Party (BSP), once articulated this primary concern when he stated that 'Our problem is Humiliation, not Deprivation.'[48] This became the key source of political mobilization for his party. His ideological position was rooted in the experience of the SC employees in public sector. However, the young educated boys from families of educated parents, as the author observed from close contact, are beginning to be less touchy about that, even flaunting their Dalit or *jati* identity. They seem to take occasional incidents of that kind in their stride often ready to insult the other in retaliation.

The relatively less advantaged Dalits and social activists commonly ridicule or/and condemn the class of the rich or educated Dalits for turning their backs on the rest of their less fortunate people. It is believed that such 'upstarts' are caught in a difficult situation, neither accepted by the upper castes as equals nor respected by their own people. In a study conducted in district Hoshiarpur, the people of that class of SCs were found to have not only a preference for the male child but also the tendency to prevent the birth of a girl child in their families.

That points out to a social regression for they had a much better gender ratio earlier.[49] Another study of the SCs in Punjab reveals that the economic prosperity of a small section of the SCs in the post-Green Revolution period led them to emulate the upper castes, not only in terms of asserting masculinity and tightening their control over their women but also in terms of violence against women. It is found that such a tendency among the SCs exceeds the extent of that tendency among the non-SCs.[50]

A vast majority of rural SCs are, on the other hand, focused on the day-to-day economic hardship. In spite of considerable improvement under the state's social welfare schemes, they remain poor. According to one estimate, SCs constitute more than 50 per cent of the total people below the poverty line. Among the SCs, about 66 per cent belong to that category.[51] They are the major sufferers of the decline in government spending on education and public health during recent years. A very high rate of drop-out of SC children from schools is only one indication. One notices considerable incidence among them of belief in spirits and ghosts in the districts of Amritsar and Gurdaspur. Faith healing practices and preaching is reportedly a major reason for conversion of Mazhabis to Christianity in some of the villages.[52]

One of the key reasons for their deprivation and backwardness is believed to be their landlessness. In a society where a person's status and capabilities are determined by the ownership of land, the landless are not only powerless but also without dignity. Not many of them have any hope of introduction of land reforms in Punjab in the future. Therefore, education and employment are generally identified as two basic needs of the SCs. And on that count, a vast majority live with a palpable apprehension of bad times ahead. In the words of Comrade Swaran Singh:

> Because of non availability of employment, the young boys were joblless . . . even after education. Children wander about without anything to do; have taken to intoxicants. . . . Intoxication of smack is prevalent among those with money; our children use things containing chewing tobacco, . . . *sukkha ragarr ragarr ke piende ney* (they go on grinding hemp for drinking), five rupees for a glass of hemp juice; this has spread so much, there is no limit. Earlier, home-made liquor was available; kinship groups used to brew their own; one could buy a

bottle for five rupees. Now that is not available. In some homes the addicts beat their working women for money to buy intoxicants. Some women are standing up to confront the male members. But, for their sons, they would readily hand out money and then curse them and their fate.[53]

Rising incidence of caste atrocities is another development. A survey of press reports on atrocities on Dalits between 1998 and 2003 brought up over a dozen cases of rape, gang rape and stripping and walking Dalit women naked through the village.[54] Cases of social boycott of Dalits have also been rather frequently reported during the last decade. Punjab's *Dalit Dasta Virodhi Andolan* prepared an inventory of Dalit bonded labourers and fought for their liberation. Most of these were cases of men and women at brick kilns who took an advance amount or a loan on interest which they were never able to repay through labour wage. Caught in an endless bondage, hard labour, physical torture and rape of women was for them a form of punishment for non-payment.[55] Punjabi writers point out that 'Before the 1980s you rarely heard of registration of a case of rape of a dalit woman.' Dalits did not have the courage to lodge a complaint; the police were never inclined to register their complaints and media took no notice. At present, public demonstrations, *dharnas,* and efforts to draw the attention of the media and political leaders are common first for getting cases registered and then for arrest of the culprits. Dalits believe that a major reason for a rise in the incidence of rape, social boycott and other forms of atrocities, is that of the Jat population's reaction against the upward mobility and assertiveness of the SCs in the villages.

Determined resistance of Dalits against discrimination is a most noticeable phenomenon now. One marker of that was the proliferation of separate religious temples and gurdwaras and also separate cremation grounds. Until the end of 1960s, all cremated their dead at one place. Now practically each village has separate cremation grounds. In a long series of articles in *Nawan Zamana*, Des Raj Kali analysed incidents of caste clash centred on newly contested claims on ownership of such religious places as had been for ages considered as belonging to the village as a whole.[56] The assertion by the SCs in that regard appears to signify a struggle for their own spaces of autonomy and a distinct identity. A thumbing of their nose at the 'other' or at the symbols of the dominant caste, and often a palpable readiness for confrontation seem to be one of the marks of their transformation, particularly among the young men.[57] Many rural Jats find it difficult to come to terms with the shift in social equations in the village. They dominate both the Congress and the Akali parties in the state. 'Since leadership was with the Jats, the poor Jats were never able to overcome the illusion of their superior caste, even though their conditions of living may be worse than those of the lower castes. That was the reason that the main contradiction emerged between Jats and Dalits.'[58] People of both categories, in other words, tend to assert their caste identity more than earlier.

III

The transformation is evidently partial, and reflects contradictions. The issue of identity appears to have become more salient for Dalits than the issues of redistribution and of access to opportunities and social justice, which were earlier central to the lives of a vast majority of their poor and illiterate fellows. The consciousness of identity, on the other hand, took varied forms. Instead of a Dalit identity, the discrete *jati* consciousness strengthened an internal caste hierarchy. One may notice a milder form of untouchability in the relations of Ad Dharmi and Kabirpanthi with the Mazhabi and the Balmiki. Kanshi Ram's BSP in Punjab remained mainly an Ad Dharmi-Chamar organization, practically excluding other segments. The Mazhabis of village Heran in Ludhiana district who had, eight years earlier constructed a separate gurdwara in collaboration with Ramdasia (another SC of the village), resolved in 2002 to construct another, exclusively Mazhabi Sikh gurdwara. The reason?—they were incensed over humiliation of their women by Ramdasia women who had threatened the former of violence in case they entered the gurdwara.[59] In the recent widespread Balmiki protest in Punjab against the incident of setting on fire houses in a Balmiki colony of Gohana (Haryana), the Ad Dharmi Chamars in

Jalandhar and Amritsar virtually kept away from the protest by the Balmikis. Similarly, during the long drawn Ad Dharmi agitation in Boota Mandi relating to a gurdwara in Talhan village of Jalandhar, the people from nearby Megh colony of Bhargava Camp and from the Balmiki colony kept a distance. A majority of people of each SC community usually prefer living in their separate colonies in practically all towns and villages. All SC communities are strictly endogamous groups.

Another aspect of identity-based aspirations is related to increasing inclination towards following the religious route to status. 'Which is most useful for our community—religion or politics?' was a question seriously raised much earlier. The particular *jatis* are also seen to be engaged in a process of inventing and strengthening distinct *jati*-based religio-cultural markers, giving themselves distinct religious symbols, rituals, ceremonies, festivals, *jaikaras* (religious cries) and salutations.[60] Large sections of the SCs seek solace in joining sects like the Radha Soami, the Sacha Sauda *dera* of Sirsa (Haryana), *dera* Wad Bhag Singh, Nirankari and Namdharis sects, *dera* of Sachkhand Ballan and many others. An interim list of Ravidasi sants and *deras* in Punjab prepared by a researcher mentions 64 such *deras* at the last count.[61] A Radha Soami Balmiki regarded his identity to be different from that of other Balmikis, and status higher. The Ambedkarites, such as L.R. Bali, on the other hand, ridicule the shift towards religion as obscurantism and also a hurdle in the structuring of Dalit solidarity.

Looking at the present in comparison to the past, the SCs of Punjab recognize the change in their lives to be significant, even 'remarkable'. Many of them referred to a sense of liberation from the scourge of untouchability and exclusion, feel proud of a new kind of personal dignity and visibility in the public spaces. They are highly conscious of their rights as also of their importance in electoral politics. No longer are they the only poor in the village for they witness, in comparison, the poverty and sufferings of a section of the upper castes. But overall, there is little sense of empowerment. The mental baggage of the past seems to loom large.[62] Instead of the desired annihilation of caste, the salience of hierarchy among the SCs appears to reflect almost a Brahmanical pattern, even a form of untouchability.

Dalit writers routinely condemn the reservation-benefited class for cultivating an upper caste mentality towards their own people, something akin to what has been described in another context as 'secession of the successful'. There is a wide lag between material change and the change in the habits of mind of the SC and non-SCs. But nothing has come as a greater blow to the meagre hopes of the poor and backward SCs than the accelerated withdrawal of the State from its obligations in the social sector and its declining capability for good governance. '*Saadi tek sarkar te si, oh ne palla jhaarta, tan asi kithey jaana*?' (our hopes are on the government; if the government washes its hands off from its obligations where do we go?). The dialectics of empowerment and oppression have created a variety of contradictions.

NOTES

1. Prominent among them being Lahori Ram Bali of Jalandhar, an old and well-known Ambedkarite and editor of *Bheem Patrika;* Attarjit Singh of Bathinda, a well-known Punjabi short story writer; Jai Singh, the chief of Dalit Dasta Virodhi Andolan: Satnam Singh Kainth, former Member of Parliament (BSP) and now president of Bahujan Samaj Morcha; Harinder Singh Khalsa, formerly a diplomat, an MP and the member of the National Commission for Scheduled Castes and Scheduled Tribes; and Comrade Swaran Singh Nagoke, secretary, Dehati Mazdoor Sabha, Amritsar.
2. The author has benefited from a reading of Peter L. Berger and Thomas Mann, *Social Construction of Reality: A Treatise in the Sociology of Knowledge,* London, 1967.
3. See Ritu Menon and Kamla Bhasin *Boarders and Boundaries: Women in India's Partition*, New Delhi, 1998 and Urvashi Butalia, *The Other Side of Silence: Voices From the Partition of India*, New Delhi, 1998.
4. Butalia, 1998, pp. 223-58.
5. Ibid.
6. Sardar Harnam Singh, 'Arguments of the Sikhs', in Mian Muhammad Sadullah et al. (eds.), *The Partition of the Punjab 1947: A Compilation of Official Documents*, vol. II, Lahore, 1983, p. 125. See also Paul Brass, 'The Partition of India and Retributive Genocide in the Punjab, 1946-47: Means, Methods, and Purposes', *Journal of Genocide Research*, 2003, vol. V(1), pp. 96, 101.
7. Sadullah et al., 1983, p. 125; Brass, 2003, pp. 96, 101.

8. Brass, 2003, p. 96. The argument was, in fact, stretched further. If these (non)-persons were to be counted rather than discounted, then there could be an exchange of such non-persons. In other words, as Brass stated, 'the non-persons among the Muslims in these districts could be exchanged with the SC non-persons from the western Punjab districts for the sake of preserving the claimed Sikh homeland'.
9. Balbir Madhopuri, *Chhangiya Rukkh*, Delhi, 2002, p. 175.
10. Ambedkar told his audience at Jalandhar in 1951, 'Pakistan did not bother so much if the Hindus left; but who would do the dirty work of the scavengers, sweepers, the Bhangis and other despised castes, if the Untouchables left Pakistan? I requested Pandit Nehru to take immediate action and strive for the removal of the ban on their migration.' Text of his speech in D.C. Ahir, *Dr. Ambedkar and Punjab*, Delhi, 1992, p. 21.
11. Butalia, 1998, pp. 223-58.
12. Ahir, 1992, p. 227.
13. Ibid., pp. 228-30.
14. Lal Singh Dil, *Dastan: Swajeevani* (autobiography in Punjabi), Ludhiana, 1998, p. 24.
15. In this regard, Lal Singh Dil, writes candidly, 'I cannot recall even one incident of the past which I felt happy about.' Ibid., p. 38.
16. Ditt Singh, *Mera Pind* (Punjabi) n.d., pp. 43-54; Amandeep Hira, *Rachna: Dalit Paripekh* (Punjabi novel), Amritsar, 2004, pp. 101-5; Ninder Gill, *Dastan Dalitan Di,* n.d., p. 308.
17. Madhopuri, 2002, p. 75.
18. Comrade Swaran Singh Nagoke, tape-recorded interview, Amritsar, 21 August 2002.
19. Gurcharan Singh Rao, *Mashaalchi*, Mandi Mullanpur Dakha, 1986, p. 27.
20. When the author checked up with his colleagues from rural back ground, it was confirmed that up to the end of 1970s the non-Dalit young boys in the villages routinely bragged about their sexual access to one or the other Harijan girls in the village. See also Mark Juergensmeyer, 'Cultures of Deprivation', in Harish K. Puri (ed.), *Dalits in Regional Context*, Jaipur, 2003, p. 49.
21. H.S. Sachdev, in one of his interview sessions with the author.
22. Gurcharan Singh Rao, pp. 125-6.
23. Nicholas Dirks, *Caste of Mind: Colonialism and the Making of Modern India*, New Delhi, 2002, pp. 176-7; Mukul Kumar, 'Relationship of Caste and Crime in Colonial India: A Discourse Analysis', *Economic and Political Weekly*, vol. XXXIX, no. 10, 8 March 2004, pp. 1081-6.
24. Kumar, 2004, p. 1085.
25. Lal Singh Dil, 1998, p. 26.

26. Ibid., pp. 24, 38.
27. Ibid., p. 26.
28. Indera Paul Singh, 'Caste in a Sikh Village' in Harjinder Singh (ed.), *Caste Among Non-Hindus in India*, Delhi, 1977, p. 70.
29. Harish K. Puri, 'Scheduled Castes in Sikh Community', *Economic and Political Weekly*, no. 26, 2003.
30. Talvinder Singh, 'Jaat Sade Avchetan Ch Hai' *Lakeer,* no. 95, October-December 2005, ref. from original, pp. 38-40.
31. Ajmer Singh, 'Jattvad ik Deeragh Rog: Veehvin Sadi di Sikh Rajniti' (Punjabi), Ludhiana, 2003, pp. 292-300.
32. *Punjab Census Report*, 1931, Part A, p. 199.
33. Interviews with Com. Swaran Singh, Bali, Kainth, Attarjit Singh, Amandeep Singh and many others.
34. Indera Paul Singh, 1977, pp. 76-7; Paramjit Singh Judge, 'Interrogating Caste Status of Dalits in Punjab', in Puri, 2003, pp. 100-31.
35. Com. Swaran Singh, recorded Interview, Amritsar 21 August 2002.
36. S.S. Jodhka, 'Prejudice' Without 'Pollution'? Scheduled Castes in Contemporary Punjab', *Journal of Indian School of Political Economy,* XII, 3 and 4 (July-December 2002), pp. 71-2.
37. Com. Swaran Singh's estimate of the percentage of SC agricultural labourers was practically the same as was found by Jodhka in his study.
38. Com. Swaran Singh, interview. Amritsar, 21 August 2002.
39. Madhopuri, 2002, p. 53.
40. Report of NCSCST, 1997-8
41. Interview with Ardaman Singh Dhillon, Amritsar, 1 September 2003.
42. Javed Alam, *Who Wants Democracy*, New Delhi, 2004, p. 48.
43. Paramjit Singh Judge, *Peetu,* Jalandhar, 2003, pp. 82-6.
44. Amandeep Hira, 2004, pp. 170-202.
45. A recent survey made by the quarterly magazine *Lakeer* listed by name, 45 of the notable Punjabi writers as belonging to the SCs.
46. Ram Sarup Ankhi, 'Malwal Pendu Samaj Vich Jaat-Bradri dian Jadaan', *Lakeer*, 2005, p. 41.
47. Hira, 2004, 72, pp. 199-200.
48. Kanchan Chandra, 'The Transformation of Ethnic Politics in India: The Decline of Congress and the Rise of Bahujan Samaj Party in Hoshiarpur', *The Journal of Asian Studies*, vol. 59, no. 1, February 2000, pp. 36-40.
49. Shalini Sharma and B.K. Aggarwal, 'Educating Dalit Women for Development: A Study in Hoshiarpur District', in Harish K. Puri, 2003.
50. Parmod Kumar and Rainuka Dagar, 'Gender in Dalit Identity Construction in Punjab', in Harish K. Puri, 2003.

51. R.B. Singh, *Scheduled Caste Welfare: Myth or Reality*, Delhi, 2003, p. 72.
52. Unpublished Report of a survey conducted by R.B. Singh in districts Amritsar and Gurdaspur in 2006.
53. Interview with Comrade Swaran Singh.
54. Puri, 2003, pp. 2699-2701.
55. Tarsem Peter, *Nawan Zamana*, 3 October 2004.
56. Des Raj Kali, *Nawan Zamana*, 27-31 August and 1-4 and 14 September 2003.
57. Prominently visible during the Talhan agitation 2004.
58. Judge, 2005, p. 26.
59. Puri, 2003, p. 2700.
60. Juergensmeyer 1982, pp. 260-8.
61. Som Nath Bharti, *Jagat Guru Ravidas Sampraday: Sant te Sadhna Sthal*, Jalandhar, 2004, pp. 1-112.
62. A number of short stories by Dalit writers such as Attarjit's '*Bathloo Chamar*' and '*Thooan*' (Scorpion), Jinder's '*Sorry*' and Prem Gorkhi's '*Arjan Safaidiwala*' powerfully capture the irony and contradictions.

EUROPE AND ASIA

CHAPTER 14

The Frontiers of European Modernity

BARUN DÉ

Professor V.N. Datta is a stalwart of the Indian historical profession who has never failed to ignore the Western coordinates—whether Asian or British—of our cultural traditions. Ignoring the chauvinism that led the now-defunct NCERT 2000 national curriculum framework to characterize the entire second millennium CE as one of degeneration due to 'Islamic' and 'Christian' domination of global history after the 'Golden Ages' (of a presumed 'Hindu' first millennium), Professor Datta directs our attention to British and Indo-Islamic cultural influences on subcontinental culture. These have shaped modern India as much as Sanskrit did. It is in that spirit that my contribution is presented, an extempore presentation of which was earlier made at the History department of Jadavpur University. My ideas about the forces that led to the creation of modern Europe rest tenuously on the slim experience of studying it more than fifty years ago at Presidency College in the inspirational classes of Professor Susobhan Chandra Sarkar as well as those of Professor Abdul Wahab Mahmood. I later read European history during the half century between the fall of the second Bonaparte Emperor and the origins of the Second World War.

*I am grateful to Professor K.L. Tuteja of Kurukshetra University for his courtesy in enduring my interminable requests for fresh, typed copies of my spidery handwriting. I also thank Dr. Jayanta Sengupta and Professor Kunal Chattopadhyay of Jadavpur University, the first for his invitation to me to speak at the Orientation Course of European History, the second for encouraging me to write out my views.

Professor Sarkar's classes tempted many of us to a simplistic Marxian 'model' chronologizing geographical data, 'facts' as we called them, specifically about contestation for political authority at the state level, i.e. realpolitik in late medieval and early modern European dynastic interests. These were supposed to be poised above class struggle in relatively autonomous terms. Over the years, one has realized, 'facts' failed to include cultural relations and social and individual creativity. Many complexities inherent in 'class struggle', complexities created by variant modes and paths of historical change, have since then appeared in our intellectual horizon.

I propose to depart from that smoothened out method of following only the Eurocentric path of transformation by raising some doubts and questions. My first premise is that much of the thematics have been obscured by historiographical usages that are implicit in the unproblematic idioms of 'Europe', 'transition' and 'modernity'. We may start with the first term.

1. MODERNITY

The adjective 'modern' can be applied to any epoch, era, or longer-term historical period that is generally supposed to be most recent in a three-stage periodization of general history. Specifically it is the last in succession in the progression 'ancient-mediaeval-modern'. Is the reification of an adjective to a noun signifying a tangible historical period (with presumably historical terminal points) very much more than a sociological solecism? What does 'modern*ity*' (emphasis as part-italicized, mine) mean in simple language? Is it a concrete category, with a clear beginning and a clear end? What are the exact terminal points of social, economic and political formation: what are the cultural attributes of ideational tradition that either progress or transit from earlier periods, and act as a stabilizing social force or retard it?

These questions are begged by a recent terminology 'alternative modernity/ies'. I have not been able to find the book with this title edited by Dilip Parameshwar Gaonkar (Durham, N.C., Duke University Press, 2001) which has articles by *avant-garde*

Anglo-American and Commonwealth anthropo-historical theorists: but one can get an idea from a recent statement in which I found the reference:

> The number one problem of modern social science [is] modernity itself . . . *modernity* means that historically unprecedented amalgam of new practices and institutional forms (science, technology, industrial production, urbanization) of new ways of living (individualism, secularization, instrumental rationality) and of new forms of malaise (alienation, meaninglessness, a sense of impending social dissolution). Is there a single problem here, or do we need to speak of multiple modernities, the plural reflecting the fact that non-Western cultures have modernized in their own ways and cannot be properly understood if we try to grasp them in a general theory that was originally designed with the Western case in mind.[1]

In the opinion of Professor Taylor, a social philosopher who uses historical data but not as a historian *per se*—like many of the writers in the journal referred above—'The central(ity) of Western modernity (is in) a new conception of moral order of society'. More old-fashioned historians themselves, on the contrary, always emphasize the hybrid intermingling of continuities and changes in the precise social, economic and political relations and forces of production and culture that originate and lead to further changes.

The current use of 'modernity' is in the plural, emphasizing its multiplex formations. Each formation is a set of practices including ideas and institutions that span different continents, different countries, different ethnicities/regions/social communities, with different terminal boundings (in the sense of secular time-spans). A particular continental category like 'Asian modernity' is too loose. By no stretch of imagination can modern Chinese trends be synchronized with pre-1947 British Indian ones (let alone with the incipience of modern trends in British India's native states, such as Rajputana's many different ones on the one hand, and Travancore-Cochin or Pudukkottai and Ramnad on the other). Nor can there be exact synchronization in the Turkic world (stretching from Kazakhstan to Turkey) or the Afro-Arab one (Egypt on the one hand and the entirely different Maghreb on the other). The plural variety of 'modern' time as distinct from medieval or ancient (whose periodization has similar problems) precludes a neutral adjective being first turned into a noun with specific attributes and then being used in a grammatically plural way. Consider for instance the neologism implicit in the usage 'construction of alternative modernities'.[2]

We may also look at the problem of translating the historicist usage of 'modernity' into Bengali, or for that matter into any other north Indian language. *Adhuniktaa* is an attribute, which has no specific historical periodicity. The root word *aadhunik* tallies with the adjectival meaning of 'modern', though its literal translation *of adhunaa*, i.e. 'of today' or 'now' is closer to 'contemporary', i.e. the recent part of modern. This is perhaps what Euro-American or Westernized Asians among the cultural theorists and literary sociologists call 'post-modern', by using an unhistorical solecism. After all history, dealing with the past, extends till the last minute before it is written. By definition, modern history is the process of 'becoming', the latest unraveling—not of having been—of the most recent stage of development.

Each beginning, for different constructs of the modern process in different communities, societies, ethnicities or politics, can be defined or determined by a consensus about the *differentia specifica* of new processes, distinguished from earlier, more traditional stages. This determination in the sense of process of happening is the substance of transition from and earlier stage to a later one. To reiterate, modernity is not a past historical period. It is merely the neutral attribute of recent periodicity in historical development. The point then arises, in each pattern of modernity, how, in which sector/region/or classes, and with what velocity does 'transition' and ultimately 'transformation' from one stage to another take place. Here come the rub: what does the usage 'historical transition' itself signify?

2. Transition

During the last half-century, in the English language—at least in British and post-British Indian research—the verbal usage of 'transition' (meaning 'the processes within historical change from one predominant tendency to another') has become somewhat identified with one narrow, and now largely forgotten, controversy about conceptual aspects of its manifold paths.

This is a debate collated in 1954 by Anglo-American old Marxists arguing about the view that only internal contradictions within feudal relations of production created conditions for the transition to world capitalism. That view had been expressed by Maurice Dobb in *Studies in the Development of Capitalism.*[3] The paperback *Transition from Feudalism to Capitalism*[4] was basically Eurocentric, with only one Japanese scholar, Professor Takahashi from Asia, writing, and that too within a largely European framework. Only the American Marxists, Sweezy and Baran considered the possibility of general wider-than-European 'laws' of development. That feudalism could exist under different circumstances in China or India was then skirted by most Western Marxists, except a few like Daniel Thorner. The non-European aspect of historical *differentia specifica* has been swept under the carpet of universalist Stalinist fiat (after the 1931 Leningrad discussions on the mode of production in Asia) seeking to occult Marx's sketchy thoughts on 'Asiatic despotism', 'the Asiatic mode of production', or 'the self-sufficient village economy' in India. These fiats were then twisted by 'once-Marxist, turned occasionally into critics of it', like Karl Wittfogel, into fantasies about 'hydraulic society' as the basis for 'Oriental Despotism'.[5]

More recent research and attempted generalizations about the character of mediaeval societies in Asia, as well as about the relatively scattered nature of Marx's views on pre-colonialism there, have made the old 'transition debate' academically dated and indeed obsolete. More general conceptualization, yet specific particularity, is necessary for connoting 'transition of socio-economic and political formations'. Indeed a strict reading of 'transition' should particularly stress its core word 'transit', i.e. fleeting from one point to another. This means—in this context of the logic of socio-economic terminology—the process and events during that process that are consequent on prior events and/or cause later events before or after the moment. Such events are not necessarily determinate or even linear. They may halt ahead of, recede from, or pick up 'latecomer' speed towards, the predominance of new guiding ideas, which create changed class clusters of power. Feudalism is one such indeterminate set. It is part of, but not equal to, medieval tendencies.

In fact, the adjective 'mediaeval' is the most explicit of the three-state periodization model. Its exact meaning is 'that which pertains, without any necessary determinacy, to any event, trend or formation, *between* two others'. The world 'between' is emphasized since it gives the precise sense more than 'middle' or 'middling'. Whatever does not appear to be really ancient, whose vestiges have become very small in modern times, whatever has forms that appear semi-feudal, primitive or antiquated, lumps into such a median phase. Its roots lie in antiquity, but its tendrils creep into modernity and even contemporaneity. The forms of 'bonded labour' as part of the feudal mode of production are very much a case in point.

As in all concepts of periodization, the question of transition in the mediaeval sense can really be determined by clarity about what existed at its inception, and what forces led to its dissolution. The question of *when* these things happened, or *what* was the broad cluster of dates for such conjunctures, requires not just logical, but hard empirical work. This in turn may lead to unsettling of what were previously supposed to be definite categories.

Without claiming a vestige of empirical research beyond standard English texts, or even a definite position about the social relations or forces that led to transition from medieval to modern Europe, it may still be acceptable to consider some inferences and tentative conclusions about the changes in the significance of the third term of the title of our subject, 'Europe' itself.

3. Europe, Eurasia, Islam

Europe was hardly considered a geographical entity in ancient times. This is fairly well-known. Rome, its imperial frontiers and the peripheries beyond its marchlands to the east, north and extreme west, i.e. Ultima Thule, was the territoriality of an imperial ancient *imaginaire*. This extended from Britannia, Gaul and Germany through Rome to the African littoral and the Middle Eastern coastline as well as some land beyond the Jordan

River. The intellectuals of Hellas and Rome saw the Mediterranean as a great bounded inland sea interconnected with older Afro-Asian cultures. In those ages, what later came at the end of the second millennium to be the determining continent, was perhaps, then, seen from Asia and North Africa as a set of subcontinental promontories, with distinct identities certainly, but also with umbilical roots stretching into the two great continents to its east and south. The territorial distinction as a composite continent was a late Christian, i.e. second half of the second millennium idea.

The dissolution of the Roman Empire in the three or four hundred years after Christ proceeded not only from internal contradictions, but also external attacks by the *Barbaroi* (bearded wild ones) beyond the eastern horizon. In the latter case, Eurasian population movements westwards were crucial beginning from about the times of Attila the Hun (nowadays hailed as an ancient world conqueror by Kazakh historical chauvinism, at least in Almaty strategical studies university anniversary celebration in early 2001), and petering out several centuries later after the stabilization of the non-Islamic Mongol Empire of Chengiz Khan and his earlier successors in China, Iran and Tatarstan.[6] Pre-modern Europe was neither culturally separate nor wholly distinct from the Levant Coast, the North African littoral, or the Black Sea hinterlands.[7] After the barbarian pressures had spent themselves, Islamized Arabs and Berbers extended their dominion over southern Spain, and their cultural influence even further east into Sicily. Turks conquered the Balkans much later in medieval times, while Catholic potentates of Castile and Aragon were conducting the *reconquista* of Spain.

Islam played a cultural role in European civilization, most notably in the early centuries of the second millennium that we have just left behind. One of the most percipient recent scholars of Indian Islam has written about this in the context of world history:

> Already by the late seventh century Muslims were regarding themselves as carriers of a new civilization and not just members of a Arab culture of autonomous and self-regulating religious communities—Greek Orthodox Christians, Monophysites, Nestorians, Copts, Zoroastrians,

Manicheans, Jews—as well as a plurality of linguistic and literary traditions including Greek, Coptic, Syrian, American, Middle Asian and various dialects of Aramaic. Either they could constitute themselves as one more autonomous community modeled on those they ruled—thereby preserving Allah as a Arab deity, Islam as a Arab culture and Arabic as the language of the ruling class—or they could try to bring all these diverse communities and traditions together into a new, cultural synthesis. By the eighth century, they had turned to the latter alternative. Convinced of the political imprudence of a tiny, ethnic minority ruling indefinitely over an enormous non-Muslim minority, the Caliphs openly encouraged their non-Arab subjects to convert.[8]

Koranic injunctions to Jews and Christians to return to the monotheism of Abraham, their common ancestor, are inscribed around Islam's earliest surviving monument, Jerusalem's Dome of the Rock, built in 691:

> O mankind! The messenger hath come unto you with the Truth from your Lord. Therefore believe; [it is] better for you. O people of the Scripture. Do not exaggerate in your religion nor utter aught concerning Allah, and his word, which He conveyed to Mary, and a spirit from Him. So believe in Allah and say not 'Three'—Cease! [It is] better for you—Allah is only one God. Far is it removed from His Transcendent Majesty that he should have a son. His is all that is in the heavens and all that is in the earth. And Allah is sufficient as Defender.[9]

These words point to the unifying and integrating role that the Muslims saw themselves as playing amidst the older religious traditions of the Middle East. This iconoclastic monotheism is what fanatical revivalists among the more reactionary forces in the Arabized sectors of Islam in the modern world (notably in the Saudi Kingdom, Pakistan and southern Afghanistan, Indonesia, and the Sudan) seek to revive, as if it is the only message of twenty-first-century Islam in crisis.

What was far more remarkable in the medieval world was that the Islamicate globalized itself from Sind to the Pillars of Hercules. For instance, the Islamization of Central Asia was not the only result of the Arab victory over a Chinese army in the mid-eighth century CE. Chinese prisoners of war taught the Abbasids paper-making. By the twelfth-century paper was manufactured in Morocco and Spain, and thence spread to

Europe. Eaton also demonstrates the worldwide diffusion of agricultural products to, through, and from the early Muslim world. The Arab conquest of Sind in 711 swivelled knowledge of crops such as hard wheat, rice, sugar cane, new varieties of sorghum; fruits like banana, sour orange, lemon, lime, mango, watermelon, coconut products; vegetables such as spinach, artichoke, eggplant, and the key industrial plant, cotton, familiarized in the Fertile Crescent and (except for the mango and coconut) thence all the way up the Mediterranean coasts. This led to corresponding changes in Europe in hydraulic technology and to water use in larger quantities, leading to further technological changes. The diffusion and qualitative transformation of scientific knowledge was inseminated by Indian and Greek texts: with improvements in the evolution of science, medicine and mathematics.[10]

This was a period in which India exercised the role of a bridge between China from which scholars travelled in search of Indian secular as well as religious knowledge in Buddhist tracts on the one hand, and to the Arab domains with magnates of Indian origin like the Barmakids influencing Baghdad thought on the other. The global outreach of this Asian inter-connection of culture in a time when Europe was supposed to be in its Dark Ages has recently been emphasized by Amartya Sen in his recent essay 'China and India'.[11]

Old twentieth-century European historical writing posited two cultures, one facing west, the heirs of the Graeco-Roman tradition, the other supposedly looking east, the Arab theological-cum-Perso-Turkic secular tradition. This view has to be limited to the post-Renaissance, post-sixteenth-century European expansion only, four centuries of the second millennium. Before that, the role of Middle East/southern Europe interaction was to create a zone of material culture stretching on an east-west axis from Sind to Spain, and on a south-north axis from the Hejaz and Egypt to the Danube and the Rhine. That was the pre-Renaissance and post-Roman imperial dissolution epoch in Western and Central Europe. Earlier European historiography castigated it as 'Dark Ages' from which West European revivalism was supposed to have brought about a 'twelfth-century renaissance'! If Europe is not to be limited to just a medieval Christian concept, if the dialectical interconnections of Hellenism and Islam, Islam and India, and further east, India and China are to be acknowledged, then the immensely significant copula of Indian and Islamic world-historical universalism in early mediaeval cultural history must be explicitly signified. The European Dark Ages recede into conceptual insignificance in the context of Islamic-Indian-Chinese connectivities in the early mediaeval countries.

This, of course, does not mean that the importance of Christianity in the crystallization of early (and indeed recent) European ideas of sovereignty and ethics of power should be denied, or even deflated. However, its estimation needs much more depth of focus on the extra-European influences on Christendom—the proximity of the Nile basin in antiquity, the cultural pressures and attractions of Eurasia, the lands of the Islamicate and the land route to Cathay from the Middle East, and later of the seaward routes to the east. If Emperor Constantine had not shifted temporal empire in the transition from antiquity to early medieval authority, from Rome to Byzantium and thus held back first the Sassanids, then Islam, from delivering a *coup de grace* to Hellenistic civilization, neither the Roman Papacy nor the Frankish Holy Roman Empire would have enjoyed isolation from the cultural and armed heyday of the Orient. Nor would Europe's new Viking and then Venetian adventurers from the north and the west have been able to stabilize a new civilization to roll back the Moors all the way from Spain, the Adriatic approaches to south-eastern Italy and the upper reaches of the Danube. Byzantium which spanned Mediterranean Europe and Western Eurasia created a bulwark and marcher space for the developments within Europe proper. This transformed and originated modern forces within its culture.

Within this new confine of culture, north of the Mediterranean and its Alpine barrier, the space that gained importance was Burgundy, the Rhineland, and even further north, the Norse Lands from where sailed south the Vikings, and later by the twelfth and thirteenth centuries, the northeastern inland post of Bruges, and across the Channel, England. Even then these were outreaches of the intra-European socio-economic contacts with

Byzantium and on to the Eurasian routes to the Mongol great Yurts at Karakoram, and east to Khanbaliq in Khitai. This east-west part of the so-called Silk Route lost its importance only about the early fifteenth century after Marco Polo's overland journey to China from where, significantly enough, he returned not by land, but by the southern seas to Persia, and then through the Middle East to Venice.

The early middle ages of European cultural history can also be visualized in the clear distinction between southern France and central and north France—Avignon, the Rhone Basin and Provence where forms of Christianity existed quite 'alternative' to, and in contestatory mode, *vis-à-vis* Roman orthodoxy (the emphasis on the Virgin Mary juxtaposed against paternalism). Central and northern France from Normandy and Picardy to Anjou was contested between its native rulers and the successors of the Norman conquerors of England during the Hundred Years War. These were followed by the internecine feuds within the English ruling class, known as the War of the Roses. These local distinctions were subordinated to absolutist power only after the mid-fifteenth century.

In 1453, the fall of Byzantium to the Ottoman Turks blocked Eurasian land routes to the firm Turkic power. Even more than the flight of old Greek scholarship to Italy sparking the 'rebirth' of antique humanism, this new geopolitical trend opened the way to the riposte of Western seafaring—Portuguese, then Dutch, then French, and English from the fifteenth to the seventeenth centuries around Africa, across the Indian Ocean defeating Turkish admirals in the Arabian Sea, shifting from the 'Silk Route' to the 'Spice Route'. All this led to the rise of Western colonialism, enrichment, loot and plunder. Without this expansion Europe might not have gained its modern identity.

Before that happened, the rise of the Ottoman power in Eastern Europe and the Southern Mediterranean coastline was Eurasia's reply to the several century old violence and rapine in the Levant and lately in Spain, beginning with the Crusades and ending with the late fifteenth-century Spanish *reconquista*. From the Western European mass hysteria since the days of the English ruler Richard Coeur-de-Lion to the military ventures finally repelled by Salahdin and Saljuqs in Filistiniya (Palestine), what modern European romanticism has called War for the Cross, has now degenerated into the US-British idiom that USA's President George W. Bush on 11 September 2001 chose to trivialize by calling as 'crusade'—the war that his establishment was already engaged in planning against Islamic subaltern challenge to Western domination of the international security system. The Crusades were the first strictly European popular breakout, as distinct from Roman *imperium* for colonializing plunder. They were an eastern breakout that ultimately failed, as Anglo-American neo-colonialism indeed may over-reach itself by 2025.

4. The Precursors of Colonialism

It is necessary to note this dialectic of the destructive as well as regenerative aspects of Islam-Christian interaction as the prehistory of modern colonialism. There were Levantine Crusader castles in ports like Acre, and Tyre on Sidon. The Crusader castles were the direct ancestors, though much previous, to the 'factory' forts of the European Companies (Fort St. George in Madras, Fort William in Calcutta and Bombay Castle) in the Indian subcontinent in the seventeenth and eighteenth centuries. Ottoman outreach from inner Anatolia into the Aegean and the Balkans did not halt till the eighteenth century. At the turn of fifteenth-sixteenth century, Selim the Grim's pincers swept southwards at the time when Columbus or Vasco da Gama were sailing west and south-east along the inner lines of Levant-Egyptian eastern Mediterranean communication. Selim the Grim took for the Turks the holy places of Christianity as well as Islam, Cairo and Upper Nile Valley. They were an effective barrier to European easy communication with India and Indonesia. This also gained the Ottomans the succession to the titles of Kadhim-al-Haramayn (Protectors of the Venerated Places) and Khalifa (Caliph, the claim to represent the seniormost secular as well as Koranic authority to arbitrate over Muslims, which the Egyptian Sultans had claimed after the Mongols killed the last Baghdad Caliph). This second blockage forced the initiatives of trade, and following it, the flag, away from Venice, Genoa and Livorno in northern Italy, and ultimately from western

Spanish ports like Barcelona and Cadiz, in the same way as the desiccation of the Silk Route had earlier led to the collapse of Bruges and Ghent's early medieval nodal prosperity.

These diverse connections of Islam with discrete elements in southern European geopolitics make the concept of a composite continent from the Urals to Ireland and from Muscovy to the Straits of Gibraltar quite problematic till the seventeenth-century. Portugal and Spain sought outposts in the Maghreb, i.e. in Islam-dominated northwest Africa, and then in either southern Africa or the Atlantic islands. Turks controlled the Balkans till the third quarter of the nineteenth century. Till the sixteenth century, Muscovy, Kiev and the Crimea were under Tatar Turkic control. All this led central and eastern Europeans to be dominated by a heterodox Islamicate under conditions of in-depth feudalism. It also led to many Islamic ideas, symbols or concerns to be familiar to most Europeans (except perhaps Scandinavia and the northern plains) throughout the middle ages.

This interaction, culturally fruitful as well as inimical, began to change only after western Europe began to expand navally and militarily into the wider world. This turned the Eurasian continental flank away from just what one of the fathers of modern European geopolitics in the early twentieth century, Sir Halford Mackinder, would have called the north-western rimland. The *reconquista* of Moorish Spain, the African and American expeditions, the Portuguese stranglehold over the Indian Oceanic trade of the sixteenth century and the circumnavigation of the world by Magellan and Drake via the Pacific all outflanked Ottoman expansion. This made it possible for European culture to contest Turks and their Tatar civilization in the Balkans, Ukraine and heartland Russia. These developments were not quite the same as the process of Christian renaissance in Italy, Germany, France, Netherlands, England or the Western efflorescence of a spirit of capitalist venture, military enterprise, and racial and ethnic distinctiveness amounting to xenophobia. This in time led to a sort of superiority complex regarding other religions, non-Graeco-Roman languages, and alien ethnic identities in other continents. The later distinctiveness of European continentality grew after the development of colonialism in late medieval and early modern Europe.

The Renaissance originated in western urban centres like Florence, Rome, Venice, Augsburg, Paris, Rotterdam or London. The first seaborne empires also came out of western urban ports like Genoa, Cadiz, Bristol, Bordeaux, Antwerp, or Amsterdam. The common points about these littoral and maritime empires of first trade, then the flag, through the two hundred and fifty-years between 1453 and 1707 were twofold. On the one hand, the Islamic empires that had held the old continent west of China together—the Mughals in India and Afghanistan, the Safavids in Iran, and with much less central authority, the Uzbeks in Bukhara, Khiva and Khokand—atrophied with of course one exception—the Ottomans in Turkey. On the other, specific European consciousness having brought the continental land from the Elbe and the Oder Rivers to the Urals into its periphery, was now firmly culturally based in the centre (Germany and Italy), in the west (Britain, France, the Netherlands) and across the Atlantic in Quebec, the Thirteen Colonies, Mexico, Rio de Janeiro and Buenos Aires. Cultural compositeness was marked by the growth and development of the religious, i.e. ideational consciousness of Christendom with which Europe had come to be associated, both within itself and in the minds of non-Europeans. To non-Europeans, it seemed to be broadly common, though not yet ecumenical, faith in Christianity. This bestraddled the early modern differences of the Reformation and Counter-Reformation.

The capitalist venture was not at all internal to Europe. It was marked by a threefold westward thrust. Having failed in the Levantine Crusades, it switched towards what would become Latin America, i.e. Mexico, Cuba, Meso-America, and South America, systematically despoiled by the Iberian monarchies. After that, colonial capitalism from north-western Europe turned its attention to the rest of the West Indies and the Atlantic littoral of North America. Simultaneously, Portugal and later Holland, France and Britain began to move into the Indian and Indonesian lands between the Middle East (which was held by Turkey till the early twentieth century) and China. After two centuries of seaborne trade, an imperialist bridgehead was found into the Indian hinterland from Bengal in the second half of the eighteenth century. And thirdly, Africa, similarly probed by global trade till the second half of the nineteenth century, was 'scrambled for' in the next seventy years then 'Mandated' by the League of Nations, and finally 'decolonized' into its present immiserization in the second half of the twentieth century.

The dynamics of early modern capitalist imperialism have been analysed lucidly by Irfan Habib's 'Capitalism in History'.[12] Disposing of various misunderstandings that have surfaced since the old 'transition debate', Habib clarifies the Marxist position in this regard:

> There was strictly no sanction in Marx' for either the old tendency to extend the 'feudal mode' to all agrarian regions of the world, or the interpretation of seeing changes in it due to 'internal contradictions'—the second tendency leading Mao Zedong in 1939 to declare that pre-colonial China, left to itself 'would of itself have developed into a capitalist society even without the impact of foreign capitalism.

Habib stressed real historicity:

> . . . the actual genesis of capitalism, the role of force and of subjugation of external economies on the world scale. . . . There were two major pillars of primary accumulation, internal exploitation, constituting alone all the expropriation of the peasantry, and external plunder, linked to global colonial dominance. . . . It is not possible to imagine how a credible history of capitalism can be constructed without comprehending colonialism.[13]

Colonialism and mercantile capitalism are inextricably intertwined in the historical record of the late medieval and early modern eras. As strands in the braid of socio-economic change, they are not necessarily equal at any given point of time. Although they originated in interdependence, their subsequent history was often different.

Seafaring nations like the British or the Dutch exported their capitalist practices to different parts of the world. But once their European citizens formed subordinate state structures in colonialized territory—whether the North Atlantic seaboard or in British India, or in the Netherlands East Indies, the socio-political cultures of the colonialized areas appeared far more feudal then in their European metropolitan capitalist homelands. On the other hand, before capitalism fully spread over the nineteenth century *bourgeois conquerance* (as Charles Moraze would have termed an earlier phase of globalization), many central European and Mediterranean nations, such as the Italians or the Germans were hardly colonialist, being involved in internecine disputes or local isolation. Their colonialism was merely latecomer emulation of Western European colonial penetration of Africa.

There was also the problem of 'internal colonialism'. Ruling elites setting the tone for nationality treated marginalized ethnic groups within the same state or nation as *herrenvolk* treat *untermenschen*—in conditions of socio-economic subjection. The English landlord, Scot laird and highland ghillie relationship, north of the Forth River in Scotland, is a British case. So is the British-Irish relationship till the formation of the Irish Free State. The case becomes more explicitly racial with white European settlers-Red Indians, or Boers-Negroes, or Australian-aboriginal relations. The braid of socio-economic change thus tangles into a twisted skein in the modern historical period when combinations of uneven development in diverse conditions become apparent in nationality formation and national movements in various European dependencies.

Progress towards modern tendencies was always associated with regression of the socio-economic conditions of the subjugated or under-entitled communities or 'lower' classes in Europe itself. In the era of globalization it became associated with bourgeois dominance. What sociologists, political scientists or 'cultural studies' people today call 'modernity', as a finite historical category, was produced at the cost of many parts of the world—within Europe (as for instance, the Gaelic-language areas of the British Isles and much of northern Scandinavia, parts of north-west France or south-east Spain, southern Italy and its western islands, Sardinia and Sicily, and pockets of remnant Turkic identity in the Balkans, such as Bosnia, Albania or Macedonia) as well as outside Europe. This process of the growth of prosperity of one class as a product of and related to the impoverishment of another one is known to theorists of economic growth—since the term was coined by Karl Marx for processes in capital accumulation—as 'immiserization'.

Modernity too has had in history, its own costs of cultural immiserization, reared by imperialism as a Leviathan on the corpus of crushed or desiccated indigenous traditions. The impact of eighteenth and nineteenth century colonialism on the loose framework of pre-British civilization in India is well known. What is notable is that this sort of impact of modernity at the expense of indigenous economies and cultures took place—of course at an uneven and variegated pace—all over Europe and the world where the European model of 'transition to modernity' took place. Such 'immiseration modernity' was mainly a nineteenth-century product in Latin America, India and other parts of Asia and Africa. The trends of sectoral cultural immiserization concomitant with national modernist trends were mature by the middle of the twentieth century. Later, i.e. more recent trends, elaborated by neoconservative imperialism attacking new Asian nations are now a feature of transition within modernity.

NOTES

1. Charles Taylor, 'Modern Social Imaginaries', *Public Culture*, 14(1), Winter 2001, pp. 91-2.
2. Statement of objectives printed on the inside back cover, *Public Culture*, 10(1), Fall 1997.
3. Maurice Dobb, *Studies in the Development of Capitalism*, London, 1946.
4. Rodney Hilton (ed.), *Transition from Feudalism to Capitalism*, London, 1959.
5. Karl Wittfogel, *Oriental Despotism: A Comparative Study in Total Power*, New Haven, 1957, pp. 402-4.
6. Barun De, *Secularism at Bay: Uzbekistan at the Turn of the Century*, New Delhi, 2005, p. 169.
7. Neal Ascherson, *Black Sea*, London, 1995.
8. Richard M. Eaton, *Essays on Islam and Indian History*, New Delhi, 2005, p. 25.
9. Ibid., p. 26.
10. Ibid., pp. 26-9.
11. Amartya Sen, *The Argumentative Indian*, London, 2005, Chapter 8.
12. See Kesavan Veluthat and P.P. Sudhakaran (eds.), *Advances in History: Essays in Memory of Professor M.P. Sridharan*, Calicut, 2003.
13. Ibid., pp. 238, 242-3.

CHAPTER 15

Colonialism, Modernization and the Asian Identity

IRFAN HABIB

Herodotus, the Greek 'father of History', writing in the fifth century BC begins his *Histories* by saying that he wished to 'put on record the astonishing achievements both of our own and of the Asiatic peoples; and, secondly, and more particularly, to show how the two races came into conflict'. One may see in the latter statement a premonition of what two thousand years later would come to be regarded as the normal state of relations between the two continents. But we must remember that Herodotus's notions of Europe and Asia were both very constricted. For him the Greeks represented 'Europe', and the Persian and other peoples across the Agean and the Mediterranean Seas, belonged to Asia: the geographical notions of both Asia and Europe were still understandably vague. The limitation of knowledge can be seen from the way the physician Hippocretes (*c.* 400 BC) held that the temperaments of the Asiatics and Europeans were different owing essentially to Asia being possessed of a moderate climate and Europe of an extremely varying one.

This contrasting picture of Europe and Asia, however factually erroneous, was transmitted, with classical learning, to Renaissance Europe. When after the discovery of the New World, global maps began to be made, Asia at last began in European maps to assume the outlines that are given to it in the present day. Hondius's map of the world (1607), for example, marks the entire tract from Japan, across China and India, to Arabia as part of the continent of Asia. The French traveller Francois Bernier (travelled in Asia between 1656-68) was perhaps the first to lift the contrast between Europe and Asia from a mere climatic or religious (Christian/non-Christian) level to that of a fundamental difference in political institutions: the difference to him lay in the absence of absolute despotism in Europe, and its total predominance in Asia. In his *De l'espirit de lois* (*The Spirit of Laws*) (1748), Montesquieu further underlined this contrast, and henceforth 'Oriental Despotism' became a part of the commonly accepted assumptions about Asia in modern European thought (including, to some extent, that of Marx).

In whatever form, Asia yet lived only in European thought. No concept of Asia as a continent, with or without any common features or values, developed within any Asian civilization. Indeed, while it seems natural for a concept of Europe to have evolved, Europe forming a distinct geographical unit, a peninsula jutting out of the Eurasian land mass into the Atlantic, Asia possesses no such geographical validity. For the people of Europe it, in turn, became natural further to consider the whole of the East, as a single continent. Had geographical conventions been shaped out of Chinese, Indian or Perso-Arab cultures, it is doubtful if a continent of such an immense size as of Asia could have been conceived. Indeed, it is probable that East Asia, South Asia, and West Asia, that are large regions in themselves, each with as geographically valid limits as Europe, might have been thought of as so many distinct continents, along with Europe.

What would grow, instead of a spontaneous Asian consciousness, was the knowledge of the existence of neighbouring civilizations in each of these distinct subcontinents. The great unification of China under the Qin (Chin) dynasty (221-207 BC) led to the whole of China coming to be known in India as 'China' or 'China-*bhumi*', China-land. The northern-Chinese dynasty, Qidan (Chhi-tan) (AD 907-1119) produced the name 'Khita' (Cathay) for China in Persian and Arabic. The Mongol conquests of the thirteenth century had the result of bringing to the Islamic world a large body of knowledge about China, some of which entered the great history of the world by Rashiduddin Fazlullah, in Persian and Arabic (early fourteenth century).

On its part China (and Japan) obtained, through the spread of Buddhism, a knowledge of India, whose Chinese name 'In-tu' or 'In-du' was borrowed from the Old Persian name for India, 'Hindu'. Xuan Zhuang (602-64) wrote a detailed account of India in Chinese, such as is not extant in any language including Indian languages, prior to that date. He also carried to China a short but valuable account of Iran.

Between India and the Perso-Arab world, geography made contacts easier. The Indians in the eleventh and twelfth centuries used the term 'Tajik' indifferently for Persians and Arabs. Abu Raihan Alberuni (*c.* 1035) wrote an account of India in Arabic, the first occasion, perhaps, when one of the finest representatives of one civilization studied the sciences and learning of another, at the highest levels of rationality.

There thus existed by the Middle Ages a fairly large storehouse of knowledge in different parts of Asia about its other parts, which these examples of inter-civilizational contacts illustrate. There was a sense, in other words, of a common world, though not a specifically Asian world. It was indeed, colonialism which, by putting Asian countries under a common system of oppression, laid the initial groundwork for the emergence of an Asian consciousness.

II

When the Portuguese navigator Vasco da Gama rounded the Cape of Good Hope and crossed the Arabian Sea to appear in south India in 1498, he inaugurated the long period of European dominance over Asia. An Indian historian and statesman K.M. Panikkar has chronicled the history of this process in a pioneering work *Asia and Western Dominance* (London, 1953). There is hardly any country in Asia which does not have its own major incidents of defeat or humiliation to recall from the history of colonialism: for example, for Indonesia there is the Dutch seizure of Batavia (1619); for India, the battle of Plassey (1757); for China, the Opium Wars (1840-2, 1856-60); and for Japan, the expeditions of Commodore Perry (1853-4). In a conventional political narrative, such as Panikkar's, colonialism appears as a continuous emanation of European aggression and dominance. One should, however, recognize that the configuration of colonialism itself was deeply affected throughout by the pressures exerted by the genesis and growth of capitalism in Europe.

In the first long phase from 1492 when Columbus reached America (1492) to about the end of the eighteenth century, colonialism basically followed the short-term aims of obtaining from the subjugated countries as much plunder as possible, the process being strikingly summed up by Karl Marx in a passage in *Capital* (vol. I):

> The discovery of gold and silver in America, the extirpation, enslavement and entombment in mines of the aboriginal [Amerindian] population, the beginning of the conquest and looting of the East Indies, the turning of Africa into a warren for the commercial hunting of black skins, signalised the rosy dawn of the era of capitalist production. These idyllic proceedings are the chief momenta of primitive accumulation [of capital].

Colonialism in its first three centuries resulted in an enormous transfer of wealth from Asia, Africa and Latin America taken in the form of precious metals, enslaved human power and products of human industry. The last was drawn especially from Asia, where European powers, notably, the Netherlands and then Britain, could employ the revenues of subjugated territories to acquire craft and agricultural products—which, therefore, came to them free of cost in larger quantities, year after year. Marx had a much clearer notion than, apparently, many later economic historians like Maurice Dobb, that a part of this wealth (in both money and commodity form) became available for capital (hence the term 'primitive accumulation' used for it by Marx) in western Europe, especially Britain. Other circumstances like the Scientific Revolution and a reserve labour army created by the Enclosures being also present, this infusion of capital helped to put the English Industrial Revolution on its course and so usher in the age of full-blown capitalism.

Once Britain, as the first capitalist nation, had been industrialized, the colonies had to fulfil an additional function, that of serving as markets for Britain's industrial products, and sources of raw materials and primary wage-goods. This new function of colonialism, so clear to both Marx and Engels, unfortunately escaped attention in Lenin's analysis of imperialism (1917), which seems to have been far too greatly influenced by J.A. Hobson's well-meaning pioneering work *Imperialism* (1902), written from a free-trade point of view. Though the germs of this perception are already to be found in the writings of Marx and Engels, one need not deny full credit to John Gallagher and Ronald Robinson for their seminal delineation of the 'Imperialism of Free Trade' in an essay of this title (1953). The impact of this phase which lasted throughout the nineteenth century was felt mainly by the 'coloured', that is, the Asian and non-white African colonies. To these colonies, unlike the white colonies, there were made no great exports of capital—the feature that Lenin especially ascribed to 'Imperialism' of his time. In these colonies it rather became of interest to Britain, the leading colonial power, to provide capital only for transport infrastructure, and thereafter to prevent, by means of tariff as well as administrative measures, the genesis of any indigenous industry able to compete with metropolitan industry. In their 'counter-factual' work (*Mammon and the Pursuit of Empire—1860-1912*, Cambridge, 1986), Lance E. Davis and Robert A. Huttenback completely ignore this fundamental feature of free-trade colonialism. They, therefore, profess surprise that in India Britain took no steps to encourage and patronize 'business', as did the governments of Britain's white colonies. If the two authors had cared to look further at the British official policy in India, by far the largest colony in the world (in terms of population), they would have found that the British in fact sought to kill the only modern industry the Indians tried to develop, viz., cotton textile manufactures, first, by removing all import tariffs on textiles (1878-80), rupee revaluation (1891) and, finally, by enhanced excise (1894, 1896). In every sector the official policy remained solidly one of 'Buy British'. To embellish a well-known statement of Marx, colonialism fundamentally played a destructive role not only because it shattered the pre-colonial social order, but also because it strove to destroy the industrial future of the colonies as well.

There was no alteration in this feature when 'New Imperialism', the phenomenon studied by Hobson and Lenin, intertwined with colonialism from the days of the Great Depression (1873-96) onwards. By hindsight one can attribute the intensification in the struggle for colonies during the period preceding the First World War (1914-18) essentially to the fact that Britain was no longer the sole workshop of the world. Germany, US and France had begun to compete with it for markets; and neither for Britain nor for its rivals was free trade a safe 'open door' formula to be extended from China to one's own colonies. A 'protectionist' colonialism took over, but we must remember that no colony was protected against its own ruling country. Other phenomena that emerged in the capitalist world at this time, namely, finance capital, monopolies and export of capital, gave enormous strength to capitalist oligarchies within the major industrialized countries; but the 'Third World' colonies remained only on the periphery of these momentous processes. If any 'colonies' were involved, these were the nominal white 'colonies' of Britain, such as Canada, Australia, and the white-dominated South Africa, which were parts not of the colonial but of the capitalist world. It was only there that capitalism was now installed by capital exported to them. These 'colonies' could, and did, set up protective tariffs against imports of consumer goods, and so made foreign capital investments in them especially profitable. Such distinction between the two sets of colonies, did not enter the cores of the analysis of contemporary capitalism, whether by Rosa Luxemburg (*Capital Accumulation*, 1913) or Lenin (*Imperialism the Highest Stage of Capitalsm*, 1917), despite their numerous other brilliant insights. However, the issue of protection was of vital importance to the future development of the colonies.

If the colonial regimes would not allow protection, then for even capitalistic development of colonies, liberation from the tutelage of western powers became an essential requirement. Frederick Engels made this point when in 1892 in a letter to N.F. Danielson he contrasted the conditions of Czarist Russia which, being independent, could develop its industry under protection, to those of India, a totally subject country with no such privilege. A few years later he might well have cited the example of Japan, for its great success in industrialization because of its independence. Obviously, then, resistance and national liberation offered the only course by which economic modernization would be possible. Modernization, however, necessarily requires a change in the set of prevailing ideas, and we must examine briefly how this change came about in Asia.

III

Edward W. Said in his *Orientalism* (1978) propounded a thesis which, allowing for some marginal reconsiderations by him in his 'Afterword' (1995), can be summarized as follows: Europe *in tandem* with colonialism, evolved a hostile and censorious picture of Asia, which it not only propagated among Europeans, but also imposed on Asiatic minds, so as to combine its political subjugation with an intellectual hegemony over the latter. Those who speak in the increasingly popular idiom of post-modernism designate the communication of modern values from the West essentially as a part of such 'colonial discourse'.

There is no doubt that much writing in the West about Asia accepted the assumptions about Asia's intrinsic inferiority. This can be seen even in such widely read late text as H.A.L. Fisher's *History of Europe* (1935). Here we are told, for example, that 'to the conquest of nature through knowledge the contributions made by Asiatics have been negligible'. But there has also been another component of European 'orientalism', which springs from the application of scientific methods of enquiry and modern social values, notably, the rejection of racial inequality. Thus alongside the colonial constructs about Asia, there have arisen within 'Orientalism' objective reconstructions of Asia's past, which stand in contrast to the kind of 'Orientalist' depictions that Edward Said deals with. This other side of 'Orientalism' that Said all but closes his eyes to can be seen in a large array of works from Edward Gibbon's chapters on Asia in his *History of the Decline and Fall of the Roman Empire* (1776-88) to the splendid series of Joseph Needham's *Science and Civilization in China* (beginning, 1954).

Said's one-sided exposition of 'Orientalism', in fact, mirrors a long-established confounding of the colonial with the modern. The modern values that received their final imprint in Europe, namely, the supremacy of rationality and science, the ideas of equality in social, political and gender spheres, and of national independence, democracy and socialism, were created in Europe in the midst of struggles and battles on the streets, obtaining their sharpest expressions in and around events like the French Revolution (1789-94) and the Soviet Revolution of 1917. These values have become the common possessions of mankind through a similar mode of internal conflict and struggle, and not just by a simple mode of ideological diffusion.

There is no doubt that in so far as colonialism had to create a local administrative structure, it needed to accommodate or even create a local elite familiar with the language and ways of the rulers, in other words, a partly westernized class. In India this necessitated the establishment of schools for instruction in English, the official policy in this respect being proclaimed by Macaulay's resolution on English education (1835), though the Hindu College at Calcutta (Kolkata) for a similar purpose had been established some twenty years earlier. Such education was designed to provide the services of low-level native officials for the British administration. With this limited end in view, the British government was extremely parsimonious in spending money on English education, leaving it largely to private effort by Indians. The palm was taken by the Dutch in Indonesia, where in 1940 out of a population of 70 million there were only 637 'natives' in colleges and only 37 graduates with B.A. degrees.

However limited the extent of modern education thus imparted, it could not escape opening the gates to the storehouse of ideas and knowledge generated in Europe. This, in turn, resulted in a dual process: the rejection of those elements of the past culture of the colonial country which did not accord with modern values; and the use of European economic and political ideas by colonial intellectuals to develop a critique of colonialism itself. In India, the first can be said to begin with Raja Rammohun Roy (1770-1832), the proponent of scientific education and opponent of oppression of women in Indian society; and the second, with Dadabhai Naoroji (1825-1917), the 'Grand Old Man' of Indian nationalism. The two aspects were interlinked: India, as Keshav Chandra Sen pointed out in 1870, could become a 'nation' only to the extent that its social inequities and divisions were removed. The two streams came to find a common representative in one man, Mohandas Karamchand Gandhi (1869-1948), social reformer, national liberator and martyr. Gandhi professed that most of his ideas had sanction from India's past, but it is obvious from his own autobiography that to him they came initially and almost entirely from the West (from the modern interpretations of the New Testament, and from Tolstoy, Ruskin, and Irish nationalists, among others); he was, therefore, as much a product of modern thought as any other figure in the Indian national movement.

Analogous trends could be observed in other Asian countries. In China, laid low by the collective aggression of colonial powers, there arose the 'Modernization movement' of Kang You-wei (1858-1927) and Liang Qichao (1873-1929), which pursued the objective of internal reform for strengthening China to meet imperialist aggression. It reached its high water mark in the Hundred-Day Reform (1898), ending in tragedy and producing its own martyrs. Despite its failure, it lit the path for the great Sun Yat Sen (1866-1925), the Revolution of 1911 and China's subsequent titanic struggles. The Communist triumph of 1949 can be characterized as both a triumph of modernization and national unification, however much Mao Zedong's socialist vision might appear different from the concerns of today's seemingly westernized China.

Like any great event, the Meiji Restoration of 1868 in Japan would always invite diverse interpretations. Its leaders' declared aims of internal modernization and saving Japan from colonial subjugation were undoubtedly products of remarkable insight. The success of a policy based on these objectives enabled Japan to enter the club of the colonial powers by World War I, on the basis of its own industrial development and militarization. This proved that capitalism as a system need not be an exclusively European phenomenon, and also, unfortunately, that colonialism too was not tied to any particular set of races.

IV

What thus happened in India, China, Japan and other Asian countries, in response to the dominance of European colonialism, was precisely what Karl Marx had divined in 1853 as a future 'regeneration', which colonialism, despite its own designs, was bound to bring about in Asia (Marx in his two *New York Tribune* articles was specifically discussing India). Crucial to this process of regeneration has been the emergence of the 'nation' as the central entity commanding, over all other claims, the loyalty of those belonging to it. Conventional history teaches that 'nation-states' began to form in western Europe in the sixteenth century (Spain, Portugal, England, France, and the Netherlands), as developing commerce transformed the economies of these countries. But it was the French Revolution that, faced with the hostility of the monarchical powers ranged against it, proclaimed the right of all nations to independence, a principle, which, ultimately, did not only redraw the map of Europe, but also redrew the map of the whole world.

By giving to his study of the history of the idea of 'nation', the title of *Imagined Communities* (London, 1983), Benedict Anderson has underlined the fact that a nation is not created by geography or spoken language, but is a product of popular 'imagination'. There is of course no doubt that a nation has to be perceived as such by the bulk, or at any rate, a very large number of those who inhabit it. This is why quite variant definitions of 'nation' yet bring in the factor of the 'feeling' of oneness among the inhabitants (J.S. Mill) or the 'psychological make-up' of its people (J.V. Stalin), neither of which are material factors but belong to the realm of consciousness. Where one cannot go along with Anderson is his supposition that this imagined notion is essentially implanted by the phenomenon of 'print capitalism'. From the very case of Latin America which Anderson examines in some detail, it is clear that the Hispanic nations of South America were born out of the struggle led by Bolivar and San Martin against Spanish colonialism. It is true that their revolt, despite its banner of national 'patriotism', was basically that of the 'creoles' (old white settlers), and not of the Amerindian populations. But one must remember that the concept of 'nation' does not necessarily involve either equality or democracy, although as political consciousness spreads, these values may be invoked more and more strongly to reinforce a national cause.

As one traces the genealogy of the idea of 'nation', one goes back inevitably to Revolutionary France and the preceding political and ideological developments in Europe. This presents, perhaps, the clearest case where a western idea, once grasped by tens of millions in Asia, could make it impossible for Western rule or dominance to continue in the old way.

It was not, however, only the idea of the nation, but what the nation should be like, that made Asian peoples draw heavily on ideas that had their origins in the West. The Indian National Congress, when it met in December 1885 for its first session at Bombay, was and remained for some decades an organization of middle-class men. One is reminded of the Creoles fighting under Bolivar in the name of the whole population of Spanish South America. The middle-class Indian nationalists too wished to speak on behalf of the entire people of India. They, therefore, analysed the grievances of the Indian poor, and for this purpose, used all the instruments of modern economic science that came to them from Adam Smith, Ricardo and John Stuart Mill. Dadabhai Naoroji's *Poverty and Un-British Rule in India*, with materials published over the period 1876-1901, was the most notable effort of this genre. From here, the second stage arrived with Gandhi's mobilization of the poor (especially, peasants) as participants in the national movement from his Champaran campaign (1917), onwards. In his footsteps came the Communist movement and socialist groups, with ideas derived from European socialist thought, notably Marxism. The influence of these ideas, especially as articulated by Jawaharlal Nehru, predominates in the Karachi 'Fundamental Rights' Resolution of the Congress (1931), outlining the programme of action after India would win its freedom. From now on it was this programme carrying a vision of India as a semi-socialist secular democracy, that would serve as the main platform of the nationalist cause.

The same process could be seen in the Arab world. Confronted by the occupation of the bulk of the Arab countries by Britain and France after First World War, the growth of nationalism took first a liberal form, notably with the formation of the Wafd of Egypt under the leadership of Zaghlul Pasha in 1919. But socialist ideas too percolated, and in 1941 the second major secular stream in Arab nationalism, represented by the Ba'ath movement, came into being at Damascus. Its major theoretician, Michel Aflaq created the vision of a single Arab nation along with a strong commitment to socialism. The western mainsprings of the ideologies of both the Wafd and the Ba'ath are manifest.

The concept of a 'nation' was not at all prominent in early Marxist thought, the proletariat being held to belong to no nation. In practice, however, the nation asserted itself. Lenin sanctioned the theory of national self-determination. Later, Communists in Asia tended to combine the aim of national liberation with that of an ultimate socialist transformation. This took place most successfully in China and Vietnam, where the long armed struggles took the appearance of successful peasant wars.

V

If the present independent nations have been the result of the twin impact of colonialism and modernization—one provoking resistance, the other shaping the aims of that resistance—then, where does it leave Asia, within which these nations have been created?

Perhaps this question ought not to be so worded. As I argued in the beginning there was in fact no perception of 'Asia' as a continent among Asian peoples, so that one cannot expect there to have been the sense of an Asian identity before the ideas of European geography reached us, along with colonialism. That geographical designation took a living form only when, confronted by European colonialism, there arose a perception of Asian solidarity. Its beginnings lay initially in widely scattered expressions of fellow feeling. I offer here a few illustrations of such expressions of feeling drawn from India.

The British exploitation of India in the form of the annual 'drain' or 'tribute' was made possible by India having a huge annual export surplus, whose proceeds were transferred to England. Throughout the latter half of the nineteenth century the Indian export surplus was made possible by her exporting enormous quantities of opium to China, which was compelled to admit the drug after the two Opium Wars Britain fought with her. This made Indian nationalists see the Chinese as fellow-victims of the same colonial regime. Dadabhai Naoroji expressed their sentiment in 1880 in the following words:

> Because India cannot fill up the remorseless Drain; so China must be dragged in to make it up, even though it be by being 'poisoned'. . . . This opium trade is a sin on England's head and a curse on India for her share in being the instrument.

Great sympathy was similarly aroused for Turkey when Britain and France began to put pressure upon the Ottoman Empire from the late 1890s. The Young Turk Revolution of 1908 was followed by the Italian invasion of Libya (1911-12), and the Balkan Wars (1912-13). Indian sympathies took the practical form of an Indian Medical Mission to Turkey (1912-13), funded by voluntary effort. When after First World War and the Treaty of Sevres (1920) Turkish independence was in jeopardy, the Indian National Congress initiated the Non-Cooperation Movement (1920-2), of which the major demands were self-rule for India and restoration of Turkish independence under the Caliph. The agitation prevented any despatch of Indian troops to Turkey by Britain, and so partly facilitated the decisive Turkish military success of 1922.

Another issue was created by the Balfour Declaration (1917), by which Britain invited European Jews to settle in Palestine, recently seized by her. While opposing Hitler and his persecution and massacre of the Jews, Indian nationalist leaders, notably Gandhi and Jawaharlal Nehru, consistently took the side of the Arabs, especially in the 1930s, considering it a matter of victimization of a fellow Asian people by Britain.

Like Turkey, Japan, at the other end of Asia, was an object of great nationalist interest. Japan became a model for Indian nationalists once it attained the status of an important industrial power around 1900, and its success in the Russo-Japanese War (1904-5) created great excitement, since it showed that an Asian country could indeed defeat a great European power. The Indian leader Lala Lajpat Rai declared that 'Japan had vindicated the honour of Asia'. There was expectation that Japan would assist Indian nationalism, and one of the early revolutionary Indian leaders Barkatullah Khan spent some years in Japan (1910-14); so too did Rash Behari Bose, Mahendra Pratap, and A.M. Sahai.

Between 1942-5, one of India's major nationalist leaders Subhas Chandra Bose organized the Indian National Army with the objective of liberating India from the British, with Japanese assistance.

After First World War, China once again occupied India's attention. It was an unfortunate source of perplexity for those who believed in Asian solidarity that China's troubles now should emanate chiefly from the actions of Japanese imperialism. India's great poet Rabindranath Tagore travelled to Shanghai and met Lu Hsun in 1924. He also visited Japan. The Indian National Congress sent the Indian Medical Mission under Dr Atal to China (1938-43), for which Mao Zedong wrote a letter of thanks to Nehru in May 1939.

These facts from the history of the Indian national movement show that the sense of Asian identity began to form as result of the recognition of the fact that India as well as other nations of Asia were the victims of colonialism, and it was important that they should aid each other. The strength of this feeling is reflected in so moderate an Indian scholar-politician as K.M. Panikkar sitting down in the early 1950s to write the history of Western dominance over Asia. It was perhaps inevitable that there was also an attempt to glorify Asia's past. Thus, Gandhi himself used to say with some pride that all the major religions of the world had originated in Asia.

Undoubtedly, such sentiments grew in other countries as well. I do not have access to material from the writings of China, Iran or the Arab countries about Asia to present the evidence here; but I expect that references to the common plight of Asian countries were frequently made and even a pan-Asian consciousness projected.

This sentiment needs, however, to be distinguished from an appeal to the Asian identity made from the motive of justifying parity with colonial powers. Since Japan developed as the first capitalist nation in Asia, it is not surprising that such a stance should have been taken so vigorously by some circles in Japan. Benedict Anderson quotes Kita Ikki, an influential ideologue, as demanding in his *Nihon Kaizo Hoan Taiko* (1924) that Japan should have equal rights to possess other territories, at par with

Britain and Russia; he laid claims to Australia and Eastern Siberia on behalf of Japan. In fact, Imperial Japan's colonial acquisitions were perforce confined to Asian countries, and such slogans as 'Asia for Asiatics' or 'East Asia Co-Prosperity Sphere' could hardly conceal the inter-Asian conflicts its policy of expansion generated.

VI

The end of World War II created a new groundwork for Asian solidarity. Imperial Japan being defeated, its colonial framework was destroyed. The destruction was huge in human costs because of the atomic attacks by the US on the civilian populations of Hiroshima and Nagasaki on 6 and 9 August 1945—an attack all the more reprehensible since the USSR's joining the war was imminent by previous agreement. There was a feeling engendered immediately (as I remember the reaction of my parents and my own at the time)—and, nothing has come to light since to show it was wrong—that Japan was chosen as a testing ground because those who would suffer were, after all, Asians. It may be recalled that for this very reason the Indian judge on the War Crimes tribunal could not join in the condemnation of the Japanese accused when those who perpetrated Hiroshima and Nagasaki were going scot-free.

Another factor was the attempt of the European colonial powers to re-establish the position they had lost in South-East Asia and to retain it elsewhere, the flash points being Indonesia and Vietnam. The Inter-Asian Relations Conference at Delhi, in April 1947, organized under the auspices of the Provisional Government at Delhi, was certainly in part a reaction to this attempt. The Central Asian republics of the USSR also participated in this conference. An effort was made at Delhi to build up a feeling of Asian brotherhood by publishing portraits of Indians leaders like Gandhi and Tagore, and of Sun Yat Sen, Kemal Ataturk and Count Okakura, who were all deemed to have been advocates of Asian unity. This conference, though not, perhaps, a landmark in itself, was nevertheless an attempt to express the need for Asian solidarity at a moment of crisis of old-style colonialism. Such efforts certainly added to pressures on the Dutch, who finally recognized the independence of Indonesia in 1949.

Opposition to colonialism naturally brought in Africa, where after its 1952 revolution, Egypt had begun to play a prominent role. The defining moment came with the conference of heads of governments of 29 Asian and African states at Bandung (Indonesia) in 1955. Here, defying Cold War alignments, both China and India played a prominent part in calling for the removal of all vestiges of colonialism in Asia and Africa and for safeguarding the independence of the post-colonial nations. Sukarno, the Indonesian leader, was to later describe the latter task aptly as a struggle against 'neo-colonialism'.

Subsequent events, however, disrupted these developments. The pressures of the Cold War led to the emergence of the 'non-aligned' camp, which cut across Asia, in that China, the largest Asian country, was excluded from it, along with countries, on the opposite side, like Japan and the SEATO countries aligned with the USA. Territorial disputes between Asian nations, like India's with Pakistan and China, or Iraq's with Iran and Kuwait, blown out of proportion by local nationalisms, thwarted the growth of an Asian spirit. It seems a small mercy that institutions like the Asian Games or the Asian History Congress nonetheless survived.

It is, therefore, ironical that after the collapse of the Soviet Union, and the West's victory in the Cold War, there should now be again raised the spectre of a 'clash of civilizations', *a la* Huntingdon, or of a challenge to the West seen in the economic growth of Asian nations, first, Japan, and, now, China and India. It would seem as if once again 'Asia' is more the mental construct of the West (as the 'Other') than of the Asian peoples themselves.

There are, however, two sets of facts that ought once again to lay the foundations for some form of Asian solidarity. The first set of facts are essentially of an economic character. These derive from the fact that once the Asian countries' internal stagnation let Western colonialism dominate Asia, the continent's economic status declined precipitously. I here draw upon the data which Angus Maddison collects together in *The World Economy: A Millennial Perspective* (Paris, 2001), a publication of the Organization of Economic Cooperation and Development. Maddison estimates that Asia (excluding Japan) accounted for 62.1 per cent of the World GDP around 1500, but for only 15.5 per cent in 1950. Despite 'decolonization', the percentage remained at 16.4 in 1973. Thereafter, Asia's share increased to 29.5 per cent in 1998, which, though a considerable improvement, is still far behind its share in world population, viz., 57.4 per cent. Even if Japan is added, Asia's share in world GDP in 1998 would have been 37.2 per cent as against its share in world population at 59.5 per cent. (It must be remembered that the figures for the GDP of Asia, excluding Japan, have been raised considerably by use of the Purchasing Power Parity converters replacing market currency exchange rates, for stating the GDP in 'International Dollars'.) It is, therefore, obvious that for a very large part of Asia the sheer removal of poverty remains a shared problem. (In contrast to Asia, Western Europe with 6.6 per cent of the world population contributed 20.6 per cent of world GDP).

There is acute dissatisfaction among many with the notion that a mere introduction of 'globalization' or unqualified openness to foreign investment and commercial penetration is an adequate solution to the economic difficulties of independent Asian countries. It is time to remind ourselves of Arghiri Emmanuel's thesis of 'unequal exchange' (*Unequal Exchange: A Study of Imperialism of Trade*, 1969; transl., 1972), though we may, perhaps, replace his argument about the cause of it, viz., high wages in 'developed' countries, by the higher capital-intensity in the industries of those countries. The GDP per person employed in the US rose from 23,615 in 1950 to 55,618 in 1998 in terms of 1990 international dollars, while the corresponding figures for China were 1,297 and 6,181, and for India 1,377 and 4,510. The current hue and cry in Western countries about the 'out-sourcing' of certain services and production to relatively labour-intensive service and industrial sectors in Asia underline the kind of relationships that are now developing with the advanced countries practically enjoying a monopoly of capital-intensive technology.

This monopoly gets broken only where Asian countries use their independence to take special measures to develop and protect their capital-goods industries, as, indeed, China and India did through building up huge sectors of public-owned industries by the late 1970s. Owing to rapid technological changes, such 'public sectors' need continuous renewal and expansion, often by measures that cannot be deemed 'profitable' under ordinary market considerations. There is much anxiety among Western countries, especially the United States, to prevent such measures being adopted by developing countries through invoking instruments like the WTO and by applying open political pressures. The US opposition to the Iran-India gas pipeline, to which India seems currently to be succumbing, is one illustration of how the economic freedom of Asian countries is being daily endangered.

It must be realized that the USA's ability to exercise this kind of power does not come solely from its economic strength. Since 1988 it is no longer a nation with net assets abroad. By 1998 its foreign assets deficit had reached $1.5 trillion or 20 per cent of its national income. As its economic strength has faltered, USA's military power has become correspondingly important for it.

This brings us to the political set of factors we have mentioned earlier. Ever since the beginning of this century it has been recognized, with almost no protest from any Asian powers, that the US and its allies have a right to intervene at will in Asia. The 2003 invasion of Iraq by the so-called 'Coalition Forces', led by the US, was a brazen illegal invasion of an Asian country by western armies. Earlier Afghanistan was brought under not only the US but also the NATO's sphere of operations. Syria is being threatened with similar military action, and Iran by sanctions. President Bush's repeated announcement that the USA is entitled to bring about 'regime change' has not met with any challenge from any Asian government, apart from the governments immediately threatened ('the axis of evil' countries)—and by Malaysia.

Unfortunately, popular resentment against these neo-imperialist actions is increasingly taking a religious colour in West Asia and partly in South-East Asia, as if what the Asian countries are faced with today is exclusively a Western crusade against the religion and culture of Islam. There is no doubt that nationalisms have often invoked religion to fortify patriots, who are ready to sacrifice themselves for the cause with still greater conviction. Catholicism was used to mobilize the Irish people for freedom by Irish nationalists, and similarly, Hindu sentiments in India were appealed to by the nationalist leader Bal Gangadhar Tilak. It is understandable that there should be widespread admiration for the bravery shown by certain militant organizations in Palestine, Labanon, Iraq and other countries in standing up to the US and its allies iike Britain and Israel. Yet it needs to be recognized that by constantly appealing to Islamic peoples only, the leaders of these resistance movements show a total indifference to the cause of the solidarity of Asian and other peoples, which is crucial for restraining and resisting the growing dominance of Western powers over the world. It is worth recalling the advice that Jamaluddin Afghani, the founder of Pan-Islamism, gave to young Muslims of Calcutta in 1882: he asked them to be loyal to India in order not to divide the ranks of people opposing British imperialism. That kind of vision is needed if we hope to convert the hurt that we felt yesterday over Vietnam and must feel today over Iraq into a sense of Asian identity, which can then help all of us to unite and give 'Asia for Asians' a new democratic substance—a craving for the continent's complete liberation.

If Asia has to achieve the necessary transformation of its consciousness for this end, as rapidly as circumstances demand, then the role of Japan as the most advanced nation of Asia in terms of material circumstances and scientific attainments, is also very important. Japan has already done so much to teach us. Especially to be saluted is the memory of those in Japan who before 1945 laid down their lives or faced imprisonment and persecution for their opposition to expansionist wars. The suffering of the people of Hiroshima and Nagasaki is a constant reminder to us of the sheer ruthlessness of imperialism. The fortitude and determination with which the Japanese people rebuilt their country and made Japan the second biggest economy in the world have been a source of inspiration to all other Asian peoples. And, finally, the defiant spirit with which the Japanese people, with Japan's intellectuals and scientists in their front ranks, have opposed the revival of militarism and upheld the cause of freedom and peace has a message for the conscience of people throughout the world. In constructing Asian solidarity with a new vision, so as to serve the cause of safeguarding national independence, preserving peace, and furthering equitable development, the contribution of the Japanese people, from whom the slogan of Asian solidarity had first come, could be of crucial significance today.

HISTORIOGRAPHY

CHAPTER 16

The *Keralotpatti* as History: A Note on Pre-colonial Traditions of Historical Writing in India

KESAVAN VELUTHAT

The form in which historical consciousness expresses itself varies from society to society, sometimes to such an extent that one society, used to its own particular notions of history, may fail or even refuse to recognize historical consciousness expressed in other forms as pertaining to history at all. In the case of India, writers of the colonial era held that India had neither a consciousness of history nor a sense of the past. They explained this lack variously: the greater concern of India with the spiritual than the material, the changelessness of Indian society, Muslim vandalism, and so on were thought to account for history being a weak point of this otherwise splendid civilization. However, the fact seems to be that for those scholars brought up in the Rankean tradition of historical writing, any statement that was not authenticated by 'evidence' from 'contemporary sources' was less than history. What was presented as history had also to look like 'what actually happened'. Indian forms of historical writing fell short of these standards. Naturally, India was stated to have 'produced no Herodotus or Thucydides . . .'—a statement repeated *ad nauseum* by every third-rate textbook of Indian history.

Such refusal to accept Indian forms of historical writing as valid need not be taken as entirely innocent either: it often formed part of a larger project of rejecting a whole knowledge before establishing another in its place. The 'secure and usable past' which the colonial masters had 'invented' for the colony had to pass for, and be used, as *the* knowledge that would help them establish and maintain control and dominance over the colony. A necessary first step then would be to repudiate Indian forms of historical writing and knowledge, which they did in a consummate way. It came to be generally accepted that India was an ahistorical society, lacking in a sense of history and not given to maintaining authentic and accurate records of the past. The manifold specimens of historical writing from any part of the country were variously ridiculed as superstition, legend and nonsense. It will be interesting in this context to look at the instances of historical reconstruction attempted by the colonial masters. In his justly famous *Malabar Manual*, William Logan pooh-poohs the narrative called *Keralotpatti* as a 'farrago of legendary nonsense'.[1] It is not altogether beside the point that Logan, nonetheless, leans heavily on the statements in the *Keralotpatti* for his own reconstruction of the history of Kerala. Thus, even while there was a refusal to accept 'native' forms of historical writings as reliable, there was also a tacit acceptance of them, if in an attempt to pin events and personages in them down to points in space and time. What is more important in this case is the publicized rejection of the 'native' tradition than the secretive use to which they were put when it suited those scholars to do so.

In recent years, however, the statement that India was an ahistorical society has been called into question. It has been shown that India did have a sense of history; but the form in which historical consciousness expressed itself in India was not the same as what one finds in the Greco-Roman or Judaeo-Christian or post-Enlightenment traditions of Western historiography. The privileging of these Western traditions is not just a matter of Eurocentrism; it is part of the baggage of colonialism. This baggage and all that it contains are being challenged and rejected effectively in the context of the post-colonial self-understanding of the former colonies. At another level, not only is it doubted whether the expressions of a historical consciousness in the Western tradition can be really taken as *the* standard, but it has also been demonstrated that other societies, too, had an equally strong or stronger tradition of historical writing.[2] No society can be really said to be devoid of a sense of history. In fact, it is even persistently argued that pre-modern societies all over the world had a greater sense of history than modern societies.[3]

Since the whole debate veers around the question of an understanding of what a sense of history is, it may be useful to begin by something of a definition. Romila Thapar defines a sense of history as 'a consciousness of past events, which events are relevant to a particular society, seen in a chronological framework and expressed in a form which meets the needs of that society'.[4] There are inadequacies about this view; but the essentials, such as the relevance of particular instances and the choice of the form, are important. If this view is accepted, it can be seen that India too, like most other ancient societies, had a clear sense of history although literature that can be specifically called historical may be lacking there in the earliest periods. Historians have prised out and appreciated veins of history embedded in the Vedic, Buddhist and Jain literatures, not to speak of full-length texts of what could be described as externalized history dating from a later period.[5] The purpose of the present paper is to look at a few expressions of such historical consciousness in narratives from pre-colonial Kerala in an attempt to identify the notions of history which obtained in this part of India. In the course of the discussion the needs of that society, which prompted the preference of certain specific forms to certain others to express that consciousness, also will be taken up for examination. I intend to consider specimens which are specifically from Kerala, leaving out songs from the Tamil '*Sangam*' or *Bhakti* literature which are products of a cultural idiom not typically Keralan, although they are heavily historical and extremely relevant to Kerala.

I want to begin by speaking about an absence before I take up the presences for discussion. Typical of south India, or nearly the whole of Indian subcontinent, in the early medieval period[6] is a profusion of what are known as *prasastis*. This genre of literature has been a form in which historical consciousness found its expression in early medieval India. The *prasastis* form largely prefaces to inscriptions recording grant of land and contain, generally, a supposedly historical account of the dynasty of the donor in whose honour they are composed. Usually there is a recitation of the tradition, real or invented, regarding the origin of the dynasty, a somewhat detailed description of the 'career and achievements' of the immediate ancestors of a patron, and then a dwelling at some length on the patron himself.[7] All these items use a particularly manufactured image of the past, and, in every case, that image would be used in the validation of the new political forms that came into existence in different regions in the subcontinent in the early medieval period. The *prasasti* begins to make its appearance as a form of expressing historical consciousness from the time of the Guptas (AD fourth century AD) onwards in early medieval India. It went a long way in legitimizing the new monarchical state and the monarch in it in south India in the period of the Pallavas (seventh century AD) and later.[8]

It is interesting that there is a conspicuous absence of such *prasasti*s in Kerala, even while a new state, contemporaneous with and comparable to other early medieval states of the deep south, was very much in existence in the Cera kingdom of Mahodayapuram. This enigma cries out for an answer. M.G.S. Narayanan, an acknowledged authority on the history of this kingdom, has suggested that the Ceras had little to boast of in their ancestry since they followed the matrilineal order of succession.[9] This argument does not hold much water because ancestry is ancestry, whatever the system of succession. Any system is as good or as bad as any other, and there is nothing that makes patriliny better than matriliny except under the tutelage of a particular discourse. The one in Kerala, if anything, was in favour of matriliny. In fact, in the *Mushikavamsakavya*, a dynastic chronicle from the northern part of Kerala dating from the period of the Cera kingdom itself (AD eleventh century), the poet describes elaborately the genealogy and also the fact of matrilineal succession in the chiefly house of Kolam in the historical period.[10]

An alternative possibility, therefore, is that the form in which Kerala society expressed its consciousness of past events, and the events themselves which it chose to record, were different from what obtained elsewhere in south India. The needs of society seem to have been different in this case. It is clear that the nature of state that came into existence in Kerala under the Ceras of Mahodayapuram was characteristically different from its contemporaries in other parts of south India.[11] For one thing, there was a much heavier Brahmanical presence in the political economy of Kerala—the Brahmanas are presented as the 'power behind the throne' in that kingdom—and, more than the genealogy and status of the ruling house or its claim to legitimacy through a particular origin myth or celebrated ancestors, it was the fact of the subservience of the ruler to the Brahmana groups that needed emphasis and sanction. The kind of legitimacy that those in power in Kerala wanted to seek was hence different from what it was elsewhere. The *prasasti*, with its concern with the origins and succession of the ruling house, was hardly the tool for this. Naturally, therefore, the ruling sections in Kerala society avoided this form of expressing the consciousness of the past as it failed to meet the specific needs of society. The *prasasti* therefore failed to take roots there.[12] There were, however, other forms of expressing a consciousness of the past.

I shall now turn to the much-maligned *Keralotpatti* and show it as one such form through which the elite in Kerala chose to express its historical consciousness from time to time. The *Keralotpatti* is a narrative in somewhat Sanskritized Malayalam prose, giving an account of Kerala's history from the creation of the land by the inevitable Parasurama, expressed in the style of Puranic exposition. There are many versions and more copies of this book, at least half a dozen available in print and many more that number in palm leaf manuscripts. In fact, many old houses of landlords and local chieftains had in their collection one or more copies of it, a fact which has its interest for us. Even a Tamil translation is available. It is also important that the standard way in which the book ends is by saying that it is the work of Thunchatthu Ramanujan Ezhutthacchan, the seventeenth century Malayalam poet who was responsible for popularizing the Puranic lore among the non-Brahmana aristocracy of Kerala through his translations of *Mahabharata* and *Ramayana* in Kilippattu meters.

Historians in the past have taken widely varying positions, ranging from describing *Keralotpatti* as 'a farrago of legendary nonsense' and as 'having attained the rank of authentic history'.[13]

Attempts to study it were centred on the question of accepting or rejecting the veracity of statements related to heroes (or villains) and events in this narrative. Thus, Parasurama, Sankaracarya, Ceraman Perumal or Patamel Nayar the creation of Brahmanical settlements or the conversion of the last Perumal or the partition of Kerala were all variously accepted, rejected or explained away by those who worked on the history of Kerala using the narrative. In other words, the concern of those scholars was with the *historicity* or otherwise of the narrative, rather than the *historical consciousness* expressed in it or its social function. Thus, they failed to identify or appreciate the narrative as an expression of the sense of history shown by Kerala society.

The *Keralotpatti* is, to be sure, not to be taken for a work that would satisfy modern sensibilities of chronology, causation and generalization. Its chronology is not absolute, and where there is mention of absolute chronology in terms of the Kali era or the Christian era (as in Hermann Gundert's edition). The dates are hopelessly inaccurate, abounding in anachronisms and impossible correspondences. There are minor confusions in terms of geography as well. It has, naturally, failed to make the grade as 'history' in the assessment of modern historians. However, after scholars of an earlier generation dismissed it as a bundle of legends, there has been an increasing appreciation of the fact that the *Keralotpatti* is

> not to be rejected outright but to be used with caution. The statements made there should not be accepted at their face value. However, they contain references which supplement and clarify evidence obtained from other sources of information though it reflects interest and prejudice and suffers from interpolation as well as misinterpretation.[14]

This is a great leap forward. In fact, M.G.S. Narayanan has brought out many instances mentioned in the narrative which get attested by other sources, thereby showing the validity and authenticity, if not accuracy, of the statements there. Moreover, there is an attempt to appreciate the social function of the narrative in Narayanan's work, although he does not develop it to the logical conclusion. His exercise, pioneering as it is, remains nevertheless at the level of looking at *Keralotpatti* yet as a *source* of history, accepting or rejecting the historicity of individual statements contained in it.

My purpose here is to look at the *Keralotpatti* as a narrative of history which tells the story of Kerala right from the creation of the land. I will argue that it exhibits a sense of history inasmuch as there is in it 'a consciousness of past events, which events are relevant to a particular society, seen in a chronological framework and expressed in a form which meets the needs of that society'. An examination of these events and how they are represented here will clarify the extent of historical consciousness that it exhibits. Which of the past events were thought to be more relevant than others will also show the interests and concerns of society and explain, at least partly, the choice of the form for expressing them. The discussion will show also that history was used here as elsewhere as 'a handmaid of authority'.[15]

Different versions of the *Keralotpatti* are available. All of them, however, share the same structure with a more or less uniform chronological scheme. It falls into three broad periods, namely 'the Age of Parasurama', 'the Age of the Perumals' and 'the Age of the Tamburans'.[16] The variations in the different versions are related largely to the third period, i.e. the age of the Tamburans, namely the period of the petty locality chieftains in the post twelfth-century period of Kerala history. There are also variations in relation to the position that different castes are given in different versions of the *Keralotpatti*, with a clear social purpose where the position of particular castes is sought to be defined as something of a charter of social validation. The details in relation to the earlier periods tally in a broad manner, probably showing a common source of the tradition in those two sections. I have used here the version related to the kingdom of the Zamorins in Calicut.[17] I make cross-references to a few other versions where relevant, particularly to the one related to the Raja of Kolattunad in the north.[18] I confine myself to statements of a political nature, the social aspects being the subject of a separate study.

The *Keralotpatti* begins with an account of Parasurama's creation of Kerala, the land between Gokarna and Kanyakumari, by raising it from the Arabian Sea with a fling of his axe and settling it by Brahmanas brought from the north in 64 *gramas*, of which 32 are in Tulunad and 32 in present-day Kerala. Scholars in the past have looked upon this as an attempt to explain some mysterious geological phenomenon in terms of a divine intervention. However, it is important to see that this is not a tradition prevalent in Kerala alone. One sees this, at dates earlier than the references pertaining to Kerala, in relation to regions further north on the west coast. In fact, it is seen first in relation to Gujarat. Then it moves down to the Sopara region in Maharashtra, and further south to what is known as the *Sapta-Konkanas* before reaching the Canarese coast. Scholars have noted the moving character of this legend.[19] It has been suggested that a legend migrated from the north to the south along the coast, which is indication that it represented a moving chain of group migration, the migrants carrying with them the tradition that Parasurama created *their* land and donated it to *them*. The Brahmanical groups wanted to remember this as an important item in relation to their past, as the control they had in large areas of land received considerable sanction from this memory.

Speaking about the way in which Parasurama peopled the land of Kerala after raising it from the sea, the *Keralotpatti* says that the Brahmanas who were brought and settled in the first instance would not stay; they returned to their original home in Ahicchatra for fear of serpents in the new land. Parasurama brings a second wave of Brahmanas from Ahicchatra. In order that they would not be accepted if they returned, he had their hair style and style of clothing changed. He also persuades them to accept matriliny so that he could expiate for his own matricidal sin; but only those of one village, namely Payyannur, would oblige. Parasurama also establishes 108 temples each for Shiva and Durga. He selects 36,000 Brahmanas from the different *gramas* and confers on them the right to arms (*sastrabhiksha*), so that they could protect their land themselves.

Following the battle between historians who rejected *Keralotpatti* as legendary nonsense on the one side and those who accepted it as authentic history on the other, there have been attempts of another kind in the historiography of Kerala going on for the past two or three decades now. For instance, the story of the creation of the land by Parasurama by raising it from the sea is identified as something which was not exclusive to Kerala, and that it indicated the fact of a long chain of migration along the west coast of peninsular India. All the speculation about the story being an explanation of some geological phenomenon is put to rest, as it should be now applied to other parts of the peninsula. Similarly, all the 32 *gramas* mentioned in the text, except one, have been identified with the help of inscriptions, literature, monuments and surviving ethnic traditions. The meetings of their committees are now better known from other records, which correspond to the indications in the *Keralotpatti*. The curious group of fighting Brahmanas, on whom Parasurama conferred *sastrabhiksha*, are identified with the prominent group of what are known as the *cattirar* or *cattar*. Their organization of the *salai*, where military training was part of the curriculum, has been studied extensively. Their presence in inscriptions and medieval literature has been a subject of engaging study.

In this context, a comparison of the Parasurama tradition obtaining in South Canara and Kerala will be interesting. The story in relation to South Canara is told in the Kannada text, *Gramapaddhati*.[20] The account of the creation of the land and its donation to the Brahmanas occurs in both regions, but the latter part is not represented in the *Gramapaddhati* with as much importance as it is in the *Keralotpatti*. In the *Gramapaddhati* version, the sage creates Brahmanas from fishermen and donates the land to them. Subsequently, as they turn out to be ungrateful to him, he curses them and turns them into untouchables.[21] According to the *Gramapaddhati*, the Brahmana settlements in coastal Karnataka are, thus, not survivals of the ones created by Parasurama. They date from a much later period, and are established by Mayuravarman Kadamba or even later. Here is the crucial difference between the situations in Kerala and South Canara, and it is a significant indication of the difference in the role of the Brahmanical groups in the two societies. The landed wealth in South Canara was not under the control of the Brahmanical groups as much as it was in Kerala and, therefore, the importance that the Brahmanas of Kerala had in polity and society was not matched by what their counterparts in South Canara had. As it was much greater in the case of Kerala, it would take none less than Parasurama to be not only the creator of the land but also the donor to the Brahmana groups. So also the exceptional importance attached to the arms-bearing Brahmans called *sastrabrahmanas* or *cattirar* and their group meetings[22] is another instance of the use of the past in seeking validation for the Brahmanical groups in Kerala society. Parasurama establishes a *Brahmakshetra* in Kerala, where Brahmanas looked after the work of the Kshatriyas, with every arrangement for the welfare of the people, including religion, administration and law. The Brahmanical authority in Kerala was so great that it took a Brahmanical *avatara* of Vishnu, with sufficient Kshatriya pretensions, to do the job.

In the period that followed, too, it is interesting that the text shows that the Brahmanical groups had played a major role in society and politics. Representatives of the Brahmanical establishment govern the land gifted to them by Parasurama as *Brahmakshetra*. In course of time, however, they realize that the business of governance has corrupted them, and they themselves decide to get a Kshatriya as their ruler. Accordingly, a Kshatriya and his sister are brought; the brother is anointed king who is made to swear habitual allegiance to them. A monarchical state was established in Kerala. The sister is married to a Brahmana and it is agreed that the progeny would be Kshatriya according to the matrilineal system of succession. The descendants of this sister would be the successors to the throne. The conviction that the business of governance is not the Brahmanas' cup of tea and that it belongs to the Kshatriya is very much in tune with the Brahmanical principles and the theory of *varnasramadharma*, which expressed the ideology of the ruling class in early medieval India in general. At the same time, there is no attempt to latch the origin of the dynasty on to one of the reputed Kshatriya lineages of Puranic fame; nor is an origin myth in the tradition typical of the medieval court literature in Sanskrit invented or the heroic deeds of the ruler or his ancestors recited. On the other hand, the progeny of a union between a Brahmana male and a Kshatriya female is recognized as Kshatriya, even at the expense of contradicting the *Sastra* rules of *Sankirnajati*, obviously following the matrilineal system of succession obtaining in Kerala. That the ruler was himself both a Kshatriya through matrilineal inheritance and the son of a Brahmana by birth was sanction enough! After this, the kings were enjoined to listen to what the representatives of the Brahmanical establishment would dictate to them through their body of the *Nalu Tali*, which acted as a council of the king.

Many details here have lured historians in the past; but in the absence of what the Rankean tradition of historiography would call 'corroborative evidence', it was not quite possible for any of them to accept or reject these statements, except at the level of assertions and wishful thinking. From the middle of the previous century, however, a number of inscriptions dating from the ninth century onwards have been discovered and published. They have been subjected to a critical study within the discipline of historical method as well. They bear out many statements contained in the *Keralotpatti*. For instance, Mahodayapuram or Kodungallur was the capital of Kerala. The members of the dynasty which ruled from there followed matrilineal descent. The ruler was known as the Perumal. He was under the habitual tutelage of the Brahmanical establishment. He had a council of advisors called the *Nalu Tali*, every detail of which corresponds in the inscriptions, medieval literature and the *Keralotpatti*.

A definitive and exhaustive study of the history of the Cera kingdom of Mahodayapuram has brought out several interesting details about the nature of polity there. It has effectively brought out the overwhelming importance of the Brahmanas there, who functioned as 'the real power behind the throne'.[23] This position of theirs has been shown as owing to the fact that they controlled the best agricultural land in the fertile river valleys of Kerala; and the resultant command they had in economy and society reflected itself in the political structure as well. The polity with such overwhelming importance of the Brahmanical groups in it required a legitimation different from what was used and found successful elsewhere in contemporary south India. Thus, the story of Parasurama creating the land and donating it to Brahmanas, the Brahmanas carrying out the governance of the land upon the bidding of Parasurama, the Brahmanas themselves creating the ruler in every sense of the term and the ruler being habitually obedient to them are all motifs which would be extremely useful in this unique means of legitimation. The difference between the Kerala tradition in expressing a sense of the past on the one hand and its Tamil or Kannada counterparts on the other lay in this difference in the composition of the two societies: the predominance of the Brahmanical groups in the former. The *Keralotpatti* is unique in relation to this period. It is a Brahmanical document *par excellence* and as such records those events of the past which it thought were relevant to the Brahmanical groups of Kerala society. The form that it chose, too, was most suited to the needs of the Brahmanical groups in society.

There are other aspects of the *Keralotpatti* that are important and relevant in relation to the age of the Perumals, i.e. the second chronological phase. The ways in which Namputiri heroes like Azhvancheri Tamprakkal[24] or Vasu Bhattatiri[25] or, most of all, Sankaracarya[26] are treated are cases in point. Of particular interest is Sankaracarya. If we are to believe the biographies of the great teacher ascribed to his own disciples, he owed hardly anything to Kerala and it had no claims on him to boast about.[27] But after he became a celebrity, he was shamelessly appropriated and the origin of anything that needed sanction in the Brahmana-dominated society of Kerala was attributed to him. Thus, the beginning of the Kollam era, the introduction of the graduated scale of untouchability for different castes, the peculiar codes of conduct for the Brahmanas of Kerala, etc., were all gifts of the great *advaita* philosopher! The fact that the *Keralotpatti* is a Brahmanical document aimed at the validation of the Brahmanical groups through a particular use of history is underlined in all these instances. The way in which the arms-bearing Brahmanas who had a major presence in medieval Kerala society and their group meetings[28] is presented in the accounts is another instance of the use of the past in seeking validation for those groups which enjoyed and sought to perpetuate their status.

The account about the end of the Perumal regime is also interesting. The *Keralotpatti* says that as the last Perumal over-stayed and thus incurred the sin of misappropriating the wealth of the Brahmanas. He wanted to expiate for it, but since it was too serious an offence to be expiated according to the provisons of the four Vedas and six Shastras, he decided to accept the fifth Veda. Accordingly, he abdicated the throne, divided the kingdom among his sons and relatives, and left for Mecca after accepting Islam.

Writers from at least the sixteenth century have repeated and commented on this tradition in one way or the other. Suggestions that would support one or the other aspect of the story are there in the sources. They include a sense of guilt which the last Perumal had about wronging the Brahmanas, his attempts to atone for it, the chronological sequence of the disappearance of the last Perumal and the appearance of independent rulers in many principalities, the appearance of the first datable mosques in Kerala at the same time, and so on. And nearly all rulers of what could be described as the 'successor states' claimed a gift of the last Perumal at the beginning of their kingdom and dynasty.

The next chronological phase in the *Keralotpatti* is related to 'the age of Tamburans'.[29] Historically, this corresponds to the period following the end of the Perumal era in twelfth century AD. The character of the narrative suddenly changes in this section in a big way. The role that the Brahmanical groups have to play is little if any. It is the newly emerging political power, and the support it had from trading groups, that are highlighted in this section. In Gundert's version, for example, the fortunes of the kingdom of Calicut are taken up. A gift of the last Perumal to two Eradi brothers is presented as marking the origin of the kingdom: of a strip of useless land and a few equally insignificant symbols of royalty such as a piece of rusted sword and a broken conch. The throne (or any piece of ramshackle furniture that pretended as one) of any ruler in the post-Cera period was presented as a similar gift from the Perumal. Again, when the growth of the kingdom of Calicut is taken up, the military aggrandizement of the Zamorin comes in, unlike in the case of the Perumal in an earlier period. The Eradi brothers push forward, following the Perumal's leave 'to annexe [territories] by dying and killing'.[30] The support that they got from the trading groups, especially the Muslims, is treated at some length.[31] So also, the various nodes of power in the localities with the Nayar landed elements occupying a crucial place in the power structure is acknowledged. The medieval festival of *mamakam* is described elaborately, where the Zamorin of Calicut is presented as the veritable sovereign of the whole of Kerala.[32]

As I have suggested above, there are many differences in the nature and content of the narrative from this point on. For one thing, there is the recognition that political power is more a function of military aggrandizement. Secondly, in a region with few Brahmanical settlements and therefore limited Brahmanical control over agricultural land, the real power behind the throne was different from what it was under the Perumals. At the same time, there were a large number of local landed magnates who were incorporated into the political system as *samanta* 'feudatories', civil and military functionaries of the state in the localities, managers looking after the private estates of the ruler and other members of his family in different parts of the kingdom and other elements of the 'bureaucracy', such as it was.[33] There was also the considerable wealth that trade, particularly Arab, fetched to the port of Calicut. At the same time, the relatively inferior ritual status of the family of the Zamorins was something that they cherished not exactly with pride. Rituals in temples such as the *pattattanam* or the *mamakam* helped somewhat in getting over this disability as also the royal courtly rituals, where the Brahmanas condescended to bless the Zamorin and the junior princes. A historical narrative had to take all these realities into consideration; and the *Keralotpatti* promptly did it. The down-to-earth political, and to a considerable extent secular character of the historical narrative is hard to miss in this section of the *Keralotpatti*.

Interestingly, this section in the Kolattunad tradition of *Keralotpatti* follows the period of the *Mushikavamsakavya*, another specimen of historical writing from the same region. The latter is a typical dynastic chronicle and has been written about elaborately by scholars since its discovery.[34] It typically participates in the tradition of historical writing in India known as dynastic chronicles that came up in the post-Gupta period, legitimizing the newly emerging kingdoms in the regions. The function of the *Mushikavamsakavya* too was not different. It is significant that the *Mushikavamsakavya* pertains to a *nadu* division that contested, with varying degrees of success, the overlordship of the Perumals of Mahodayapuram. The way in which it related itself to the Perumals was different from that of other *nadus* in Kerala in this period.[35] Is it possible that, given the proclivity of this *nadu* to claim autonomy, it used well-known, successful techniques of political validation? One is tempted all the more when one considers that *Udayavarma-caritam*, the first 'historical biography' from Kerala, is related to a king of this house ruling immediately after this period.[36] These two aspects, namely the existence of a separate dynastic chronicle and the fact of the first 'historical biography' in Kerala coming from this region, however, need further elaboration and analysis.

My argument here is that Kerala too had a sense of history, which it expressed in forms that were found most suitable for its needs. History being generally a record of the activities of socio-political status groups, those that have status at different times find a place in recorded history. Social groups like the Brahmanas which enjoyed power and wielded control over resources thus found themselves in the centrestage. When in a later period status came to be defined in different terms, an alternative form for expressing historical consciousness is devised. In the earlier sections of the *Keralotpatti*, one sees what seems to be a larger than life picture of the Brahmanical groups. Later on, when political power was in the hands of other groups which had less respect for the Brahmanical groups, the concern of historical writing also gets shifted to those who are at the different nodes of power. Hence we see in the *Keralotpatti* a large number of non-Brahmana chiefs figuring with prominence in the 'Age of Tamburans', whether it is in the kingdom of Calicut or of Kolattunad. As history is basically a charter of validation for status groups in society, there is a greater concern at this later stage with these non-Brahmana sections as much as there was with the Brahmanical sections in an earlier period. In short, I beg to submit in this preliminary report on a reading of *Keralotpatti* that

(a) Kerala, or India for that matter, was not a society entirely devoid of a sense of the past and
(b) that the different forms which that sense of history took to express itself eminently suited the needs of society from time to time.

I do believe that there is a case for taking up all expressions of historical consciousness from the region and subjecting them to analysis within the social and political context in which they were written. Such exercises in relation to different parts of the country will bring out the way in which Indian civilization perceived the past. Apart from giving the lie to the statement that India was an ahistorical society, it will also hopefully throw light on one of the significant systems of knowledge in Indian society and the function that it had to serve.

NOTES

1. William Logan, *Malabar Manual*, Madras, 1887 (ed. P.J. Cherian with detailed studies and notes, Thiruvananthapuram, 2000), Chapter III, 'History', esp. pp. 221-44. In spite of this rejection, much of Logan's formulation on the early history of Kerala with 825 as a central date hinges on accepting the statements in *Keralotpatti*. For situating Logan within the historiographical context of colonial India, see Kesavan Veluthat, 'Logan's *Malabar*: Text and Context' in above-mentioned work edited by Cherian, pp. xxxvi-xlvii.
2. J.H. Plumb, *Death of the Past*, Harmondsworth, 1973, esp. pp. 17-33.
3. Ibid., esp. pp. 34-50.
4. I borrow this definition from Romila Thapar, 'The Tradition of Historical Writing in Early India', in Romila Thapar, *Ancient Indian Social History: Some Interpretations*, New Delhi, 1978, p. 268.
5. This geological analogy is proposed by Romila Thapar, 'Society and Historical Consciousness: the *Itihasa-purana* Tradition', in Romila Thapar, *Interpreting Early India*, New Delhi, 1992, p. 137.
6. For an engaging discussion of 'the early medieval' and the rise of regional states there, see B.D. Chattopadhyaya, *The Making of Early Medieval India*, New Delhi, 1994, esp. pp. 17-34 and pp. 183-222. I have taken up this problem, if slightly differently, in my Presidential Address to the Medieval Indian History Section of the Bangalore Session of the Indian History Congress. Kesavan Veluthat, 'Into the "Medieval"—and Out of It: Early South India in Transition', *Proceedings of the Indian History Congress*, Bangalore, 1997.
7. For discussions on the *prasastis*, J.G. de Casparis, 'Inscriptions and South Asian Dynastic Traditions', in R.J. Moore (ed.), *Tradition and Politics in South Asia*, New Delhi, 1979; George Spencer, 'Heirs Apparent: Fiction and Function in Chola Mythical Genealogies', *Indian Social and Economic History Review*, vol. XXI, no. 4, 1984. I have examined how the *prasastis* were used in the validation of the newly

emerging political context of south India in the early medieval period. Kesavan Veluthat, *Political Structure of Early Medieval South India*, New Delhi, 1993, pp. 29-69.

8. For further details about this function of the *prasastis* in early medieval south India, Veluthat, ibid., pp. 29-69.
9. M.G.S. Narayanan, *Perumals of Kerala: Political and Social Conditions of Kerala under the Cera Perumals of Makotai (c* AD *800-*AD *1124)*, Calicut, 1996, p. 85.
10. K. Raghavan Pillai (ed.), *The Musikavamsakavya of Atula*, Trivandrum, 1977, *sarga* XI, vv. 62-90, presents a story of a shift from patriliny to matriliny in the succession in that house. Historians in the past, in fact, have taken this as 'historical' and explained it as resulting from the conquest of the Mushika territory by the Ceras of Kerala who were followers of the matrilineal system. What is more likely is that the Sanskrit poet explained what to him and his readers would look like an 'aberrant phenomenon'—the case of matriliny in a Kshatriya house—by means of a mythical incident placed in the twilight of the remote and the recent pasts. In any case, what is important here is that the fact of matriliny being the system of inheritance in that house in the historical period does not stop the court poet from singing the praise of the ancestors of the patron and preparing elaborate genealogies. For a study of the *kavya*, C. Girija, 'The Mushikavamsa Kavya: A Study', unpublished M.Phil. disseration, Mangalore Uni-versity, 1990.
11. I have brought out this difference in Kesavan Veluthat, *Political Structure of Early Medieval South India*, passim.
12. In fact, it will be wrong to believe that Kerala did not know the *prasasti* at all. A copper plate record from Kerala dated AD 1188, contained in the Kollur Madhom Plates, describes itself as a reissue of an earlier *prasasti*. *Travancore Archaeological Series*, vol. IV, no. 7, pp. 22-65. However it is not a *prasasti* in the strict sense of the term, as none of the elements related to the structure and functions of the *prasasti* is present there. The term is used in the sense of a grant!
13. For the former statement, Logan, n. 1 above. The latter statement is of V. Nagam Aiya, *Travancore State Manual*, Trivandrum, 1906, p. 210. Elamkulam P.N. Kunjan Pillai, *Caritrattinre Pascattlattil*, Kottayam, 1961, p. 37 believed that the *Keralotpatti* contains 'stories concocted by a Namputiri on a fine morning with a view to supporting the story of Parasurama'.
14. M.G.S. Narayanan, *Perumals of Kerala*, p. 20. Narayanan has established the historicity of many statements contained in the text. Ibid., passim. The present writer followed this line in an attempt to identify the Brahman settlements mentioned in Kerala. Kesavan

Veluthat, *Brahman Settlements in Kerala: Historical Studies*, Calicut, 1978, pp. 20-38.

15. Plumb, *Death of the Past*, p. 33.
16. Hermann Gundert (ed.), *Kerlotpatti (The Origin of Malabar)*, Mangalore, 1868, has, in fact, given these as three sub-headings, probably a contribution of the editor. Although the other versions do not give these sub-headings, the neat division, without overlap, is hard to miss in them. The references below are to the edition of eight works of Gundert brought together with a prefatory study by Scaria Zacharia, *Kerlolpathiyum Mattum*, Kottayam, 1992.
17. Ibid.
18. M.R. Raghava Varier (ed.), *Kerlotpatti Granthavari* (*the Kolattunad Traditions*), Calicut, 1984.
19. Many scholars have studied the Parasurama tradition in relation to the West Coast. F.E. Pargiter, *Ancient Indian Historical Tradition*, London, 1922, pp. 106ff; V.S. Sukhtankar, 'The Bhrugus and the Bharathas', *Annals of the Bhandarkar Oriental Research Institute*, XVIII, 1-76; A.D. Pusalkar, 'Parasurama and the Konkan', in P.K. Narayana Pillai (ed.), *Kerala Studies*, Trivandrum, 1955; B.A. Saletore, *Ancient Karnataka: History of the Tuluva*, vol. I, Poona, 1936, pp.1-30. The work of Saletore is of particular interest to us as he deals with the region neighbouring on the north. A recent study by Pradeep Kant Chaudhary, 'The Cult of Parashuram: The Making of an Avatar', Ph.D. thesis, Delhi University, 2001, makes an analysis of the Parasurama tradition in its various aspects. M.G.S. Narayanan, *Perumals of Kerala*, has made a brilliant analysis of this in relation to Kerala. See also Kesavan Veluthat, *Brahman Settlements in Kerala: Historical Studies*, Calicut, 1978.
20. There are various versions of the *Gramapaddhati*, too, like *Keralotpatti*. For a study, Nagendra E. Rao, 'The Historical Tradition of South Canara and the Brahmanical Groups: A Study of *Gramapaddhati* and *Sahyadrikhanda*', unpublished M.Phil. dissertation, Mangalore University, 1995. I have used the version Krishniah Holla (ed.), *Gramapaddhati*, Balanadu, 1924.
21. Kesavan Veluthat, 'Non-Brahaman Protest in Brahmanical Literary Expressions: The *Gramapaddhati* from South Canara', an unpublished paper, 1995.
22. Zacharia, pp. 156-7, 172-5. This group of arms-bearing Brahamanas was an enigma in the history of Kerala. Elamkulam Kunjan Pillai was the first scholar to explain it sensibly. He presented it in the context of education, where brahman boys were given instruction in both the use of arms and in the 'academic' disciplines. M.G.S. Narayanan pursued it further and brought out the significance of the Brahmana groups in the historical records of Kerala, in the process appreciating

the significance of the statements in the *Keralotpatti*. For details, M.G.S. Narayanan, *Aspects of Aryanisation in Kerala*, Trivandrum, 1973, chapter 'Bachelors of Science'. Following the trail suggested by him, I have sought to explain the existence of the phenomenon all over India, something which earlier writers had missed out. Kesavan Veluthat, 'The Cattas and Bhattas: A New Interpretation', *Proceedings of the Indian History Congress* Aligarh, 1975.

23. Narayanan, *Perumals of Kerala*, passim.
24. Zacharia, pp. 176 and 179-80. Azhvancheri Tamparakkal is a Brahaman of great religious merit and spiritual traditions, and is held in high esteem in the Brahmanical establishment in Kerala.
25. Ibid., p. 177. Vasu Bhatta was a Brahman poet, celebrated for the *yamaka kavya*s he wrote in Sanskrit.
26. Ibid., pp. 182-7.
27. For situating Sankara in the history of Kerala, Narayanan, *Perumals of Kerala*, p. 214 and the notes on p. CXXXIII.
28. Above, n. 22. Inscriptions from the period of the Cera kingdom record the proceedings of the Brahmanical bodies known as *sabha*, *ur*, *kanam*, etc. Narayanan, *Perumals of Kerala*, chapter 'Local Bodies'; Veluthat, *Brahman Settlements in Kerala*, chapter 'Organisation and Administration'. There is an elaborate statement in the *Keralotpatti* as to how the meeting of one of these, the *gana* or *kanam*, was to be held.
29. Zacharia, pp. 193-211. In this section of this version, the Zamorin is invariably referred to as 'our lord'. Interestingly, this version has a Tamil translation of unknown date. T. Chandrasekharan (ed.), *Keraladesa-Varalaru*, Madras, 1960. Does it mean that it wanted to appeal to the Tamil elements also? Varier (1984) contains two versions of the *Keralotpatti*. The first is more or less a copy with only minor variations of the 'standard' version which Gundert has edited except for the lack of details in relation to the Zamorin. The second summarizes the earlier two parts relating to Parasurama and the Perumals and elaborates on the Kolattiri, the Raja of Kolattunad. The other versions of the *Keralotpatti*, likewise, elaborate the history of other principalities in this third phase.
30. Zacharia, p. 191. The accounts of the Zamorin's conquests are contained in pp. 193-8, 199, and 201.
31. Ibid., pp. 198-201.
32. Ibid., pp. 201-2.
33. For an account of the state of affairs in the kingdom of Calicut, K.V. Krishna Ayyar, 'How the Empire Was Governed', *The Zamorins of Calicut*, Calicut, 1938, esp. pp. 261-96: Ayyar wrote long before the history, or even the sources for writing one, of the Cera kingdom of Mahodayapuram had been published. There is a later work which

gives further details from the documents of the Zamorin's archives. N.M. Nampoothiry, *Samutiricaritrattile Kanappurangal*, Edappal, 1987. This book is no better in terms of the methodology and rigour of analysis. There is a work in progress: V.V. Haridas, 'The King, Court and Culture in Medieval Kerala: The Zamorins of Calicut'. Ph.D. thesis in progress, Mangalore University.

34. It was T.A. Gopinatha Rao who discovered, and published extracts of, the *kavya* for the first time. *Travancore Archaeological Series*, vol. II, part II, pp. 87-113. Many scholars have commented on it. C. Girija (1990), gives a summary of these earlier works and an elaborate bibliography.
35. For details of the history of Kolattunad under the Cera kingdom, Narayanan, *Perumals of Kerala*, pp. 91-4. For the differences of Kolattunadu from other chiefly territories, Veluthat, *The Political Structure of Early Medieval South India*, pp. 113-17. For the *Mushikavamsakavya* as legitimizing the king and the kingdom, Romila Thapar, 'The Mouse in the Ancestry', in S.D. Joshi (ed.), *Amritadhara: Essays in Honour of R.N. Dandekar*, Delhi, 1984.
36. For the significance of historical biography in early medieval India, Romila Thapar, 'Of Biographies and Kings', *The Book Review*, vol. XXI, no. 8, 1987, pp. 5-9. Thapar takes up the case of the well-known historical biography, the *Harshacarita*. It will be interesting to consider the situation in Kerala with the help of the insights available here.

CHAPTER 17

Interpreting Sikh History: A Study of Gokul Chand Narang's *The Transformation of Sikhism*

K.L. TUTEJA

Reading of text alone is not sufficient to draw historical conclusions, it is equally important to know the context of the text—the purpose, the function, the audience and the patron, all go in the making of a text.

ROMILA THAPAR

Colonial policies of divide-and-rule and political machinations of Sikh, Hindu and Muslim elites, competing with each other for colonial patronage, resulted in the creation of notions of Hindus, Muslims and Sikhs as neatly-separated communities having little or nothing in common with each other, which is really an inversion of social reality.

HUSAIN ALTAF, Social Activist, Pakistan

Gokul Chand Narang's *The Transformation of Sikhism* was indeed recognized as an authoritative study on the history of the Sikhs for a long time. First published in 1912, its revised and enlarged versions appeared from time to time.[1] This study was originally submitted as doctoral thesis to the Oxford University but was not approved for the award of the degree. The author, however, did succeed in securing a Ph.D. degree from one of the universities in Switzerland.[2] The book is based on a large number of contemporary writings and secondary sources. A list of the source material used by the author is given at the beginning of the first edition of the book. Narang claims that he had consulted 'every important book or manuscript dealing with Sikh history that he could find in the Bodleian Library of Oxford, and the libraries of the India Office, British Museum and the Royal

Asiatic Society in London'.[3] The main object of this study, according to the author, was to present to the 'general reader a concise but complete view of the processes which led to the transformation of Sikhism from a religious sect into a political organization'.[4] The book begins with the emergence of Sikhism under Guru Nanak and covers the period up to the rise of Sikh *Misls* in the late eighteenth century. Later, the author added more chapters which updated the history of the Sikhs to his own contemporary times in each subsequent edition.[5]

A cursory reading of Narang's book clearly reveals that his historical method was largely shaped by the empirical—positivist approach which was a dominant historical trend in the West at the turn of the twentieth century. Narang, keeping in view the spirit of liberal historical tradition, claimed that he had dealt with the subject 'neither in the spirit of hostile critic nor as a votary of Sikhism'.[6] He further asserts that his study was, therefore, an 'impartial account' of the Sikhs based on the evidence culled out by him from a variety of original sources.[7] Moreover, following the Rankean tradition, he pleaded that as a historian his first 'loyalty is to truth', and considered it 'improper to take sides in history'.[8] Yet, it is quite evident from the narrative that he was quite sympathetic towards the Sikh gurus for whom he had deep and abiding reverence since his childhood.[9] It is also important to mention that Narang privileged religion in history. In support of his contention, he cited a number of instances where religion was shown as playing a pivotal role in determining the course of history. In particular, he contended that 'nowhere in the world has the relation of political movements to religion been so close as in India'.[10] Further in this regard, Narang's position appears in a way quite close to that of the Orientalists when he says: 'They (Indians) have since times immemorial been religious people, and religion, therefore has been the chief motive power in all their great undertakings and achievements'.[11] It is with this frame of mind that Narang explored the history of the Sikhs. In the present paper the object is twofold. First, it examines how Narang's own ideological framework deeply infused with Hindu consciousness shaped his approach in writing the history of the Sikhs. Second, in a wider perspective, it argues that a section of

Hindu intelligentsia which included Narang made a selective use of historical consciousness in a manner that would contribute in consolidating Hindu identity and, at the same time, project the Muslims as the 'other' (or the enemy) in the past as well as in their own contemporary times.

I

Gokul Chand Narang belonged to a Hindu middle class family of Arora caste. After his studies in Punjab and Calcutta universities, he pursued his higher education abroad. He started his career as a teacher of history at DAV College, Lahore, but soon shifted to the legal profession. He was also closely associated with a number of business houses in Punjab. Apart from this, he was deeply interested in journalism and politics. Narang was a prominent member of the Hindu Mahasabha for a long time. He did not take part in the nationalist movement spearheaded under the leadership of the Congress although the British were suspicious of his role in the Rowlatt Satyagraha of 1919. On the whole, Narang represented liberal-bourgeois views with a strong Hindu orientation.[12]

It is generally believed that Narang's Hindu consciousness was the product of his association with Arya Samaj. However, this aspect of Narang needs to be understood in the backdrop of Hindu resurgence which, in particular, was witnessed in Punjab in the second half of the nineteenth century.[13] Recently some historical writings have clearly established that the consciousness of a trans-territorial Hindu identity was gradually constructed under the colonial rule in the nineteenth century. Before this period, Hinduism as a distinctive and codified religion did not exist in India, nor did the Hindus have a well-established common social identity. In the early phase of colonial rule, the Orientalists and Evangelicals played a significant role in forging Hinduism as a coherent religion comprising a vast body of shared beliefs, myths rituals and laws.[14] This projected view of Hinduism arbitrarily attributed a monolithic unity to groups and sections of society which were actually disparate and were bound by a very vague sense of identity.[15] The new Hindu middle classes which emerged under British rule appropriated the homogeneous version of Hinduism and filled it with new content to suit their specific requirements. Actually under the colonial conditions there was acute cultural pressure on these people to redefine their traditional identity in accordance with the needs and requirements of their new historical being. They sought to reform their inherited religious tradition in the light of new notions of rationality, justice and progress which they had imbibed from western education and which also supported their class aspirations and goals. The pressure of their class role was forcing them to go beyond the strictly local and narrow affiliations which formed an integral part of the diverse traditional identities they had acquired through religious and social practices grounded in the realities of an earlier historical period. Thus, the new Hindu middle classes which included persons like Narang played a crucial role in constructing consciousness of a broad Hindu identity in the Indian society.[16]

The Brahmo Samaj can be cited as the pioneer organization that aimed at reforming Hindu religion and reconstructing Hindu religious identity that supported the aspirations and goals of the newly educated middle classes. In Punjab, however, its influence was mainly limited to a small section of Bengali elite who went there in the early years of the colonial rule. A notable attempt to reform and recast Hinduism in this province was actually made by Swami Dayananda, the founder of the Arya Samaj. This organization aimed at purging Hinduism of those elements, which were contrary to the progressive and rational ideals adopted by the emergent Hindu middle classes. An important feature of this reconstruction of the religious tradition was a pronounced assertion of its indigenous character and superiority in contradistinction to the religious belief of the foreign rulers. This exercise of reconstructing Hindu identity was done by Swami Dayananda ostensibly in the name of recovering the essentials of Vedic culture by removing contamination that had occurred in the post-Vedic period. The revivalism of the Arya Samaj played a pivotal role not only in demarcating the religious particularism of Hinduism but also heightened a sense of pride among the Hindus.[17] The ideology of the Arya Samaj had great appeal for a cross-section of Hindu middle classes comprising merchants, moneylenders, small entrepreneurs, professionals and service persons. In the sensibility of these middle class persons and the mode of social existence in which they were rooted, many pre-capitalist features had persisted. This was particularly the case among the small urban centres of Punjab. The aspirations and ideals of such middle class groups could not get articulated in a fully developed bourgeois form; they had, therefore, to express themselves through a reconstructed and modified version of their traditional Hindu identity. The ideology and programme of the Arya Samaj were in particular suitable for their purpose. A section of this Hindu middle class followers of the Arya Samaj would ultimately become the carriers of Hindu consciousness in the specific conditions that prevailed in the early twentieth-century Punjab.[18]

Narang belonged to this section of Hindu society in Punjab. He was deeply conscious of the belief that the Hindus formed a pan-Indian community, and had a highly 'glorified past' in the ancient period. In arriving at this conclusion, he was influenced by the Arya Samaj, and the famous Orientalist writer, Max Müller. Narang makes a special mention of Max Müller's book in the list of works consulted by him for his study of the Sikhs.[19] A close reading of *The Transformation of Sikhism* clearly reveals that Narang's understanding of Hinduism was largely derived from Max Müller. As a matter of fact, the writings of Max Müller and other Orientalists decisively contributed in constructing the ideology of the Arya Samaj, which 'laid stress on Vedic culture as the root of Indian tradition, and, made it the ideal'.[20] For Narang and other Hindu middle class Arya Samajists, Max Müller's glorified description of Hinduism was ideologically highly relevant since it was not only found useful in asserting the superiority of Hinduism but also heightened their sense of pride, which certainly made them more 'susceptible to communal propaganda'.[21] Along with this, Narang firmly believed that the 'golden age' of Hinduism was later seriously threatened by Islam that came to India in the form of invading armies. Throughout his book, Narang projects Islam as a 'barbaric and aggressive religion' which only preached hatred against the Hindus and the Sikhs. In other words, he took an essentialist view that the Muslims were inherently oppressors and there could never be harmonious relations between the Hindus and the Muslims—

which later became the basic argument in support of the two-nation theory. This kind of historical understanding, described as communal interpretation of Indian history, has a fairly long tradition, at least going back to the colonial times. In particular, it was James Mill's *History of British India* (1819) that actually laid the foundation of communal approach and 'had an abiding influence on Indian historiography, with a large number of Indian historians of vastly different ideological persuasions rather uncritically internalising this interpretation'.[22] Narang was one of those historians who had consciously adopted a Hinduized communal framework for his study of the Sikhs.

It is also necessary to take a close look at the role of the Arya Samaj in shaping Narang's attitude towards Islam. Swami Dayananda, the founder of the Arya Samaj in his famous work *Satyarth Prakash* had decried Islam, describing it inferior to Vedic religion.[23] However, Kenneth W. Jones is correct in saying that Dayananda's understanding of Islam was merely limited to 'scriptural exegesis', and was not based on the study of its actual historical evolution.[24] A careful analysis of his views would show that in making this criticism, Dayananda did not wish to create communal hatred against the Muslims at the social level. As a matter of fact, his attempt was to 'explore religious truth through a comparative understanding of different religions. Dayananda after all was as trenchant a critic of the practices of Sanatani Hinduism as of other religions'.[25] However, it needs to be clearly recognized that the emergent Hindu middle classes found the ideology of Arya Samaj, deeply embedded with the belief of cultural superiority of Hinduism, highly significant in asserting their position *vis-à-vis* the Muslims in the socio-political structure created under colonial rule. In particular, this kind of ideological impact of the Arya Samaj was quite visible in a section of urban Hindus who were engaged in an intense competition with the Muslims for wresting concessions in the civil society in Punjab since the second half of the nineteenth century.[26] In such a situation of rivalry and bitterness between the Hindus and Muslims, a number of Hindu *pracharaks* and middle class persons who were associated with the Arya Samaj not only made efforts to heighten communitarian consciousness among the Hindus but participated in activities which could be described as anti-Islamic, resulting in communal hatred and violence. For instance, in 1897, Lekh Ram, an Arya Samajist, was killed by a Muslim for his pronounced anti-Islamic position. This polarization on communal lines was also evident in the press and in other writings of a number of the Hindus and Muslims at that time.[27] Narang's work appears to be a part of such writings published in Punjab in the early twentieth century. However, it is important to mention here that not all Hindus associated with the Arya Samaj were communal in their approach. As a matter of fact, a number of prominent Arya Samajists like Lajpat Rai and Rambhuj Datta carried communitarian-nationalist perspective according to which the primary task was to participate in the struggle against the colonial rule along with the people of other communities, particularly the Muslims, without giving up communitarian interests in the civil society. But this perspective was not acceptable to the communal Hindus like Narang for whom the Muslims were the main opponent, and were to be projected as the sole 'enemy' of the Hindus both in the past and present. This kind of ideological framework of Narang became more evident at the later stage when he not only kept himself away from the joint struggle of the Indian people against the colonial rule but preferred to carry communal hatred against the Muslims through the programme and policies of the Hindu Mahasabha.[28]

Here it is important to take note of the relations of the Arya Samaj and the Sikhs in the late nineteenth century, which indeed had a strong bearing on the views and writings of many Hindus including that of Narang. In *Satyarth Prakash*, Swami Dayananda described Sikhism a cult that originated from Hinduism. In his opinion, Guru Nanak, the founder of Sikhism, had noble aims but he failed to bring a real change in society since he lacked Vedic knowledge.[29] However, the Arya Samaj in Punjab in the initial stages attracted a number of Sikhs because of its rejection of caste distinctions and other orthodox social and religious practices. But this association proved a temporary phenomenon because of the growing tension between the Arya Samaj and the Sikhs at the turn of the twentieth century. Although this issue has already been explored in detail in a number of writings, it is however necessary to mention that the growing revivalist trends in the Arya Samaj, and the aggressive postures adopted by some of its members towards the believers of other religions were largely responsible for increasing acrimony between the Arya Samajist Hindus and the Sikhs.[30] Along with this, from late 1870s the new Sikh leadership associated with the popularly known Singh Sabha movement was attempting to define and construct a Sikh identity both by emphasizing the basic tenets of Sikhism and by purging those elements that had any kind of connections with Hinduism.[31] In support of this position, Kahan Singh wrote a book entitled *Ham Hindu Nahin* with the object of asserting a distinct character of Sikhism. Of course, this was equally contested by those who believed that the Sikhs were an integral part of the Hindu community.[32] However, the tension between the Arya Samajist Hindus and Sikhs did not take a serious turn though the debate continued in a contentious manner on the issue of a separate Sikh identity both in the press and at other platforms.[33] As a matter of fact, many Hindus did not perceive Sikhs as 'the other', because unlike Christianity and Islam, the origin of Sikhism was seen as rooted broadly in Hinduism. This aspect was clearly present in the mind of Narang who once remarked that 'anybody who followed a religion whose founder was an Indian was a Hindu'.[34] Therefore, he zealously maintained that the Sikhs were an integral part of the Hindus. At the same time, he expressed concern over the increasing efforts being made to establish a distinct identity of the Sikhs which, in his view, would ultimately weaken the unity of the 'Hindu race' especially against the Muslims. This issue shall be discussed later in detail.

II

Narang began his study by saying that it was necessary to understand the historical process that led to the 'transformation of Sikhism from a religious sect into a political organization'.[35] This transition in Sikh history, according to the popular tradition, took final shape with the establishment of the Khalsa by Guru Gobind Singh. However, Narang believes that the beginning in this direction was made by Guru Nanak himself. In this connection, he writes:

The sword which carved the Khalsa's way to glory was, undoubtedly forged by Gobind, but the steel had been provided by Nanak who had obtained it as it were, by smelting the Hindu ore, and burning out the dross of indifference and superstition of the masses, and pharisaism [*sic*] of the priests.[36]

In other words, his contention is that Nanak's concern to reform and revitalize the contemporary Hindu society could be described as the *raison d'être* of the emergence and growth of the Sikh movement in Punjab.

In Narang's view, the condition of Hindus was 'most deplorable'[37] when Guru Nanak came on the scene in Punjab in the late fifteenth century. Because of his Arya Samajist background, Narang firmly believed that in the age of Vedic civilization, socio-religious life of the Hindus was pure and simple.[38] But with the increasing dominance of the priestly classes, corrupt and dogmatic practices gradually crept into Hindu society resulting in the overall decline and unpopularity of Hinduism. Along with this, Narang held the advent of Islam in India responsible for the decline of Hinduism. He states:

The spring of true religion had been choked by weeds of unmeaning ceremonial, debasing superstitions, the selfishness of the priests and the indifference of the people. Form had supplanted the reality and the highly spiritual character of the Hindus had been buried under the ostentatious paraphernalia of sects. The centuries of invasion, foreign misrule and persecution had produced the greatest depression, and the spiritual subjection and stagnation had aggravated the demoralization to an enormous degree.[39]

By providing such a depressing and gloomy account of the Hindu society, Narang was trying to reiterate the point that there was a strong need of a reformer who would restore Hinduism to its pristine purity and thereby make it strong enough to check the onslaught and 'proselytising zeal of Islam'.[40]

Nanak, as the author shows, seemed to have thoroughly 'diagnosed the case of the Hindu community of his times and found out that religious revival was the only remedy which could save it from impending destruction'.[41] In pursuance of this objective, Nanak made up his mind 'to devote his life to the service of the nation, and by percept and by example, bring his people back to a religion of simplicity and sincerity, to wean them from the worship of stock and stone, restore them to pure worship of their ancient forefathers and make them once more able to stand on their ground as a nation'.[42] In this manner, Narang argues that the first guru tried to 'emancipate the Hindu mind completely from the fetters of mythology'.[43] Further he observes that Nanak, despite being an illiterate, was 'endowed by nature with a powerful intellect and strong common sense'.[44] It was 'his [Nanak's] practical wisdom and strong common sense that always prevailed the logic and theology of opponents making his task of reforming Hindu society much easier'.[45]

Narang's considered view is that Nanak's success was the result of two factors. First, unlike the reformers who preceded him, the first guru was 'not sectarian' in his approach and methods of reforms.[46] Secondly, he rejected the path of renunciation, and showed to the Hindus that the 'highest worldly ambition was not incompatible with the purist and godliest life'.[47] Narang was, therefore, convinced that the first guru achieved his objective as his ideas and teachings 'leavened the whole Hindu thought in the Punjab and improved the moral and spiritual tone of the whole people'.[48] In totality, it appears from this work that Nanak rejuvenated Hinduism, and aroused a consciousness of 'common nationality' among the Hindus.[49] Therefore, Nanak, in Narang's opinion, was a 'hero whom every Hindu could call his own, and of whom every Hindu could feel justly proud'.[50]

Nanak was born in a Hindu family and his life carried the imprints of the socio-religious system that existed in the rural society of central Punjab at that point of time. He was of course critical of some of the prevailing social and religious beliefs, which he related to the age of *Kaliyuga*. He denounced the priestly class, abhorred caste distinctions, rejected idol-worship and reading of scriptures as essential for human salvation.[51] Since a detailed discussion of Nanak's thought is outside the purview of the present paper, it is however necessary to mention that the essence of his message was more universal in content. For him, 'God alone is the bestower of life upon all living beings'.[52] Therefore, he held supreme faith in God, emphasized the path of truth and repeatedly preached the message of spiritual regeneration. W.H. McLeod, who has placed Nanak in the Sant tradition, sums up the central aspect of Nanak's philosophy by saying that 'the first guru stressed on the interior nature of devotion, dismissing as false and dangerous the kind of external ritual associated with conventional Hindu tradition or the orthodox Islam of the Mullah'.[53] On the whole, Nanak's views and activities laid emphasis on morality and simplicity. They thus appealed to a cross-section of people especially when their social and religious lives were more governed by local customs and traditions. It is also necessary to mention here that Hinduism at that stage was merely a loose conglomeration of desperate social groups and sects having varied rituals and belief systems. The concept of a larger Hindu collectivity on the basis of a distinct and well-defined religious system was quite vague in Punjab in pre-modern times. Under such conditions, Nanak's concern was neither limited to the reformation of the existing Hindu society nor aimed at arousing a consciousness of 'common nationality' amongst the Hindus as contended by Narang. McLeod, as a matter of fact, has rightly observed that 'Sikhism cannot be wholly located within the area of Hindu tradition'.[54]

As far as the origin of Sikhism is concerned, Narang believes that Nanak in reality 'intended to leaven the social and religious thought of the Hindus' and did not plan a separate church having a distinct social and religious code from the very beginning.[55] In this connection, he writes that 'Nanak did not want to cut himself off from the Hindu community. He wanted to live in it, work with it, and by his noble examples and lofty teachings to raise it to a higher level of social and religious life'.[56] However, he decided to appoint his successor (Guru Angad) who could carry his mission 'after his [Nanak's] death'.[57] Guru Angad, according to Narang, like the first guru, was equally committed to the cause of Hindu society in Punjab. But at the same time he realized that 'Nanak's mission should nevertheless possess a distinctive character and his followers though forming a part of the main, should have an individuality of their own'.[58] Narang continues:

In order that the influences started by Nanak might continue to work, it was essential that those influences should be perpetuated and a community created which, though forming a part of the same host, should march a little apart of its advance guard.[59]

By 'advance guard' Narang meant that unlike the mass of superstitious Hindus, the followers of Nanak would possess 'faith, devotion and earnestness'.[60] It was by virtue of these qualifications that 'they (Nanak *Panthis*) led the way and drew the whole Punjab after them'.[61] It can thus be concluded that Sikhism in Narang's opinion, emerged essentially out of the efforts made to reform and rejuvenate the contemporary Hindu society.

Narang further observes that the followers of the gurus gradually expanded and were spread all over the province. In particular he mentions that the Hindu peasants living in the Bari-Doab region were attracted towards the Sikh gurus.[62] Along with this, Sikhism quickly spread among the Jats,[63] who after their migration to Punjab had changed from pastoralists to peasant cultivators. As convincingly argued in some recent writings, the cultural traditions of the Jats deeply influenced the nature and growth of Sikh *Panth*.[64] Narang believes that some early initiatives taken by the Sikh gurus made a substantial contribution to the popularity of the new church which eventually led to the carving out of a distinct Sikh community. The first step in this direction, as mentioned by him, was the use of the Gurmukhi script by the gurus.[65] Besides, Narang records that the institution of *langar*, which largely evolved during the period of the second guru 'served as a strong bond of union among the new brotherhood of the Sikhs'.[66] Further, he adds that the third guru, Amar Das, in order to provide an organizational structure to the expanding Sikh community, 'divided the whole country inhabited by his followers in twenty-two deices or *Manjas* to be headed by pious and influential persons who would act as bishops or viceregents of the gurus'.[67] Along with this, Narang also mentions that the emergence of religious places like Kartarpur, Gobindwal, and Amritsar as popular centres of pilgrimage in Sikhism, contributed in the further establishment of a distinctive position of the followers of the Sikh gurus.[68] Moreover, his opinion is that it was the compilation of the *Adi Granth* and the building of the Harmandir Sahib at Amritsar during the period of the fifth guru, Arjan Dev that actually led the Sikhs to view themselves as a different religious community.[69] Finally, Narang echoes the popular tradition saying that the establishment of the *Khalsa* by Guru Gobind Singh that laid down some rules of conduct and body symbols to be observed by the Sikhs, produced among them a sense of a cohesive community. In this regard, he says, 'the observances singled out the genuine Sikhs from the mass of lukewarm Hindus and produced a cohesion in the internal body of the *Khalsa* which was in a short time to make a united nation of them'.[70] Thus, it is quite evident from Narang's account that by the end of the gurus' period in the early eighteenth century, the Sikhs appeared to have constituted a community with a distinct set of beliefs system and practices.

But having said all this, Narang rhetorically maintains that the Sikhs were essentially an offshoot of the 'Hindu race'. It is important to mention here that he strongly refutes J.D. Cunningham's view that Sikhism emerged out of the union of Hinduism and Islam.[71] At the same time, he reiterates, 'it [Sikhism] is a phase of Hindu religious development and has in consequence, great similarity with main features of Hindus'.[72] In this regard, it is forcefully argued that the central doctrine of the unity of God in Sikhism essentially grew out of Hindu philosophy.[73] Further, while pointing out the similarities in the two religions, Narang interestingly goes to the extent of saying: 'To me the constitution of the *Granth* appears to resemble that of the Rigveda much more than any other book. . . .'[74] At the same time, he also mentions that there was practically no dissimilarity in the social ethos of the Hindus and the Sikhs in their daily life. He was conscious of the differences between the Sikhs and Hindus on some philosophical and social issues, which according to him, were merely in form and not in essence. Narang was perhaps well aware of the debate that was taking place on the issue of Sikh identity in Punjab since the late nineteenth century. As stated above, a section of Sikhs intelligentsia deeply infused with the spirit of *Tat Khalsa* (pure Sikhism) were seriously engaged in defining the Sikh identity with special emphasis on establishing a clear line of demarcation between the Sikh and Hindus. Narang certainly appeared concerned about the ideology and activities of such Singh Sabha activists who were trying to establish a separate nature of Sikhism. In this regard, he mentions with disdain, the Anand Marriage Act (1909), by which the newly evolved system of marriage in Sikhism was accorded legal approval. This legislation in Narang's view, was clearly a manifestation of a 'separatist' approach which was followed by the *Tat Khalsa* Sikhs.[75] Yet, it is significant to note here that despite the growing acrimony on certain issues between the Sikhs and Hindus in the early twentieth century, Narang was not disturbed by this phenomenon since he was more concerned with the issue of the Hindu-Muslim divide. It is quite evident from the following section that Narang firmly held the view that it were only the Muslims and not the Sikhs who were the main opponents (or the 'other') of the Hindus both in the past and in contemporary times.

III

The transition of Sikhism from a sect of peaceful devotees to a community of warriors began during the period of the sixth guru, Har Gobind but actually matured only with the establishment of the *Khalsa* in 1699. Narang believed that it was a necessary step for the Sikhs as they needed to defend themselves against Islam in general and the Mughal empire in particular. In fact, Narang constructed his whole account of the origin and growth of Sikhism by juxtaposing Islam, mainly its political form as the main opponent. At the outset, Narang was convinced that there was nothing common between Islam and Sikhism and the latter was 'not Islamic to any extent whatsoever'.[76] He contested the view that the concept of monolithic God, as propounded by Nanak, was borrowed from Islam. In his view, as stated earlier, the very idea of unity of God was present in Hinduism from ancient times and Nanak, like a number of other reformers, inherited it as a legacy from Hindu religious tradition. Moreover, Narang does not accept the view that Nanak ever came in contact with any Muslim teacher who shaped his ideas in an effective manner.[77] Above all, he rhetorically argues against those historical writings that had constructed Sikhism as a mixture of Hinduism and Islam which in his view was nothing more than a myth that needed to be exploded in totality.[78] His final comment in this regard is that 'Sikhism owes nothing to that religion (Islam)'; instead it has retained all essential features of real Hinduism.[79]

However, Narang at the same time argues that 'Islam had something to do with the advent of Sikhism. In fact there might have been no Sikhism or it would have probably never appeared in this form if Islam had not crossed over the boundaries of India'.[80] His whole argument revolves around the point that the emergence Sikhism in Punjab was closely related to the threat posed by Islam which came to India as a 'religion of sword' causing immense cruelties on the local people. Narang writes:

> This (Punjab) province was first to be conquered. It lay between the two powerful capitals, Delhi and Cabul. The Muslim government was most thoroughly established here. The wave of proselytism had spread there with an overwhelming force and the Punjab contained largest number of converts to Islam. Hindu temples were leveled to the ground. Hindu schools and colleges had made room for the mosque. All vestiges of Hindu greatness had been obliterated.[81]

According to Narang, since the primary object of the Muslim rulers was to spread Islam, the Hindus were left with only one option, that is, either to convert to Islam or face death. He maintains that in the absence of strong Hindu rulers in Punjab, it was impossible to resist the onslaught of Islam. The local Hindu society was extremely vulnerable since upper caste Brahmans 'entrenched in dogma and superstition' were incapable of providing moral and spiritual leadership to the common people, who easily fell prey and were converted to Islam.[82] Narang states that the first Sikh guru felt that the only way out in such a situation was to infuse the masses with fresh spirit with a view to strengthening the moral and philosophical aspects of Hinduism. This indeed could make them once 'more able to stand their ground as a nation'.[83] In this manner, it is argued, that Nanak's central concern was to safeguard the Hindus who were threatened by the advent of Islam. Narang's position on this issue is best reflected in his observation stating that 'Islam necessitated the birth of Sikhism' but 'the latter did not form part of it (Islam)'.[84]

Narang is unambiguously communal in approach when he explores the relations of the Sikh gurus with the Mughals, which constitutes a major part of his work. At the outset, it is necessary to mention that he offers a stereotyped account both of Islam and the Mughal state. For instance, his construction contains: (a) Islam is an aggressive and fanatic religion; (b) the believers of Islam constitute a monolithic community irrespective of their social and spatial variations; (c) the Muslims (described as *Mlechchha*) are different in all respects from the non-Muslim sections of society; (d) and, there is an innate enmity between the Muslims and the Hindus (including the Sikhs). Along with this, Narang like a number of European writers holds the belief that the Mughal state was essentially Islamic in nature and it wittingly discriminated against the Hindu inhabitants in a number of ways. His endeavour was to show that barring the period of Akbar, the Hindus suffered enormously under Muslim 'tyranny'. This point is illustrated by giving a number of cases of the Sikhs and Hindus who were 'persecuted' on the basis of religion by the 'Muslim government' of the day.[85] Narang says that this, however, did not deter the Sikhs, and their resistance against the state ended by their ultimate success about which he writes: 'Not only did they succeed in founding a church which claims the allegiance of the majority of the Hindus in the Punjab but established a kingdom which gave a magnificent sunset to stormy days of Hindu glory.'[86]

According to Narang, Guru Nanak was the first among the Hindus to raise his voice against tyranny and oppression.[87] It is mentioned that Nanak 'expressed himself very strongly against aggressive fanaticism of Islam' and regretted the suffering of the Hindus.[88] In support of his contention, Narang quotes what Nanak had once observed: 'The age is a dagger, the rulers are butchers. Dharma has taken wings to itself and has flown away. The *amavasya* or darkness of falsehood reigns supreme. No one can see the moon of truth.'[89] According to Narang, Nanak however, fully understood that it was not possible to directly confront the forces of Islam, and it would be more appropriate to raise the moral and spiritual power of the Hindus which, as stated earlier, could make them strong enough not to yield meekly before the proselytising zeal of Islam.

Narang, however, does mention about the cordiality that existed in Mughal-Sikh relations during the period of Akbar who had once paid a personal visit to Guru Amar Das. This gesture of the Mughal emperor, in Narang's opinion, added to the popularity of the Sikh guru which was quite evident by the meteoric rise in the numbers of his followers. However, as is well known, the growing prestige and power of the Sikh movement especially under the fifth guru, Arjan Dev was perceived as a 'disturbing phenomenon' by the Mughal state under Jahangir. Narang on the basis of well-known contemporary work *Dabistan-i-Mazahib* by Muhsin Fani narrates the circumstances leading to the arrest of Guru Arjan Dev and later of his death.[90] The martyrdom of Guru Arjan Dev has been described as the starting point of the 'persecution of the Sikhs' by the Mughal state on the basis of religion which in his view, was a clear manifestation of its fanatical religious character.[91] At the same time, Narang considers that within the Sikhs too, this event was a turning point as it not only strengthened the bond of community but also inspired the sixth guru, Har Gobind and his followers to take up arms against the Mughal state, with the object to 'defend the Hindus from the threat posed by the forces of Islam'.[92] In this regard, he approvingly cites the British historian John Malcolm who had recorded that Har Gobind girded two swords saying 'one to revenge my father and the other to destroy the miracles of Mohammad'.[93] This approach of the sixth guru, in Narang's opinion, unequivocally reveals his determination for the 'destruction of Islam and the Muslim government'.[94] In pursuit of his object, Har Gobind is believed to have exhorted his followers to bear arms and 'be always prepared to fight the enemies of true religion'.[95] At this stage, Narang's narrative highlights the anti-Islamic nature of the Sikh movement that started taking a militant form during the period of the sixth guru and this phenomenon continued until the eighteenth century.

Along with this, Narang's rhetoric continued saying that the Sikh gurus were essentially fighting for the cause of the Hindus. For instance, he has narrated the story of a woman who had sought protection of Guru Har Gobind believing that the latter was a 'champion of Hindus'.[96] He regards Guru Tegh Bahadur as an acknowledged head of Punjab Hindus, and also describes him as an obstacle in the way of Aurangzeb's 'Islamic zeal'.[97] Narang further wrote that the execution of the ninth guru by the Mughal government was 'universally regarded by the Hindus as sacrifice for their faith', and as a result 'the whole Punjab began to burn with indignation and revenge'.[98] In his description of the tenth guru, Gobind Singh, as a 'defender of Hindus', Narang states:

> The object that the Guru set before himself was to infuse a new life into the dead bones of Hindus to make them to forget their differences and present a united front against the tyranny and persecution to which they were exposed, in one word, to make once more a living nation of them and to enable them to regain their lost independence.[99]

Along with this, while recognizing the significance of *Khalsa* in giving the Sikhs a distinct character, Narang's emphasis appears to be more on the ideological function of the *Khalsa* that infused a spirit of sacrifice and heroic devotion among the followers of the guru, especially in the context of the on-going confrontation with the Mughal state.[100] Besides, he also mentions that the guru cherished the sword as an object of worship as well as of necessity in his 'contemplated war upon the enemies of his race'.[101] Narang finally gives a detailed but eulogistic account of the activities of Guru Gobind Singh against the Mughal state with a view to projecting it as a part of a larger 'struggle' waged by the Hindus against Islam and the Muslim rule in India. In this regard, he writes that Gobind had seen what was yet vital in the Hindu race 'and he relumed it with Promethean fire'.[102] Viewed in this manner, Guru Gobind Singh has thus been placed along with Shivaji as 'defender of the Hindu race' against Muslim rule.

Narang's understanding of Islam was myopic since he neither examined its scriptures nor evinced any interest in the historical evaluation of Islam which of course was yet to be more critically explored. His stereotyped description of Islam as a 'dogmatic or fanatic religion' was based on his selective reading of some medieval chroniclers and European writings.[103] However, this kind of representation of Islam was in reality an ideological need of Narang who was trying to establish that the Hindu-

Muslim divide was an essential characteristic of Indian history. Moreover, Narang's concern was limited to political Islam and he did not take into account the cultural manifestation of Islam in India. The latter phenomenon, described as cultural 'efflorescence', can be easily discerned in the writings of Amir Khusro and Abul Fazl, which provide useful information on the synthesis of Hindu-Muslim traditions that enriched composite culture and the inclusive character of Indian society.[104]

In the case of Punjab, it is believed that Sufism was largely responsible for the spread of Islam. It is well known that the Sufi saints had a strong mystic appeal; they were perceived as mediators between God and the believer. Many a time, the Sufi saints and their shrines were patronized by the state in Delhi which certainly added to their influence and prestige in the local society. In particular, the Sufi shrine of Baba Farid at Pak Pattan was deeply revered. Its contribution to the spread of Islamic ideas is widely recognized. Richard M. Eaton has convincingly argued that the Sufi saints did not make any conscious attempt or adopt coercive tactics to convert the local population to Islam. However, there are instances where a large number of people living in different clans (outside the fold of Brahmanical Hinduism) came under the influence of Sufism and willingly embraced Islamic faith, making necessary adjustments in their own local cultural systems. For these local communities, Islam was not an alien or a closed exclusive system to be accepted or rejected as a whole.[105] It is equally important to record that many people, especially in south-west Punjab, after their transition from pastoral to sedentary agriculture also found religious linkages with sufi shrines as a crucial factor to establish their own higher position in the existing socio-political system. Thus, the Sufi shrines, 'gave clan leaders and their followers not only access to Islam but the honour of participating in the reflected splendour of the Sultan or Mughal court without actually being subservient to the authority in Delhi'.[106] On the whole, it is logically concluded that Islamization in Punjab was not the logical consequence of invading armies of the Muslim rulers as contended in a number of conventional writings including the work of Narang. It is rightly observed in a recent study that 'there were no programmes of mass, much less forced conversion'. Many people, as noted above, were actually just attracted to the Islamic faith propounded by Sufi saints, leading to their gradual 'assimilation' to Islam.[107]

Apart from this, frequent visitors to Sufi shrines, especially to Baba Farid's shrine at Pak Pattan, also included a large number of Hindus and Sikhs, who of course did not intend to be 'educated in Islamic theology'.[108] Their primary concern in undertaking such pilgrimages was to get relief from illness or sufferings since in popular imagination the Sufi shrines were known for healing and supernatural powers. However, it also needs to be clearly recognized that a large number of non-Muslims had deep reverence for the Sufi saints because of the mystic and spiritual appeal attributed to them.[109] They often participated in *Urs* celebrations of the the Sufi shrines, and in many cases, the Hindu traders, as a part of their customary tradition, offered *nazrana* 'out of respect for a local institution of great repute, and perhaps also out of a sense of civic responsibility'.[110] It was this kind of popular culture deeply embedded with syncretic practices that Nanak had actually inherited and breathed into the rural society of Punjab.[111] In other words, the historical reality was quite different from what Narang has shown with regard to the Hindus and Muslims, as totally distinct monolithic communities having nothing in common with each other.[112]

Besides, it is necessary to examine closely Narang's contention that the Sikh movement was essentially anti-Islamic in character from its inception. Narang, as stated earlier, actually failed to recognize the cultural influence of Islam that had a strong bearing on the society in which Sikhism had emerged in the early sixteenth century. Nanak was of course aware of the fact that Islam was the religion of those who were ruling Punjab and Delhi at that point of time. It is also believed that he made a 'direct denunciation of contemporary rule' and considered *jizya* and the pilgrimage tax imposed on non-Muslims as unjust.[113] Moreover as already mentioned, Nanak was highly critical of Muslim *Mullahs* for laying emphasis on dogmas and external rituals and giving little attention to the interior nature of devotion. But, at the same time it is also true that Guru Nanak was impressed by Sufi saints and their ideas, especially those related to mysticism.[114] It is generally believed that Nanak had borrowed the idea of unity of God, transcendent as well as immanent, from Islamic faith. Apart from this, his idea of *Naam Simran* was closely related in some respect to the religious ideas and practices of Sufism. Besides, Nanak's vocabulary included words that were frequently used in Sufi writings and thought. All this has perhaps led a number of writers to believe that Nanak's endeavour was primarily to synthesize Hinduism and Islam.[115] W.H. McLeod has, however, persuasively argued against it saying that there were no such conscious attempt on the part of Nanak.[116] However, it is necessary to mention that a number of Islamic ideas were passed on to him because of his association with the Sant tradition which had actually carried some features of Sufism as a part of its own belief system. Moreover, some of the Islamic ideas inextricably mixed with the local culture were unconsciously accepted by Nanak as a part of his own world-view.[117] In other words, the first guru did not consciously attempt to borrow any Islamic ideas, yet the imprints of Islam were quit visible in his thought. Therefore, it can be concluded that the Muslim contribution was not of fundamental importance in the origin of Sikhism but its influence cannot be 'dismissed as wholly insignificant'.[118]

It is quite evident that Narang in his construction of the Mughal-Sikh relations signified religion as the guiding factor in determining relations on both sides. As stated earlier, he stereotyped all Mughal rulers except Akbar as 'fanatic Muslims', who discriminated against non-Muslims on the basis of religion. In particular, Narang on the basis of scanty sources focused upon the bigotry of Aurangzeb and on the persecution of the Sikhs and other non-Muslims during his reign. Under such circumstances, he further argues that it became necessary for the Hindus, including the followers of the Sikh gurus, to resist the 'Islamic Mughal State'. This kind of description, both of Mughal rule as well as of the resistance offered by the non-Muslims on religious lines, was actually a legacy of the colonial historiography which was uncritically accepted by a number of Indian historians including Narang. However by now it is well established that the Mughal state was not Islamic in nature where *shariat* prevailed; instead, it has been described as supra-religious in nature.[119] It is beyond doubt that it was not Islam but exigencies of the empire that largely guided the functioning of the state, especially when the non-Muslims constituted the major part of the population living in the Mughal empire. Moreover, it is widely accepted that the cultural synthesis produced by Islam's contact with non-Muslims in India was largely responsible in shaping the supra-religious character of the Mughal state. As far as religion is concerned, there are clear cases of variation in the attitude of the Mughal state, especially in relation to their non-Muslim subjects. For instance, the case of Akbar is remarkable in the sense that he took a highly rationalist position saying that 'no man should be interfered with on account of religion, and any one is to be allowed to go over to a religion that pleases him'.[120] The other trend, as mentioned earlier, was obviously represented by Aurangzeb who in the later period of his reign appeared to have adopted an approach which is generally described as more Islamic in content. But it is important to note that the Mughal state refrained from adopting any uniform policy on the basis of religion in the case of non-Muslims, including the Sikhs. Therefore, Narang seems to have over-emphasized the Islamic factor and paid little attention to the socio-political processes that were more relevant for understanding the nuances of the Mughal relations with the Sikhs gurus.

At the same time, it is difficult to accept Narang's contention that the Sikh gurus were motivated by their desire to oppose Islam as well as to safeguard the Hindus from the 'tyranny of Muslim rule'. As stated earlier, neither Guru Nanak nor any one of the other Sikh gurus was opposed to Islam in principle. It is well known that some Muslims were followers of Guru Nanak but their number was small. Besides, the very fact that Baba Farid's sayings form part of the *Guru Granth Sahib*, the most sacred text of the Sikhs, shows that the Sufi saints were highly respected by the early Sikh gurus. Moreover, the popular view that Guru Arjan Dev had invited Mian Mir to lay the foundation of Har Mandir Sahib is worth mentioning. It is of course true that the active resistance that started against the Mughal state from the period of the sixth guru, Har Gobind became the dominant characteristic of the Sikh movement. But this resistance was not a fight against Islam. Har Gobind was never inspired to oppose Islam or fight for the cause of Hindus as stated by Narang. On the contrary, it is believed that he got built a mosque at Har Gobindpur and maintained close association with a number of Muslims. His confrontation with the Mughal state did not mean that he harboured any kind of hatred for Islam. It is true that the martyrdom of Guru Tegh Bahadur on his refusal to embrace Islam stirred the Sikh community and 'strengthened their resolve to oppose Aurangzeb's bigotry and work for the overthrow of his rule'.[121] But Narang's plea that Guru Tegh Bahadur by defying the state order, sacrificed his own life for the wider cause of Hindus appears a simplistic explanation. J.S. Grewal, however, offers a more convincing interpretation saying that the ninth guru's action actually revealed his commitment to 'freedom of conscience'.[122] Finally, Guru Gobind Singh's resistance against the Mughal state took a more organized form with the establishment of *Khalsa* which as a 'military formation identified with highest spiritual and temporal authority represented by the Guru and Holy Granth'.[123] But, as pointed out by Khuswant Singh, the tenth guru 'made sure that his crusade would not be wrongly construed as one of the Sikhs against the Muslims'. It is important to note here that he had engaged 500 Pathans in his army for deployment against the Mughal rule. In this connection, recently Iqtadar Alam Khan has forcefully argued that the tenth guru in his work *Zafar Nama*, while denouncing Aurangzeb's 'conduct and behaviour in exercising political authority, did not criticize his faith Islam'.[124] Moreover, it is stated that there is no remark in the *Zafar Nama* 'that may be considered as directly or even obliquely against Islam'. On the other hand, the guru appears to refer to the Koran and Prophet Muhammad with respect.[125] Finally, there is no evidence to support the view that the guru was ever inspired to forge a trans-territorial unity of the 'Hindu race' against the force of Islam as contended by Narang.

IV

Narang's work, on the whole, represents a curious example of Hinduized consciousness which was fast gaining strength, especially in north India at the turn of the twentieth century. His sympathetic accounts of the Sikhs carried two different trends which at times appear contradictory to each other. Yet, Narang's endeavour was to present his narrative of the Sikh past in a manner that could easily accommodate divergent trends at the same time with much ease. Like *Tat Khalsa* Sikhs, Narang gave precedence to 'faith' over other factors which could be relevant for explicating the complexities of Sikh history in a more critical and scientific manner. His work at times appears quite close to the writings of *Tat Khalsa* Sikhs, largely based on a popular religious tradition and legends, which did not necessarily converge with the actual historical reality. Nevertheless, it is quite easy to discern a vital difference between Narang and the *Tat Khalsa* writings. As stated earlier, the *Tat Khalsa* Sikhs were trying to assert that Sikhism since inception had its own distinctive character. Besides, their concerted effort was to construct a Sikh identity by clearly laying down rules, rituals and belief system which would establish their demarcation from the Hindus. This, as is well known, was equally contested in some Hindu writings which emphasized upon the inseparable bond that existed between the two at social and religious levels from the very beginning. Narang, as stated earlier, also believed that the roots of Sikhism lay in Hindu religion and, therefore, it can best be described as a Hindu sect (in some way similar to the Arya Samaj) which gradually evolved into a socio-political community by the end of the eighteenth century. This phenomenon became more explicit by his ideological conviction which was based on the assumption that all those who followed a religion whose founder was an Indian were Hindus. Keeping this in mind, Narang describes the Sikhs as 'Hindus' many a times in the whole text in an unproblematic manner. Yet, at the same time Narang did not get himself actively involved in the acrimonious debate which was witnessed at that time between the different sections on the contentious issue of the Sikh identity. However, he was critical of some of the steps taken by the *Tat Khalsa* Sikhs as regard to the Sikh identity which, in his view, would certainly widen the gulf between the Sikhs and the Hindus. Nevertheless, his belief was that such type of manifestation of Hindu-Sikh tension was a temporary phenomenon which could be resolved in an amicable manner. Therefore, his work on the

Sikhs appears to be one of the ways to underline the fact that there was an inherent bond between the Sikhs and Hindus and both at the same time had a common enemy in the Muslims. In other words, the Sikh past was presented with a Hinduized perspective positing Hindu-Muslim divide as a central aspect of Indian society, both in the past and contemporary times.[126]

Finally, Narang's work for obvious reasons also differed from the writings which offered a nationalist perspective on the Sikh past. It is well known that since the late nineteenth century, the rising new intelligentsia imbued with the vision of a pan-Indian identity, often chose to write on issues of common cultural heritage including the history of the Sikhs. They highlighted the humane and spiritual content of Guru Nanak's message with a view to asserting the rich cultural heritage of the Indian nation. It was indeed perceived as a powerful instrument to reassert their self-respect under conditions of colonial subjugation. The sense of alienation provoked by British rule could find expression through a proud glorification of one's own cultural heritage. Moreover, the nationalist writers selectively invoked those aspects of Sikh history that could be used to instill patriotism and to strengthen the forces of anti-imperialist struggle. For instance, Guru Gobind Singh was portrayed as a selfless person who resisted oppression and fought for justice. The central concern of such writings infused with nationalist ideas was to project the guru's image in a manner that could be emulated by the Indian people in their struggle against colonial rule.[127] However, this kind of representation of the Sikhs was contrary to the Hinduized framework of Narang. Therefore, it is quite evident that Narang selectively invoked the past in a manner that could help in bringing necessary changes according to his own conviction and concerns in contemporary times, which indeed had long-term implications for the Indian nation both in pre-and post-independent times.

NOTES

1. This paper is largely based on the first edition of the book published as *The Transformation of Sikhsim and How the Sikhs became a Political Power,* Lahore, 1912.

2. S.P. Sen, *Dictionary of National Biography,* vol. III, Calcutta, 1974, pp. 229-30.
3. Narang, 1912, Preface, fn.
4. Ibid.
5. Narang originally intended to bring out a second volume on the Sikh history with the rise of Ranjit Singh but it was never published. It may be mentioned here that all subsequent editions are updated with sketchy accounts of Sikh history. Besides, these are not well documented and are more polemical in nature.
6. Narang, 1912, Preface.
7. Ibid.
8. Narang, 1945, 2nd edn., Preface.
9. Narang at the outset records 'the author . . . has been since his infancy, a devoted admirer of the Gurus, and has made Sikhism his life-long study'. Ibid., 1912, Preface.
10. Ibid, p. 2.
11. Ibid.
12. For a biographical background of Narang, see S.P. Sen, 1973, vol. III, pp. 229-30; *Oral Transcript of Gokul Chand Narang,* Nehru Memorial Museum & Library (hereafter NMML).
13. For the Hindu resurgence in north India, see Kenneth W. Jones, *Arya Dharma: Hindu Consciousness in the Nineteenth Century Punjab,* New Delhi, 1975. K.L. Tuteja and O.P. Grewal, 'Emergence of Hindu Communal Ideology in Early Twentieth Century Punjab', in *Social Scientist*, vol. 20, nos. 7-8, August 1992, pp. 1-28. Christopher Jafferlot, 'The Gensis and Development of Hindu Nationalism in the Punjab: From the Arya Samaj to Hindu Sabha', in *Indo-British Review,* 21(i); Richard Gordon, 'The Hindu Maha Sabha and the Indian National Congress 1915-1926', in *Modern Asian Studies*, vol. 9, August 1975, pp. 143-208. John Zavos, *Emergence of Hindu Nationalism in India*, Oxford, 2000.
14. See P.J. Marshal (ed.), *The British Discovery of Hinduism in the Eighteenth Century*, Cambridge, 1970.
15. Romila Thapar, 'Imagined Religious Communities? Ancient History and the Modern Search of Hindu Identity', in *Modern Asian Studies,* vol. 23, no. 2, 1989, pp. 228-31.
16. Tuteja and Grewal, 1992.
17. Swami Dayananda, *Satyarth Prakash* (English translation), Delhi, 1970; also see Jyotirmaya Sharma, *Hindutva: Exploring the Idea of Hindu Nationalism,* New Delhi, 2003, pp. 39-41.
18. Jones, 1975.
19. It is reasonably believed that a number of Indian intellectuals largely acquired their knowledge about Indian history and culture from the writings of the Europeans; Narang was not an exception. Bernard

Cohn has rightly remarked in a different context: 'Educated Indians were to learn about their own culture through the mediation of European ideas and scholarship'. Bernard Cohn, *An Anthropologist Among the Historians and Other Essays*, New Delhi, 1987, pp. 632-82.

20. Romila Thaper, 'Communal Interpretation of Ancient Indian History', in Romila Thaper, Harbans Mukhia and Bipan Chandra (eds.), *Communalism and the Writing of Indian History*, New Delhi, 1969, pp. 1-13.
21. For an incisive analysis of religiosity and communalism, see Bipan Chandra, *Communalism in Modern India*, Delhi, 1984.
22. K.N. Panikkar, 'Politics of Writing History Text Books', *Frontline*, vol. 18, no. I, June 2001. It is well known that James Mill's pioneering work was widely accepted as the first standard text book on Indian history for a long time. In his introductory chapter to the reprinted version of the book *History of British India*, London, 1975, p. XXXVI, William Thomas writes that James Mill was regarded as a highly informed expert on Indian affairs.
23. Swami Dayananda, 1970, pp. 507-70.
24. Jones, p. 146.
25. K.N. Panikkar, 'Outsider as Enemy: Politics of Rewriting History in India', in K.N. Panikkar, *An Agenda for Cultural Action on Other Essays*, New Delhi, 2006, pp. 95-112.
26. For details on the Hindu-Muslim tension in Punjab since late nineteenth century, see K.L. Tuteja and O.P. Grewal, 1992.
27. See Gerald Barrier and Paul Wallace, *The Punjab Press, 1880-1905*, Michigan, 1970.
28. For growth of Hindu Maha Sabha in Punjab and its communal politics see K.L. Tuteja, 'Hindu Consciousness, Communalism and the Congress in Pre-Partition Punjab', Presidential Address (Modern India Section), 58th Session of the Indian History Congress Proceedings, Banglore, 1997.
29. Swami Dayananda, pp. 355-8.
30. Ganda Singh, 'The Origin of Hindu-Sikh Tension in the Punjab', *The Punjab Past and Present*, vol. XI, pt. II, 1977; K.W. Jones, '*Ham Hindu-Nahin*: The Arya-Sikh Relations', in *Journal of Asian Studies*, XXXII, 3 May 1973, pp. 1995-2005.
31. For a recent authoritative study of the Singh Sabha Movement, see Harjot Oberoi, *The Construction of Religious Boundaries: Culture, Identity and Diversity in the Sikh Tradition*, Delhi, 1994.
32. It is important to note that apart from some urban Hindus, a section of Sikhs headed by Khem Singh Bedi (one of the descendents of the Guru Nanak) at a meeting in Lahore in 1897 had openly supported a resolution saying that the Sikhs were part of the Hindus. This was,

however, strongly resented by the *Tat Khalsa* (Pure Sikhism) ideologues of the Singh Sabha movement. In this regard Harjot Oberoi observes:

When Sanatan Sikhs used the term Hindu to encompass Sikhs, it possessed meanings rather different from those we understand today. On the one hand it was for them on ethno-territorial category which applied to people who inhabited the subcontinent; on the other hand it was an umbrella word encompassing a body of indigenous religious beliefs, as distinct from exogenous religions like Islam or Christianity. . . . A favourite analogy of Sanatan Sikhs to express the intertwined status of Hinduism and Sikhism was that Sikhism was like a wing within a large inn called Hinduism. It shared the same foundation and courtyard but had its own separate rooms and terraces. Thus, it could simultaneously be distinct from and in unison with Hinduism. In support of this view Sanatan Sikhs cited the history of the Sikh tradition. Ibid., pp. 395-6. In a way, the position taken by Khem Singh Bedi was not much different from the view point of Narang on the issue of Sikhs as part of Hindus.

33. See G. Barrier, *The Sikhs and Their Literature*, Delhi, 1970.
34. *Oral Transcript of Gokul Chand Narang*, NMML, New Delhi.
35. Narang, 1912, Preface.
36. Ibid., p. 1.
37. Ibid., p. 3.
38. Ibid., p. 26.
39. Ibid., pp. 5-6.
40. Ibid., p. 4, fn.
41. Ibid., p. 3.
42. Ibid., p. 6.
43. Ibid., p. 11.
44. Ibid., p. 9.
45. Ibid., p. 10.
46. Ibid., pp. 13-14.
47. Ibid.
48. Ibid., p. 13.
49. Ibid.
50. Ibid., p. 8.
51. For life and teachings of Guru Nanak, I have made use of the writings of J.S. Grewal and W.H. McLeod.
52. J.S. Grewal, *The Sikhs of the Punjab*, New Delhi, 1994, p. 29.
53. McLeod, *Who is a Sikh?: The Problem of Sikh Identity*, Oxford, 1989, p. 13.
54. McLeod, *Exploring Sikhism: Aspects of Sikh Identity, Culture, and Thought*, Oxford, 2000, p. 1.
55. Narang, 1912, p. 15.

56. Ibid., p. 16.
57. Ibid., p. 15.
58. Ibid., p. 17.
59. Ibid., p. 17.
60. Ibid., p. 17, fn.
61. Ibid.
62. Ibid., p. 33.
63. Ibid.
64. See Irfan Habib, 'Jatts of Punjab and Sind', in *Proceeding of the Punjab History Conference,* Patiala, 1972; McLeod, *The Evolution of the Sikh Community,* Oxford, 1976.
65. Narang while underlining the significance of the Gurmukhi script says, 'The very name of script, therefore, reminded those who employed it of their duty towards their Guru, and constantly kept alive in their mind the consciousness that they were something distinct from the common mass of Hinduism, that they were regenerated, liberated and saved'. He, however, also records that later on the issue of Gurmukhi script was raised to establish the separate nature of Sikhism which caused difficulty in 'consolidating the Hindu race.' Ibid., pp. 17-18. In this regard, Harjot Oberoi observes that in medieval Punjab, the majority of the Hindus, Muslims and Sikhs 'spoke welter of Punjabi dialects without any religious distinction'. It was only in the second half of the nineteenth century that the new Sikh leadership made the Gurmukhi script and the Punjabi language exclusive emblems of Sikh identity. Harjot Oberoi, p. 348.
66. Ibid., p. 19.
67. Ibid., p. 23.
68. Ibid., pp. 31-3.
69. Ibid.
70. Ibid.
71. Ibid.
72. Ibid.
73. Ibid.
74. Ibid.
75. Ibid.
76. Ibid., Appendix II, p. IX.
77. Ibid., p. XI
78. In particular, Narang was critical of Cunningham who had observed, 'The Sikhs are converts to a new religion, the real of the double dispensation of *Brahma* and *Mahomet*'. Ibid., p. IX.
79. Ibid., p. XVI.
80. Ibid., p. IX.
81. Ibid., p. 3.
82. Ibid., p. 5.

83. Ibid., p 6.
84. Ibid., Appendix II, p. X.
85. Narang has devoted two full chapters describing the persecution of the Sikhs and Hindus in a highly commuanlized manner. See chapters V and VI.
86. Ibid., p. 39.
87. Ibid., p. 12.
88. Ibid., fn.
89. Ibid.
90. For a recent translation of *Dabistan-i-Mazahib*, see J.S. Grewal and Irfan Habib (eds.), *Sikh History from Persian Sources*, New Delhi, 2001.
91. Ibid., pp. 39-40.
92. Ibid., pp. 54-5
93. Ibid., p. 54.
94. Ibid., p. 55.
95. Ibid.
96. Ibid., p. 57 fn.
97. Ibid., p. 66.
98. Ibid., p. 67.
99. Ibid., p. 76.
100. Narang underlined the significance of the rule of conduct laid by the tenth guru for observance by the members of *Khalsa* as body symbols (especially five 'Ks'). In this regard, he observes that 'Guru had thoroughly realised the hypnotizing power of certain external forms and symbols and knew what an inspiration men often derives from a change in their outward appearances.' Ibid., p. 81.
101. Ibid., p. 86.
102. Ibid., p. 102.
103. It is necessary to mention here that the representation of Islam in negative was largely taken from those European writings which dealt with the Crusades. But such kind of judgements, as has convincingly been argued 'were based on little or no evidence since the history of Islam in India had not been investigated at this time'. Romila Thapar, *Early India,* Penguin, 2002, p. I.
104. See Ather Ali, 'Encounter and Efflorescence: Genesis of Medieval Civilization', General Presidential Address, *Indian History Congress Proceedings,* Gorakhpur, 1989, Irfan Habib (ed.), *India: Studies in the History of an Idea,* New Delhi, 2004; Barbara D. Metcalf and Thomas R. Metcalf, *A Concise History of India,* Cambridge, 2002, Chapter 1.
105. Richard M. Eaton, *Essays on Islam and Indian History*, New Delhi, 2000, sections 3 and 4.
106. Ibid., p. 216.

107. For a crucial difference between the 'expansion of Islam', and 'assimilation to Islam', see Richard Eaton, p. 35.
108. Oberoi, pp. 155-6.
109. Ibid., Eaton, pp. 204-46 (Chapters IX and X).
110. Eaton, p. 241.
111. W.H. McLeod, *Exploring Sikhism: Aspects of Sikh Identity,* Oxford, 2002, p. 28.
112. Harjot Oberoi has convincingly argued that the division between different religious systems was quite blurred and fuzzy in Punjab in medieval times. He writes: 'In the case of the subcontinent, the either/or dichotomy is not to be taken for granted, for the religious life of the people, particularly in the pre-colonial period, was characterized by a continuum. There was much interpenetration and overlapping of communal identities', Oberoi, 1994, p. 12.
113. See Grewal, 1984, pp. 28-9.
114. See Tara Chand, *Influence of Islam on Indian Culture,* Allahabad, 1963.
115. Khushwant Singh, *History of the Sikhs,* vol. 1, Princeton, 1963.
116. McLeod, 2002, pp. 3-18.
117. In this regard, McLeod makes a perceptive comment:
'The primary influence appears to have been indirect. Sufism had already exercised a limited influence upon Sant belief, and such influence was subsequently mediated to Guru Nanak as a part of the Sant synthesis. The secondary influence was communicated by means of direct contact. In some small measure this direct influence may have come through contact with exponents of a relatively refined Sufism, but the principal source of the direct influence appears to have been the popular variety which had blended with orthodox Islam and was to some extent indistinguishable from it.', McLeod, 2002, p. 10.
118. Ibid., p. 4.
119. Iqtadar Alam Khan, 'State in Mughal India', in *Social Scientist,* vol. 29, January 2001, pp. 16-45. Also See Sanjay Subodh, 'Temples, Rulers and Historians' Dilemma: Understanding the Medieval Mind', in *Social Probings*, vol. 15, nos. 3-4, Winter 2003.
120. Cited in Amartya Sen, *Identity and Violence: The Illusion of Destiny,* New Delhi, 2006, p. 64.
121. Iqtadar Alam Khan, 'The Khalsa of Guru Gobind Singh: Its Soldiers' in Himadri Banerjee (ed.), *The Khalsa and the Punjab: Studies in Sikh History to the Nineteenth Century*, New Delhi, 2002, pp. 21-32.
122. Grewal, 1994, p. 72.
123. Khan, 2000.
124. Khushwant Singh, vol. 1, p. 79.

125. Khan, 2002.
126. For a brilliant critique of this genre of writings described as 'Hinduised history', see the introduction in K.N. Panikkar (ed.), *The Concerned Indian's Guide to Communalism*, New Delhi, 1999.
127. For details, see Himadri Banerjee, *The other Sikhs: A View from Eastern India,* New Delhi, 2004. Also see K.L. Tuteja, 'Vernacular Writings on the Sikhs', in *Economic and Political Weekly,* XVL, 1, 7 January 2006, pp. 35-9.

CHAPTER 18

History Textbooks: Narratives of Religious Nationalism

K.N. PANIKKAR

The debate about history textbooks during the last five years has brought to the fore a large number of issues about the practice of the discipline. The debate was occasioned by the steps initiated by the government led by the Bharatiya Janata Party (BJP) to withdraw the books then in use and replace them with a new set of books. Periodic revisions or even change of textbooks normally should not arouse much opposition, as it is a necessary practice, if advances in knowledge are to be incorporated in them. It was, therefore, not so much the revision or change that occasioned the debate, but the nature and purpose of the exercise. Changing the textbooks was intrinsic to a reorientation of education, which the Hindu fundamentalist forces have been advocating. The reorientation was intended to inculcate political and cultural values, which would impart ideological legitimacy for a Hindu nation. The discipline central to this project was history, because a nation's identity is inevitably enmeshed with its historical consciousness.

I

All governments in India, beginning with the colonial rule, have been alive to the importance of textbooks as a means to ensure their future interest by hegemonizing the young. Taking keen interest in the nature of instruction they tried to shape the textbooks according to their ideological needs. The British, for instance, had set up textbook committees in the beginning of its rule in order to oversee their content and character. These committees laid down guidelines for the preparation of textbooks and to orient their character to compliment the colonial world-view.[1] Apart from the official agencies there were also unofficial organizations like the schoolbook societies, engaged in the preparation, production and dissemination of textbooks.[2] All of them, both official and non-official, helped further the interest of the colonial rule by crafting the textbooks, in conception and content, to fulfil a legitimizing role for colonialism. The textbooks prescribed in states ruled by Indian princes also fulfilled a similar role by disseminating the notions of dynastic patriotism and loyalty. In other words, the textbooks carried in them the political purpose of creating consent in the mind of the subjected.

The growth of education during the nineteenth and twentieth centuries, both through the initiative of the state and private agencies, made textbook production an extremely challenging task, particularly because of the number of languages in which education was imparted. Textbook production was a predominantly private enterprise, with the government exercising a modicum of control in the form of approving the textbooks. The government did not directly enter into the preparation and production of textbooks and permitted private agencies, whose interest was primarily commercial, to monopolize it. The government was concerned not so much with quality as with the image of the colonial rule the textbooks projected, as education was looked upon essentially as an instrument for bringing the 'natives' under its hegemony.

The colonial textbooks performed this assigned task not merely by idealizing the British through the narratives of their political and military achievements but more by exposing, even if indirectly, the contemporary state of Indian civilization. The work of Orientalists had such an implication as it highlighted the past achievements of Indian civilization in contrast to the degradation of the present. The colonial presence drew its rationale from this contrast. Colonialism had intervened in a chaotic society, divided into religious communities which were interminably in conflict with each other. This view of Indian society also informed the colonial conception of the past, which acknowledged religion as the motor of Indian history and social consciousness. As a consequence the colonial ideologues invoked religious identity as the distinguishing characteristic of Indian history. Hence, James Mill's periodization using religion as the marker. The influence of this interpretation has been so overriding that it continued to persist for a long time, with some of its vestiges present even today. The importance of Mill's view of Indian history, however, was not that he followed the religious affiliation of the rulers to characterize a historical epoch, which he indeed did, but his conception of society as constituted by religious communities continuously in conflict. Such a view became central to colonial historiography with the textbooks incorporating it as an axiom.

History is often invoked as a source of legitimacy by all regimes. The preparation and promotion of textbooks by ruling powers reflect this political interest. The growth of historiography in India during the last two hundred years comprehends within it the influence of changing contours of power and politics. Most of the writings on India authored by the colonial administrators and ideologues were intertwined with the interests of the colonial rule.[3] Delegitimizing the pre-colonial, even if colonial strategies of domination were not without an element of appropriation of the 'native' past, was one of the objectives they had pursued. The familiar themes of colonial historiography like the despotism of Indian rulers and the characterization of the pre-colonial era as a dark age are integral to this quest. The racial explanation of the British conquest of India and the debilities of Indian character, which the colonial historiography so eloquently narrated, had the same intent. The Indians lost out to the Europeans, it was argued, not because of the technological superiority of the latter, but because of the racial inferiority of the former. The innumerable histories of British military conquest bears testimony to this. What they highlighted as reason for British success was the European character in contrast to that of the Indian. The intellectual make-up of generations of Indian students was influenced by this coloured version that the colonial textbooks imbibed in them. The sense of inferiority, which the Indian intelligentsia suffered in relation to the West, can be traced, at least partially, to the ideological and cultural influences that the school textbooks initially brought to bear on the young minds.

Equally important was the political message. The colonial textbooks conveyed the idea that India, inhabited by an agglomeration of religious and caste communities antagonistic to each other, was neither a nation nor had the potential to be one. The Indians did not share a national sentiment or a sense of patriotism, but were involved mainly in their personal or group interests. India, to borrow a popular expression from colonial historiography, was nothing but a geographical expression. The Indian history that the colonial textbooks projected was, therefore, a record of sectarian strife.

II

The teaching of history in India after independence in 1947 was burdened with this religious-communal baggage bequeathed by colonialism. The new government was quite alive to the colonial character of education and urgent need to reform it, as evident from several education commissions it had set up. The reports of these commissions recommended steps for evolving a national policy of education, which would help decolonize the education system. The production of new textbooks replacing the ones in circulation during the colonial rule was a necessary precondition, if education were to meet the demands of the new nation. With this in view the government set up the National Council for Educational Research and Training (NCERT) in 1961, entrusted mainly with the mission of preparing school-level textbooks.

Among the textbooks prepared by the NCERT, the history books had attracted considerable attention both for academic and political reasons. Academically they marked a distinct departure from the then current textbooks, both in content and interpretation. They followed a scientific approach and adopted an interpretative frame distinct from the colonial and the communal. Written by some of India's well-known historians—Romila Thapar, Ram Sharan Sharma, Satish Chandra and Bipan Chandra—they incorporated, to the extent possible within the limitations of school textbooks, the advances made in the discipline. In place of the dynastic political history, which occupied the centrestage of earlier texts, they tried to locate historical developments as a part of the social process. The new NCERT books were, therefore, welcomed widely by historians and teachers.

Despite their academic quality these textbooks attracted the ire of the Hindu fundamentalist forces. They alleged factual inaccuracy and biased interpretation. The Aryan migration to India and their beef eating habits were particularly contentious, as these historical facts undermined the Hindu nationalist claims. Therefore, in 1977 when they became partners in the government an attempt was made to withdraw these books, which had to be eventually abandoned due to the protest of the academia and the opposition of liberal sections within the government. However, the intention of the fundamentalist forces was clearly revealed. Whenever they succeeded in having a more effective control over the government the textbooks would be so recast to project a Hinduized view of the past. Within twenty years of the initial attempt this possibility in fact became real. During this period the political climate in the country turned in favour of the Hindu fundamentalist forces, which enabled them in 1998 to lead a coalition government in which the Ministry of Human Resource Development which dealt with education was headed by Murli Manohar Joshi, a long standing cadre of the Hindu fundamentalist organization, Rashtriya Swayamsevak Sangh (RSS). Under his stewardship the government spared no effort to change the content and character of education, of which the introduction of new textbooks was perhaps the most prominent and indeed controversial.

III

The preparation or revision of textbooks undertaken by the successive governments was part of their larger educational and political vision. For instance, the educational system that the post-independent government led by the Indian National Congress tried to bring into being was integral to its commitment to a secular—democratic polity and society. Such a commitment evolved out of the struggle against colonialism and from a perception of multi-cultural and multi-religious national identity.

Seeking a fundamental change from the colonial system—in objectives, in teaching methods, in programmes, in the size and composition of the student body, in the selection and preparation of teachers, and in organization—the government envisioned education as an instrument for creating a sense of common citizenship and culture, and for strengthening national integration. Even if this intention was not fully translated into practice and the vestiges and influence of the colonial system continued to persist, initiatives were taken to realize a modern system of education. In doing so there was no attempt to adopt the Western or to resurrect the traditional as the ideal. Instead, the concern of all those involved with educational reform, from the early nineteenth century onwards, was to marry the traditional with the modern. A national system of education envisaged by them was based on a possible synthesis of all that is advanced in the West with all that was socially healthy and abiding in the traditional. In other words, the national policy was not lodged in dichotomy between the indigenous and the Western. The impact of such a policy was the internalization of a universal outlook and the location of the indigenous in the wider matrix of human history. The educational system that evolved in independent India, despite severe limitations, had a liberal and universal outlook.

Such a trajectory of educational development suffered a major setback with the emergence of Hindu fundamentalist forces and their control over the government.[4] The freedom from British rule, they argued, did not bring about any change in the system of education, for the new rulers were the product of the colonial system, 'the children of Macaulay', as they were derisively described. Therefore, the education system of independent India, it was contended, continued to be colonial and Western. The real reason for opposition, however, was the liberal and secular character of education, which did not serve the fundamentalist cause. The advocates of Hindu fundamentalism, therefore, wanted the existing system to be dismantled in favour of the traditional and the indigenous. A national system of education, in their reckoning, should be anchored in Hindu religious ethos and indigenous knowledge. M.S. Golwalkar, the leader and ideologue of the RSS, had advocated such a system, which is essentially religious in character with emphasis on tradition, discipline and military training. Following the principles enunciated by its intellectual mentor, the BJP government set upon implementing an inward looking system, largely ignoring the achievements of other civilizations. Identity, national pride and attachment to the past were the qualities the government wanted to develop in the students:

> A sense of belonging must be developed in every individual learner by focusing on India's contribution to world civilization. It is high time that India's contribution in areas like mathematics, sciences, maritime, medicine, trade, architecture, sculpture, establishment of institutions of learning is emphasised and made known to the learner to develop a sense of belonging to the nation with respect and an attachment to the past.[5]

The BJP's prescription to achieve these objectives was an 'Indianized, nationalized and spiritualized' system of education. The prerequisite for the implementation of such a system was the reordering and reorientation, if not a complete dismantling, of the existing curriculum and syllabus, which were by and large secular in character and universal in outlook. The alternative proposed had an unmistakable Hindu religious orientation with an emphasis on indigenous knowledge and practices. The focus was to 'privilege the innovative experiments and experiences emanating from the indigenous context and thus to bring to notice the contribution of India to the world wisdom.[6] These ideas were put into practice through the government agencies at all levels of teaching and research. The NCERT prepared a new curriculum statement, the University Grants Commission (UGC) announced new programmes for financing and research-funding agencies like the Indian Council for Historical Research and Indian Council for Social Science Research supported projects with a fundamentalist flavour. The NCERT curriculum statement effectively used the pretext of value education to impart a Hindu religious character, in place of the values the existing system had enunciated: honesty, kindness, charity, tolerance, courtesy, compassion and sympathy.[7] The UGC, at the same time, liberally financed and promoted subjects that contributed to obscurantism and superstition like astrology and Hindu priest craft, in the name of preserving indigenous knowledge. A new philosophy of education, backward looking and fundamentalist, was being put in place. In this endeavour the textbooks, particularly of history, were of crucial importance, for history was central to the concept of religious nationalism as championed by the Hindu fundamentalist forces in India.

IV

The introduction of new textbooks by the NCERT was inspired by the political purpose of seeking rationale from history for constructing India as a Hindu nation. The textbooks were, therefore, recast as narratives of Hindu religious nationalism. Claimed as an effort to retrieve the true nationalist history from the motivated distortions of colonial historiography they attribute to Indian nation an exclusively Hindu character. As such the new textbooks are not a continuation but a departure from the 'nationalist' history the anti-colonial movement had advocated, which countered the colonial misrepresentations by underlining the historical evolution of India as a multi-cultural and multi-religious society. In contrast, the communal version shares the colonial view of Indian civilization being static. Therefore, the ancient civilization of India was depicted as the living present. What characterized the Indian civilization, according to these textbooks, is continuity as many practices, both religious and social, of the earliest civilization continued to persist without change. The continuity is traced in the worship of gods, in social customs and political practice.[8] Although reminiscent of the colonial conception of unchanging India, such a view of the past being modern and the present being a replica of the past lent credence to the argument in favour of India being a Hindu civilizational state.

The idea of India being a Hindu civilizational state runs through all the texts, either directly expressed or indirectly suggested. The question of the indigenous origin of Aryans and the identity of Harappan civilization with the Vedic society has some bearing on this issue. The former is quite central to the fundamentalist agenda of claiming the nation as Hindu, as the migration theory would deprive the Hindus of indigenous lineage.

Therefore, against the widely held scholarly opinion Aryans are credited with indigenous origins, subscribing in the bargain to the colonial view of the Aryan race. In the former case the textbooks put forward the view that the Aryans were indigenous to India and that the opinion widely held by scholars about their migration was dismissed as inconsequential. In defense of indigenous origin no substantial evidence is adduced, except negative reasoning. It is asserted that the 'the oldest surviving records of the Aryans, the *Rigveda*, does not give even an inkling of any migration. It does not have any knowledge even of the geography beyond the known boundaries of Ancient India. It further says:

> Many scholars think that the Aryans were originally inhabitants of India and did not come from outside. It has been argued by such scholars that there is no archeological or biological evidence, which could establish the arrival of any new people from outside between 5000 BC and 800 BC. This means that if at all there was any migration of Aryans or for that matter of any other people in India, it may have taken place at least eight or nine thousand years ago or after 800 BC to both of which there is no evidence. Further, the skeletal remains found from various Harappan sites resemble the skeletons of the modern population of the same geographical area.[9]

The theory of the indigenous origins of Aryans serves multiple purposes in the Hindu nationalist agenda. For one, it is the ground in which the identification of the Vedic with Indus civilization is constructed. The identification starts with a change in the name itself. The Harappan civilization is rechristened as Saraswati—Sindhu after the Rigvedic river, suggesting thereby the Vedic association of the Harappan civilization.[10] The similarity between the two civilizations is then dealt with in great detail. It is suggested that the 'Harappan and the Rigvedic knowledge of geography covers the same extent, from Afganistan in the north to Gujarat in the south, Ganga in the east to Kubha (Kabul), Pakistan, in the west'.[11] This shared knowledge about territory is invoked as a proof for the identity of two civilizations. The second reason given is that most of the animals known to the Indus people are also known to the Rigvedic people, such as sheep, dog, buffalo, bull, and so on. The animals hunted by the Rigvedic people were antelopes, boars, buffaloes, lions, and elephants, most of which were also familiar to the Indus people. As regards animals the crucial evidence could be about the presence of horse, which is associated with Aryans and the Vedic society. It is stated that 'horse bones and terracotta figurines have been found in some Harappan sites', for which no evidence exists. One Mr. N.S. Rajaram, who claims to be a US-trained scientist engaged in historical research, made an attempt to transform the unicorn of the Indus seals into horse through computer manipulation. This attempt was exposed as a fabrication by historians, particularly by Prof. Michael Witzel of Harvard University.[12] Yet, the Harappan civilization is credited with the presence of horses in order to prove its Vedic association. The similarity is also extended to almost all other aspects of life, including worship, use of metals, treatment of hair, and so on. On the basis of these 'similarities' the author suggests that a number of scholars have come to the conclusion that 'the Harappan civilization is the same as the Vedic civilization and the Aryans did not come to India from outside'. The similarities thus invoked do not take into account the basic difference between the two: Harappan civilization was urban whereas the Vedic was pastoral. The author, however, concedes that there are 'other scholars who consider Vedic culture as different from that of the Harappan civilization'.[13] Why they consider so is not discussed at all and therefore the former is presented as a settled fact. Such an assertion in a textbook becomes particularly objectionable when there are hardly any scholarly research and opinion to support it.

The identity of Harappan–Saraswati civilization with the Vedic society has been marshalled to trace the lineage of the nation to a Hindu past which cannot be done by predating the Harappan to the Vedic. The Harappan being the oldest known civilization of India, its association with Aryans would alone lend credibility to the Hindu origins of the nation. Secondly, it would also antedate the chronology of Vedic civilization at least by a couple of millennia, which would locate it not as one of the old, but as the oldest in the world. This is part of an India-centric view that the Hindu fundamentalist forces have been trying to project, according to which humankind evolved and diffused from the upper Saraswati region. The Indian civilization, the textbooks affirm, has an 'unbroken history of about 8000 years' and its cultural and intellectual achievements both antedated and surpassed others.[14] To substantiate this view, the chronology of Indian civilization has been revised without any respect for evidence. As a result, the Vedic and the Harappan civilizations are sought to be placed around 5000 BC. More importantly, new civilization sites are being discovered which are claimed as flourishing as early as 10,000 BC. Such revisions have not been taking place after scholarly investigation or consensus.

The purpose of this revisionist history, which has been incorporated into the textbooks, both implicitly and explicitly, appears to be the creation of an inward looking chauvinistic self-view in the impressionable minds of the young. The running theme in all textbooks prepared by the NCERT is the relative antiquity of Indian civilization and its qualitatively superior achievements, in both philosophical and material fields. The textbook meant for class VI students entitled *India and the World*, which provides the initial introduction to human history, is a good example of this tendency. The chapter on world civilizations is titled 'non-Indian civilizations', which suggests India as the point of reference to understand all other civilizations. The change in the title of the book—from *World Civilizations* to *India and the World*—is itself symptomatic of the change in perspective. The focus is not on India *in* the world, but on India *and* the world, which in a way defeats the purpose of studying world civilizations, which can only be to create a universal outlook. By reorienting the syllabus to an India-centric framework the superiority of Hindu-Indian civilization is foregrounded. Such an aim seems to be inbuilt into the introductory statement itself, which modifies nomenclature, establishes antiquity and indicates greater geographical extent:

> In the northern and Western parts of India and Pakistan there developed a civilization along the Indus and Gagghar/Harkara (ancient Saraswati) rivers which is known variously as Harappan, Indus or Indus-Saraswati civilization. It started developing around 4600 BC but reached its peak around 2600 BC and lasted at its peak for about 600 years. It started declining by about 2000 BC. In geographical extent it was the largest civilization in the world. Its geographical extent was almost 20 times of Egyptian civilization and Mesopotamian civilizations combined.[15]

The superiority, it is suggested, is not in geographical extent and antiquity alone, but more so in intellectual achievements, cultural practices and scientific pursuits. The ancient period of Indian history, identified as the golden-Hindu, is depicted as the era in which Indians not only excelled in many a field but also surpassed all others. The suggestion of Indian superiority is an undercurrent in the selection and description of facts as well as in the analysis and argument. As a result, the textbooks carry an unmistakable Hindu religious flavour. It begins with the emphasis on the sacred and religious character of the Vedas and Upanishads. The Vedic literature is described as 'Hindu religious literature and is revered. But it must be remembered that the Vedas or the Vedic literature does not signify any individual religious work like Koran or Bible. The word Veda means Knowledge or the sacred spiritual knowledge.'[16] In a similar vein Upanishads are described as the 'works of most profound philosophy in any religion'. Evidently the descriptions are consciously so crafted to include an explicit comparison suggestive of Indian superiority.

In science and technology the achievements of Indian civilization is credited with much greater advances than others and favourably compare with modern science, particularly in arithmetic, algebra, geometry, astronomy, alchemy, medicine, and so on. The textbook on social sciences for class sixth students sets the tone:

> In the Vedic period, astronomy was well developed. They knew the movement of heavenly bodies and calculated their positions at different times. It helped them in accurately preparing their calendars and predicting the time of solar and lunar eclipses. They also knew that the earth moved on its own axis and around the sun. The moon moved around the earth. They also tried to calculate the time period taken by bodies from the sun. These calculations are almost the same as calculated by the modern scientific method.[17]

This assessment of the scientific achievements of Indian civilization is carried forward in subsequent textbooks. The class XI textbook states: 'In the field of mathematics, astronomy and medicine India had much advanced knowledge during this period in comparison with any other country in the world.

These developments in science and technology in India were first borrowed by Arabs and then by the Western world.'[18] The implication is that India is the original home of knowledge in science and other countries in the world had benefited from the achievements of Indian civilization. The Indian youth could therefore take legitimate pride in this past.

V

In contrast to the repeated references to the 'Hindu' achievements in science and technology the textbook on the medieval history of India is conspicuously silent about the new developments in the field during the medieval period. An impression is conveyed that there were no scientific pursuits or technological innovations worth mentioning in this period. This is part of a general view that with the coming of the Muslims Indian history passed into a dark age, losing in the process all that Indian society had achieved earlier. As a result, the syncretic tendencies manifested through the coming together of different cultural streams, which created a new cultural ambience, are overlooked.

Exclusion as a strategy of denial of history is most effectively practised in the case of architecture and religion. Very few fields of cultural production have been more creative and innovative than architecture, as it developed during the Sultanate and Mughal periods. The blending of the Islamic and Hindu traditions heralded new styles in conception and execution. The textbook on medieval history turns a blind eye to this significant tendency in the cultural history of India. While the Islamic character of medieval architecture is emphasized, the syncretic tendency, which developed during this period as a result of the coming together of two different systems does not find any mention. Some of the magnificent buildings resulting from this interaction have been completely ignored, except Man Mandir built by Man Singh, the ruler of Gwalior, in the sixteenth century. But the influence it exercised over the Mughal architecture, which would highlight the procees of cultural synthesis, finds no place. Catherine B. Asher observes:

Man Mandir is rightly regarded as having influenced Akbar in the design of his own palaces. Its exterior influenced the inlaid mosaic façade of the Delhi gate in Akbar's Agra fort, the interior of this palace had an even greater impact on Akbar's architecture. The main body of the palace consists of a series of small connecting courtyards around whose perimeter are galleries containing rooms. These rooms are never arcuated, but have essentially flat roofs, a type that reappears in Akbar's Agra and Fatehpur Sikri palaces.[19]

Similarly Islamic architecture had exerted decisive influence over the buildings constructed by Hindu rulers.[20]

Despite this interaction, which characterized the medieval architecture as a whole, the textbook on medieval history pays no attention to it. Instead architecture is invoked as another example to underline religious division. The evolution of architecture during the Sultanate period, which is credited to have evolved in three distinct stages, is a good example. The initial phase is 'characterized by destruction', second by dismantling of buildings to 'provide readymade material for new structures' and third by building of 'Islamic structures with specially prepared stone'.[21] The suggestion that the grandeur of the medieval architecture was achieved at the expense of the existing Hindu structures is unmistakable and reminiscent of the campaign for the construction of the temple at Ayodhya on the plea that the mosque was constructed by destroying a temple. This idea is repeated as the general policy followed by all Muslim rulers, who, it is emphasized, not only forbade the construction of Hindu temples but also destroyed the existing ones.

Among the several syncretic religious movements that had emerged in Indian society during the medieval period, the Bhakti and the Sufi are the most popular and influential. Both of them came into being in a multi-religious context and as vehicles of monotheism and universalism. Their import can hardly be understood if isolated from their multi-religious context and syncretic character. Yet, the textbook on medieval history attempts precisely that by locating them as movements emerging from within each religion, without any external influence. The Bhakti movement, it is asserted, was 'not a Hindu response to the egalitarian message of Islam' but only the continuation of the tradition from the time of Upanishads and *Bhagavat Gita*.[22]

In the same vein Sufism is described as a 'movement that arose independently within the Muslim world and not as a consequence of its interface with Hinduism'.[23] Naturally the Bhakti and Sufi saints who epitomized in them the syncretic tendencies do not figure at all in the text. The absence of *Nirguna Bhaktas* like Kabir and Ravidas who have made a major impact on Indian society through their ideas of a casteless egalitarian society is particularly conspicuous. The attitude of Sufi saints towards Hinduism and their attempts to promote cultural synthesis are also absent. The silence is perhaps not accidental, but part of a design to foreground religious exclusion and difference as the characteristic of Indian society for which historical facts are suppressed, distorted and invented. An undercurrent of religious identity is thus attributed for almost everything that happened in the past.

The underlying assumptions and the interpretative structure of the textbooks prepared by the NCERT thus impart an unmistakable religious character, privileging the Hindu as the embodiment of the nation on the lines of the ideas and arguments earlier advanced by communal ideologues like V.D. Savarkar and M.S. Golwalkar. This is inspired by the political project of Hindu fundamentalism, to transform the multicultural and multireligious Indian nation into an exclusively Hindu state. What the textbooks have attempted is to reshape the Indian past to derive legitimacy for this political project and to communally reconstruct the historical consciousness of the coming generations. In the process the generally accepted norms and methods of historical discipline have irreparably suffered.

Although there is considerable concern in the country about the fundamentalist turn in history textbooks produced by the government agencies, it is often forgotten that they form only a small part of the textbooks actually used in the schools. In fact, the textbooks produced by the NCERT are used only in 3 per cent of the schools. The textbooks used in the remaining schools suffer from the same malady, perhaps they are much worse. A national steering committee, which reviewed the textbooks, noticed communal influence quite pervasive in the reading materials used in almost all states.[24] More so in schools managed by Vidya Bharati, the educational wing of the Hindu fundamentalist forces. The reading material in schools run by Muslim communal outfits are equally so. They subscribe to the view that religion alone played crucial role in moulding the course of history and therefore, considers the advent of Islam as a marker of historical epochs. They divide history into two phases: pre-Islamic and Islamic. The report observes: 'These textbooks present an extremely narrow view of the subjects they deal with. In the name of developing an Islamic viewpoint and religiosity, these textbooks foster all kinds of irrational and obscurantist and narrow sectarian ideas and, in many ways, a communal outlook'.[25] This is precisely the problem with most textbooks. What is objectionable in them is not factual errors, as is often projected by many,[26] which indeed is deplorable, but the worldview it imbibes and the social ideals it upholds.

In no other discipline communal influence has been so well pronounced as in history. In recent times popular historical discourse has considerably changed in favour of the communal; the debates in history have tended to revolve around communal distortions and interpretations; the teaching in universities has increasingly come under communal influence. Even research establishments have promoted communal history. Such an all out assault on history is indicative of the importance the fundamentalist forces assign to the discipline. In fact, communalism invokes history as an ideology and uses it for multiple purposes: to gain legitimacy for the construction of India as a Hindu nation, to cast the 'outsider' as enemy and for creating a religious cultural identity. Above all history is the source from which cultural nationalism, foregrounded as the real and positive nationalism, derives its justification as rooted in the historical experience of the people.

The textbooks in history have thus become a matter of contention in India. The fundamentalist forces have been trying to transform history as a narrative of Hindu religious nationalism. In the bargain they have violated the generally accepted norms of historical discipline, which has aroused much opposition from a large section of historians who have been trying to retrieve the discipline from the distortions and misrepresentations of the religious revisionist history. The debate about history in India is a contest between these viewpoints. The textbooks are the terrain in which this contest is most evident.

NOTES

1. Amitabh Mukerjee, *Reform and Regeneration in Bengal, 1774-1823*, Calcutta, 1968.
2. *The First Report of the Calcutta School Book Society*, Calcutta, 1818.
3. C.H. Philips, *History and Historians of India, Pakistan and Ceylon*, London, 1961.
4. K.N. Panikkar, 'Whither Indian Education' in *Before the Night Falls: Forebodings of Fascism in India*, Bangalore, 2002.
5. J.S. Rajput, 'Values in School Education', *Journal of Value Education*, New Delhi, November 2003, p. 43.
6. *National Curriculam for School Education: A Discussion Document*, New Delhi, 2000, p. 10.
7. Report of the Education Commission, vol.1, 1964, New Delhi, 1971.
8. The similarity in the objects of worship like the *peepal* tree, *linga*, fire, sun, wind, and sky during the Harappan and contemporary times is cited as an example. The figures in the seals of Harappa are identified as Hindu deities like the Mother Goddess and Shiva, even though these identifications are not accepted by archeologists and historians. Similarly in another seal the contemporary practice of using vermilion mark in the parting of the hair by married Hindu women is traced. In case of political institutions the Sabha and Samiti of the Vedic period are identified as the prototypes of the modern parliament. *India and the World*, Social Science textbook for Class VI, pp. 81-6 and *Ancient India,* textbook for Class XI, pp. 65–81.
9. Ibid., p. 89.
10. *India and the World*, p. 80. Also see K.S. Valdiya, *Saraswati: The River that Disappeared*, Hyderabad, 2002.
11. *Ancient India*, p. 90.
12. Michael Witzel and Steve Farmer, 'Horseplay in Harappa: The Indus Valley Decipherment Hoax', *Frontline*, vol. 17, issue 20, 30 September–13 October 2000.
13. Ibid., p. 92.
14. *India and the World*, p. 58.
15. Ibid., p. 80.
16. Ibid., p. 89.
17. Ibid., p. 91.

18. *Ancient India*, p. 207.
19. Catherine B. Asher, *Architecture of Mughal India*, Cambridge, 1992, p. 15.
20. Tarachand, *Influence of Islam on Indian Culture*, Allahabad, 1963, pp. 229-57.
21. *Medieval India*, a textbook for Class XI, pp. 114-15.
22. *Medieval India*, pp. 123-4.
23. Ibid.
24. Report of the National Steering Committee on Textbook Evaluation, 1993.
25. Ibid., p. 71.
26. The Indian History Congress has compiled a long list of factual errors in the NCERT textbooks, without giving adequate attention to the ideological dimension of these books. Irfan Habib et al., *History in the New NCERT Textbooks: A Report and an Index of Errors*, Kolkata, 2003.

NOTE

CHAPTER 19

A Note on the Spread of Islam in India

AMRIK SINGH

Islam came to India a century or so after it had consolidated itself not only in Saudi Arabia but in several other Middle Eastern countries as well. Even before the rise of Islam, Arab traders had been sailing across the Indian Ocean off and on and were visiting the western coast of India quite often. The Mapillas of Kerala for instance belong to this category. The conquest of Sindh in the early eighth century did not lead to a real penetration of Islam into India. That happened two centuries later when Mahmud of Ghazni led seventeen invasions into India, one after another. These events have been written about in considerable detail, including the fact that two centuries after the first invasion of Mehmud of Ghazni, a Muslim sultanate had got established in Delhi. Though the dynasties got replaced every few decades, Islam kept growing and expanding all the time. A couple of centuries later, the Mughal Empire was established in India and made a mark on history, both nationally and internationally.

All this is known and has been written about. But one thing that has not been discussed or analysed is why Islam did not spread to all parts of India but only to certain parts and amongst certain sections of the population. This was against the general trend. No other religion has spread so fast as Islam did. What happened in India was contrary to the pattern of growth and development of Islam, if it may be said. The overall picture was highly uneven. It was mainly in the north-west and the north-east of India that Islam spread in a significant way so that, when in 1947 the country was partitioned, these two parts of India had a sufficiently large Muslim population to be able to claim a separate homeland. All kinds of questions arise and it is an odd omission that no one has chosen to articulate or investigate them.

After more than a thousand years of presence in India, Islam remains a minority religion. In 1947, when the partition took place, the proportion of Muslims in India was about one quarter of the total population. After the establishment of Pakistan, it got reduced to half that figure and that is where it stands.

The general pattern of the spread of Islam was that, in most cases, Arab armies conquered countries in the neighbourhood of Arabia. This happened in the wake of the rise of Islam. Till then, the Arabs had been divided into a large number of tribes who were seldom at peace with one another. What Islam did, amongst other things, was to unify them. Once they got unified and also militarized, within a hundred years, they had conquered the entire Middle East. Iraq, almost a next-door neighbour of Arabia, became the seat of a powerful and vibrant Muslim Empire which extended to many other Middle Eastern countries, both near and distant.

Islam expanded its influence more into Asia than Europe. Spain, however, came under Muslim domination when the Moors of North Africa who had embraced Islam crossed the Mediterranean and occupied Spain. But some centuries later, a reverse operation took place. That was contrary to the general trend in terms of which a country once occupied by the Muslims continued to be Muslim. This did not happen in the case of Spain. Today, all that remains of the long and creative Muslim rule in that country are the countless monuments that they left behind.

Islam had spread to some of the African countries. When it came to Persia, there was prolonged resistance and it took the Arab armies almost two-thirds of a century to conquer Persia. While doing so, the Arabs had to concede a good deal to the rich Persian culture. As is well recognized, it was the Persian-Arab culture which spread into India though the job of conquest was actually done by the Turks.

In terms of the spread of Islam, the penetration into India came later. It is not necessary to go into further details here except to underline one point. Despite all the advances made by

Islam in India, Islam failed to convert the local population beyond a point. To put it bluntly, even after six centuries in the north of India, half that period in western India and a little less than that in southern India, the overall picture in terms of population growth was as described already.

In almost all other countries where the Muslims captured political power, they were able to convert the local population to Islam. This may not have happened entirely in countries like Egypt, Lebanon and one or two others. But the overall picture generally was that wherever Islam went and captured power, it dominated completely and was seldom thrown out or displaced (Spain being the only exception).

This issue might not have arisen in this manner but for the fact of the British occupation of India after the decline of the Mughal Empire. The British brought a very different approach to the problem of governance in India. One of the things they did was to gradually introduce their own legal system into India. A relatively less important feature was the introduction of local self-governments in the cities and the gradual extension of the principle of a new electoral system of representation to Indians. For reasons, which should not be difficult to understand in the context of their history and the system which they had evolved for themselves, it was the system of one-man-one vote. For the Muslims in India, this was a total innovation. In terms of how they had functioned till then, this was a complete break with their past.

Once this principle was extended to India, it became clear to people like Sir Syed Ahmed Khan that this was a game which they could not win. Several other Muslim thinkers before him had been becoming apprehensive about what would happen in that case. They recognized the fact that as long as the Muslim rulers were in power, it did not matter that the Muslims did not constitute the majority of the population. But once they had lost power, the situation underwent a qualitative change. It was with the establishment of the Indian National Congress and the dawn of the political consciousness in the later half of the nineteenth century that more and more people started thinking about these issues and along these lines.

While the Muslims of Bengal, Kashmir and Gujarat have to some extent been studied by scholars, there is a total absence of any such study in respect of the other states. The case of Bengal has been studied in detail by an American scholar Richard Eaton, but no one has yet undertaken a similar study in respect of Punjab which constituted the hub of what is known as the north-west of India. Neither I.H. Qureshi, nor Peter Hardy, nor K.A. Nizami for that matter—to mention some of the better known scholars who have worked in this area—have anything worthwhile to say on the subject. While perceptive and outspoken, Mohammad Habib did not have anything meaningful to say as regards this issue, M. Mujeeb in his magisterial volume on the Indian Muslims has said a good deal about a wide range of issues but hardly anything meaningful about the issue of conversions to Islam and the multi-layered dimensions of this problem. The only two exceptions are Irfan Habib who in his article on the Punjab Jats offers a few leads and K.M. Ashraf who touches upon some of the relevant issues.[1]

India is highly heterogeneous in ethnic and sociological terms. Over the centuries, groups of migrants have been pouring into India, mainly from the north, and settling down in various parts of India. Most of them who came at different stages did not have a set of distinctly defined beliefs, religious or meta-religious. In other words, they were at a stage of cultural and spiritual development where they were open to any kind of influence. When they came to India, depending upon where they settled down, they got assimilated into the local population. This included also becoming, in a sense, part of the Hindu community in the midst of which they found themselves. Several of them retained some of the characteristics that they had brought with them and their acceptance of Hinduism, in whatever version it was popular in that area, did not penetrate their thinking deeply enough.

Muslims were perhaps the only group of people who had a well-developed and clearly defined set of religious beliefs. Equally important, they had a fairly well-defined legal system, indeed systems, which they had brought with them. Conversion to Islam had become an established practice in their historical tradition by then. In keeping with this tradition, the Muslims in

India attempted to convert the local population to Islam.

One question that arises here is whether they did it systematically or not. Had they done it systematically as per practice in other Muslim countries, the outcome would have been different; that is to say the bulk of the Hindus would not have continued to subscribe to their faith as they actually did. Perhaps, the grip of the traditional caste system was so firm, even inflexible to some extent, that Islam failed to make the kind of impact that it had made on other societies and countries. There was however, continued interaction between the Muslim rulers and the Hindu subjects all the time. But that was either on the social plane or in terms of administrative contacts. In terms of religious beliefs, they influenced each other only up to a point.

On the whole, a kind of coexistence developed between the two. It was disrupted only after the advent of the British. How and why that happened does not have to be discussed here. One thing however, is definite. Despite all kinds of setbacks and diversions, a kind of composite culture began to develop. There is a good deal to be investigated here however. Whoever undertakes to do this job would have to extend his enquiry into areas which are much too complex to be reduced to a mere category or two. In a sense, Richard Eaton has done a pioneering job. Apart from his work on Sufis in south India, his analysis of Sheikh Farid's work and performance in the Punjab has shown the direction in which other scholars have to move.

The pattern of the spread of Islam in Bengal has been analysed by him with a wealth of local details and in terms of the history and geography of that area.[2] On the whole, that analysis has won general acceptance. Nothing of the same kind has been done in respect of Punjab, to repeat what has been stated already. In this context, one crucial thing needs to be understood. The structure of the society in the area to the north of the river Jhelum where it first spread was not organized along the lines of what is generally described as the caste system. On the contrary, the social structure of that part of the country was tribal in character. Once, as a result of whatever happened, the chief of the tribe embraced Islam, everyone followed suit. That is why it has been argued by several people, and not wrongly, that by,

AD 1200 the entire area to the north of that river had gone Muslim whereas in its south the social pattern that prevailed was as in the rest of India. In other words, the caste system prevailed completely and the dominance of the Brahmins was universally accepted.

To illustrate this phenomenon in respect of Guru Nanak's career would be instructive. Had he been born 50-60 miles to the north of where he was born, he would have been completely out of place in that social set up. Heir to the Upnishadic tradition as he was, he talked in an idiom that was understood. That could not have happened if he had been living in the tribal belt of north-west India. One may not fully agree with the argument put forward in the *Indus Saga* by Aitzaz Ahsan but of this there can be no doubt that the social structure in that part of the country was not exactly the same as in the rest of India.[3] This is not the occasion to expand upon this argument any further except to call attention to the fact that if a certain proportion of non-Muslims was to be found to the north of Jhelum in the post-AD 1200 period, that was entirely because of the trade which had started taking place between the rest of India and the countries located to its north. As a part of this process, the Hindus who carried the caste system with them started migrating form the rest of India and settling down even in those areas, which at one stage had embraced Islam to the last man.

The caste system has survived in Indian society for a very long time, somewhere around two and three thousand years. Even though it has undergone some changes since its origins and emergence, its grip has not significantly diminished. It is only during the last century or so that it has started undergoing some real change. When some sections of the Hindu population moved over to Islam, in quite a large number of cases, they carried their earlier caste baggage with them so much so that even the Muslim society got infected by the caste virus. Even though this was in direct contradiction of what Islam stands for, this happened, and continued to happen for several hundred years.

Allied to it was another phenomenon which is not to be found in any other Muslim society to the extent that it was found in

India. A kind of social cleavage developed between Muslims who came into India from Arabia, Iran, other countries of Central Asia or the Middle East and those who converted to Islam from within India. This cleavage was so pronounced and unmistakable that not to take it into account in the history of medieval India would be completely misleading. A good deal has been written about it. The process needs to be analysed still further. Equally important to study is the role played by the *Ashrafs*, as they are usually described, both in the conceptualization and the struggle for Pakistan. Indeed their role in virtually taking over the governance of Pakistan and almost becoming the new ruling class of that country calls for a still deeper study.

An analysis of the ethnic and social composition of those who embraced Islam in different parts of India also need to be undertaken in some detail. Generally speaking, those who embraced Islam were people who had skills in certain areas like dyeing, weaving, iron smithy, carpentry, leather work, and so on. The situation varied from area to area. It is difficult to generalize, therefore. In any case, India is so heterogeneous that whatever formulations are made are likely to encounter all kinds of exceptions to them.

What has been stated above is in the nature of general observations. But this much is clear that these issues have a direct bearing on medieval Indian history and need to be studied both in considerable depth and detail.

II

In our limited attempt to understand this problem, we come to the tentative conclusion that while some of the Muslim rulers in India did attempt the task of conversion to Islam, not each one of them was inclined to do so. Most of the Muslim rulers were satisfied with the political power that they wielded and did not undertake this task of conversion in a manner in which it had been possibly undertaken in other countries.

Perhaps the size of India, the complexity of the social situation and the highly malleable character of Hinduism and its various other facets made it difficult for the Muslim rulers to ensure the conversion of the bulk of Hindu population to Islam. In this connection, a detailed reference to the work of the Indian Sufis cannot be overlooked. A substantial proportion of the spread of Islam in India was the outcome of the remarkable job done by them. While Sufism has been a recognized dimension of Islam in almost every Muslim country for more than a thousand years, and has been studied in some depth, in India the Sufi movement became more diverse and multihued than elsewhere. The majority of the Sufi saints did not believe in converting people to Islam. But some of them did choose to do so. After what they saw for themselves and the manner in which the Sufis conducted themselves, a certain number of the Hindus did embrace Islam though, perhaps, their number was not all that large.

In any case, the conduct and performance of the Sufis impressed the local people and some of them did decide to convert to Islam. It created a kind of atmosphere in the country, which, in the long run, facilitated a certain spirit of coexistence. The belief in holy men, their miracle-making powers, the whole system of shrine worship and the extensive use of amulets, etc., were different aspects of what was happening mainly in the countryside. There is considerable evidence of what was happening about these issues in medieval Punjabi literature. If there is similar evidence in some of the other modern Indian languages which received the same kind of impact of Islam as Punjabi did, this would be logical rather than surprising.

If this state of affairs got disrupted at a later stage, that was owing to certain other reasons which cannot be gone into here. Evidently, these issues need to be analysed further. Something has been said about what the Sufis did and how much they achieved but a lot more needs to be investigated. Their achievements were significantly influenced by the fact that the Sufi saints merged with the local population and wrote and preached in the local language. In certain cases, some of them influenced the evolution of those languages.

Altogether, this is a vast area of research which needs to be undertaken in the near future. If no notable contributions have been made to it so far, it is largely because of the highly charged political situation through which India, Pakistan and Bangladesh have been passing through for over half a century now. Indeed they are still not out of it. It is only when the political temperature cools down and inflamed identities revert to their original proportions that something of this kind will be attempted. Perhaps one way of bringing down the temperature would be to undertake such studies and make them as widely known as possible.

At the same time, the enduring character of folk memory is also to be taken note of. Folk perception consists mainly of what has been handed down generation after generation for several hundred years. That is one thing and what is written in books of history is another. Even when the school textbooks are written as they should be written—objectively and fairly—there would still be a certain degree of conflict between what would be taught at school and what children would pick up at home. Of the two sources of information, as anyone can see, it is the folk memory which is likely to prove more decisive. Therefore, if public attitudes are to be influenced, without a significant re-orientation of the character of public consciousness, things will not change.

III

To conclude there is a case for going deeper into this issue and investigating the whole process of how Islam spread. In India, the pattern of its spread was different from the pattern followed elsewhere and did not lead to the conversion of a large number of people to Islam. This was a peculiar situation with which the British dealt in their own way. The problem now is how to bring about a change of outlook and conduct so that antagonism between the two communities, such as it is, is replaced by accommodation and a spirit of coexistence.

Towards the end, a more detailed and less biased view of what happened in medieval India is important. In making out a case for understanding the phenomenon of the spread and role of Islam in India needs to be studied in any case. But some of the considerations referred to above cannot be left out of reckoning.

NOTES

1. See M. Habib, *Sultan Mahmud* of *Ghazni,* Delhi, 1951; M. Mujeeb, *Indian Muslims,* London, 1967; M. Habib and K.A. Nizami (eds.), *A Comprehensive History of India,* vol. V, Delhi, 1970; K.A. Nizami, *Religion and Politics in India During the Thirteenth Century*, Bombay, 1961; I.H. Qureshi, *The Muslim Community of Indo-Pakistan Sub-continent,* Hague, 1962; Irfan Habib, 'Jatts of Punjab and Sind', in *Proceedings of the Punjab History Conference,* Patiala, 1972; Richard M. Eaton, *Essays on Islam in Indian History,* New Delhi, 2000; Peter Hardy, *The Muslim in British India,* Cambridge, 1972; K.M. Ashraf, *Life and Conditions of the People of Hindustan*, New Delhi, 2001 (rpt.).
2. Richard M. Eaton, *The Rise of Islam and the Bengal Frontier*, Delhi, 1994.
3. Aitzaz Ahsan, *Indus Saga and the Making of Pakistan*, Karachi, 1996.

Selected Publications of Professor V.N. Datta

I. Publications

1. *Amritsar: Past and Present* (Municipal Committee, Amritsar), 1967.
2. *Jallianwala Bagh* (Lyall Publishers), 1969; translated into Hindi and Punjabi. A film based on it was shown by the BBC, London on 1 January 1992.
3. *New Light on Punjab Disturbances 1919*, vols. 1 & 2 (Institute of Advanced Studies, Simla), 1975-6.
4. *A Muslim Nationalist and Indian Politics* (in collaboration) (Macmillan, Delhi), 1977.
5. *The Punjab Elite* (Punjabi University, Patiala), 1977.
6. *Madan Lal Dhingra and National Movement* (Vikas, Delhi), 1977.
7. *History of Kurukshetra* (in collaboration) (Vishal, Kurukshetra), 1985.
8. *Sources of Nationalist Movement, 1919-20*, vol. I (in collaboration) (ICHR, New Delhi), 1985.
9. *SATI: Social, Historical and Philosophical Enquiry into the Hindu Practice of Burning Women* (Manohar, Delhi), 1988; published in UK and America.
10. *Maulana Azad* (Manohar, Delhi), 1990.
11. *Jallianwala Bagh Massacre*, ed. VN. Datta and S. Settar (ICHR, New Delhi), 2001.
12. *Maulana Abul Kalam Azad and Sarmad* (Rupa & Co., Delhi), 2007.
13. *Gandhi and Bhagat Singh* (Rupa & Co., Delhi), 2008.

II. Articles and Addresses

1. General President Address, 'Interpreting Partition', Indian History Congress, 27-9 December 1996.
2. Presidential Address (Section III, Modern India), 'Interpreting Indian Nationalism', Indian History Congress, 28-30 December 1981, Bodh Gaya.

3. 'Jawaharlal Nehru and the Partition of India (1947)', in *Nehru Revisited*, ed. N. Ram, Nehru Centre, Mumbai, 2003.
4. '*Nehru in Biographical Dictionary of Modern Peace Leaders*', Editor-in-Chief, Harold Josephson, London, 1985.
5. 'Lord Mountbatten and the Punjab Boundary Award', in *The Parting of Ways*, ed. S. Setter & Indira Baptista Gupta, New Delhi, 2002.
6. 'An Intimate Relationship: Maulana Azad and Jawaharlal Nehru', in *Haksar Memorial Lectures*, vol. II. *Contributions in Remembrance: A Homage to P.N. Haksar*, Chandigarh, 2004.
7. The Mohammad Mujeeb Memorial Lecture, 'Mohammad Mujeeb, A Portrait from Memory', Jamia Millia Islamia, 30 May 2003, New Delhi.
8. The Athar Ali Memorial Lecture, Aligarh Muslim University 'Iqbal, Jinnah and India's Partition', later published in *Economic and Political Weekly*, Mumbai, vol. XXXVI, no. 50, 14-20 December 2004.
9. 'Mulana Azad's Perception of Modern Education', in *The Contested Terrain: Perspectives on Education in India*, ed. Sabyasachi Bhattacharya, New Delhi, 1998.
10. 'Interpreting Partition', in *The Partition in Retrospect*, ed. Amrik Singh, New Delhi, 2000.
11. 'Punjabi Refugees and the Urban Development of Greater Delhi', in *Delhi Through the Ages: Essays in Urban History*, ed. R.E. Frykenberg, Delhi, 1986.
12. 'English Education' in collaboration with R.C. Majumdar and K.K. Datta in chapter II, *The History and Culture of the Indian People: British Paramountcy and Indian Renaissance*, Part II, General Editor R.C. Majumdar, Bombay 1965.
13. 'Jallianwala Bagh', in *We Fought Together for Freedom: Chapters from the Indian National Movement*, ed. Ravi Dayal, New Delhi, 1995.
14. 'The Vitality of India: A Historical Perspective' at International Conference on *The Vitality of India*, Chandigarh, 2004.
15. 'The Message of Iqbal in Persian and Urdu Poetry', in *A Shared Heritage: The Growth of Civilization in India and Iran*, ed. Irfan Habib, New Delhi, 2000.
16. 'Mountstuart Elphinstone: His Training, Method and Intellectual System', in *Kunwar Mohammad Ashraf: An Indian Scholar and Revolutionary (1903-1962)*, ed. Horst Kruger, Berlin, 1966.
17. 'Towards Freedom: Inside story', Paper for Symposium '*Towards Freedom*', Indian History Congress (62nd) Session, Bhopal, 2001.

18. Presidential Address (Modern Section), 'Local and Regional History,' delivered on 26 April 1975 at the IXth Session of the Punjab History Conference, Panjabi University, Patiala.
19. Convocation Address: D.A.V. College (Lahore), Ambala City, 20 March 1974.
20. 'Chapter 4, part III 'Social Reforms', in the *Gazetteer of India: Indian Union*, vol. 2, *History and Culture*, ed. P.N. Chopra, New Delhi, 1973.
21. Chapters XV, 'Education and Culture' in *Delhi Gazetter*, ed. Prabha Chopra, Delhi, 1976.
22. 'Amritsar and the Growth of National Consciousness', in *The City of Amritsar: A Study of Historical, Cultural, Social and Economic Aspects*, ed. Dr. Fauja Singh, New Delhi, 2000.
23. 'Introduction', in *Jallianwala Bagh Commemoration Volume*, ed. Gursharan Singh, Patiala.
24. 'Reflections on Jallianwala Bagh', in *Jallianwala Bagh: A Saga of Sacrifice*, ed. Kamlesh Mohan, Chandigarh, 1995.
25. 'Macaulay Reconsidered', in *Cultural Forum*, December 1959, Ministry of Scientific Research and Cultural Affairs, New Delhi.
26. 'Notes on the Soviet Union', in *Cultural Forum*, Ministry of Scientific Research and Cultural Affairs, April 1963, vol. III, New Delhi.
27. 'Jawaharlal Nehru', in *Indian Historical Review,* vol. XI, July 1984-January 1985.
28. 'Maharaja Duleep Singh', in *Maharaja Duleep Singh: The Last Sovereign Ruler of Punjab*, ed. Prithpal Singh Kapur, Amritsar, 1995.
29. 'The Image', in *Century Special,* New Delhi, January 1965.
30. 'Islam and Pakistan', in *Economic and Political Weekly*, vol. XXXIX, no. 39, 25 September-1 October 2004.

Contributors

K.L. TUTEJA is Director, Academic Staff College, and former Professor of History, Kurukshetra University, Kurukshetra.

SUNITA PATHANIA is former Professor of History, Kurukshetra University, Kurukshetra.

K.M. SHRIMALI is Professor of History, Delhi University, Delhi.

BHAIRABI P. SAHU is Professor of History, Delhi University, Delhi.

INDU BANGA is Professor of History, Panjab University, Chandigarh.

J.S. GREWAL is former Vice-Chancellor, Guru Nanak Dev University, Amritsar and former Director of Indian Institute of Advanced Study, Shimla.

ANIRUDDHA RAY is former Professor of Medieval Indian History, Calcutta University, Kolkata.

SHIREEN MOOSVI is Professor of History, Aligarh Muslim University, Aligarh.

SABYASACHI BHATTACHARYA, former Professor of History, Jawaharlal Nehru University, New Delhi, and former Vice-Chancellor of Viswa Bharati University, is currently Chairman of the Indian Council of Historical Research, New Delhi.

SUDHIR CHANDRA is former Professor of History, Centre for Social Sciences, Surat.

SATPAL SANGWAN is Senior Scientist, NISTADS, New Delhi.

DEEPAK KUMAR is Professor at Zakir Hussain Centre of Educational Studies, Jawaharlal Nehru University, New Delhi.

RADICA MAHASE is a research scholar at the University of West Indies, Trinidad.

SURANJAN DAS is Vice-Chancellor and Professor of History, University of Calcutta, Kolkata.

HARISH K. PURI is former Professor, Ambedkar Chair, Guru Nanak Dev University, Amritsar.

BARUN DÉ is former Director of Centre for Studies in Social Sciences, Kolkata and former Director of Maulana Abul Kalam Azad Institute of Asian Studies, Kolkata.

IRFAN HABIB is Emeritus Professor of History, Aligarh Muslim University, Aligarh, and former Chairman of the Indian Council of Historical Research, New Delhi.

KESAVAN VELUTHAT is Professor of History, Mangalore University, Mangalore.

K.N. PANIKKAR, former Professor of History at Jawaharlal Nehru University and former Vice-Chancellor of Sree Sankaracharya University, is currently Chairman, Kerala Council for Historical Research.

AMRIK SINGH is former Vice-Chancellor, Panjabi University, Patiala.